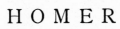

HOMER

HOMER

AND THE EPIC

BY

ANDREW LANG

AMS PRESS
NEW YORK

Reprinted from the edition of 1893, London
First AMS EDITION published 1970
Manufactured in the United States of America

SBN: 404-03845-X
Library of Congress Catalog Card Number: 71-109918

AMS PRESS, INC.
NEW YORK, N.Y. 10003

DEAR MONRO,

If anything could increase my gratitude to you for giving some of your valuable time to my Homeric essays, it would be your kindness in letting me dedicate them to yourself. The weak arrows of the literary skirmisher may now be shot, as it were, from under the shield of the Scholar.

Yours very truly,

A. LANG.

St. Andrews: December 1892.

PREFACE

The Homeric question, the question of the unity of authorship, is a literary problem, yet attempts are constantly made to solve it by other than literary methods. Here are two poems : does each bear the mark and stamp of a single authorship, in harmony of tone, in a preconceived catastrophe to which all tends, in dramatic consonance of character, in grandeur of style ? These are matters of art, but they are often approached, not in the spirit of art, but in that of a cross-examining barrister, or of an historical student testing the accuracy of a statement of facts. The habit of minute analysis, as Signor Comparetti says, produces a mental short-sightedness, and Homeric commentators see the mote immensely magnified, but have no eyes for the beam. They pore over the hyssop on the wall, but are blind to the cedar of Lebanon. They pick out, or invent, blemishes all but invisible, discrepancies which must exist in every fictitious narrative, and they regard these as only to be explained by diversity of authorship, and by the redacting, patching, and combining into a mechanical whole, of lays, fragments, and mutilated epics wrought by many hands in many ages.

This method, we argue here, is erroneous. It has its origin in the arguments of Wolf against the possible existence of a long continuous early Greek epic. These arguments led men to look for the traces of joins in the poems, and to find them, to hunt for the resulting discrepancies, and to discover them. But Wolf's *a priori* arguments, we try to show, are no longer valid. It is not impossible that a long early Greek poem might have been composed, and might survive. This being so, we plead for wider and more generous views of the Iliad and Odyssey, for a study of poetry as poetry, not as a dubious clause in a Bill, or a doubtful statement by an historian.

In one way the prevalent literary taste is adverse to a correct judgment of Homer. It is plain to every reader that long narrative poems are now out of fashion. In all English literature only four or five long narrative poems are widely read, if even they are widely read, *The Faery Queen, Paradise Lost*, Scott's *Lay* and *Marmion*, and *Don Juan*. Our taste is such that Edgar Poe denied the existence of such a thing as a long poem ; there are only moments of poetry, he said, in a mass of verse which is unpoetical. It is this kind of taste which makes Wilamowitz Moellendorff observe, about the author of the Iliad, that ' if he made the *Patrocleia*, or the Λύτρα, he was a great poet, but if he made our Iliad, was a *Flickpoet*—a botcher.' [1]

Now, with all admiration for the critic's great learning, research, and brilliance, he seems here to be simply stating Poe's paradox in a concrete form. The remark would apply as well to Milton, Byron, Scott, or Spenser, not one of whom is always on the level of his best passages, which

[1] *Hom. Untersuch.*, p. 380.

alone, in Poe's theory, deserve the name of poetry. But
Homer lived in an age, whatever that age may have been,
when long narrative poems were in vogue. His generation,
his audience, were not at the point of view of Poe and
Wilamowitz. They did not cry

Indignor quandoque bonus dormitat Homerus,

and deny that the drowsy passage was by the true Homer.
We must read him as his audience listened ; we must not
pore over him with microscopes. That is our argument,
though we try to show that even the discoveries of micro-
scopical criticism have less importance than the microscopists
imagine. Into the linguistic question, the supposed
Ionicising of an Æolic epic, the author has not ventured to
go. It is a matter for experts in language, not for the mere
literary student.

As far as this problem of language affects the other
problems as to the original home and time of the epics,
whether in continental Greece, or on the coast of Asia
Minor, whether before or after the colonisation of the
Asiatic shores, the author is inclined to agree with Mr. Leaf
in his introduction to his *Companion to the Iliad,* and with
Mr. Monro in his paper on *Homer and the Early History
of Greece.*[1] That is to say, the poems, or the bulk of them,
were first sung in continental Greece, Argolis, Thessaly, or
Bœotia, before the founding of the colonies on the other
side of the Ægean. It is pleasant to be able, in spite of our
total difference as to the composition of the Iliad, to agree
here with Mr. Leaf. As to the question of one author or
many authors, the question of the unity of the Iliad, we are
never likely to convert each other. If there be here and

[1] *Historical Review,* No. 1, 1886.

a

there a needless vivacity in our attempts to answer his
arguments, we would say, with Euryalus,

ἔπος δ' εἴ πέρ τι βέβακται
δεινόν, ἄφαρ τὸ φέροιεν ἀναρπάξασαι ἀέλλαι.

To the Provost of Oriel, Mr. Monro, I must here
express my thanks for his kindness in reading my proof-
sheets. I almost doubt if I should name him, 'pour ne lui
point donner une part de responsabilité dans les fautes que
je suis seul coupable d'avoir laissé subsister.'[1] But every
reader who detects an error will know that I only am
responsible. Nor is it to be assumed that Mr. Monro
agrees with all the views expressed. On the matter of the
tenth book of the Iliad, for example, we are not at one:
though I have no great confidence in my attempted
defence of its originality.

I have also to thank Mr. Edmund Gosse for examining
what is here said about the Northern lays and the *Volsunga
Saga*, assistance most valuable to one who only reads the
Sagas in translations. Mr. A. S. Murray and Mr. Cecil
Smith have, with unwearied kindness, imparted to an
amateur some inkling of archæology. The gem engraved
on the cover, which seems to represent an Achæan
Mrs. Gamp and Mrs. Prig, is from a gold ring published
by MM. Furtwaengler and Loeschke in their work on
Mycenæan vases. The part of the discussion of the Iliad
which deals with book xvi. appeared in the *National Review*,
and most of the chapter on 'Homer and Archæology' in
the *Quarterly Review*. The author has to thank the con-
ductors of these periodicals for permission to reprint his
observations here.

---

[1] Gaston Paris, *La Littérature Française au Moyen Âge*, p. vi.

CONTENTS

HOMER AND THE EPIC

—◆◆◆—

CHAPTER I

HOMER'S PLACE IN LITERATURE

In an age full of other, and otherwise pressing, questions, it may be held that the Homeric question should be allowed to go by ; that Seneca was right when he said life was too short for it, that we should dally no longer with this ancient Gordian knot. It is not practical, it does not affect the well-being of society. We can read Homer, if we choose, without asking when he lived or where were 'his city and they that begat him,' or whether, indeed, his name is not a noun of multitude, and his poetry a collection of elegant miscellanies. To this we must answer that, whatever the urgent practical problems and distractions of an age, men of letters are enlisted to keep flying the colours of the highest literature, of all that makes and records the flower of civilisation. Pessimists may prophesy that our public oratory, far unlike the elaborate rhetoric of Louvet and Robespierre and Vergniaud, will decline into mere bandied abuse. They may frighten themselves by a vision of our poetry seeking the Fountain of Youth in the idioms of the costermonger and the dialect of Cokayne. Even were there good grounds for these apprehensions, are we not engaged

B

to maintain, as best we may, the ever new and fresh love of what is old and excellent, the admiration of that divine poetry which, during three thousand years, has been the delight and the consolation of the world? Now, though the poetry abides unaltered, the conditions of its readers are eternally changing. We cannot study Homer as Xenophanes did, or Socrates, or Nero, who died with a Homeric line on his lips, or as Eustathius did, or as Pope and Boileau did, or even as Wolf or Lachmann studied him. New knowledge keeps coming in, knowledge drawn from the records of Oriental empires, from comparative study of customs, from the graves of the royal dead in Mycenæ. New theories are raised, prevail, and fall obsolete ; we have often to ask ourselves where we stand in our knowledge of the Bible of Greece.

To forget Homer, to cease to be concerned and even curious about Homer, is to make a fatal step towards a new barbarism. Mankind exists, or should exist, not to live only, but, as Aristotle defines it, to live nobly. A noble and enjoyable life demands an imaginative participation in all that the human race has done, or said, or thought, which is excellent. The outcasts of Poker Flat, in Mr. Bret Harte's tale, consoling their last hours with the story of *Asheels,* in Pope's Iliad, were living a nobler life than the comfortable citizen, who reads newspapers, and nothing but newspapers all day, and wakens with a fresh appetite for his morning journal. To keep up, to diffuse, as far as we may, interest in the best literature, is the duty of all who have been educated and called to this task.

Inopportune as their endeavours may seem, their work is like that of the copyist monks in the Middle Ages. They, too, were out of harmony with their age, but they were working for the age which was to come. If, in the future, an age of general well-being is to arrive, its children will turn, as all men who have the opportunity must, to what is best in human art, to the literature of Greece. It is our business, in our degree, to applaud and to elucidate it, to clear it, if we can, from doubts and erroneous theories, to see it as it is, and as it was in its origins, to keep reminding the distracted age of those Islands Fortunate sleeping in the ocean of times dead and gone.

In the front of all poetry stands the poetry of Hellas, and in its foremost rank stand the epics of Homer. If we were offered the unhappy choice whether we would lose Homer and keep the rest of Greek poetry, or keep the rest and lose Homer, there could be little doubt as to our choice.

We would rescue the Iliad and the Odyssey. How much and how invaluable the remainder is, we know. The stately tragedies, the immortal comedies, the triumphant odes of Pindar, the pictures of hill and glade, river and well, and the pastoral life in Theocritus, the passion and patriotism of Sappho and Simonides, all the mirth, the love, the laments of the Anthology, would be known and heard no more. But as, if a similar choice were put before us in English literature, we should keep Shakspeare, and let Spenser and Shelley, Scott and Wordsworth disappear, because Shakspeare in a sense includes them all —includes the romance of Keats, and the speculation of Wordsworth, the humour of Scott, and his delight in battle — includes the flower of all lyric melody, every mood, and all thought —so Homer includes, in essence, the sum of all Greek poetry. It is a whole world, with all its possibilities of joy and sorrow that lives in the Iliad and Odyssey. The tragedian avowed that his own plays were only 'scraps from the great Homeric banquet.' The funereal wails of Meleager in the Anthology are present already in the half lyric laments of Andromache and Helen over Hector slain. The figures of

B 2

Eros and Anteros are here, in the noble affection of Andromache and Hector, in the shameful, the repentant, the agi-
tated passion of Paris and Helen. The solemn thoughts of
human fortunes, and the justice of Heaven, which Æschylus
ponders beside the Titan's bed of pain, on the rocks of
Caucasus, are already meditated by Homer. His Atê,
which blinds men, his Ægisthus and Clytæmnestra, who
draw down sorrow beyond their doom, his fate, which
controls both mortals and gods, Homer's reflections, in the
Odyssey, on the lot of man, 'the most unhappy of all
creatures,' his stoical conclusion in the resolute valour of
Hector and Odysseus, anticipate in simple terms the results
of all later speculation. Already the problems are stated, and
the Homeric answer is given in the words of the Lycian
Sarpedon, 'Ah, friend! if once escaped from this battle, we
were for ever to be ageless, and immortal, neither would I
fight myself in the foremost ranks, nor would I send thee
into the war that yieldeth men renown; but now—for
assuredly ten thousand fates of death do every way beset
us, and those no mortal may escape or avoid—now let us
onward!' Zeus has given to man an enduring mind.
The tides of mortal fortune must come and go. Great
Ilios must perish on its day, the city of Priam of the ashen
spear. 'But now, since I have heard the voice of the
goddess, and looked upon her face, I will go forth, and her
word shall not be void. And if it be my fate to die beside
the ships of the mail-clad Achæans, so would I have it; let
Achilles slay me with all speed, when once I have taken in
my arms my son, and have satisfied my desire with moan.'

We too, in Homer, see the face and hear the voice of
the goddess, of the Muse, and are heartened to go forth and
meet our destiny. The philosophy of Homer, simply as
his problems are stated, is fortified against all vicissitude.
His mind, like the mind of Herodotus is constantly occu-

pied by the thought of change, how the ancient city must fall, and fall, too, must its conqueror, slain on his own hearthstone in the full fruition of victory. Nay, the very civilisation of which Homer sings, with all its valour and art and gold, is to go down before the assaults of the Dorians. His Achilles is the type of triumphant youth, but of youth with sheer doom before its eyes. To him

> 'One crowded hour of glorious life
> Is worth an age without a name.'

His eyes are open from the first, and his choice is made. This, then, is the philosophy of Homer, and to what other better philosophy have the schools of three thousand years brought their disciples? It is for this clear vision, this lucid insight into the ultimate questions, that Greece chose Homer for the master of masters, the teacher of all philosophers, 'the first of those who know.'

His theory of life might thus be called melancholy. Even at home, after all his wanderings, the curse of the sea god yet hangs over Odysseus, his troubles are not over, he must set forth again into the unheard of lands. There is no continuance of mortal happiness, 'here we have no abiding city,' but against this Homer does not repine. With his clear vision of the end of all living, he combines the gladdest enjoyment of life. To him the world is full of joy. Storms, and snow, and sea, the ruinous rains, the noisy torrents that divide the hills, the eyes of lions, the peaceful piping of the shepherd, the murmur of man and maid from rock and oak-tree, the woven dance, the tribunal, all the arts of ship-building and sea-craft, of weapon-forging, of chariot-building, of gold work, of weaving and embroidery, all the life of peace, of the chase and the festival and the song, all the life of war, ambush, and siege, and march, clashing of shields, and countering of chariots, all is alike dear to him, all makes part of the eternally

moving, the eternally absorbing spectacle. His work-a-day
world is on every hand environed with the divine, as the
refluent stream of Oceanus girdles the earth. The gods
appear in beautiful shapes of young men and huntress
maidens ; in the unsailed seas, the untrodden isles, the
goddess burns her fragrant fire, and sings her magic song,
as she weaves at the immortal loom. Everything is full of
possibilities, every adventure tempts him, whether here he
meets the courteous and clement Egyptians, by the river
Ægyptus, or there the cannibal Læstrygonians, by their
fiord in the land of the midnight sun. This world that is so
hard, this life that must end in death, are yet rich in the
beautiful and the strange. Man's days are wealthy in
works and deeds, he is a warrior, a counsellor, a hunter, a
shipwright, a smith, a mower in the fields of hay, a plough-
man behind the steers.

This is life, as Homer paints it, life cheered by women
as fair as the heroes are bold, ladies loyal, staunch, wise,
tender and true, fit mates for the heroes. When the men
are dead in battle and eaten of dogs, before the women lies
the day of captivity, 'to strew another's bed and bring
water from another's well,' but the hour is their own.

Thus Homer takes all experience for his province, in his
similes he gives us idylls, 'little pictures' of pastoral or
hunting days, encounters with lions, adventures in the
mountain mists, wars with the sea waves for home and for
dear life, labour in every kind, sketches of children, building
houses of sea sand, or clinging to their mother's gown, and
crying to be taken up in her arms. He has humour, too,
as in his pictures of the squabbles of Olympus, the speeches
of Thersites, the arrogance of the wooers, the girl in thought
about her wedding day, the easy luxurious Phæacians.
'His lyre has all the chords'—now the triumphant Achæans,
bearing Hector dead break into a pæan, now the women

shrill the dirge, as even yet they do in Corsica. The epic
is thus the sum of all poetry—tragedy, comedy, lyric, dirge,
idyll, are all blended in its great furnace into one glorious
metal, and one colossal group. Another style of composition Homer offers us, which nowhere else we receive from
Greece, till we get it, in decadent though still beautiful shape,
in Greece's dying age. The epic, in the Odyssey, becomes
a romance, the best of all romances, and the most skilfully
narrated. No later tale can match, in sheer skill of composition, with the Odyssey.

This is not all. The epics are not only poetry, but
history, history not of real events, indeed, but of real manners, of a real world, to us otherwise unknown. The heroic
and sacred poetry of other peoples, as of Vedic India and
of Finland, goes back into the years before history was.
But the Vedas have but little of human interest, the Finnish
Kalewala has no composition, and is merely a stitching together of disjointed lays of adventure, or of popular songs.
The Iliad and the Odyssey, keeping all the fresh vivacity
and unwearied zest of 'popular' poetry, are also master-
pieces of conscious art. Homer does not wander in a
poetic chronicle along the ages, or all through a hero's
career; he seizes on a definite moment in the Siege of Troy,
a set of circumstances centring in one heroic passion, or he
tells a clearly circumscribed tale of Odysseus' return. Many
peoples have heroic lays, or poetic chronicles of legendary
events. Greece alone had a poet who could handle these
with the method of a master. We readily see how Homer
can rise above his time, while remaining true to his time.
His age, though rich in minor decorative arts, had no
accomplished statuary. The poet could not inspire himself
from sculpture. On the other hand, it is his description of
Zeus that inspired the colossal work of Phidias in a later
day. The statues he knew were probably rude ancient

idols, covered with sacred robes. But when he describes
Athene arming, we see the polished body of the Goddess, the
gleaming armour, the immortal raiment, 'as in a picture.'
It is thus that Homer rises above the age whose ways,
whose arms, whose ships, whose chariots, whose golden cups,
and necklets, and ornaments of amber he paints so firmly.
He tells us plainly of a civilisation far advanced, when
women were honoured and listened to as the equals of men
though they were ceremonially purchased in wedlock. It
was an age when religion, apart from mythic and scandalous
anecdote, was comparatively clean. We hear of no foul
rites of purification with pig's blood ; the Mysteries, with
their mingling of the lewd, the barbaric, and the sublime,
are never the subject of an allusion.

The Gods do not make love in the guise of eagle and
ant, of dog, and swan, and bear, as in the mythology of a
later and more cultivated time. The worst moral stain on
later Greek character is never mentioned even in a hint.
In many ways, Homer's age is divided from the historic age
by a great gulf, and much of the Homeric social excellence
was never revived by pagan Greece. All this is history, of
a kind, and, but for Homer, all this would have been for
ever forgotten.

The relics of his own, or of a yet earlier period, which
the spade has revealed at Mycenæ and elsewhere, would be
indecipherable if the epics had not survived among the
ruins of many civilisations. This gives another charm and
value to Homer, in addition to his poetic worth. This
makes his poems a yet more priceless and unique possession
of humanity. His own age cherished them, and they
escaped in the fall of the Achæan empire. Later Greece
adored them ; Rome received and imitated them ; the
Middle Ages took them from Rome in the shape which
Virgil gave them, and in curious perverted tradition. Even

ancient Ireland had its own singularly altered version of the
Odyssey. The Renaissance woke to the enjoyment of
Homer, Petrarch dying with a copy of the book which he
could not read in his hands. Homer became more than
ever what he had always been, the master and teacher of
poetry. Faint and distorted echoes from him had inspired Chaucer, he had been the guide of Virgil, who, again,
was the guide of Dante. With the renewal of Greek, he
came forth into the daylight, though it was rather a revival
or avatar of his genius than the knowledge of his works
which gave inspiration to Scott. Not till the French
Revolution, and the storm of changed opinion which blew
with it, did scholars seriously doubt whether there had
indeed been any Homer, and seriously try to think that his
magnificent unity of thought, of style, of manners, was the
result of a congeries of atoms, the work of many minds, in
many ages. These questions have not injured Homer; nay,
they have stimulated to a more constant study of his
poems, and have kept interest in them alive. The ages of
Anne and Louis XIV., in spite of the translation by Pope
and the defence by Boileau, had little of the Homeric spirit.
A more general, a more vivid appreciation of him was
excited by the very causes which impelled Wolf to criticise
him, namely by the revived love of romance and of old
popular poetry. Meanwhile the question as to whether
Wolf's doubts are justified, is the matter which this book, in
its degree, tries to discuss. Thus far we have spoken of
Homer as we speak of Shakspeare, taking pride in so
great and delightful a triumph of a single human spirit,
listening in wonder to one lyre of so many various and
harmonious chords. But our triumph must pass, and only
our wonder remain, if the Homeric poems, their music,
their pictures, their consistent philosophy of life, are to be
explained as a mass of old and new, of interpolations, of

dovetailings, of essays by rhapsodists and 'diaskeuasts,' Achæan minstrelsy, and Ionian imitation, all combined, no man knows how or by whom, offered to Greece as the work of a single artist, and accepted, by the jealous and isolated communities of Greece, for what they pretended to be. Certainly our wonder abides, and is greatly increased, if this literary miracle can be established, in a world where miracles do not happen. If there were so many great poets, almost all so much alike, all with one theory of life, all with one knowledge of manners, institutions, arts, and of the world; if, despite these congruities, they lived in different epochs, in different states; if their effusions could be combined into the epics, and if all Greece could be persuaded to accept the combination as one artist's work, then miracles after all do occur.

In discussing the possibility or probability of these ideas, we shall begin, where the Homeric question, properly speaking, commences, with a statement and criticism of Wolf's famous *Prolegomena*. We shall then examine the composition of the Iliad, and of the Odyssey, taking for chief texts the conclusions of Mr. Leaf, in his excellent edition of the Iliad, and the latest German criticism. Next we shall consider the archæological theories of Homer's date and civilisation based on recent discoveries. We shall then compare Homer with certain other early national poems, such as the *Chanson de Roland*, the *Kalewala*, and *Beowulf*, trying to show in what respects his work resembles, and in what it transcends and differs from, these interesting lays. We shall then state the conclusion to which we have been guided by the whole process—namely, that the Homeric epics, in spite of certain flaws, and breaks, and probable insertion of alien matter, are mainly the work of one, or, at the most, of two, great poets. Their place in literature has already been defined, they contain the voice of a whole lost world, they are full of

the prime vigour of the Greek genius, and may be accepted
as the sum, in an early and vigorous form, of all that the
Greek genius was able to accomplish. What all ancient
literature offers us, namely the sense of living a more opu-
lent life, enriched by sympathy with a life spent under widely
different conditions of society, climate, knowledge, and
religion, Homer, by virtue of his antique date and perished
civilisation, offers yet more abundantly. He communicates
to us the common thrill of humanity ; for his men face, in
other guises than ours, the same problems as we—the eternal
problems of death and life, of war and peace, of triumph
and defeat, of pleasure and pain. Our own sense of vitality
is thereby in a measure increased, and, as it were, there is a
kind of transfusion into our veins of the heroic blood, of the
vigour in the limbs of the sons of Gods. Even if we doubt
concerning our portion and lot in the future, by the knowledge of Homer our share in the past is secured, and we are
made conscious partakers in his heroes' immortality, sharers
in the joy of all who have loved him, of Archilochus and
Virgil, of Plato and Goethe. In this, there is a truth more
than rhetorical, and in this joy an inalienable possession.
As men, after all, are so made that they desire to be grate-
ful for a poem to a poet—a sentiment of which Longinus
appreciated the generous enjoyment—and not to a vague
Société des Gens de Lettres, it is hoped that the argument may
help to strengthen the belief in one author, not in a college
of collaborators, and so may add, however slightly, to the
pleasure taken in the Iliad and Odyssey. For it does not
appear to us that the question of the single or the composite
authorship of the poems, is of no æsthetic importance, that
the epics are just as excellent whether they be the work of
one genius, or a patchwork, a mosaic of different pieces,
derived from different ages. In that case, much of the poems
must be sham antiques, the manners must have been arti-

ficially reconstructed by minstrels who did not live in the world of the earlier lays. The characters will not have been conceived by one master genius, but Achilles will be in origin the creation of one mind, Odysseus of another, Helen of a third ; and many other poets must have adroitly kept up the unity of characters which they did not invent or create. Thus we have to allow for at least two Achilles's, the second acting in direct contradiction of the character of the first, according to the separatist theory. We can never be sure that some new poet is not making a hero act as his first creator would not have had him act ; we may believe that the original poet, had he foreseen the future, would have killed all his personages, as Addison killed Sir Roger de Coverley to keep him out of the hands of Steele. We have seen, in late days, attempts to continue Coleridge's *Christabel* and the greatest novels of Dumas. These efforts are egregious failures, hence we more distrust the hypothesis of Homeric continuators, working throughout several centuries. Where we have been wont to admire the unity of one genius, we are now asked to censure 'diaskeuasts,' editors, younger poets, and to grope among a perfect Almanack of the Muses. If these criticisms be correct—if the original poet of the Odyssey, for example, never dreamed of the hero's adventures among the wooers, and his meeting with the old hound Argos —we cannot but feel our confidence shaken, and our pleasure turned to pain and bewilderment. This is no argument in favour of shunning analysis ; 'the truth must be sought at all costs,' but it is not certain that the truth, when found, will prove to be disenchanting. About Homer it is just possible that the Poets may be right, and the Professors may be wrong.[1]

---

[1] In 1778 Allan Ramsay told Johnson that he 'supposed Homer's Iliad to be a collection of pieces written before his time.' In 1773, Mr. McQueen, in Skye, 'alleged that Homer was made up of detached fragments.' Johnson denied this.

CHAPTER II

THE Homeric question has always been discussed, in various aspects, since literature became conscious and curious as to its own origins. A portion of the Homeric poems is alluded to in the fragments of Archilochus, and the comparison of the life of man to the forest leaves is quoted by Simonides, and attributed to 'the Man of Chios.' Pausanias, in the second century of our era, tells us that Callinus, about 700 B.C. supposed Homer to be the author of a poem on the heroic legend of Thebes.[1] Herodotus, in the fifth century B.C. (ii. 117) denies to Homer the authorship of the *Cypria*, and speculates as to his date, which he places some four hundred years before his own (ii. 53). Popular songs and riddles, and humorous or satiric poems like the 'Battle of Frogs and Mice' and the *Margites*, were attributed to Homer, as also were the hymns. The so-called 'Lives of Homer' were based on remarks in these works. Nothing is certain, except that men of letters in Greece knew nothing about the personality of Homer, and guessed much. After the founding of Alexandria, as we shall see in the chapter on Wolf's *Prolegomena*, acute criticism was busy with the editing of Homer and the purification of his text. The chief traces of ancient doubts concerning Homer are to be found in the vague tradition, later to be investigated, that

[1] Paus. ix. 9, 5.

his poems had become 'scattered,' and were reunited in
Athens about the time of the Pisistratidæ.   Again,
Josephus (90 A.D.), in defending Hebraic against Hellenic
antiquities, mentions an opinion that Homer could not
write.   There are vestiges, in ancient notes or *scholia*, dating
in part from the Alexandrine age (200 B.C. and onwards) of
a paradox, or theory dividing the authorship of Odyssey and
Iliad.   The believers in this view were called ' Chorizontes,'
or 'Separatists.'   After the revival of letters the remark of
Josephus, that, in general opinion, Homer could not write,
was commented on by Casaubon (1559-1614) in a note on
Diogenes Laertius (ix. 12).   Perizonius (1684) in his
Animadversiones Historicæ (p. 209), made observations on
the late Greek use of writing for historical purposes, and
conceived that Homer himself did not write his lays, but
committed them to memory.   In his remarks we have the
kernel of the later Homeric controversy, but, as Volkmann
says, even Wolf does not seem to have known the work of
his predecessor.   He was acquainted, however, with an
obiter dictum of Bentley, in *Remarks upon a late Discourse
of Free Thinking* (1713), where Bentley declares that
' Homer *wrote* a sequel of songs and rhapsodies. . . . These
loose songs were not collected into the form of an epic poem
till about five hundred years after.'

Charles Perrault doubted if there was any Homer at
all.   ' Il y a des savants qui ne croient pas à l'existence
d'Homère, et qui disent que l'Iliade et l'Odyssée ne sont
qu'un amas de plusieurs petits poèmes de divers auteurs
qu'on a joints ensemble.   C'est l'avis de très habiles gens.
L'Abbé d'Aubignac n'en doutait pas, il avait des mémoires
tout écrits.'   The Abbé d'Aubignac, Boileau says, had but
a moderate knowledge of Greek.   However, he wrote his
Conjectures, published posthumously in 1715, and, according to M. Rigault, invented all that the Germans only

obscure.[1] Fénelon had just been demonstrating the existence of a Deity, by that of Homer. Here is a poem, therefore there is a poet ; here is a universe, therefore there is a God.[2] Now the Abbé said in his haste that there was no poet. It was a kind of constructive atheism. The Abbé had to be the Darwin of the Homeric world, and explain how it was evolved, as he had got rid of its creator. He imagines, about fifty years after the fall of Troy, a set of lays by various hands on the subject of the war, lays sung by 'rhapsodists'—of course an error in literary history. These men were often blind : Homer's name means 'blind : ' 'Homer's poems' mean 'songs of a blind crowder.' Some-one collected these fragmentary pieces ; perhaps he was Lycurgus. His collection was imperfect ; not till the edition made for, or by, Hipparchus and Pisistratus had Greece her Iliad and Odyssey. On the whole, the Abbé d'Aubignac is only the Empedocles, or at most the Lamarck, not the Darwin, of Homeric evolution.

In 1715, the Abbé d'Aubignac regarded the Homeric poems as a mere collection of loose lays, but his learning was not equal to his audacity.[3] Vico (1725) looked on Homer as no real historical personage, and believed that the loose lays were collected, as in the vague ancient legends, and written out under Pisistratus. The very name of Blackwell's book, *An Inquiry into the Life and Writings of Homer* (1757), shows how little these speculations affected him—'I do not say that Homer and Hesiod had no learning of this sort,' namely 'from books' (p. 129) ; and Blackwell speaks of this or that ' part of Homer's *writings*.' 'Letters were then but little known,' however (p. 82), Blackwell, by the way, does observe. ' These poems, they tell you, Homer did not commit to writing himself, but his

---

[1] *Querelle des Anciens et des Modernes*, p. 413.
[2] *De l'Existence de Dieu*, i. ch. 1.   [3] Wolf, *Proleg.* p. cxiv.

posterity in Chios ; and the rhapsodists, who were for ever
reciting them, came at last to have them by heart, and
Cynæthus, their chief, while he preserved Homer's verses,
did intermix a good many of his own invention,' such as the
Hymn to Apollo (p. 110, 111).   He scouts the authority of
' a nameless scholiast of Pindar,' who is the evidence for
this notion.

The influence of Macpherson's Ossian (1760–1765) was
all in favour of a belief in rude uncultivated ' nature-poets,'
and the tendency now was to reduce Homer to their ranks.
In 1775 appeared the posthumous *Essay on the Original
Genius and* Writings *of Homer*, by ' the late Robert Wood,
Esq.' [1]   In this work (p. 248) Wood asks, ' How far the use
of writing was known to Homer.'   He denies that any
' idea of letters or reading is to be found in Homer.'   The
famous letter of Bellerophon [2] is ' symbolical, hieroglyphical,
or picture description ' (p. 250).   It may have resembled,
Wood thinks, the picture-writing of the Aztecs.   But Wood
does not conclude from Homer's silence to Homer's ignorance, ' a manner of reasoning which has been carried too
far on other occasions.'   But there are, in Homer, no
written treaties, no inscribed tombstones.   Even when
writing did reach Greece, ' it was attended with much difficulty.'   ' The materials, too, were very rude, and inadequate
to the purpose ' (p. 252).   Writing would come in gradually,
and almost unnoticed, from the Phœnicians.   Prose composition is late in Greece, a proof of tardiness in writing.
' The common familiar use of an alphabet ' must be about
the same date as prose composition in Greece, about 550
B.C.   The earliest written laws were late, and were
monumentally inscribed.

---

[1] There was an earlier edition of 1769.   Wolf used, apparently, the
edition of 1775.

[2] Iliad, vi. 168.

This argument, to which various objections are to be urged, was the inspiration of Wolf. In Macpherson, too, collecting and writing and publishing the so-called Ossianic lays, he had a parallel for the work mythically assigned to Pisistratus. Heyne and Tiedemann (1780) were turning their thoughts in the same direction. Chesterfield was comparing Homer's heroes to 'porters.' As early as 1779, in a college essay, Wolf entered on his sceptical career. He was snubbed by Heyne, but persisted, being specially moved by his detection of a fresh and incongruous tone in the last five books of the Iliad ; while this tone recurs in the Odyssey.

In 1788 appeared Villoison's edition of the Iliad, containing the previously unpublished scholia or notes of the Venice manuscript, which, again, are rich in excerpts from Aristarchus and the great Alexandrians. This was a mine of information for Wolf. How hard and thoroughly he worked we shall learn from his own confessions in the analysis of his *Prolegomena* to the Iliad,[1] a tract hastily composed while the printer's devil waited for 'copy.' *Jacta est alea!* he cries, he has crossed the Rubicon, and the modern Homeric question has begun to rage. Over the reception and contemporary criticism of the *Prolegomena* we need not linger. Goethe was at first carried away by the tide, and toasted 'the man who has delivered us from the name of Homer.' But on May 16, 1798, he wrote to Schiller : 'I am more than ever convinced of the indivisible unity of the Iliad ; the man lives not, nor ever shall be born, who can destroy it.' With the exception of Coleridge, poets have usually sided with Goethe against Wolf, and Mr. Matthew Arnold was a staunch defender of the epic unity.[2]

[1] Halle, 1795.

[2] Volkmann's *Geschichte und Kritik der Wolfschen Prolegomena* (Leipzig : 1874) has been followed in this chapter.

C

CHAPTER III

WOLF'S THEORY

THE *Prolegomena* begin with some general remarks on the editing of ancient texts. 'A true recension,' says Wolf, 'with all the aid of the best materials, seeks everywhere for the very hand of the original author' (p. iv), and everywhere relies, not on taste, but on evidence, reasoned examination of the sources of the texts compared. The assiduous study of texts, of as many and as good as possible, is absolutely necessary. On this topic, in general, there is no difference of opinion. But Wolf finds that, in the case of Homer, there is some doubt as to whether much should be made of the differences in the manuscripts. The Homeric manuscripts older than the eleventh and twelfth centuries of our era are few and far to seek. 'If the doubts expressed go so far as to imply that from these sources, these late manuscripts, we can never recover the words of the poet as they first flowed from his divine lips, I shall show later how gladly I acquiesce in this doctrine' (p. vi). But our manuscripts of Herodotus and Plato are of much the same date as our oldest Homeric manuscripts. Herodotus and Plato we read 'almost in their true splendour,' so why not Homer? Then the Alexandrian critics gave much labour to Homer ; probably our text is better than that on which they worked. The ancient authors who quote Homer quote him, on the whole, allowing for slips of memory, as we know him.

Our criticism will hardly construct for us a better text than Plutarch and Longinus read and used. We shall never see the primitive form of the Homeric poems. We can only do our best with our materials, and Wolf has done his best in his new edition. Homer has hitherto been too negligently edited. His very lucidity has lulled the editors to a drowsy repose, save when they were roused by a stray various reading, or a casual *scholium*, or a remark of Eustathius. The Italian editors had the Venetian manuscript of Villoison and the scholia at hand, but never used them.

The various readings in ancient lexicographers have also been, on the whole, overlooked. Wolf now criticises the editions of Etienne and Barnes, and he thinks that the second Aldine editor and he of Rome did not use Eustathius studiously. Clarke was indolent, Ernestius deserved better of Homer; but it is only in the last seven years, since 1788, that we enjoy the wealth of Homeric lore provided in the edition of Villoison, the Venice manuscript with the ancient scholia. The Venice manuscript is 'more valuable than all our other sources together,' though it includes much that is trivial, and does not offer much that we desire.

Villoison's edition, however, is a book which there are few to praise and very few to read. 'Indeed, as we say now, the book is *unreadable*.' It must be mastered by hard labour. Much of old learning is lost, but much remains. We only have extracts from the famous Alexandrians, but these are priceless.

Wolf now traces an interesting picture of his own exhaustive Homeric studies. He read, and re-read, and analysed Eustathius, the then known scholia, the old lexicographers, the ancient grammarians, and all classical literature in which he might hope to find a trace of the text

of Homer.   Then the Venice scholia appeared, and all his
work had to be done over again.   But he did not regret his
researches in the work of ' that wordiest of men,' Eustathius,
his labours in the collation of manuscripts and old
editions, nor lament the years when 'ground he at grammar'
in the ancient grammarians.   It is easy, he says, to neglect
and ridicule the minutiæ of grammar, easy to discourse on
the barbarity of Homer's age, or on myths, or on the
opinions of Aristotle.   But grammar is not to be contemned,
at all events by those who have never taken the trouble to
learn it.   In linguistic research we enter, as it were, the
honourable company of the ancient critics of Alexandria.
In brief, Wolf thinks that his colossal industry has not been
heavier than the nature of his work as an editor of Homer
required.   ' Willingly have I toiled, whatever the value of my
toil.'   His object, as an editor, is to give a text that would
satisfy any ancient critic, who knew how to employ the
commentaries of the Alexandrians.   To exhibit the nature
and difficulties of his task, he will give a brief history of
Homer's text.   This he divides into six ages (p. xxii) :—

　　1. From the origin of the lays, say 950 B.C. to the time
of Pisistratus (550 B.C.).

　　2. From Pisistratus to Zenodotus, the early Alexandrine
critic.

　　3. From Zenodotus to Apion, whose fame as an interpreter of Homer Seneca attests.

　　4. From Apion to Porphyry, the disciple of Plotinus, an
allegorising writer on Homer.

　　5. From Porphyry to Demetrius Chalcondyles, editor of
the first printed edition.[1]

　　6. From 1488 to the end of the eighteenth century.

　　Wolf next shows the badness of the ordinary or vulgate
text, by a series of examples.   The ordinary text had its ortho-

---

[1] Florence, 1488.

dox fanatics : even in classic times, Lucian asks Homer, in Hades, a question about the supposed interpolations. Homer answered that they were all his own. But surely no one would wish to preserve the solecisms and printer's or copyist's blunders. And there must be far greater departures from a primitive text, for Hippocrates, Plato, and Aristotle quote whole verses of which not a trace remains in our copies, or in the scholia.[1] Wolf thinks that the famous edition 'of the Casket' made by Aristotle for Alexander the Great never came into the hands of the Alexandrian critics, who make no quotations from it. But the Alexandrians must have had most of Aristotle's materials. Thus it is plain to Wolf that we have not before us even the text which Aristotle and Plato knew. And what relation to the primitive text had that with which Aristotle was acquainted? Here, at last, Wolf comes to his point ; he tries to show that primitive *text* there was none, the poems were lays orally recited. His argument as to the trustworthiness of our text of Homer runs thus :—

Trust it we may, unless these poems have endured peculiar corruptions, and borne far more and more serious alterations than others. But suppose that, judging by the very early appearance and popularity of Homeric emendation in Greece, the Greeks themselves lacked really genuine examples, whence he who would might make fresh copies. Suppose, again, that the earliest recensions, the efforts of criticism not yet perfected, differed often and widely from each other. Suppose that grammarians in the later and more learned Greece introduced a vulgate some time after

[1] Wolf himself brought into the speech of Phœnix four new lines (Iliad, ix. 458-461) from Plutarch's tract, *De Audiendis Poetis*. These were in none of our extant manuscripts, nor named in the scholia. Who excised them ? Plutarch says Aristarchus did, on account of the terrible 'realism' of Phœnix. Our text is, however, not that of Aristarchus, but the vulgate common in his day.

Aristotle. Suppose, again, that we have not even a perfect
example of the text of Aristarchus, which the ancients
for long very highly preferred, but only a text re-edited
in the centuries immediately after our era, and restored
according to the judgment of various critics, and afterwards covered with blemishes in the ages of increasing
barbarism, may we not gather from all these considerations the idea which I have already promulgated, that the
text of Homer is as to purity in a very different condition
from those of Lucretius and Virgil ? As to the difference
between the condition of the older texts of Homer and those
of the Alexandrine critics, it is enough to say in passing
that in Hippocrates, Plato, Aristotle, and other authors of
that time, we can find, not only variations in single words,
but even many remarkable verses of which no trace survives
in Eustathius, nor in the oldest and most learned scholia.

'So far I believe I shall win the ready assent of all who
have learned to trust their own eyes. But if the suspicion
of some scholars is true, namely that the Homeric and
other lays of those times were not written at all, but were
first composed in the memory, and sung from memory by
the poets, that they were next carried abroad in song by the
rhapsodists, whose business it was to learn them by rote, it
necessarily follows that many alterations must have been
made in the poems by accident or design. Then suppose
that, as soon as they began to be written, they were thus
full of different renderings, and next suffered many more
changes from the rash conjectures of those who tried
emulously to reduce the lays to their own idea of polish
and to bring them into conformity with the best laws of the
art and style as then understood. Finally, suppose that the
whole context and order of the two epics were not due to
the genius who usually receives credit for it, but to the skill
of a more lettered age and the combined efforts of many ;

suppose too that the very lays, out of which the Iliad and Odyssey were put together cannot be proved by probable argument to have had a single author—in short, suppose that on all these matters we must hold opinions very unlike the prevalent ideas, what then will be the labour of restoring to the songs their original splendour and genuine form ! [1]

Wolf thus briefly sketches his doctrine. The Homeric poems were originally mere lays composed and handed down without the use of writing. Later they were committed to writing, and in the process were combined by the editors into continuous wholes, and were also polished and emended in accordance with the taste of a more advanced age than that which gave them birth. Next they suffered many things of many editors, Alexandrine and Imperial, and, finally, ran the gauntlet of Byzantine scholarship and of Byzantine ignorance.

In advancing this theory, Wolf has to combat, he says, the opinion of antiquity, though not, as it will appear, of all antiquity. The question which meets us on the threshold, the question of early writing in Greece, 'has lately been brought forward, or rather revived.' This was done by Robert Wood, in his work *An Essay on the Original Genius of Homer* (second edition, 1775). The Homeric lays show 'much genius, less art, and no deep learning.' The art of the poems, noble as it is, is in a way *natural*. The lays differ as much from the native wood-notes wild of mere balladists as from the manner of poets in cultivated ages. They stand between the ballad and the learned epic, between *Chevy Chase* and the *Æneid* or *Paradise Lost*, as we may say. Wolf does not deny to Homer all knowledge of writing, but only the habit of using it.[2] He does not regard appeals to the muse and to the memory as proofs

---

[1] Pp. xxxvi–xxxix.

[2] 'Non tam cognitionem litterarum quam usum et facultatem.' P. xliv.

of want of writing. These might be traditional formulæ. On he other hand, the word γράφειν, meaning merely 'to scratch,' does not imply that writing was known.

If we look for ancient evidence as to the origin of writing in Greece, we find the subject veiled by the mists which conceal all such beginnings. The Greeks did not practise the *comparative* method of studying analogous institutions in many different countries, of examining races widely severed, which are yet in the same stage of culture. They reposed on valueless myths about the earliest inventors. Modern authors have too hastily concluded that the introduction of letters and their general use must have been nearly simultaneous. No inquiry has been made into the degrees of advance, the modifications that must have existed. We must dismiss late and credulous legends about Phemius, about Homer's schoolmaster, and the other fables of the so-called 'Lives of Homer.' Let us examine the reasons for holding that, even if letters were introduced to Greece before Homer's day, there was almost no use made of them till the beginning of the Olympiads (776 B c.). That there was an introduction of Phœnician characters corresponding to what we gather from the myth of Cadmus, constant report and the form of the letters themselves declare. But the date is most uncertain. We have no information about the period when the Phœnicians began to use writing, nor about the uses to which they applied it. Greek fables have darkened the whole topic. The Greeks delighted in tracing all origins to the remotest ages, and in attributing inventions to their own mythical heroes : as, to Prometheus, by Æschylus ; to Palamedes, by Euripides ; to Cadmus, by Herodotus (v. 58), who gives it as his own opinion that previously letters were unknown to Greece. Supposing that the art was soon used for brief inscriptions, that does not imply a large use of writing for long poems.

Wolf surmises that Herodotus was deceived by the Theban heroic inscriptions on helmets and other votive offerings. The language and metre of these is clearly late.[1] Wolf detects in all these a 'pious fraud' of the priests. The evidence of Herodotus only amounts to this : the art of writing was known so long before his time, and was so familiar, that it might be attributed to extreme antiquity. As for Cadmus, the myth of his invention of writing may merely indicate the time when a vague rumour of such an art was abroad; after a long period would follow rude attempts to imitate it, and these, again, were succeeded by the general use of letters.

Wolf lays great stress on the probable slowness of any progress in writing. The letters were foreign, they needed adapting to a new tongue, vowels and other characters had to be introduced. After this labour writing would be confined to brief inscriptions on hard materials. Lastly would come writing for literary purposes. Perhaps six centuries would be needed for the development of literary writing. There would be a prejudice against copying out popular poetry, as if writing would deprive it of its life and spirit.[2] Wolf now turns to an argument from the assumed lack of writing materials in early Greece. Papyrus was not introduced till the sixth century B.C. He disbelieves in writing on leaves of trees or on potsherds. Stone, wood, and metal would be the earliest materials. These would only be used for public records. Wolf rejects Pausanias's story of the very ancient copy of Hesiod's *Works and Days* on thin sheets of lead.[3] The Greeks did not, like the Romans, write on linen

---

[1] Wolf compares Pausanias, ix. 11.

[2] The Ettrick Shepherd's mother urged that Scott had ruined the Border Ballads by publishing them.

[3] ix. 31, p. 771. Imprecations scratched on very thin sheets of lead are not uncommon.

(*libri lintei*). The Ionians introduced writing on skins. This Wolf regards as late, about 776 B.C., but gives no reason for his opinion (p. lxii). He says there could be no volumes written on waxed tablets. The Ionic alphabet of twenty-four letters, itself late, was not adopted at Athens till 403 B.C., before which the long vowels H and Ω were not employed.[1]

The Ionian colonists in Asia Minor were probably the first to make general use of writing. The Æolic and Ionic lyric poets before Simonides and Epicharmus can scarcely have dispensed with the art. As to public documents, Zaleucus appears to have been the first who introduced written laws, about 664 B.C.[2] The laws of Solon were written *boustrophedon*, alternately from right to left and from left to right, on rude materials, about 594 B.C. Thus writing for literary purposes was probably used earlier in Ionia and Magna Græcia than in continental Greece. Archilochus, Alcman, Pisander, could certainly write. But, as far as the writing of books in Greece generally is concerned, we cannot put the practice earlier than the period of Thales, Solon, Pisistratus, and the commencements of prose composition. Taking Pherecydes Syrius and Cadmus of Miletus, contemporaries of Pisistratus. as the earliest writers in prose, we may say that the making of books in Greece, and among the Ionians, is not prior to their date.

Homer may be said to prelude to prose composition, which, for lack of writing materials chiefly, was not evolved till three centuries later. (This would place the origins of the Homeric poems about 850 B.C.)

Wolf now denies that any learned Greek critic regarded

---

[1] His authorities are Ephorus, Theopompus, Andron Ephesius, in Euseb. *Chron.* ad Ol. xciv. 4; Cedren. and Pasch. *Chron.* ad xcvi. 4, and scholium to *Phœnissæ*, 688.

[2] Scymnus, *Perieg.* 313; Strabo, vi. p. 259.

the 'baneful tokens' of Prœtus as a letter. It must have been from the discussions of the Alexandrine learned that Josephus drew his famous statement, ' Late, and laboriously, did the Greeks acquire their knowledge of letters. . . . They say that even Homer did not leave his poetry in a written text, but that it was afterwards put together from oral recitations ; hence its many discrepancies.' [1]

Homer himself says nothing about writing. This argument from silence may, of course, be abused. Other poets, who could write, have not mentioned writing. But Homer is full of pictures of the arts, and Hesiod dwells especially on the domestic arts. Of writing, neither has a word to say. [2]

Two Homeric passages have been supposed to refer to writing. The first is Iliad vii. 175 ff. In this the princes are casting lots. Each marks his own, they are thrown into a helmet, Nestor shakes it, a lot leaps out, the herald shows it to each prince, none recognises it for his own but Aias. He knows the σῆμα, or private mark, which he had scratched on his lot. This clearly does not mean writing.

The other passage is vi. 168. Prœtus is in the position of Potiphar as regards his wife and Bellerophon. ' To slay Bellerophon he forbore, but he sent him to Lycia, and gave him tokens of woe, graving in a folded tablet many deadly things, and bade him show these to Anteia's father, that he might be slain.' (Anteia was the wife of Prœtus ; her father was King of Lycia.) Bellerophon goes to the Lycian king, and ' on the tenth day the king questioned him, and asked

---

[1] *Contra Apion.* i. 2. p. 439.

[2] Neither poet alludes to signet rings, which recent discoveries prove to have been very common in very early times. The graves of Mycenæ are rich in rings. Seals, again, being used as signatures by their owners, imply documents that had to be signed ; they can be used for other purposes, but in Assyria and Egypt their first use was to stamp the owner's signature.

to see what token he bore from his son-in-law Prœtus.
Now when he had received of him Prœtus's evil token, first
he bade him slay Chimæra, the unconquerable.' Here the
word σήματα, ' tokens,' suggests writing, as we hear of
Φοινικικὰ σήματα Κάδμου. Then πίναξ πτυκτός, ' a folded
tablet,' suggests a letter, and the word γράφειν, to scratch,
came to mean ' to write.' But these suggestions are false.
Eustathius was following Alexandrine authorities when he
says, on this passage, that the very early Greeks used hieroglyphs, much like the Egyptians.[1] The Venetian scholia (A)
also declare that the σημεῖα were εἴδωλα, not γράμματα ; it
was picture-writing, not alphabetic writing. This, Wolf says,
is the right Alexandrine interpretation, though Plutarch
' chatters ' about the ' letter' of Bellerophon. The Alexandrine critics were probably led to this opinion by the
word δεῖξαι, to ' show ' the token. No Greek or Latin poet
could talk of *showing* a letter.[2] Wolf will listen to no argument on the other side. Is it not better to adopt the interpretation of the ancients (in Eustathius and scholia A) than
to twist and pervert the language of Homer ? The folded
tablet was no letter, but a wooden *tessera* or *symbolum*,
with deadly marks (whatever they may be) rudely incised.[3]
Wolf thinks kinsfolk had secret marks, which they understood and sent to each other. He quotes a French author,
who has ' these most facetious observations : ' ' If this was
really a written letter, it is odd that so useful and well known
an invention should have disappeared two generations later,
when its employment would have been otherwise important.

---

[1] This would prove nothing in Wolf's favour. Books of any length
might be written in hieroglyphs ; or even, perhaps, in picture-writing,
εἴδωλά τινα.

[2] We, however, talk of producing, presenting, or displaying credentials.

[3] Schol. A. To ' write' is to engrave ; he *engraved images*
(εἴδωλα).

Was it only good for letters of introduction that tended to get people devoured by the Chimæra?'

So Homer never mentions writing. But how, we may be asked, was the composition of the epics possible without writing? Rousseau conjectures that the letter of Bellerophon was interpolated by the compilers of Homer. 'The Odyssey is a tissue of silly absurdities, which a letter or two would have dispelled in smoke, if we suppose that the heroes could write. Homer did not write, he sang; had the Iliad been written, it would have been much less recited.' [1]

Wolf is brought to consider the question of rhapsodes, or reciters, because, if there was no writing, the poems can only have been preserved by oral recitation. It is, therefore, most important to understand how they were handled by reciters, whether pains were taken to keep them in their pristine state, or whether there was much licence of inter-polation, addition, and alteration in general. Wolf's main idea is that the Homeric age was young, buoyant, *natural*, indifferent to 'a paper immortality.' Then he seems occasionally to regard the original lays as on a footing with *Volkslieder*, popular oral songs, concerning which nobody asks 'who composed them?' This attitude of mind was natural in a period influenced by Rousseau, and by the first researches into popular poetry. The original bards would be content with the praises of their audiences, and Wolf does not regard the Homeric minstrels, Phemius and Demo-docus, as on a footing with the late reciter in the *Io* of Plato. The world hardly understands, he says, that we really owe Homer to the rhapsodes, who are, however, not to be con-founded with the paid professional reciters of Plato's time (p. xcvi). Nor did the rhapsodes, though their name be derived from 'stitching' or weaving songs, compile mere

---

[1] Wolf quotes Rousseau, from his collected works, xvi. 240 (Geneva, 1782).

centos out of Homer. Nor were rhapsodes like the ' blind crowders' and ballad singers of modern life. Recitation was every ancient poet's only mode of reaching his public. The Homeric poems, however, were recited more than all others. 'Many testimonies confirm the fact that there was a kind of family (or guild) of Homeridæ, exercising their art, first at Chios, afterwards elsewhere' (p. xcviii). These Homeridæ were not a clan of descent from Homer, or if ever there was such a clan, the name was transferred to reciters, interpreters, and admirers of Homer.[1]

The name Rhapsode is later than Homer. The profession in his time was much more distinguished than in subsequent ages. The less education there was, the more illustrious were the reciters. The reciters originally chanted their own poems, and even till the time of Cynæthus (69th Olympiad, beginning of the fifth century), every rhapsode was likely to be himself a poet (p. xcix).

In the Homeric age, the minstrel's was a distinct profession, whether the poet stayed at a prince's court or went about to festivals, being dear to the Gods and honourable among men. 'The life and position of the rhapsodes was the same,' till, in the changes of society, they became mere mercenary entertainers (p. xcix). Did they recite from written books, and, if not, how did they learn their lays? Doubtless they used memory alone, and, even in the days of Socrates, did not read from a book. There is nothing to marvel at in their memory, a professional memory, carefully cultivated. Their sole business was to make poems, or learn and recite the poems of others (p. cii). One rhapsode would carefully instruct another. As much is even now committed to memory, for example, by actors : as great feats of memory are possible.

[1] The passages on the Homeridæ in Strabo, Pindar, and the scholia, Harpocration and his authorities, Ælian, and others will be later discussed.

Wolf thinks that, granting proper instruction, the Homeric poems need not have been at once deformed and altered, even though they were unwritten. However, even the ancients saw that recitation had been a source of various readings (p. cv). He relies on Josephus, as, in his opinion, giving the view of the Alexandrine critics.[1] Wolf proceeds inconsistently, after saying that the poems would not be altered in recitation, to show that they would be corrupted, that they would suffer from excisions, additions, alterations (p. cv). Many rhapsodes would venture on improvements of their own, and would insert fresh material. Their object would be to please their audience, not to preserve the lays. The family of Cynæthus is especially accused of taking these liberties.[2]

The Homeric hymns, Wolf thinks, represent what the rhapsodes were likely to compose, with no intention of literary imposture.

After all this disquisition on rhapsodes, whose memory and fancy alone preserved Homeric poetry before writing was used, Wolf declares that, without writing, no genius could have composed the epics *as we now possess them.* Nor would it have paid him to compose the epics if he had been able to do so. They would have been like huge ships built inland, and in no way to be launched. If he could not be read, the poet's epics, as we possess them, would have been worthless to him. Nobody could hear them out at a sitting, nobody could read them; so the idea of making them could never have occurred to him (p. cxii).

Hence the poem 'came otherwise,' not by the art of one ancient minstrel.

Here Wolf meets objections naturally raised by the unity

[1] *Contra Apion.* i. 2. p. 439 : ' They say that even Homer did not leave his poetry in writing ; hence its many discrepancies.'
[2] Schol. Pind. *Nem.* ii.

of plot and character in the Iliad and the Odyssey. Is that
unity so perfect in each poem as it is thought to be? The
discussion delays his argument, which ought at this point
to have shown *how* the poems came into their present
shape if they were not composed by one author. We must
remember that he will return to this problem, and must
follow him into the digression, whither, as Socrates says, the
λόγος leads him. Wolf will leave to others, he says, the
difficulties which the marvellous beauty and structure
of the epics can be made to yield. It is not enough to
admire the artistic character of the two poems as we possess
them, the simplicity of the action, so conspicuous in such a
mass of varied detail, the choice of one chief event and one
hero from the whole story of the Trojan war, the skilled
addition of ornament; how all in one poem bears on the
wrath of Achilles, all in the other on the return of Odysseus.
Many of these qualities undeniably merit just praise, especially in the case of the Odyssey, the 'admirable composition of which is to be reckoned the proudest monument of
the Greek genius.' As to the Iliad, the learned still dispute
about its original argument and chief motive. The difficulty
is that the προέκθεσις, or statement of the topic in the
prelude, does not demand the unfolding of all that the
Iliad contains, if the Iliad is only to tell of the wrath of
Achilles and its results. A few battles, just to show how the
Greeks fared without Achilles, would be enough. The
promise made by the seven verses of prelude might easily
be fulfilled in eighteen rhapsodies. The rest of the poem
is a mere appendix to the story of the wrath. Indeed, the
topic of the poem as it now stands is not the *wrath*, but
the *glory* of Achilles. Wolf kindly offers four verses of
prelude of his own composition, which he thinks would be
more appropriate than the actual prologue (p. cxviii). They
might readily be recognised as the work of a German rhapsode.

Sing of the *glory*, Goddess, of Achilles, son of Peleus,
Who while he lay by the ships in wrath with the king, Agamemnon,
Brought on the Greeks and himself griefs manifold, but when he rose
    thence
Woes did he bring on the Trojan array and on knightly Hector.[1]

Wolf thinks it may be no effect of art, but of nature, that one episode in the war was capable of being produced in an harmonious poem. 'Do you suppose,' he asks, 'that the poem would have come out very different from what it is, if not one poet but four had woven the web?' (*telam de-texuissent*) (p. cxx). The structure of the Odyssey could not be the work of a wandering minstrel. The several parts, however, may have been separately made and sung long before some one, in a more polished age, observed that by a few changes, omissions, and additions, all might be brought into a complete and perfect shape, to be a new and more splendid and perfect literary monument (p. cxxi). The opinion of Aristotle, to be sure, is adverse ; but by Aristotle's time their unity had been given to the poems.

Thus the composition of the poems is not an argument against Wolf's theory. That composition is the art of a later and more polished age, not the work of an illiterate early minstrel. And the composition is not really such a marvel of excellence as has been supposed.

Wolf now examines the so-called Cyclic poems, in their bearing on this question of composition. The Epic Cycle was a body of poems by various authors, including the Iliad and Odyssey, later arranged into a chronological order, from the Hesiodic marriage of Heaven and Earth to the slaying of Odysseus by Telegonus. It is first mentioned as

---

[1] This question of the promise of the prelude still plays a great part in disintegrating criticism. On the other side, who would detach from *Paradise Lost* all the passages which are not even distantly hinted at by Milton in his prelude?

D

the Epic Cycle by Proclus (circ. 140 A.D.) in his Handbook
of Literature.   Here he gives short prose summaries of the
poems in the Cycle.   They were such works as the *Cypria*
attributed to Stasinus, about 776 B.C., the *Little Iliad*, the
Æthiopis, and other poems of from 776 to 560 B.C.

The little we know of the Cyclic poems, says Wolf,
proves that they lacked the very qualities of unity and composition which are admired in Homer.   They have sometimes a hero, but usually no central motive, nor primary action
interwoven with episodes.   This is the evidence of Aristotle
himself, in the *Poetics*.   Wolf argues that, if the Cyclic
poets had known our Homer and his art in composition,
they must have appreciated and imitated it.   But they did
not do so ; therefore they are earlier than our Homer : they
did not know our Homer (p. cxxvii).

Wolf now gives examples of passages in the poems introduced by later hands, to effect a transition.   One is Iliad
xviii. 356–368, where many of the lines also occur in other
parts of the poem.   This was suspected in ancient times by
Zenodorus, of whom nothing is known.   The lines, Wolf
thinks, were inserted by his early diaskeuast (interpolator
or corrupter) to bridge over the interval between two rhapsodies.   Another instance he finds in Odyssey iv. 620.

The Iliad and Odyssey, then, are a congeries of atoms,
but not a fortuitous congeries (p. cxxxiv).   Many ages,
many minds supplied the junctions, and imposed the
unity.   They added whole rhapsodies in which Homer had
no part.   For example, the original character of the Odyssey,
from xxiii. 297 to the end was doubted by Aristarchus, and
Aristophanes of Byzantium.   There is also dispute about the
last book of the Iliad.   Wolf himself has always doubts
about the last six books of the Iliad.   He has a feeling
that the style is different, though he will not advance his
feeling as an argument.   There are unusual words and

phrases, there is a want of Homeric spirit and vigour, there is an abundance of prodigies.[1]

Wolf next examines the little that the Greeks have reported about the early history of the poems.

First he refers to the story that Lycurgus brought the epics from Ionia into the Peloponnesus.[2] According to Heraclides, the poems were obtained from the descendants of the mythical Creophylus, in whose family, says Plutarch, they were committed to writing. In all this, Wolf recognises no more than the Spartans' previous lack of knowledge, or scanty knowledge, of the lays. Afterwards they held Homer in high honour. The next historical reference is to the regulation of Solon about the recitation of the poems at the Panathenæa. The evidence is in Diogenes Laertius (i. 57), where the question occurs with reference to the verses 557 558 in the catalogue of the ships. The Megarians had one version of these, the Athenians had another ; both parties based on their versions their claims to the isle of Salamis. The lines are : ' Aias from Salamis led twelve ships, and stationed them by the companies of the Athenians.' This was the Athenian reading ; the Megarians read : ' Aias from Salamis led his ships, and from Polichne, and Ageiroussa, and Nisæa, and Tripodi.'[3] It is in connection with the question, Were the Athenian lines an interpolation ? that Diogenes tells us about Solon : τά τε Ὁμήρου ἐξ ὑποβολῆς γέγραφε ῥαψῳδεῖσθαι, οἷον

---

[1] The darkening of the omens or prodigies also marks the close of the Odyssey, and, as we note later, of *The Bride of Lammermoor*, where the character of the romance is greatly heightened by this artifice. The opinion of Shelley was that, in the last books of the Iliad, Homer really ' begins to be himself.'

[2] Authorities :—Heraclides Ponticus, Περὶ Πολιτειῶν, in Gron. *Thes. AA. GG.* t. vi. p. 2823 B ; Dio Chrysost., *Or.* ii. p. 87 ; Reiske, *Plut. in Lycurgo*, p. 41 D ; Ælian. *V. H.* xiii. 14.

[3] Strabo, ix. 394.

ὅπου ὁ πρῶτος ἔληξεν, ἐκεῖθεν ἄρχεσθαι τὸν ἐχόμενον· μᾶλλον οὖν Σολῶν Ὅμηρον ἐφώτισεν ἢ Πεισίστρατος—here follows a corrupt passage, a blank—ὥς φησι Διευχίδας ἐν εʹ Μεγαρικῶν.

The Dieuchidas quoted was a Megarian historian. The passage asserts that Solon 'wrote a law by which Homer was to be recited *with prompting* [or in regular order] so that where the first reciter left off, the next should begin.' Then follows the remark, apparently from Dieuchidas, that 'Solon did more for Homer than Pisistratus.'[1] Wolf avers that what Solon actually ordained is rendered obscure by the brevity of Diogenes Laertius. He believes that Solon caused the cantos to be recited in order—that is, in sequence of events. The phrase ἐξ ὑποβολῆς he renders 'ita ut alius alii succederet,' one following the other orderly (p. cxli). Thus ἐξ ὑποβολῆς is equivalent to ἐξ ὑπολήψεως, the term in the Platonic dialogue, the *Hipparchus* (228 B), by which the Homeric reform attributed to Hipparchus is described. On the other hand, the translation 'with prompting' has the approval of Mr. Monro and others. Prompting seems to imply a 'prompter's book,' a written text, and is thus not in accordance with the theory of Wolf.[2] Wolf holds that no written text was used at the Athenian recitations of Solon's time. In Ionia, he thinks, the poems must

---

[1] The corrupt passage is restored by Ritschl thus : ὥσπερ συλλέξας τὰ Ὁμήρου ἐνεποίησέ τινα εἰς τὴν Ἀθηναίων χάριν, which makes Dieuchidas allege that Pisistratus collected and interpolated the Homeric poems.

[2] Mr. Jebb says : 'The only question is whether it [ἐξ ὑποβολῆς] means "from an authorised text," or "with prompting," each reciter having his proper cue given to him' (*Homer*, p. 77, note 3). In the *Corpus Inscriptionum*, ii. p. 676, Boeckh defends the opinions of Wolf at great length against Nitzsch. A passage where the phrase means 'with prompting' is quoted from Polemon, in Macrobius, *Sat.* v. 19, by Isaac Casaubon, but Boeckh supports the sense *suscipere alterius orationem*, to take up the matter where another left off.

already have been recited in an orderly manner.   In Ionia,
too, the use of writing must have already existed in the age
of Solon, at least in its *prima tentamina.*

Leaving Solon, Wolf declares that he need no longer
trust to conjecture (p. cxlii). 'History speaks. The voice of
all antiquity, and, on the whole, the consent of all report bears
witness that *Pisistratus was the first who had the Homeric
poems committed to writing, and brought into that order in
which we now possess them.'*

This may be called the key to Wolf's position, and it
has been most eagerly assaulted.   If the Homeric poems
were not even written out till the age of Pisistratus, if they
did not exist nearly in their present order till that epoch, we
must allow for a gap between their first composition and
their complete form, in which there is room for any amount
of changes.   Wolf's evidence for his very sweeping assertion
is stated thus :—

'Cicero, Pausanias, and all the others who mention the
matter, put it forth in almost the same words, and as a
thing universally known.' Cicero's remark is in his *De
Oratore,* iii. 34.   'Who was more learned in these times
than Pisistratus, or whose eloquence was better instructed
in literature than his who is said to have been the first to
have arranged, in their present order, the *books* of Homer,
previously in disarray ?'   Next we have Pausanias (vii. 26, p.
594) : ' Pisistratus collected the Homeric poems which were
dispersed, and known in memory, in various quarters.'
Then comes the familiar quotation from Josephus (*C. Apion.*
i. 2) : 'They say that even Homer did not leave his poetry
in writing, but that it was transmitted by memory and afterwards put together from the separate songs'—'that is,
by Pisistratus,' adds Wolf—'hence the number of discrepancies which it presents.'   Ælian, Suidas, and other late
authorities are then cited.   Finally, an anonymous author,

cited in Allatius, *De Patria Homeri*, quotes an epigram on a
statue of Pisistratus : ' Thrice held I the tyranny, and as
often did the people of the Erechtheidæ expel me, and
again call me back, me, Pisistratus, great in councils, who
collected Homer, that before was sung in scattered fashion.
For the golden poet was our citizen since we Athenians
colonised Smyrna.'

This is Wolf's evidence for his statement that Pisistratus
first had Homer committed to writing, and introduced
sequence and unity into scattered lays. He utterly rejects
the idea that Pisistratus collected, not oral rhapsodies, but
scattered manuscripts, and that he merely restored, and did
not make, the unity of the epics. The tradition which
assigns a library to Pisistratus—a late tradition [1]—may be so
far true that the tyrant had some copies of Homeric and
other poetry—written out, probably, by his desire. As indications of the truth of his doctrine, Wolf quotes the
passage in Eustathius, according to which the Tenth Book
of the Iliad was composed by Homer as a separate piece,
and added by Pisistratus to the general collection. Eustathius gives this on the authority of ' the ancients,' whoever
they may have been. Wolf next touches on the absurd
statements of mediæval grammarians, according to which
fire and earthquake had made havoc of the *texts* of Homer,
whereon Pisistratus, offering rewards to all who could recite
fragments, had the whole reconstructed. Seventy-two grammarians were employed in the task, a reflection of the legend
about the Septuagint, and Zenodotus and Aristarchus pre-
sided over the labour. This is the mere babble of Byzantine ignorance.

Much as Pisistratus did, Wolf does not think that he did
everything and constructed Homer as we now possess him.
After Pisistratus, between Pisistratus and the Alexandrians,

[1] Aulus Gellius, vi. 17.

came the Diaskeuasts, to whose labours much is attributed.
The Venetian *scholia* show that the Alexandrians attributed
to the Diaskeuasts various interpolations. The Diaskeuasts,
then, Wolf regards as *exactores vel politores*, of Pisistratus's
time or somewhat later (p. clii).

As to the authorities which assign Homeric labours to
Hipparchus, son of Pisistratus, Wolf imagines that he colla-
borated with his father.[1] Wolf inclines to hold that Orpheus
of Croton, the author of the *Argonautica*, Onomacritus
the forger, Simonides, and Anacreon, all, or some of them,
may have aided Pisistratus. The task of Pisistratus is compared by Wolf to the collection of ancient lays by Charlemagne, and to the *Divan* of the Arabs, put together in the
seventh century. We do not possess the collections of
Charlemagne, and the other example will not be asserted to
resemble the epic unity of the Iliad and Odyssey (p. clvi).

The next step was the removal of certain poems from
the Homeric cycle. Herodotus (ii. 117, iv. 32) disbelieved in
the Homeric authorship of the *Cypria* and *Epigoni* : the
Hymns, also, were matter of doubt. The 'Chorizontes,' who
ascribed Iliad and Odyssey to different authors, also produced what Seneca thought a vain matter of discussion.[2]

Wolf next examines the age between Pisistratus and
Zenodotus, the Alexandrian critics, 'on which we have not
much more light than on that which preceded it.' Till the
age of Pericles, Wolf thinks that reading and writing were

---

[1] The authority is the Platonic dialogue *Hipparchus*, 228 B,
where we read that Hipparchus first brought Homer into this land,
and compelled the reciters at the Panathenæa to chant the poems ἐξ
ὑπολήψεως ἐφεξῆς, ' successively, in regular order,' as they now do to
this day. The statement, taken with the other tradition about Solon,
really contradicts, and does by no means confirm, the legends about
Pisistratus.

[2] *De Brevitate Vitæ*, c. 13. The Chorizontes are frequently referred to in the Venetian *scholia*,

rare and difficult, and that Homer was best known in recitations.   About the time of the death of Pisistratus, the early
philosophers advanced allegorical interpretations of Homer.
They could not bear the literal sense of his stories about
the Gods, and, as usual in such cases, sought for symbolical
meanings.

Theagenes of Rhegium, Anaxagoras of Clazomenæ,
Metrodorus of Lampsacus, Stesimbrotus of Thasos, and
other such interpreters, are mentioned.   Others, like Xenophanes, frankly accused Homer of blasphemy, and are
followed by Plato.   Hippias of Thasos introduced a conjectural emendation in one place, to clear the character of
Zeus.[1]   These and similar facts lead Wolf to consider the
growth of Homeric criticism in Greece.   When once a few
written texts had been made, various readings derived from
recitation, or corrupted in transcribing, were sure to creep
in.   The original Pisistratean manuscript, if there were a
complete manuscript, would become the lake whence various
rivulets flowed.   Whoever made a new copy would find the
advantage of comparing older texts.   The new amateurs
would omit what they disliked, would add what they thought
worthy (p. clxxii).   There would be no critical severity of
judgment as we understand criticism.   All taste would be
'æsthetic' rather than 'critical,' relying on poetic feeling
rather than on documentary authority.   Of the early copies
which Wolf supposes to have been thus casually constructed,
we hear of several.   One was named from Antimachus of
Colophon, the poet ; another from Aristotle.   The scholiasts
call such copies αἱ κατ' ἄνδρα as distinguished from civic

---

[1] Iliad, ii. 15.   The text is Τρώεσσι δὲ κήδε' ἐφῆπται.   'With
Jesuitical art' Hippias read διδόμεν δέ οἱ κῦδος ἀρέσθαι.   'The change
of an accent (διδόμεν for δίδομεν) throws the blame from Zeus on to
Sleep.   This lusis of an Homeric problem by Hippias is quoted by
Aristotle (Poet. 25) (p. clxviii).

copies, αἱ κατὰ πόλεις, as of Marseilles, and Sinope, Chios,
Argos, Cyprus, and Crete. We know not whether they were
prepared by command of the states, nor by whom, nor in
what age. Probably they were collected by the Ptolemies
in Alexandria. The names, Chian, Massiliot, and so on,
would be given to the manuscripts by the Alexandrian
librarians. Wolf does not believe that the civic editions had
been made by the order of the several states. The real
purification and present condition of the poems are derived
from Alexandria, a filter, as it were, of the various waters.

We now reach the Alexandrian age of libraries and of
comparative criticism, the age of Zenodotus, Aristophanes,
Aristarchus and Crates. The eldest is Zenodotus, who
objected to so many passages that he may seem to banish
Homer out of Homer's poems. His was an eager and
violent kind of criticism, as was natural in the dawn of
critical science. Next came Aristophanes, the inventor of
the signs of accents. He has more learning and more
modesty than Zenodotus. Then we reach Aristarchus, the
greatest of critical names, whose work is mainly known to
us by mere citations in the Venetian scholia. Wolf maintains that Aristarchus was devoted to improving Homer, as
we may say, and thought that genuine which seemed most
worthy of his author. ' In quo nemo non videt, omnia
denique ad Alexandrinorum ingenium et arbitrium redire '
(p. ccxxxvi). Our Homer, then, is Homer as the Alexandrines
thought he ought to be. The scantiness of our evidence
makes it impossible for us to reconstruct even the shortest
canto of the Iliad exactly to the mind of Aristarchus. We
know not what novelty he may have introduced ; what respect he showed to old texts, or how he used the editions of
Zenodotus and Aristophanes. His own text swallowed the
older ones, as Aaron's rod swallowed the rods of the magicians.
We cannot say what they were like. About Aristarchus as

an interpreter of Homer, we are only certain that he dis-
approved of the symbolical and allegorical methods. He
placed his critical sign, the obelus, not so much against
the verses which he did not think were Homer's, as against
those which he held unworthy of Homer. 'Not what
Homer sang, but what he should have sung' was his chief
concern. Lessing and Wieland would change or excise
many parts of Shakspeare, as unworthy, if they were critics
in the Greek manner. Aristarchus not only put his mark
against passages, but he took many passages clean out.[1]
We know not what test or standard he used in these operations. 'He not only marked blemishes, but he cut and
cauterised ; and he set the portions which he thought were
dislocated, and so emended Homer.' The four lines in
which Phœnix says that he thought of killing his father,[2]
were taken wholly out by Aristarchus.[3] Finally, 'Our
Homer is not that which lived in the mouths of his
Greeks, but Homer as he was changed, interpolated,
reduced, and emended, between the times of Solon and
those of the Alexandrians. . . . The united voices of all
ages attest it, and History speaks. Yet our poet refutes history, as it were, and the feeling of his readers testifies against
it. Nor indeed are the lays so defaced and transformed,
as, in separate matters, to seem too unlike their original
estate. Nay, almost all in them agrees in the same genius,
the same manners, the same method of thought and speech.

---

[1] Iliad, x. 397, scholion. See Leaf's note, which puts another
complexion on the matter. 'Ammonios is stated to have said that
Aristarchus first marked the lines with στιγμαί – apparently a sign of
hesitation – and afterwards obelised them.'

[2] Iliad, ix. 458.

[3] Wolf himself restored them from Plutarch, *De Aud. Poetis*, 8.
Plutarch tells us that Aristarchus excised them. La Roche says that
the lines must have been expurgated before, as our texts represent the
Alexandrian vulgate, not Aristarchus's recension thereof.

This everyone feels who reads them closely and with intelligence. The contrast is to be felt, with its causes, in reading Apollonius Rhodius, the other Alexandrine poets, and Quintus Smyrnæus, commonly thought the very image of Homer. What if we owe the restoration of this wonderful harmony to the elegant intellect and erudition of Aristarchus? . . . What if Aristarchus and Aristophanes, by dint of comparing all relics of antiquity, grew learned in the true language and proper form of ancient utterance,' and so restored Homer (p. cclxv)?

This rather wild hypothesis, Wolf admits, cannot be demonstrated, for lack of material.

Here we may end, though Wolf adds some remarks on the *obelus* of Aristarchus, and on Crates. His main argument is, that the Homeric poems, however much of them may have been composed by a single ancient minstrel, were but scattered cantos, living in the mouths of men, till Pisistratus began the work of committing them to manuscript. They were diversely handled, till the age of the Alexandrians, when the undeniable harmony which they exhibit was imposed on them by the learning and taste of Aristophanes and Aristarchus.

CHAPTER IV

CRITICISM OF WOLF

I

IT is no reproach to Wolf that almost all his arguments may now be traversed. Time and fresh discoveries have greatly increased our knowledge of prehistoric Greek life. The comparative method, too, which he applauded rather than practised, now enables us to compare with Homer the oral or inscribed literature of many races in states of civilisation analogous to that of early Greece. These researches, indeed, yield no certain proofs, but they raise the presumption that many of Wolf's *a priori* opinions about writing, and the time required for its development and application to literary purposes, are probably incorrect. Of all his elaborate system little remains fixed, except the strong likelihood that our Homeric poems are not, word for word, the poems as they flowed from the lips of the original author. It is not to be denied that some passages bear many marks of interpolation, while it is likely enough that other parts have been lost. The problem now is : which passages are to be regarded as original, which are of later date ; at what period are they likely to have been inserted, by whom was this done, for what purposes, and, above all, how did the various interpolations gain general acceptance in Greece ? Many of these problems can never be solved. While letters endure we shall have the Homeric question with us. In this essay, the general theory is highly conservative, and attempts will be made to disprove many of the arguments in favour of frequent interpolations by many hands and at many various dates. It is admitted, however, that the poems, exactly as they were fashioned by the original author—without loss or addition of jot or tittle—cannot possibly be restored.

Coming to discuss Wolf's theory, we first examine his beliefs about early writing in Greece. Some vague early knowledge of the possibilities inherent in written characters, Wolf does not directly deny. What he does say is that even when the old Greeks came into contact with the art of writing, they would be very slow in acquiring it ; the Phœnician characters would demand changes which could only be made in a tardy evolution lasting for ages. Again, the scantiness and inadequate character of writing materials, before Greece obtained papyrus from Egypt, would delay the development of the art. For long, letters would be used for mere inscriptions on stone and wood, not for the preservation of literary documents. Perhaps six centuries would elapse between the time when the Greeks became acquainted with the foreign use of written letters and the time when they could apply them to literary uses, in the age of Pisistratus—say 560 B.C. Thus some Greeks may have had some knowledge of written characters in 1120 B.C. Yet these characters were not employed as aids to composition and literary memory till about 750-550 B.C.

These reasonings are frankly *a priori* and rest on Wolf's notions of probability. Analogy clearly tends to suggest that he is wrong. An intelligent African, after becoming familiar with our alphabet, invented (he said, in a dream) a new and complicated one to suit the needs of his native language. No one can suppose that Greeks would be slower by several hundred years than negroes, in their mental development.

As to materials again, the case against Wolf is particularly strong. The Greeks had been, as we are now told by archæologists, for uncounted centuries in close connection with Egypt.[1] They had every opportunity of seeing and obtaining papyrus if they chose to do so. Even if they did not choose, the absence of what we now consider suitable writing materials never yet delayed the art of writing when once known. The Aztecs, like the old Ionians, according to Herodotus, wrote or painted numerous documents on the skins of beasts.

The Creek Indians were in a much more backward condition than the Aztecs. Yet the ' Kasi'hta Migration Legend ' was inscribed on a buffalo skin, and handed to Governor Oglethorpe in 1735, by Tchikilli. According to the *American Gazetteer* of 1762, the legend was 'curiously written in red and black characters on the skin of a young buffalo.' The said skin was set in a frame, and hung up in the Georgia office in Westminster. The legend contained some fifteen hundred words. The skin, unhappily, is lost; nor do we know in what kind of characters it was inscribed. If it were in picture writing of any sort, the fact would be interesting ; if it were in our alphabet, this would prove that a comparatively barbarous people could and did learn to use writing for literary purposes much more rapidly than Wolf thinks probable in the case of the Greeks.[2]

That the Ojibbeways used picture writing to record on birch bark, not only their cosmogonic legends, but even brief lyrics, we learn from Kohl.[3] Analogy thus indicates

[1] Flinders Petrie, *Journal of Hellenic Studies*, 1890-91.

[2] Gatschet's *Migration Legend*. Brinton : Philadelphia, 1884, p. 235.

[3] *Kitchi Gami*, where examples are given, reproduced in *Custom and Myth*, p. 292.

that even very backward peoples, with very scanty appliances, may use these for literary purposes, and it seems improbable that the Greeks would be less apt than the Creeks. As for materials, writing has been impressed or inscribed on cakes of clay, as in Assyria; on leaves of trees, as in Burmah; on bones, as in Arabia; on tablets of wood, as in Greece; on fragments of pottery, on plates of metal, on Scandinavian staves, on everything.

There is no reason why Pausanias should *not* have seen at Ascra, as he tells us that he did, if not the original copy of Hesiod, at least an extremely ancient copy, etched on thin and mouldering plates of lead. The magical imprecations scratched on very thin slices of lead, in our museums, show us what this manuscript was probably like.

It is certain, from Homer, from tradition, and from remains of works of art, that Greece, in very early times, was in close contact with Phœnicia and Egypt. It is certain that the Phœnicians had early evolved, probably out of Egyptian hieratic characters, an alphabet. To say that Greeks would need many centuries to make this alphabet serve their purposes, and would then be hampered by lack of writing material, is to make Greeks more stupid and slow than most races. We must not make too much of the absence of inscriptions, for example, on the graves at Mycenæ. As has been already observed, in the Holy Isle of Loch Awe are many Celtic grave-stones, covered with sculptures of men and animals. But these monuments, probably of the fifteenth or sixteenth centuries, bear no inscriptions, though writing, of course, had long been familiar.[1] On a mere balance of probabilities, then, we are certainly entitled to reject what Wolf thought probable, and to hold it likely that the quick-witted Greeks rapidly made prize of

See note in *The Bridal of Caoilchearn*, by John Hay Allan, London, 1822.

the Phœnician alphabet, and were not long before they applied it to literature.[1]

Wolf argues next on the evidence of mentions of early writing in the classics. Zaleucus in Italy (664 B.C.) is said to have been the first who introduced written laws. Nitzsch controverts this opinion, founded on Strabo,[2] and Bergk declares that far too much weight is given to the evidence. ' What was new was that Zaleucus first gave a comprehensive written code (*Rechtsordnung*). . . . The beginning of writing is not to be sought in political but in religious life.'[3] Wolf argues that Solon's laws (594 B.C.) were inscribed on rude materials, and βουστροφηδόν—that is, alternately from right to left, and from left to right. But it does not follow that this manner of writing is less capable than another of literary employment. The famous inscription of the Greek mercenaries under Psammetichus, on the leg of the colossal figure at Abu Simbel, is very possibly older than 594 B.C., yet it is written from left to right.[4] It is not easy to follow Wolf's argument here, and Volkmann is not too severe in calling it ' very arbitrary.' In the eighth century, Wolf admits, some men of ingenuity may have used writing in Magna Græcia and Ionia, and such poets as Asius, Eumelus, and Arctinus may have done so, as well as the epic poets of

---

[1] Mere imitativeness leads savages in the direction of writing. Mr. J. J. Atkinson informs me that, on the sudden arrival of a friend, he wrote a message on a piece of bark, gave it to a Kaneka in New Caledonia, and sent him to the shop for some whisky. Next day the Kaneka returned to the shop with another piece of bark, on which he had scratched signs at random. He expected, but did not get, another bottle of whisky ; he had not quite understood the nature of writing, but his mind was travelling in the proper direction.

[2] vi. 260. A., quoting Ephorus.

[3] Bergk, *Gr. Litt.*, p. 195 ; Volckmann, *Geschichte und Kritik*, p. 187.

[4] Bergk, i. 194. The Egyptians remarked on the Greek manner of writing from left to right (Herodotus, ii. 36).

the first Olympiads (p. lxx). But writing for literary purposes in the whole of Greece cannot be earlier than the age of Pisistratus. Wolf is reduced to this opinion because he is determined to give Pisistratus the credit of the first text of Homer. But it is clear enough that if men were writing in the eighth century, and if the Cyclic poems were written, the Homeric poems were not likely to be left unwritten.

Modern opinion, in general, is opposed to the conclusions of Wolf about early Greek writing materials. 'The clouds of dust in which Wolf obscured the beginnings of writing are dispelled.'[1]

The progress of reaction against Wolf's denial of writing to early Greece is well traced by Volkmann.[2] In 1828 Wolf's pupil, Kreuser, maintained the ancient priestly and oracular knowledge of the art, and took, as proof of its antiquity, the slow evolution of successive alphabets. From 1828 onwards, Nitzsch busily opposed this part of Wolf's theory, and his energy was awakened again by the appearance of Lachmann's hypothesis of short scattered lays (*Liedertheorie*) in 1837.

Nitzsch relied much on the educational employment of writing in early times ; for example, on the statement that Tyrtæus was 'a teacher of letters.'[3] He also adduced Archilochus's employment of the word *skytalè*, a system of cryptic writing,[4] and Stesichorus's attribution of the art to Palamedes, in Trojan times.[5]

In 1830, Nitzsch forcibly argued for the very ancient use of prepared skins by the Ionians and Barbarians, as reported by Herodotus. He pointed to such old proverbial expressions as 'Zeus looked long into the skins,' or Books of Fate.

---

[1] *Philologische Untersuchungen*, Kiessling und Wilamowitz-Moellendorff, vii. 286 (Berlin, 1884).

[2] p. 180 *sqq.*   [3] Pausanias, iv. 15.

[4] Archil. fr. 39.   [5] Becker, *Anecd.* p. 783.

He quoted an ingenious suggestion that the Homeric phrase 'these things lie on the knees of the gods' refers to what is written in Fate's leathern roll. Moreover, the whole of archæological discovery and ethnological research, shows us peoples in the old world and the new, writing in materials not better than the Greeks had at hand, even if they lacked papyrus.

Another opponent of Wolf's doctrine, as far as writing was concerned, is Bernhardy, in *Epicrisis disputationis Wolfianæ de carminibus Homericis*.[1] The difficult expression ἐξ ὑποβολῆς, in the story about Solon's legislation on the matter of the rhapsodes, Bernhardy understood to mean 'ad fidem exemplaris probati,' 'in accordance with a good and received text.' He argued that the Cyclic poems were written and read, and believed that great part of the Homeric epics had been committed to writing by the beginning of the Olympiads (776 B.C.). But the written texts were not for a reading public but 'for a narrow circle of schools, and the guild of Homeridæ.' Bernhardy, however, does not go so far as to believe in the original writing of the epics.

Volkmann himself argues the question of early Greek writing in the light of our wider knowledge of Greek inscriptions discovered since Wolf's time, our wider knowledge of Oriental antiquity, our wider knowledge of rude races generally. Some kind of writing is a very early acquisition of man's, the first step towards and the basis of culture. All civilised peoples have writing, or some analogous system of recording by signs. The early history of such signs, we may add, is incompletely known. The Australians, perhaps the most backward race with which we are acquainted, make use of 'message sticks,' carved with lines and notches, which they can decipher. But this method answers rather to the rebuses composed of material objects,

[1] Hal. 1846.

which are used by some of the natives of India, than to
actual writing.[1] The Australian signs are probably agreed
on by the parties sending and receiving the 'message stick,'
which is their *skytalê*.[2] We find no examples of such means
of communication among the more advanced Maoris, whose
sacred hymns are preserved by regular διδασκαλία, oral
teaching in priestly colleges, answering to that of the
Homeridæ of one Homeric hypothesis. The unknown
artists of the statues in Easter Island had a very elegant
picture writing, in no way inferior, as far as appearance goes, to
Egyptian hieroglyphics, but, of course, indecipherable by us.
The Incas had nothing more advanced than knotted cords
of various colours, aids to memory which were only understood by the learned, and which answered to the wampum
belts of the North American Indians.[3] When they wished
to record any matter they 'made a knot of it.' But the
policy of the Incas was deliberately obscurantist, otherwise
they might, perhaps, have borrowed a lesson from the hieroglyphs of the Mayas in Yucatan. These are said to contain
alphabetic characters. The Aztec system included picture
signs and 'phonograms,' thus 'snake,' *coatl*, is written with
a sketch of a pot, *co(mitl)* and the sign of water, *a(tl)*.[4] As
mankind has thus always been striving after such signs, Volkmann argues that the Homeric Greeks, civilised, acute, and
in contact with peoples who could write, must not be denied
the art, and the habit of employing it for literary purposes.[5]
Bergk observes : 'Long before there was a reading public,

[1] A curious example is to be found in Mr. Kipling's book, *Plain
Tales from the Hills*. Another example, nearer home, in Allen Breck's
rebus missive, in Mr. Stevenson's *Kidnapped*.

[2] Brough Smyth, *Aborigines of Australia*.

[3] Garcilasso de la Vega, *Royal Commentaries of the Incas*.

[4] Tylor, *Early History of Mankind*, p. 93. Taylor, *The Alphabet*
i. 23.

[5] Volkmann, pp. 217, 218.

the poets made use of writing.'[1]   Bergk even thinks that the
'letter' of Prœtus may have really been a letter.

As far as writing materials go, then, the contention of
Wolf is not valid.   The date, however, of writing in Greece,
and the date of its application to literature, are different
matters, and both are obscure.   But our resources greatly
exceed those which were at Wolf's command.   As Canon
Taylor points out, in 1825 Rose's *Inscriptiones Grœcœ
Vetustissimœ* numbered less than one hundred.   There
are now more than ten thousand inscriptions in the four
volumes of the *Corpus Inscriptionum Grœcarum*, and a
complete collection might contain twice that number.   Probably there were inscriptions older than the oldest we
possess.   But, from those which are familiar, it is plain that
writing in Greece, as a not uncommon accomplishment,
may be at least as old as the ninth or tenth century B.C.

The oldest inscription which we can approximately date
is not very ancient.   It is the Greek writing on the leg of
the colossal Rameses II., at Abu Simbel, near the second
cataract of the Nile, guarding the river gates into ancient
Nubia.[2]   Some eight centuries after Rameses left The
Silent Ones, his images, to watch the Desert and the Nile,
certain Greek mercenary soldiers of Psammetichus, King of
Egypt, cut their names on the leg of the colossus.   There
were two kings named Psammetichus : the *condottieri* of
either may have chiselled the inscription.   The date of the
earlier is 654-617 B.C. ; the date of the later is 594-589 B.C.
It is more cautious to suppose that the later king is the
person mentioned in the document.   It consists of five lines
written from left to right, and in the reading of Blass and

---

[1] *Griech. Literaturgeschichte*, p. 526.
[2] Brugsch, *History of Egypt*, English translation, ii. 95, 312.
Lepsius, *Denkmäler aus Aegypten*, vol. xii. pl. 98, 99, where there are
large facsimiles of the inscriptions.

Wiedemann [1] may be translated thus : 'When the King Psamatichus came to Elephantine, these words wrote the men with Psammatichus son of Theocles. They sailed, and came above Cercis, as far as the River let them. The men of alien speech led Potasimpto ; the Egyptians, Amasis. Archon, son of Amœbichus, and Pelegos, son of Eudamos, wrote Us.' There are also *graffiti* by men of Teos, Colophon, Ialysus in Rhodes, and other Greek adventurers. If we put the date no higher that 590 B.C., these chisellings prove that the Dugald Dalgettys of Greece could read, and write neatly and intelligibly, and from left to right, and with six vowels, and three new letters, ϕ, χ, ψ, all unknown to the parent alphabet, the Phœnician—six hundred years before our era. Now, writing must probably have existed for centuries before it was an ordinary accomplishment. Moreover, the characters used, when compared with other early inscriptions, show great advance on these, and it is natural to suppose that the advance required a long period of evolution. The inscriptions at Branchidæ near Miletus are about a century later, yet in the characters evolution has had time to produce few changes. At Abu Simbel H (eta) is used both as an English H, and as a vowel, long E. At Branchidæ H is only employed as a vowel. Koppa, something like our Q, is used at Abu Simbel, at Branchidæ it has disappeared. There is no long O (omega) at Abu Simbel, at Branchidæ it is in use.

'Since it took nearly a century to bring about these three innovations, it is obvious that a century would be wholly inadequate for effecting the enormously greater amount of divergence between the Abu Simbel alphabet and the parent Phœnician' (Taylor, ii. 17). Between the original Phœnician alphabet and that of Abu Simbel there are great differences, which (unless invented in a dream,

[1] Taylor, ii. 12.

as in Africa) could not be rapidly developed. There are three additional letters at Abu Simbel over and above the Phœnician, and the vowels have been evolved.

We have examined the process of evolution downwards, from Abu Simbel to Branchidæ. Let us now look at inscriptions older than that of Abu Simbel, but not so easy to date. Cadmus ('the Man of the East') brought letters to Greece, according to Herodotus, touching at the Isle of Thera on his way. By an interesting coincidence, that extinct volcano supplies the oldest known Greek inscriptions, cut on blocks of lava or basalt. Some are written in Phœnician fashion, from right to left. Some are written alternately from right to left and from left to right (*boustrophedon*). A third kind are from left to right, as at Abu Simbel.

The first sort is little modified from the Phœnician original. In place of *phi*, Φ, as at Abu Simbel, we have HH. Thus Φ had not been invented, and H was still, as in English, an aspirate. In these early writings QH (*qh*) is used in place of X (*chi*), KH was also in vogue. Not to delay, the Thera inscriptions 'cover the whole period during which the change in direction of the writing took place.' What, then, is the date of the inscriptions in Thera? It seems only natural to believe that, between the most archaic and the more modern writings a long period of time must have gone by. Though Kirchhoff and Mr. Newton place them *all* about 620 B.C. it is easier to agree with Canon Taylor, that the various methods were slowly evolved, and even the least archaic of these is more archaic than the writing at Abu Simbel. If changes in the alphabet were made gradually, not *per saltum*, we might not exceed in allowing for several centuries between the oldest Theran inscriptions and that which is not later than 590 B.C. We might take 950 B.C. as a possible date for the beginning of writing in Greece. But when the

Greeks began to use writing for the preservation of literary compositions is quite another question.

Here we have little but analogy to guide us. Were letters used for long, as Wolf supposes, only in brief inscriptions on stone or metal? It at once occurs to the mind that the first Phœnician letters which Greeks would see at home must have been in portable documents, not inscriptions on pillars or on walls. Again, the Aztecs had large numbers of documents painted on skins, but of inscriptions on monuments they have left scarce any at all. There seems to be no good reason why Greece, or any nations, should have begun to practise the art of writing on the hardest and most difficult materials.

Once more, analogy shows that even very rude peoples, like the Ojibbeways, use their picture signs to record their brief lyric poems.[1] The Icelanders of the heroic age (*circ.* 1000 A.D.) were no great writers, but they, too, carved their songs in runes, on staves, if we may trust the Sagas. Egypt and Assyria showed to travelled Greeks the example of writing for purposes of literature. These analogies tend, as far as they go, towards the presumption that, once acquainted with letters, the Greeks would not long delay to write out their poems and other such matters. Thus Bergk is inclined to believe that writing is older than the Iliad and Odyssey, and that the original poet of these epics may also have been among the first to use writing as an aid to memory and in composition. The Odyssey according to Wilamowitz could in no other way have been composed, but he is speaking of 'our Odyssey' as it stands, in his opinion a late piece of patchwork (*op. cit.* p. 293).

Wolf next argues against writing in Homer's day, from

---

[1] It may be urged that these are magical chants, and that the picture signs are parts of the magic. But the earliest use of writing must also have seemed to possess magical efficacy.

Homer's silence. It is plain that this argument must not be too hardly pressed. As we have seen, signet rings were in existence (say 1400 B.C.) in Mycenæ, but Homer never mentions rings.[1] Two passages have been much discussed. The first is the marking of each hero's token, or lot, by a private sign (σῆμα) which he recognised when he saw it.[2] These 'signs' were not writing, or the herald would have read out the name of the owner of the winning lot. But it does not follow that writing was unknown. Ancient signs are used in casting lots for portions of common land, by persons who can write perfectly well. The other passage [3] refers to the famous so-called letter of Prœtus. We have already stated Wolf's argument. On the other side it can only be said that if the 'baneful tokens' need not have been writing, nothing proves that they were not. It is plain that they would have been intelligible to Bellerophon, for they were not in 'an open envelope' but in a folded tablet. It is plain that they were not a mere picture of a man with his head cut off, they signified '*many* deadly things.' It is manifest, too, that Iobates *expected* to receive credentials : he asked for them after ten days passed in courteous entertainment. These tokens may have been anything, from something like Aztec rebuses, to Phœnician characters. There can be no absolute certainty on the subject. The persons, too, are Lycian, not Greek. As to Rousseau's remark, that the 'silly complications' of the Odyssey would have been unravelled by a letter, the remark is imbecile. By a letter from whom to whom ? From Odysseus to Penelope ? But a message in the mouth of the swineherd would have been safer than a note which Antinous or Eurymachus might have intercepted. It was necessary to the scheme of Odysseus that his wife

---

[1] Pliny, xxxiii. 4, where Pliny says that Homer does mention *codicillos epistularum*.

[2] Iliad, vii. 175. [3] Ibid. vi. 168.

should *not* know of his arrival.   Or did Rousseau imagine that there should have been postal communication between Ogygia and Ithaca?   Wolf was too ready to accept support from the flippant ignorance of the Frenchman.

The argument from Homer's silence, then, is of slight value.   He is silent about other matters with which he must have been acquainted.   The epic, too, is a thing of old formulæ, a mass of survivals, and a poet who could write might think the mention of letters as great an anachronism in his lay as forgery seems in *Marmion*.   Thus, on the whole, the tendency of modern opinion on this matter is conservative, is opposed to Wolf's conclusions.   We may not be able to prove that Homer could write, but we see that Wolf has not demonstrated the opposite.

CHAPTER V

II

WE now arrive at the constructive part of Wolf's task. He has, as he supposes, destroyed the belief in an early written epic; how, then, did the epic survive; how did it obtain its present form? First, the lays of Homer were preserved by rhapsodes, or public reciters. But Wolf's whole argument is meant to show that these men, from Homer's own day till the beginning of the fifth century, were poets themselves. He insists that they would wilfully alter, 'cut,' lengthen, and interpolate, at will. The lays thus altered beyond hope of recognition would reach the time of Pisistratus, would then be written out, and begin to receive polish, and be welded into unity.

But what do we know about the rhapsodes? Were they really poets? Did they not only make lays of their own, but also recite and alter those of earlier minstrels? Was the instruction (διδασκαλία) of rhapsodes an accurate affair, or could the reciter mangle his original as he pleased? It is clear that, in Wolf's opinion, he might take any liberty (*Prolegg.* cv). 'There was every opportunity for changing, omitting, and adding. Their care was *not* to keep the songs intact.' He cites, as analogous to the rhapsodes, however, the Druids and bards, of whose educational system we know nothing. Two analogous cases we really know, in

New Zealand and in ancient India. In New Zealand the Maoris have, or had, regular schools of oral instruction. Boys and young men were taught to repeat, with accuracy, the long and remarkable poems containing the cosmogonic legends of New Zealand.[1]

In this case, however, as probably in that of the Druids, the hymns were sacred, and accuracy was a religious necessity. The same remark applies to the Vedic hymns, which were preserved by a thorough system of oral instruction, long before India had the means of writing.[2] But we cannot be certain that the pre-eminent excellence of the Homeric epics would, in a non-writing age, secure for them such sedulous care. Wolf's rhapsodes had nothing less in their minds, according to him, than the maintenance of a pure text. The 'teaching' they received was thus of less than no value for preserving the old songs. Now, to preserve the old songs is the one object of such schools of oral traditional poetry as we know in experience. Wolf slightly mentions the *familia*, guild, or college of Homeridæ in Chios, but he probably did not suppose that they, any more than other rhapsodes, cared about maintaining the original form of the lays. These *Homeridæ* play a great part in the hypothesis of some who do not believe in an early written Iliad or Odyssey. The darkling topic only concerns us as far as the Homeridæ, or the rhapsodists, or both, may have preserved, or corrupted, or in any way manipulated ancient lays. The theory is that the Homeridæ were a guild of poets and reciters, who, possessing ancient lays in oral memory, possessing, for example an original poem on the wrath of Achilles, composed additional pieces which they recited as Homeric, and so gradually produced the greater part of our Iliad.

[1] Taylor, *New Zealand*. White, *The History of New Zealand*, i. 11.
[2] Max Müller, *History of Sanskrit Literature*.

To this hypothesis there are several objections. As Mr.
Matthew Arnold argues,[1] we cannot believe in the existence
of a number of great poets, all masters of the grand style ;
by which, of course, he does not mean mere epic formula,
dialect, and commonplace. It is said that there are usually
several great poets when there is one, as witness the Elizabethan dramatists, the age of Louis XIV., the period of
Byron, Scott, Shelley, Keats, and Coleridge. But these
great contemporaries are always very distinct in style and
genius. Nobody could mistake Webster for Shakspeare,
Byron for Keats, Coleridge for Scott. In Molière's day,
no living man could have written an act worthy of a
place in one of his comedies. In two years' space, England was enriched by *Waverley* and *Pride and Prejudice.*
No works could be more dissimilar and distinct. It is
thus improbable that, even granting the epic commonplace, one poet told of Helen on the wall and beside
Hector's corpse, while another sang of the fall of Patroclus, and so on. Once more, all experience shows us that
great poets will not choose to father their own works
on another. ' Poet is jealous of poet,' says Hesiod. Is it
probable that, in the life, or after the death, of the composer
of the 'Wrath of Achilles,' another minstrel, equally great,
would refuse all claim to his own Helen, his Paris, his visit
of Priam to Achilles, and modestly declare that these immortal scenes were his predecessor's? It is not in human
nature to act thus, however careless an age may be of
literary property. Again, it is plain that while poets were
celebrating, under shadow of Homer's shield, their local
heroes, and glorifying their own states, other cities would
jealously watch the process, and would demur to including
the fantasies of individuals in the general glory roll of Greece.
    If even there were a guild of Homeridæ, we might as

_____

[3] *Lectures on Translating Homer.*

easily believe that they tried to preserve the lays with accuracy, as that they deliberately mangled and interpolated them. But was there ever any such guild, or clan, in Chios and elsewhere? Pindar [1] speaks of 'Homeridæ' (literally, 'descendants of Homer'), 'minstrels of stitched, or woven lays.' The scholiast explains: 'Of old they called men of Homer's clan (γένος) "Homeridæ," who chanted his lays ἐκ διαδοχῆς, afterwards the term was applied to rhapsodes not of his kin,' as the Chian Cynæthus.

Strabo [2] writes: 'The Chians, too, lay claim to Homer, offering as strong proof the so-called Homeridæ of his clan, of whom Pindar also makes mention'—that is, in the line about 'Homeridæ, chanters of woven lays.' But this connection of Chios with the Homeridæ, is a mere theory of the Chians. Neither Pindar, nor even his scholiast, mentions Chios. Harpocration, in his lexicon, has 'Homeridæ: a clan in Chios, as Acusilaus writes. Hellanicus, in the *Atlantis*, avers that they were named from the poet.' Suidas says that 'the Homeridæ were a Chian clan, named from Homer.' The evidence of Acusilaus is highly suspicious.[3] Suidas also offers an alternative derivation of 'Homeridæ,' which Harpocration too gives in very obscure language.[4] The question is, Are these Homeridæ reported to have had clan-ritual and offerings, like other clans (γένη)? Apparently Harpocration's authority, Seleucus, did not believe this, for he denied it, and insisted on the alternative etymology of 'Homeridæ' from ὅμηρος, a hostage. In brief, as Nutzhorn says: 'The word Homeridæ sometimes means men who busied themselves with Homer, sometimes appears as the title of a Chian family, who, as some thought, received their name from the poet. This is all that the ancients knew about the

---

[1] *Nemean Odes*, ii. 1.
[2] xiv. p. 645.
[3] Volkmann, p. 261.
[4] *Ibid*. p. 263-272.

Homeridæ, but it has offered stuff enough for learned combination and conjecture.' [1] We know no more, and are not
even sure what the scholiast means when he says that the
Homeridæ chanted the lays ἐκ διαδοχῆς. Does this signify that
they chanted in succession, one following the other, or that
they inherited and handed down their knowledge of the lays
from generation to generation? All is hopelessly abandoned
to conjecture. So much for the Homeridæ. They offer nothing to build or wreck a creed upon. They may have
maintained an accurate text of Homer, or may not. We
are in total ignorance. A somewhat vague use of the
hypothesis of an Homeric 'school,' perhaps indicated by
tradition as the ' Homeridæ,' is made by Mr. Leaf in his
Companion to the Iliad (p. 21)—there was 'a body to
maintain a fixed standard,' 'a central authority.' But a fixed
standard was just what they did not maintain, as each
member of the school, at his own will and fantasy, gave
'something new.' Obviously, such a school would not
preserve so much as deprave the older lays. Before poems
thus composed could be wrought into the scheme of the
Iliad, a ' Recension' would be absolutely necessary. And
when was it made if the Pisistratus legend is a fable?

As for the rhapsodes, we first hear of them as existing in
Solon's time. Herodotus (v. 67) says that Cleisthenes of
Sicyon forbade the local rhapsodes to recite Homer at the
games, because Homer praised his enemies, the Argives
(*circ.* 600 B.C.). Beyond that our historical evidence does
not go, though, no doubt, the contests of rhapsodes were
then an old institution. There is no trace of these contests
in Homer, though Thamyris competed with the Muses.
But the *Hymn to Apollo*, which was old enough to be regarded as Homeric by Thucydides, proves the antiquity of
such competitive displays. The scholion on Pindar, already

---

[1] Nutzhorn, *Die Entstehungsweise*, p. 67.

quoted, after saying that the Homeridæ were originally the reciters of the Homeric poems, adds : ' The name was afterwards applied to rhapsodes not of Homer's clan. The company of Cynæthus was particularly conspicuous. They are said to have made many lays and incorporated them with those of Homer. Cynæthus was a Chian who, of the poems attributed to Homer, is said to have written the *Hymn to Apollo*. This Cynæthus was the first to recite the Homeric epics in Syracuse, about Ol. 69, as Hippostratus says.'

Here one thing only is plain. Cynæthus, though a Chian, and in one sense an Homerid, had no claim to be of the clan of Homer. As it is hardly credible that Homer was unknown in Syracuse B.C. 504, we must imagine that he *was* known, but not recited, if the story be true. In that case, he must have been known through written texts. In Sicily, Theagenes of Rhegium had already philosophised on Homer. In Sicily, too, lived Xenophanes, who says that all men learn Homer, and who blames his mythological scandals. It is not to be believed that Syracuse knew nothing of Homer after he was so familiar in Sicily. It may be that Cynæthus was the first who, in Syracuse, declaimed Homer at a festival ; he cannot have been the first who introduced his poems there.

Against the theory that Solon first made the rhapsodes put order into the poems, Volkmann argues that, if they really were a guild for preserving the lays, it was in their interest always to have done this, and that they would not need a layman to teach them their business.

It is evident that our knowledge of the rhapsodes is far too slight to be the basis of a theory and can be of no service to Wolf. We do not know when, or how, the minstrel, chanting his own songs, declined into the reciter declaiming those of other people. We do not know how soon a sentiment in favour of maintaining favourite pieces in their original and favourite form may have arisen. We cannot estimate the jealousy which may have made a minstrel prevent his rivals from getting opportunities to learn his compositions by heart, nor can we be certain that vanity would not restrain the rivals from attempting this kind of piracy. We have no real testimony as to the existence of an Homeric guild in Chios, and, if it did exist, we cannot say whether its members strove to keep pure, or laboured to expand and alter, the lays of their eponymous hero, Homer. The few surviving traditions, vague hints, obscure and corrupt passages of lost writers bearing on these topics have been sifted, discussed, conjecturally emended at vast length, and yield nothing positive. We may try what light analogy can yield by comparing the manners of other times and nations, but that light is seldom 'dry light.' We are, in fact, as far as ever from learning whence came the unity and construction of the epics. It could not be given, Wolf holds, by the original minstrel, who, *ex hypothesi*, could not write. Nor could it arise fortuitously, when any portion of the poems might be recited, apart from its context. Wolf, as we saw, declares that a poet of Homer's age would have had no audience for such long pieces, and could have had no readers. Wolf forgets that a court minstrel might continue his narration through the winter nights of a month, if he pleased. He also makes the familiar confusion of supposing that, even if a man could write, he would not write out a poem, unless he had a reading public. The Middle Ages fortunately supply an example to the point. The *Song of Roland* exists at the Bodleian, in the manuscript book of a *trouvère*, or Old French rhapsode. His public did not read the manuscript, but he refreshed with it his own memory. Reading was a very rare accomplishment, but the *Song of Roland* was probably composed by the aid of writing, and was certainly preserved in that way, not for a reading public, but for the use of the author, and of such reciters as could obtain copies. In similar circumstances, if writing existed, but was little practised, Homer might readily have composed by the aid of writing, and used his copy to aid his memory, though there was no reading public.

A well-known and ancient Greek tradition could only have come into existence in this state of affairs. Homer is said to have married his daughter to Stasinus, and to have given her the copy of the 'Cypria' as her dowry. Now, such a gift could only have been valuable (1) in an age of copyright like our own, when the owner of the poem might make his terms with a publisher, or (2) in an age when no one could recite a poem, and obtain the rewards for reciting it, unless he had a copy of the work. The former alternative is out of the question. An example of the second is supplied by the early Middle Ages. A *trouvère* leaves, in verse, his own copy of his epic poem (*chanson de geste*) to his son. He tells the young man that he himself has lived very well by reciting it, that he has carefully prevented other *trouvères* from getting copies, and that he hopes the poem will be as valuable to his son as it had been to himself.[1]

The tradition about the dowry, of course, is not to be taken as an historical fact. But the legend could only have arisen either in an age of copyright, or in such circumstances as the *trouvère* describes : that is, when writing existed but there was no reading public. Thus both of Wolf's arguments carry no conviction. There might easily be audiences in the princely hall for a long epic, and a man who could write might, and would, write out a poem, though he had no reading public, as did the author of the *Song of Roland*. Yet Wolf says : 'If Homer had no readers, I cannot imagine how he could ever have thought of com-

[1] Léon Gautier, *Epopées Françaises*, i. 215, 216.

F

posing such long and elaborately connected lays' (*Prolegg.* p. cxii).   All this seems a wandering from the main point— how did Odyssey and Iliad come into existence?   But the argument of Wolf, hastily written, with the printer's devil always at the door, is, in fact, loose and rambling.

It occurs to him (p. cxiv) that his task will be easier if he can show that the unity is not so marvellous after all. That of the Odyssey he admits, but explains as the constructive work of a later age which put together old lays that happened to fit.   That of the Iliad he impugns, but this is not the place to defend it.   Wolf's business is to show that the unity is a very late effort of art.   The original poet wove the web so far, others completed it.   As we have seen, he argues that the Cyclic poems (of the eighth century) lack unity.   Now, if these authors had imitated Homer, they would have aimed at unity.   They did not : therefore they did not know the Homeric examples as we possess them ; therefore, too, poetical unity is the work of a later age than theirs.   To this, arguing by analogy, we might answer that the *Song of Roland* of the eleventh century, has much more unity and coherence than its languid and diffuse *remaniements* in a later and more cultivated age. On the whole point, modern scholars are directly opposed to Wolf.   Since the work of Welcker (*Der epische Cyclus*) it has been generally recognised that the Cyclic poems presuppose the existence of an Iliad, and were deliberately planned for the purpose of introducing and continuing its narrative.[1]

Wolf's strictures, which follow, on interpolations in the epics, and *juncturæ* between what had been unconnected rhapsodies or lays, will be examined later.   He has now convinced himself that writing did not exist for literary purposes in Homer's time ; that Homer could not write, and

---

[1] See Jebb, *Introduction to Homer*, pp. 150-153.   Monro, *Journal of Hellenic Studies*, iv. 305, v. 1.

would have had no motive for writing if he could ; that poems older than the epics as we have them show none of their unity and constructive art ; that this art is, therefore, later ; that the Iliad and Odyssey present signs of tinkering, and in fact they are a *congeries*, but not a fortuitous *congeries*, of poetic atoms. Their unity was the work of many minds in many ages, all labouring on the remembered lays of the original minstrels. As we saw, he adduces ancient doubts as to the originality of several books, and then examines what is reported by tradition as to the literary history of the epics. It is in this history that he must discover the *method* of the evolution. His first really important point, Solon's law as to reciting Homer at the Panathenaic games, has been discussed already. But the point is, to the last degree, obscure. As Mr. Monro remarks, in his edition of the Iliad (p. xv), our only good evidence is that of the orators Lycurgus and Isocrates. The law of ' our fathers,' according to Lycurgus, appointed Homer's to be the only poems recited at the quinquennial Panathenæa.[1] The remark of Isocrates is still more vague.[2] The garbled or corrupt evidence of Dieuchidas of Megara in Diogenes Laertius is earlier, but is interested (as there was a quarrel between Megara and Athens, which turned on a line in the catalogue of the ships) and is interrupted by lacunæ. The text has been interminably discussed, to no sound purpose.[3]

Leaving matter so disputable, Wolf at last comes to his point. He will now show us how and when the unity of construction was given and artistic merit imparted to the epics. ' History speaks. The voice of all antiquity, and

[1] *Leocr.* p. 209. [2] *Panegyr.* c. 42.

[3] Volkmann, p. 306. The value of the evidence of Dieuchidas, and the Alexandrine estimate of it, are discussed by Möllendorff (*Philologische Untersuchungen*, Berlin, 1884, p. 342) and by Ludwich (*Aristarchs Homerische Textkritik*, ii. 399).

the common consent of report avers that *Pisistratus first
committed the Homeric epics to writing and published them in
the order wherein we read them now.'*

This is the great discovery for which we have waited so
long, and to reach which we have toiled through such
jungles of learning.   But, such is the fate of literary discoveries, the part attributed to Pisistratus by Wolf is now
disbelieved in by the vast majority of scholars.

It has been obvious to anyone who read the passages
from ancient authors quoted by Wolf, that they do *not* say
Pisistratus first committed Homer to writing.   Thus Suidas
(s. v. Ὅμηρος) declares that Homer 'wrote' the Iliad, but in
fragmentary portions, leaving separate cantos in separate
towns, whence Pisistratus collected and combined them.
Tzetzes speaks of Homer's 'books,' for collecting which
Pisistratus made proclamation.   In the scholion on Plautus
discovered by Ritschl, it is said that Homer was *read*
'fragmentarily, and not without difficulty.'   Cicero avers [1]
that Pisistratus first arranged in their present shape 'the
Books of Homer.'   Josephus, who alone asserts that Homer
could not write, says nothing about Pisistratus at all.
Plutarch clearly holds [2] that Lycurgus used a written text.[3]
It is not improbable that the whole legend about Pisistratus
dates from an epigram, said to have been inscribed on his
statue in Athens.   'I collected Homer, formerly sung in
scattered lays.'   But is it likely that the Athenians allowed
a statue of Pisistratus the tyrant to stand in Athens?   'It
may be regarded as certain that the epigram is a mere literary
exercise, going back at furthest to Alexandrine times.   It
seems probable, however, that it is the source from which
the other statements are derived.' [4]   In Nutzhorn's *Die*

---

[1] *De Oratore*, iii. 34, 137.   [2] *Lycurgus*, 4.
[3] Ludwich, *op. cit.* ii. 388, note 330.
[4] Monro, vol. i. p. xxvi. note.

Entstehungsweise der Homerischen Gedichte, p. 15,[1] will be found the array of the evidence on which Wolf and, later, Lachmann relied, and a criticism of the Pisistratean hypothesis.

Though Wolf curiously exaggerated the value of his witnesses, yet he showed his acuteness by projecting a theory of this kind. Something of the sort is absolutely necessary to all who argue freely against the unity and originality of the epics. If they are in the right ; if every popular poet who chose could cut and carve the body of Homer, and could insert what he pleased of his own ; if these processes were going on for three hundred years, from Smyrna on the east to Massilia in the west, how did Greece ever obtain one generally recognised text of Iliad and Odyssey ? Would not Thessaly have one text, Thebes another, Athens a third, Colophon a fourth, all widely and irreconcilably different, as different poets, for different reasons, had modified, abridged, and enlarged?

Wolf saw clearly that, if an early written text, and copies from it, were to be abandoned as impossible, he must find a time, a place, and an editor, to whom Greece owed a *textus receptus*. Editor and place he found in Pisistratus, and at Athens. But, if separatist scholars reject his theory, as a myth without basis in evidence, how do they account for the present existence of Iliad and Odyssey ? If Pisistratus and his friends did not give unity to scattered lays, who did, and when, and where ?

We have examined the hypothesis of a kind of poetical college, a society of Homeridæ, who first recited and afterwards enlarged, and finally, perhaps, codified the casual lays, and imposed the mass on Hellas as recognised wholes. Meanwhile, Wolf's Pisistratean hypothesis is not only deficient in evidence, but in direct contradiction with

[1] Leipzig, 1869.

other old literary myths, which offer as good testimony as
that of Cicero and Pausanias.   More than three centuries
before Cicero, Ephorus and Heraclides Ponticus observe
that Lycurgus brought the Homeric poems from Asia to
Sparta.   Diogenes, we have seen, practically asserts that
Homer had already existed ' in order ' when Solon made
the rhapsodes recite him in order.   The author of the
pseudo-Platonic *Hipparchus* attributes to his hero what
Dieuchidas attributes to Solon.   These contradictory legends
cancel each other.   ' It is hardly too much to say that they
are versions of a single story, told in turn of the chief states-
men of early Greek history.' [1]

The present writer must venture, however, to express
his own opinion that where there is so much confused
smoke of tradition, there may have been some fire of fact.
All the traditions maintain that the Homeric poems were,
at one time, in a ' scattered ' state.   Most of the legends
find the place of their collection at Athens.   Now, granting that the epics, as continuous wholes, were composed
and possibly written, at a very early date, historical causes
would tend to break up their unity.   When the Achæan
courts were ruined, there would no longer be an audience
for long poems, an audience meeting night by night in a
royal hall.   To a popular audience, assembled on a day of
festival, reciters would declaim only portions of the poems.
The more striking passages would be the favourites both of
rhapsodes and listeners.   Thus the poems would tend to
degenerate into mere ' Beauties of Homer.'   To prevent
this was the object of the law attributed to Solon.   Thus
Athens, in a sense, perhaps really did collect what was being
scattered, and did restore the connection of the lays.   That
written texts should be copied out at Athens is not unlikely.
But, if it were so, we may see how little Athens, with all her

[1] Monro, vol. i. p. xxvii.

advantages, could interpolate the poems, by the very scarcity of allusions to the city. Wilamowitz (p. 245) finds an Attic interpolation in Iliad xii. 372, where Pandion (an Attic name) carries his bow for Teucer! Then there is the famous disputed line about Aias, in the catalogue, and the lines on the city of Erechtheus (ii. 546), there are a very few references to Menestheus (xiii. 195), and to Theseus, as in the Odyssey (xi. 631). If these be Attic interpolations, they show how very little even an ambitious and poetic state could do in the way of interpolating. She could not introduce the Aristeia of a local hero. How, then, and by whom, and when, were all the other innumerable 'interpolations' made?

Another problem arises, how did the successive additions win general acceptance as part of the epic? We must remember that the epic was more than a poem, it was taken as history, its evidence was quoted as justifying titles to land, and was jealously watched, as we see in the Megarian tradition that Solon interpolated certain lines, Iliad, ii. 557–8.[1] Now, if the Iliad in the time of Solon was being quoted as unimpeachable authority for territorial claims, is it likely that Pisistratus would have been allowed later to put forward, with the general consent of Greece, an Athenian edition, and that the first? If the verses, in Solon's day, only existed in memory, they would have been of little value as testimony in a court of arbitration.

The evidence as to the popularity of Homeric poetry, among all Greek-speaking peoples, in times very remote, is considerable. But, in estimating it, we are always met by the difficulty that Homeric incidents may have been known, and assigned to Homer, yet need not have existed in the shape which we now possess, in Iliad and Odyssey. Thus Alc-

---

[1] Strabo, ix. 394. Aristotle, *Rhetoric*, i. 15.

man sang of Odysseus and the Sirens ;[1] Stesichorus, in Sicily, deliberately and consciously altered the story of Helen. So, in art, the throne of the Amyclæan Apollo was decorated with scenes from Iliad and Odyssey, and also from the Cyclic poems. So decorated, with appropriate inscriptions, was the ivory and cedar chest of Cypselus (*circ.* 700 B.C.).[2] Certainly the Homer and Hesiod whose morality Xenophanes blamed, and declared to be universally taught in the education of youth, were authors whom no man, nor state, would be allowed to tamper with. Far off, in Italian Elea, Xenophanes probably read the same Homer as men in Miletus or Smyrna (*circ.* 500 B.C.). If, then, we conclude with Nutzhorn that, long before 500 B.C., Homer was universally known throughout the Hellenic world, we are further than ever from being able to believe in Wolf's Pisistratean hypothesis.[3] A single state would not be allowed to construct the canon of the Greek Scriptures. Yet some hypothesis as to the origin of a universally accepted text of the ancient Greek history and Domesday Book we must discover, unless we adopt the old view that in Homer's time, or not much later, authentic texts were written.

It is incredible that such a state as Athens was, under Pisistratus, should have imposed a Homer of her own, not only on all cities from the Euxine to Italy, but on all rhapsodes, wherever they recited. 'We are involved in a network of contradictions if we do not reject the whole Pisistratean hypothesis as a fable.'

Pisistratus, even, according to Wolf, did not leave Homer a round and perfect whole. 'To polish completely, and *ad unguem*, may seem too hard a task for a first endeavour.'[4] Pisistratus had assistants and successors. But here Wolf proves too much. If the epic is now *perpolitum et quasi ad*

[1] Nutzhorn, p. 54.   [2] Pausanias, v. 176.
[3] Nutzhorn, pp. 56, 58.   [4] *Prolegomena*, p. cl.

unguem complanatum, 'polished to the nail,' what becomes of all the talk about its inconsistencies and blunders? But, if it is not so polished, what were all the 'diaskeuasts' and other polishers who succeeded Pisistratus about? It is either polished or it is not. If it is, *cadit quæstio* as to its innumerable defects.

If it is not, what becomes of the industry of the polishers? The Venetian scholia mention several passages as interpolations by Diaskeuasts. And Wolf alleges that these Diaskeuasts were *exactores vel politiores,* 'polishers' of the text, contemporary with or rather later than Pisistratus.

But the word *Diaskeuast* means nothing of this kind. They were interpolators of fictitious lines. Homer was not the only sufferer. Aristophanes even, according to Aristarchus and Apollonius, had been the victim of diaskeuastic industry.[1] The term διασκευάζειν means 'to corrupt a genuine text,' as Galen says some supposed the text of Hippocrates to have been corrupted. A number of examples from Aristarchus's criticism of the Iliad will be found in Lehrs.[2] In each case the motive for the interpolation is assigned. The examples are of no very great magnitude or importance. Many modern critics, however, assign nearly as much of the epic to interpolators as to Homer. Among his 'polishers' Wolf thinks that Onomacritus the forger, Simonides of Ceos, and Anacreon of Teos may be reckoned.

Leaving the age of Pisistratus, Wolf presumes that early copyists would produce very various texts, partly from variations in recital, partly from mere whim. Men would treat Homer, in fact, as editors, early in our century, treated the Border Ballads, interpolating, mixing texts for purely æsthetic reasons, and generally incurring the just wrath of Ritson. To this we need only answer that the common

---

[1] Aristoph. *Ranæ,* 1439 *sqq.* Lehrs's *Aristarchus,* p. 328.
[2] *Op. cit.* pp. 329, 330.

sacred poetry and educational text-book of Greece was
hardly likely to be treated as Bishop Percy handled popular
ballads.   These were new to men of letters ; Homer was of
a holy antiquity.   These were the literature of peasants ;
Homer was the charter of kings and states. 'All men
learned Homer' as early as 550 B C., according to Xenophanes.[1] All states and priests appealed to his evidence.
To alter it purposely was no light thing, that every amateur
should try his hand on it, *ex ingeniosa libidine.*

Wolf declares that the text was altered *summa levitate,*
'with the utmost frivolity.'   Ludwich, on the other hand,
avers that never did a people preserve any language so
piously and carefully as the Greeks preserved their epic
idiom.[2]   The same writer regards the supposed fantastic
correctors and revisors as mere modern puppets of the
fancy.[3]   Assuredly this view has more *a priori* probability.
In the very nature of the case, public sentiment would not
allow every poetaster to deface, as Wolf imagines, the most
sacred national possession, by 'adding grace, where grace
there was none.'[4]   We have seen that the early copies,
which the Alexandrian critics handled under the Ptolemies,
were of two classes.   Some were styled 'civic copies,' and
were named from Marseilles, Chios, Argos, Sinope, Cyprus,
and Crete.   Others were styled αἱ κατ' ἄνδρα, and bore the
names of individuals, as of Antimachus of Colophon and
Aristotle.   As to the civic copies Wolf believes that, though
they came from Chios or Massilia, they need not have been
made specially and by public demand for these states.   We
talk of the Venice manuscript now without meaning that

---

[1] Cf. Ludwich, *Aristarchs Homerische Textkritik*, ii. 448, note
409, against Fick.

[2] Ludwich, *Aristarchs Homerische Textkritik*, ii. 458.   Leipzig,
1885.

[3] *Op. cit.* ii. 438.   [4] Wolf, p. clxxii.

it was written for the Venetian commonwealth. However
this may be, it is certain that the Marseilles text, for example, differed very little indeed from that of Aristarchus.
The scholia cite the Marseilles reading frequently : it varies
from that of Aristarchus, when it does differ, only in matters
of grammatical mint and cumin. If Wolf were right, we
should expect to find whole passages of entirely different
tenor, omissions and additions, added graces, and de-
formities purged.

But the differences in Alexandrian texts are really of
little more importance than the errors which have already
crept into the poems of Scott, and even into the novels of
Thackeray. One could point out in *Pendennis* a passage
that might keep all Germany busy with conjectures and
emendations. It is true that we do not know the date of
the 'ancient texts' mentioned by the scholiasts, nor even the
dates of the Chian and Massiliot texts. But, earlier or
later, they did not differ as two versions of *Annan Water*
or of *Clerk Saunders* differ. The fortunes of Homer's text
had ceased to be subject to the greater incidents of time
and taste before the age of the Alexandrian critics.

Wolf maintains that even these critics preferred the
guidance of their own taste to sedulous comparison of manuscripts (ccxxxi). Lehrs refuses to believe this. He finds
among Alexandrines, and among their pupils, the Romans,
'a most sedulous use of manuscripts.'[1] In fact, Lehrs
asserts that Wolf's remarks on this topic are 'pure nonsense.'[2]
And he is right.

Wolf says, 'I do not wish my remarks to be taken as if
I were denying that good and careful Alexandrine editors
used ancient and the best manuscripts, and sought, by
comparing them, to find the genuine text. But that was

---

[1] *De Aristarchi Studiis Homericis*, p. 345. Leipzig, 1882.
[2] *Op. cit.* p. 351.

'genuine' which seemed most worthy of the poet. This, as everyone sees, brings the whole matter to depend on the ingenuity and judgment of the Alexandrians.' But he had already denied that the Alexandrine critics resembled our Bentley, and Valckener. Lehrs says, 'they could not both seek the genuine reading by comparison of old and excellent manuscripts, and also abuse their private judgment.' We have, indeed, one passage where Aristarchus declared that an emendation would get rid of a difficulty, but he declined to make it, because he found the reading (which involves an inconsistency in the narrative) in most of the manuscripts.[1] If Aristarchus erred at all, in Lehrs's opinion, it was through too great caution, not through audacity.[2] We are not very much concerned with one omission of four lines, by Aristarchus, if indeed, which is more than doubtful, Aristarchus was he who Bowdlerised the speech of Phœnix. Clearly we have come, in the age of the Alexandrians, to a time when Homer's text could suffer little from carelessness, or misplaced cleverness.

We can now look back on Wolf's great work as a whole. Briefly his theory—as far as he has a coherent theory—is that writing was not used for literary purposes when first the Homeric lays were sung, nor for hundreds of years afterwards. That, through these hundreds of years, the lays floated in the memory of rhapsodes, who, being also poets, altered and added to them at will. Then they were reduced to writing, for the first time, in the age of Pisistratus. Then various copies were made, all vitiated by the caprice of the copyists. Then the age of Aristarchus revised the manuscripts, and finally gave the polish and unity which many modern commentators deny that the epics possess.

In answer to all this we have argued that writing is not

---

[1] Iliad, ix. 222. For other examples, Lehrs, *op. cit.* p. 354.
[2] Lehrs, p. 357.

proved to have been of such late use that it may not possibly
have been employed even by the original poet. We have
demonstrated that poets may write, and have written, when
there was no reading public for their works. We have
shown that about the rhapsodes, and their treatment of the
epics, whether conservative or wilful, nothing is historically
known. Without calling the Pisistratus hypothesis 'a fable'
like Ludwich, we have shown that the anecdote rests on no
certain foundation. It is unlikely, as Volkmann remarks,
that the rhapsodes, if they depended on their exclusive
knowledge of Homer for their bread, would give up their
one treasure to Pisistratus. But, however that may be, the
story is without authentic contemporary evidence, and is
discredited by the silence of all those who could scarcely
have omitted to record it. As to the supposed capricious
changes in manuscripts after Pisistratus, we have no proof of
them. The faulty citations of Plato and Aristotle may be
compared to the quotations of English poetry by Scott, who
frankly confessed that he did not know what was borrowed
and what was his own. 'As for separating what is original
from what is borrowed, I am sure it is far beyond my own
power, and probably that of anyone else.'[1] Finally, the
æsthetic caprice in alteration attributed to Aristarchus by
Wolf is plainly an error on the part of the great German
critic.

Thus the whole argument of Wolf no longer holds water.
It did not even convince himself, when he read the epics
'for human pleasure,' as Fitzgerald says we should read, not
through the microscope of the critic. Modern discoveries
have destroyed his premises, as far as writing is concerned,
and, as to the Alexandrians, later scholars are at variance
with him. If we can free ourselves from the strong grasp of

---

[1] Scott to Constable, May 28, 1822. *Archibald Constable and his
Literary Correspondents*, iii. 223.

Wolf, and admit an early written text, we need no complex
and elaborate theory to explain the existence of the epics.
A text sacredly preserved, and only suffering from such
accidents as, in such an age, all texts were subject to, is all
that we need.   If, on the other hand, we admit early texts,
we are still not free from the danger of large interpolations,
additions, omissions.   But the scholars who believe in these
will have to show how, and when, and why they were composed, and, above all, how and when they gained general
acceptance.   When they reject, as most of them do, the
Pisistratean hypothesis, or something akin to it, their
position is the more perilous.[1]

[1] On p. 65 the story of the Dowry, the *Cypria*, given by Homer to
his daughter is called ' ancient.'   For Pindar's knowledge of it Wilamowitz Möllendorff (*op. cit.* 352) cites Pindar (*Fragm.* 189, Boeckh).
That passage, however, is a grammarian's statement ; we have not the
words of Pindar.   As to Alexandrian texts of Homer, in the *Cunning-
ham Memoirs*, Royal Irish Academy, No. viii. on the Flinders Petrie
Papyri (Dublin 1891) is a fragment, iii. 4.   It contains the ends of
lines xi. 502–517, and beginnings of 518–537.   There are five lines in
the fragment not in our text of the passage.   On the other hand lines
529-530 are replaced in the fragment by one broken line beginning
κοῦροι.   This would have gladdened the heart of Wolf.   In *Index
Lectionum in Reg. Acad. Albert.* (1892), Ludwich argues against the
importance of the discovery as an example of a ' pre-Alexandrian '
Iliad.

CHAPTER VI

THE COMPOSITION OF THE ILIAD

BOOK I

IN examining Wolf's theory we have purposely neglected his argument that the unity and composition of the Iliad (obviously inconsistent with the hypothesis of multiplex authorship) are no such great matter after all. Nor have we dwelt on his extraordinary assertion that the composition of the Odyssey is at once the proudest monument of the Greek genius, and a thing which might easily be produced by joining together separate lays which accidentally happened to fit. ' Chance loves Art, and Art, Chance,' but not 'so wildly well' as Wolf's second theory, of a fortuitous Odyssey, requires. These questions of composition are literary questions, to be decided by literary taste, and can only be approached in the course of a somewhat minute study of the Epics.

In criticising the composition of the Iliad we should never forget, what critics are so unused to remember, that Homer never sang for *them*. The belief which his audience of warriors and ladies accorded to his songs 'did not wholly depend,' as Mr. Payne Knight says, 'on subtle consistencies. The old bards were not singing for minute inquirers and grammarians, but for people who freely, and even recklessly, gave play to their fancies as they listened.' [1]

---

[1] Payne Knight, *Prolegomena*, p. xxiii.

Never yet was a fiction composed in which holes could not be picked, and the works of modern novelists constantly exhibit discrepancies which any careful reader, or even a careless reader, can detect. But nobody thinks of explaining these errors (as when the moon is a crescent in the beginning of a chapter, and is full moon at the end thereof), by a theory of multiple authorship, or interpolation. Much less is it necessary to bring forward this theory. whenever the epic poet makes an error, or lapses into lines which strike an Alexandrian or a modern critic as 'unworthy.' Whether the poet could write or could not write, he certainly had no proof-sheets and no revises.

Before examining the structure of the Iliad, book by book, we may consider, as an English example of modern critical theories, the hypothesis of Mr. Walter Leaf, as set forth in his edition of the Iliad (London, 1886–1888), and in his *Companion to the Iliad* (1892). He puts his ideas as 'hypothetical and tentative' merely. In his theory, as in Mr. Grote's, 'the original poem, the work of "Homer" himself, was the Μῆνις ᾿Αχιλλέως' ("The Wrath of Achilles"), 'which related in comparatively brief but undying form the story of the quarrel of Achilles and Agamemnon, the defeat of the Greeks in consequence of the prayer of Thetis to Zeus, the partial relenting of Achilles, leading to the death of Patroklos, the final arousing of the hero, and the death of Hektor.' The original Wrath, disengaged as far as possible from the rest of the Iliad, consists of book i., book ii. 1–53, 443–483, book xi. 56–805, or perhaps to the end, omitting 665–762, the battle at the ships, now inextricably, or perhaps (vol. ii. Introduction) *not* inextricably entangled in xii. xiii. xiv. xv.; the greater part of xvi., the first part of xviii. are altered and rehandled ; pieces of xix., parts of xx. and xxi., and the killing of Hector in xxii.

Into this 'first and greatest of epic poems' additions

came. They certainly seem to have been needed. What is called 'the female interest' was entirely absent from Mr. Leaf's first and greatest of epic poems. His Homer knew Chryseïs and Briseïs, but Helen did not come into his tale, nor Andromache. The poem certainly reads the better for them, the richer, the more pathetic, though Mr. Leaf thinks 'all the dramatic interest of the story' exists —without them, and without Priam, and his interview with Achilles after Hector's death. The additions probably began, he supposes, with the exploits of Diomede (v.), the introduction of Andromache (vi.), the single combat in vii. Later came the scene on the Trojan walls, and the duel of Menelaus and Paris (iii.), the Broken Truce (iii. iv.), the Assembly (ii.). All these may be by the original poet, afterthoughts of Homer. In 1888 (vol. ii. Introduction) Mr. Leaf thought this less probable than he did in 1886. To the objection that the theory requires several great poets, identical in manner, and that such poets do not occur in history, Mr. Leaf replies that poets usually appear in groups, as in Athens, the Elizabethan age, we might add the beginning of this century, and so on. Certainly poets seem to come in groups, but one star varieth from another in glory, and, as we have said, Marlowe could not be mistaken for Shakspeare, nor Scott for Miss Austen, nor Quinault for Molière. Mr. Matthew Arnold, on this ground, disbelieved in the multiple authorship of the epics, and this is the great literary argument for a single Homer.

In the Introduction to his second volume Mr. Leaf offers, in a tabulated form, the result of his inquiries.

There are five strata in the Iliad. The first is the original poem, some 3,400 lines in length. Then come the earlier expansions ; it is very doubtful if these are by Homer. Then appear later expansions, as in xviii. the Making of the

Arms, and in viii. the Building of the Wall. Some of these are akin to the Odyssey. The fourth class contains the Greater Interpolations, as the episode of Phœnix : passages about Nestor, the Battle of the Gods, the Games. The fifth category chiefly contains the *juncturæ*, by which pieces of different ages were tacked together. Mr. Leaf admits ' the extreme uncertainty' of his scheme.

As to the date of at least the original portions of the poems, and the first additions, Mr. Leaf thinks it extremely remote. He assigns it to the time when the beehive tombs of Mycenæ were erected. The poem, in its oldest parts, is Achæan, was composed before the Dorian invasion, and on the mainland of Greece, not in Asia. It does not appear that Mr. Leaf has faith in an early written text.

It rather seems to be his opinion that the original ' Wrath' was composed by the aid of memory alone, and was preserved, added to, interpolated, and generally licked into or out of shape by the Homeridæ. As Mr. Leaf does not give credence to the Pisistratean hypothesis, it is not easy to understand how or when the later interpolations at least managed to find acceptance. Why many of them were introduced, how they were imposed on Greece, who gave its final form to the Iliad, and when, we do not learn. The discrepancies are perhaps less puzzling if we regard them as inadvertences of a poet, than if we have to account for their escaping the sedulous attention of the Homeridæ. Opportunities of discussing those questions will arise as we examine the books of the poems in detail. It may be remarked, however, that, compared with Lachmann and Wolf, Mr. Leaf is conservative. The poem is very old, it has a large nucleus of original work. In fact, the theory is a modification of Mr. Grote's, though less conservative, and perhaps more fanciful.

Taking the Iliad book by book, we find that the first

opens with a prologue, in which the Muse is bidden to sing of the wrath of Achilles, Peleus' son, 'and so the counsel of Zeus wrought out its accomplishment.' It is no more necessary that the poet should sing the wrath, the whole wrath, and nothing but the wrath, than that Milton, in *Paradise Lost*, should describe nothing but 'man's first disobedience and the fruit of that forbidden tree.' But a pedantic holding of the epic poet to the letter of his bond is a source of much modern disintegrative criticism. When he describes the Trojan side of affairs, Helen, Paris, Priam, he is thought to wander from his chosen topic, as if a poem of the Wrath could be complete without a picture of the persons whose passions caused the leaguer of Ilios. As we shall see later, a critic (German) actually denies that the Burial of the Dead is part of the original poem, because, in the prologue, the bodies of the heroes are said to be a prey to dogs and birds, and so could not have been buried!

The prologue ended, the cause of the strife between Agamemnon and Achilles is set forth. Chryses, priest of Apollo, had a daughter, Chryseïs, whom Agamemnon held as a captive in war. Chryses, imploring for her freedom, was insulted by Agamemnon. He prayed to Apollo; for nine days the arrows of the god ranged in the camp. On the tenth day Achilles called a general assembly. At his request Calchas reluctantly explained the cause of the arrows of pestilence. Chryseïs must be returned, with due sacrifice of a hecatomb, as the atonement to Apollo. Agamemnon offered to send back the damsel, but asked for another 'prize of honour.' Achilles, calling him covetous, promised him his recompense when next a city of Trojan allies was taken. Agamemnon, with a dark threat of seizing the damsel of Achilles, proposed at once to restore Chryseïs. Achilles says he will return home to Phthia, if he loses his meed of honour. Agamemnon boasts that he has others as

good as Achilles, and has Zeus to aid him. He will take
Briseïs, the mistress of Achilles. Achilles, about to draw
his sword, is restrained by Athene, who is sent by Hera
from Olympus (lines 194-5). Athene bids him put up his
sword ; on a later day threefold atonement will be made to
him in goodly gifts. This is a prophetic reference to the
disputed book ix. (line 213). Achilles sheathes his sword,
but tells Agamemnon that his arm will be sorely missed in
the day of the triumph of Hector (line 242). Both heroes
illustrate the irony of fortune. Agamemnon relies on his
chiefs, and on Zeus. But the god is to prove hostile, the
heroes are to be wounded and fail him. Achilles boasts of
the day of the wrath of Hector, which is to be mortal to his
own friend, Patroclus. Nestor in vain soothes them, and, the
assembly breaking up, Odysseus goes to carry Chryseïs to
her father (line 311). Agamemnon now sends his heralds
to lead away the lady of Achilles, Briseïs. Achilles appeals
to his mother, the sea goddess Thetis, complaining that he is
to have short life, and now has dishonour. After repeating,
in the epic manner, the whole tale of his wrong, he bids her
seek Zeus, and pray him to succour the Trojans till the
Achæans are slaughtered among the sterns of their ships
(line 409). Thetis weeps for her child, but tells him that
'Zeus went yesterday to a feast with the Ethiopians, and all
the gods followed with him' (line 423). On the twelfth
day Zeus will return to Olympus, and Thetis will kneel to
him. Thetis leaves her son, and (line 430) Odysseus
arrives in Chryse with the hecatomb and the damsel. From
line 430 to 487 the proceedings at Chryse are described in
a set of epic formulæ ; the mooring of the ship, the ritual
of the sacrifice, the feast, the sleep by the seashore, the
raising of the mast, the return, are all minutely set forth.
Achilles nurses his wrath and abstains from war (lines 488-
492) ; when the twelfth morn thereafter' was come (line

493), the gods return to Olympus. It may be remarked that, though Achilles has shunned the fight for eleven days, no particular disadvantage seems to have befallen the Achæans, nor are the Trojans in any way encouraged. But this is not singular, if the Trojans were ignorant of the cause of the hero's absence. Doubtless he had often been at a distance before, in his attacks on allied cities. Thetis mounts up to Olympus, and prays Zeus to honour Achilles by granting victory to the Trojans. Zeus, after a long silence, says that his assent will embroil him with Hera, the partisan of the Achæans. However, he will 'take thought for those things to fulfil them,' and attests his promise with a nod. The promise is rather diplomatic: Zeus will take the petition into his most serious consideration. Hera taunts Zeus, and hints that he has promised to do honour to Achilles, and harm the Greeks. 'If it be so,' says Zeus, 'then such must my good pleasure be.' Hephæstus tries to restore good humour. All go to sleep, though 'Zeus was not holden of sweet sleep,' but lay awake in thought.[1]

Simple as all this appears, Lachmann found in it a string of contradictions and anomalies, and decided that the book was a patchwork of smaller lays. The line 423, among other things, is a contradiction. The gods had all left Olympus, yet Athene was present with Achilles; Hera sent her to him from Olympus (lines 194-5). That day of the counsel was the tenth of Apollo's fatal archery; if Apollo was in Ethiopia, how could he also be dealing darts of pestilence under Troy? (48, 96, 97). In line 474, Apollo is delighted with the music at Chryse: but Apollo is with the Ethiopians! A god is not a bird, to be in two places at once. Lachmann therefore finds three elements in book i. namely: 1-347; next, 430-492; finally, 348-429 *plus* 493-611. A number of scholars, as Haupt, Naeke, Lauer,

[1] Book ii. 2.

Köchly agree, with slight modifications, in this opinion.
Köchly particularly blames the doings of Odysseus at Chryse
as a worthless mixture of reminiscences and epic formulæ.
The contradiction about the gods, in Ethiopia or at home, is
ascribed to a rhapsode, who had matter to introduce and
who forgot what went before.   Ribbeck finds in it the hand
of a Diaskeuast.   On the other hand it is argued that the
divine feast in Ethiopia gives Achilles time to nurse his
wrath ; that the scene in Chryse is a happy relief to the more
vehement action ; and Gerlach sees that contradictions about
the gods, their omnipotence and omnipresence, both very
limited, are inevitable in mythology.   The contradiction
about the presence of the gods, in one place or another, is
a mere oversight of the original poet's.   Such slips are
common enough in all fictitious narratives.   Düntzer has
observed that, even in the original lays of Lachmann and
Naeke, as by them constituted, there are other contradictions (382, 423).   In 382 Apollo is sending baneful shafts,
though (423) he is in Ethiopia.   Contradictions usually
increase as we try to disintegrate the poem.   In Mr. Leaf's
handling of book i. he leaves all intact up to line 429.
The passage now doubted (429-493) contains, as we saw,
the expedition of Odysseus to Chryse, with all that he did
there.   Why should this be omitted ?   First, because, when
the passage is completed, the poem goes on :

ἀλλ' ὅτε δή ῥ' ἐκ τοῖο δυωδεκάτη γένετ' ἠώς,

'Now, when the twelfth morning thereafter was come,'
then the gods returned from their twelve days' sojourn with
the Ethiopians, which had begun on the day before the
poem opens.   The 'vagueness' of this reference 'is
certainly not what we should expect.'   One fails to see that
the reference, if vague, is particularly astonishing.   ' Further,
the whole episode can be cut out without being missed, and
is of no importance to the story.'   Again, about half of the

lines are found in other parts of the Homeric poems. Once
more, *after* the company of Odysseus has had its fill of
eating and drinking, then (469–70) 'the young men
crowned the bowls with wine, and gave each man his
portion after the drink offering had been poured into the
cups.' 'The difficulty here is that the libation is mentioned
when the drink offering is ended, contrary to the custom.'

In answer it may be remarked that Homer's manner is
not to spare us anything. His audience wanted to know
'all about it.' They would not have been contented without hearing exactly how the sacrifice was done, and the god
was appeased. *We* do not miss this detail, but Homer
was not addressing a nineteenth century audience, but an
audience whose taste in epic was like that of the New
Zealanders.

Again, about half the lines occur elsewhere in Homer,
but the reason of that is plain. The descriptions of the
voyage, landing, and sacrifice, make what is called a ' run '
in Celtic poetry and story.[1] A ' sea run ' in a Highland
oral version begins

> They gave her prow to the sea, and her stern to shore,
> They hoisted the speckled, flapping, bare-topped sails
> Up against her tall, tough splintering masts,

and so forth. This answers to an Homeric ' run ' : ' then
they cast out the mooring stones, and made fast the hawsers,
and so themselves went forth on the sea beach,' and similar
repeated descriptions. The taste of the Maoris, as of the
Homeric Greeks and the Celts, submits to those repeated
descriptions. Probably they were at first a rest for the
memory of the reciter. Mr. Leaf regards much of the piece
as ' an unskilfully made cento,'[2] although he has previously

[1] See, for example, in Hyde's *Beside the Fire* (Nutt & Co.,
London, 1891, pp. xxv. xxviii.); cp. Campbell's *Popular Tales*, vol.
ii. p. lvi.

[2] Iliad, i. 28, note on ; 471.

said that 'the whole episode is most artistically introduced,'
and 'might have been interpolated at any time by a poet
of sufficient artistic feeling to see his opportunity.'[1] That
an artistic poet should have seized his opportunity to add
'an unskilfully made canto' seems curious enough.   There
remains the objection to 469-70, that 'the libation is made
when the drinking is ended, contrary to the rule.' But Mr.
Leaf is, of course, aware that libation was made *after* a
drinking, as well as before one.   'Now that the feast is
over, go ye home and rest,' says Alcinous in the Odyssey,[2]
and we read, 'Now, when they had poured forth' (that is
made libation) 'and drunk to their hearts' content, they
went each one to his own home to lay them to rest. But
Odysseus was left behind in the halls.' The last cup was
usually poured out in libation to Hermes.   There is thus,
perhaps, nothing contrary to Homeric custom in the passage.   Indeed, a critic of the new sort might 'athetise' and
reject as spurious Mr. Leaf's own remarks. In one place
he calls the episode 'artistic,' and says it ' is most artistically
introduced.'   In another place much of the episode is 'an
unskilfully made cento,' not only unskilful, but so late that
the poet does not even any longer understand the Homeric
customs which he means to describe. Few of the rejected
Homeric inconsistencies are so inconsistent as those observations of the commentator.[3]

Thus, on the whole, we need have no great scruple
about retaining all the First Book.   It does not cut up well
into 'lays' ; the inconsistencies are very natural and pardon-

---

[1] Iliad, i. 2.

[2] vii. 187.   The line in Iliad, i. 471, recurs in Odyssey, vii. 183.
Νώμησαν δ' ἄρα πᾶσιν ἐπαρξάμενοι δεπάεσσι.
In both cases the rite ends the festival.

[3] In his *Companion to the Iliad*, Mr. Leaf regards the arguments
for interpolation here as ' not quite decisive.'

able, and if we are told that the voyage to Chryse was a
late addition, we may ask what motive can the interpolator
have had, and how did his contribution find acceptance, if
the poem is just as excellent without it ? The poem is *not*
so excellent without 47, 48, 'And the arrows clanged on
the shoulders of the god in his going, as he descended like
the Night,' which Alexandrian and German critics, with
Bentley, wish to remove !

BOOK II

With the Second Book the serious difficulties begin. The
plot is decidedly not lucid as it stands ; whether the suggested rearrangements improve it is another question. As
it stands, the poem now introduces us to the army, and its
frame of mind after the long siege. It leads up to prepara-
tions for a general battle, and ends with the catalogue, or
muster roll, the Domesday book of heroic Greece. The
disintegrators, however, regard this book as the beginning
of distracting episodes, and wish to leave out the bulk of it,
and all that follows till book xi., where they discover the
continuation of their hypothetical original poem on the
'Wrath of Achilles.' They have some trouble in effecting
the *junctura*.

The second book opens with the statement that Zeus
was wakeful, though (i. 611) he is said to have slept. This
'inconsistency' is not worth a moment's notice. He
'slept' may mean merely 'he lay,' or 'passed the night'
beside Hera. Or anxiety as to how he was to 'honour
Achilles and destroy many beside the Achæan ships' may
have wakened him again. He determined to send a deceit-
ful dream, promising victory to Agamemnon, and bringing
on an engagement (8–15). Agamemnon woke (41) in
hope of victory, dressed himself in the garb of peace, a soft
tunic, cloak, and sandals, not in armour, took his sword

and sceptre, and went to the ships (41–47). Day dawned ;
Agamemnon bade the heralds call an assembly ; 'so did
those summon, and these gathered with speed' (50-53).
Agamemnon's costume is a point to be remembered, in
view of separatist arguments.

Agamemnon now told the chiefs in council the story of
his dream, and how he had called the assembly. But he
added that he would first make trial of the army's temper
by suggesting retreat, while the chiefs should urge staying
and fighting (72-75). Cortes, in Mexico, made a similar
experiment, with success ; but the conduct of Agamemnon
is decidedly injudicious. Nestor said a dream of Agamemnon's was worth some attention, and the assembly
met. In a long speech, Agamemnon proposed retreat.
The host rose like one man, before any could interfere, rose
like sudden waves under a sudden wind, and made for the
ships. Hera hastily sent Athene to bid Odysseus arrest the
movement, Odysseus of the hardy heart, standing in mute
indignation. Odysseus hurried about among the rushing
throng, beating some, advising others, proclaiming that
Agamemnon did but make trial of their temper. They
returned to the assembly ; and now comes the famous
intervention and chastisement of the one demagogue in
Homer, Thersites. He is beaten (265). Odysseus arises,
reminds the host of favourable prodigies and prophecies
when they left home, but says nothing of the dream, though
he refers to private words of Agamemnon when he was
driving the host to the assembly. Nestor adds a speech
with an apparently idle counsel of adopting a new model,
by arranging clan with clan, and tribe with tribe in battle.
Agamemnon repents his quarrel with Achilles, and sends
the host to arm. He then sacrifices, and prays he may take
Troy ere nightfall. The host is then summoned, and the
muster rolls of Greeks and Trojans are described in long

catalogues. So ends the book. Mr. Leaf objects to all this that the dream has nothing to do with the development of the story. Agamemnon would naturally attack at once, in force, and be disappointed. His ruse, his counsel of retreat, could only be justified by success. The description of the council is meagre, and (naturally) is made up of lines found elsewhere. The chiefs do not argue against Agamemnon—verily they had no time to argue. Except Odysseus, alway the staunchest of men, they were carried away by the tide of retreat.

Mr. Leaf at first made the delusive dream be followed by the arming of Agamemnon, and his great deeds in book xi., omitting the nine books that intervene. But, when the Iliad was enlarged, a poet wished, 'by a stroke of the highest art,' to show us the whole host ; so he made Agamemnon seriously advise flight. The art of making him do so, when he is in the brightest mood of hope, owing to his dream, seems far from high. Consequently, this poet probably dropped the dream ; but 'it was still left in its place, in order to form an introduction to book xi., if it were desired to recite that poem immediately after book i. : that is to say, the dream would lead straight to Agamemnon's arming and his heroic feats.' But book ii. and others were added, and 'to bridge over the obvious inconsistency between the despair of Agamemnon and the promise of Zeus, the council scene was interpolated, and the serious advice of Agamemnon' (to retreat) 'was turned into a mere fictitious attempt to sound the feeling of the army.' How is the junction of books ii. and xi. to be made ?

Mr. Leaf offered two suggestions. Perhaps we should stop in book ii. at line 41, where Agamemnon 'awoke from sleep and the heavenly voice was in his ears.' Thence we pick up book xi. at line 17, 'first he put his fair greaves about his legs,' and went on arming himself. Or

there is an alternative plan of Fick's.   We take the fifty-
sixth line of book xi., and join it to line 483 of book ii.,
which originally followed book ii., line 51.   The original
poem would then run thus: Agamemnon has seen the
dream, and, in high hope, gets up, puts on morning clothes,
a tunic, a cloak, sandals, takes his sceptre, and bids the
heralds call the Achæans *not* to council, but to war.   There
is this trifling objection that, when Agamemnon in the
second book (ii. 51) calls the Greeks to *council*, he naturally
does not wear his armour.   But, if we adopt Fick's own
plan, Agamemnon puts on his clothes of peace when he is
about summoning the Greeks to *war*.   Fick now reads
thus :—

'(ii. 41.) Then woke he from sleep, and the heavenly
voice was in his ears.   So he rose up, sitting, and donned
his soft tunic fair and bright, and cast around him his great
cloak, and beneath his glistering feet he bound his fair
sandals, and over his shoulder cast his silver-studded sword,
and grasped his sire's sceptre, imperishable for ever, wherewith he took his way amid the mailclad Achæans' ships.
Now went the goddess Dawn to high Olympus, foretelling
daylight to Zeus and all the immortals, and the king bade
the clear-voiced heralds summon to *war*' (in the passage
as it stands in Homer it is to *council*—a change of one word
is made) 'the flowing-haired Achæans.'   Then (skipping
to book ii., line 443), 'so these summoned, and those gathered
in all speed.'   The passage, of the gathering of armed
Achæans, is continued to line 483, where the catalogue of
the ships begins.   This and most that follows for nine whole
books, is ' cut,' till we reach book xi., line 56, where it runs
on, 'but the Trojans, on the other side, gathered them
around great Hector,' and, all in bronze, they fall to fighting,
' and in rushed Agamemnon, first of all, and slew a man.'

Was ever such a correction seen ! Agamemnon, accord-

ing to this suggestion of the learned Fick, wakes from his
dream, dresses in a soft doublet, takes no defensive armour
nor spear, but a peaceful sceptre, calls the armed assembly,
meets the Trojans, leads the charge, slays many men with
the spear (which he had not got), and is finally wounded
and retreats. The idea of an Homeric chief going into
battle in a soft doublet is unheard of. If ever there were
ignorance of Homeric custom and costume, it would be in
the poet who sang thus, yet he, *ex hypothesi*, is 'the original
Homer,' and the epic, thus queerly reconstructed, is the
original Μῆνις![1] Mr. Leaf's own first idea is clearly the
better.

In his *Companion* (p. 30), Mr. Leaf suggests much
the best transition from ii. to xi. The sequence is ii. 1–52,
ii. 442–483. Then ii. 786–810, the Trojans meet, hear of
the Greek armaments, and fly to arms. Thence we pass to
xi. 61, where Hector comes on the scene. By this plan, it
is urged, Agamemnon is neither more nor less armed than
in the Iliad as we possess it. To this we may reply that, as
the Iliad stands, Agamemnon, in dress of peace, calls a
peaceful council, but orders men to arm in ii. 382–4, which
Mr. Leaf excises. This command to arm corresponds to
ii. 808, where the Trojans, who had met in peace, 'rushed
to their arms.' Leaving the question of arming out of
sight, Mr. Leaf's final plan makes Agamemnon dream an
important dream, and say nothing to anyone about it. Yet[2]
'the hopes of the Greeks rise high, as the exploits of
Agamemnon seem to fulfil the promise of the delusive
dream,' which, unluckily, they knew nothing about. For
these reasons we prefer Homer to the reconstructed Μῆνις.

It will have been observed that Mr. Leaf does not think
the catalogue of the ships in book ii. part of the original

[1] *Die Homerische Ilias.* Göttingen, 1886.
[2] *Companion.* pp. 201–2.

poem. That may be left for subsequent consideration. We
must now see what it is that Mr. Leaf denies to the original
poet and the original poem between book ii. 51 and
book xi. 61. First, as already said, in 'the original Μῆνις,'
as reconstructed by Mr. Leaf, the dream of Agamemnon
is never more referred to. Agamemnon does not mention
it to his peers. Now, the Homeric characters are very fond
of telling their dreams, especially when the dreams are of
the first importance as indications of the will of the gods.
Agamemnon tells his in the Iliad as we have received it ;
in Mr. Leaf's Μῆνις there is nothing of the sort. For the
rest, Mr. Leaf himself expresses a justifiable uncertainty as
to what portions of our Iliad not in the original Μῆνις are
later additions by the original poet himself. 'The earlier
pieces of this class may perhaps be referred to the poet of
the Μῆνις, though I now feel much more doubt as to this
than is expressed in the Introduction to vol. i.'[1] Here, of
course, we are puzzled to know how criticism can discern
additions to a poem made by the poet himself. Again, we
cannot understand why he should be supposed not to have
composed all his poem *en bloc*. As to additions, we possess
a modern example. Lord Tennyson first wrote the *Morte
d'Arthur*, an epic fragment. Then, many years later, he
wrote the first volume of *Idylls of the King*. Then, again
many years later, he filled up the interstices with *The Last
Tournament*, *Pelleas and Ettarre*, *The Last Battle in the
West*, and *The Passing of Arthur*. As we know all about
this, we can detect differences of style in the Laureate's
complete work. But, if we did not know, and if the
Laureate's work were in a foreign language, three thousand
years old, critics might come to many various and to no
certain conclusions. This is Homer's case. We know nothing about the conditions of his literary composition, and

[1] *Iliad*, vol. ii. p. x.

we can only guess vaguely and vainly at what he himself
may have added to his work. Mr. Leaf, himself, in his
second volume, doubts very much whether the poet added
at all.

BOOK III

Even extreme advocates for the disintegration of the
Iliad accept a few lines of book ii., though they are not very
certain which of them to admit, and though their task would
be easier if they excised the whole canto. But these critics
either, with Mr. Grote, cut out all that follows, from iii. to
viii. or, with Fick and Mr. Leaf, from iii. to xi. Mr. Leaf
regards much of the intervening work as early additions,
possibly, though not probably, by the original poet. The
arguments against this wholesale excision are obvious.
Either Homer must be kept to the letter of his bond, his
epic must sing of the wrath of Achilles and the promise of
Zeus, and nothing else, or we may suppose that he describes
the whole war as affected by the wrath of Achilles. In the
former case, books iii. to xi. cannot be original, for in them
the wrath is but little in question, the promise of Zeus is
only maturing. If we take this view, we have scarce any
difficulty to meet, except that of believing in at least two
poets of equal transcendent merit and equally skilled in 'the
grand style.' One of these poets, the author of books iii.
and vi., gave us Helen and Andromache, those peerless
peers in womanhood. Now the question whether we can
believe in two poets equally great, and equally masters of
the grand style, is a matter for the judgment and imagination of every reader to decide. Mr. Matthew Arnold could
not believe in two poets of this mark; Mr. Leaf and Mr.
Grote can believe. Arguments are here of no avail.

On the other hand, again private opinion is the sole
test and standard. Does it tax our credulity to suppose that

a minstrel, who announced his intention of singing the wrath of Achilles, might be better than his word—might show us also the causes of the war, the women who wept, and the great deeds of the men, other than Achilles, who fought? Whoever cannot admit the probability of such a poetical endeavour, and who, at the same time, can believe in the existence of several poets equally transcendent, may cut out books iii. to viii., or iii. to xi., as his taste and fancy determine.

There are thus several contending parties, as regards the originality of this part of the Iliad, and, first, as regards book iii. There are those who, with Fick and Mr. Leaf and Mr. Grote, deny its originality. There are those who, with Bergk and others, find passages here by the original minstrel, other passages by a later poet, others, again, by a diaskeuast, or comparatively late interpolator. There are also the faithful who accept books iii. to xi. as Homer's own work : not necessarily word for word as he composed it, but as substantially his own.

The matter of the book may be stated thus. In lines 1-14, the hostile armies are opposing each other. In lines 15-30, Paris challenges any Achæan to single fight : Menelaus accepts. Lines 15-75, conscience or timidity makes Paris a coward ; Hector upbraids him, Paris takes heart, and offers to stake Helen and her wealth on the issue of the duel. Lines 75-110, Hector carries his challenge, which is accepted, and an armistice follows. Lines 110-120, Hector sends to Troy to bring Priam, and two lambs for sacrifice. Lines 120-244, Iris bids Helen go to Priam on the wall. She finds him there with the Trojan elders, and describes to him several of the Achæan chiefs. Lines 245-264, the messenger from the army takes Paris to the field. Lines 265-324, Paris arrives, solemn oaths of armistice are made with imprecations on the truce-breakers, Priam returns to

Troy. Lines 324–380, the duel, Paris is worsted, and carried to Ilios by Aphrodite. Lines 382–448, Aphrodite compels Helen to accept the embraces of Paris. She confesses her shame in his cowardice, and taunts the Goddess, but is compelled to submit. Lines 448–461, Menelaus searches for Paris, Agamemnon proclaims his victory, and demands the restoration of Helen.

In all this the promise of Zeus makes no way ; nor need it make any, if the poet is inclined to show us

> ' The face that launched a thousand ships,
> And burned the topless towers of Ilium.'

It is also urged that the scene on the walls, where Helen describes the chiefs, is out of place in the tenth year of the league. The duel between Paris and Menelaus should, moreover, it is contended, have occurred at the first landing of the Achæans. To this we need only reply that the *naïf* poetic perspective readily accounts for these incidents, as for the catalogue of warriors on either side, for the late advice to array the Achæans in clans, the allies in nations, and, later, for the building of the wall. Traces of later work are found in the mention of Æthra (144) and of the Amazons (189). But we really do not know that either Æthra or the Amazons were characters in sagas which only came to be developed after Homer's time. The Amazons are mentioned by the poet in vi. 186, in the legend of Bellerophon. Inconsistencies are found by wistful Germans in 134 and 326. In 134 Iris tells Helen, 'they lean upon their shields and the battle is stayed.' In 326, after the casting of the lots, ' the people sat them down in ranks.' There is no profit in arguing with such pettifogging critics. Again Köchly distinguishes himself by smelling out a discrepancy in 143 ff., and 383 f. (see, too, 411, 420). In 143 Helen, with two attendants, goes to the Scæan Gates. In 383, the duel having intervened, Aphrodite finds Helen in a high

H

tower, with many Trojan women about her ! The essential
scene of forced reconciliation between the divine one of
women and Paris (382–447) is regarded by the learned
Bergk as the diaskeuast's, an example of later work.

It is possible to give people poetry, but impossible to
give them the brains to understand and the hearts to feel
it. Helen has all charm, and every grace, but Homer
either frankly accepts her weakness of will, or (which is
much the same thing in Homeric psychology) regards her
as the victim of Aphrodite. Eustathius, as is well known,
mentions a legend that Paris, by magically assuming the
shape of Menelaus, beguiled Helen, and Eustathius thinks
that Homer was acquainted with the tradition.

As to the duel, it causes trouble owing to its parallel
in vii. Bergk thinks that Helen on the walls is sketched
by a talented later poet : the diaskeuast blended the passages. Others break the book up into small separate lays,
but this expedient has ceased to be fashionable.

BOOK IV

The story of the fourth book runs thus :—1–19. The Gods
are met on Olympus, and Zeus, for the mere pleasure of
teasing Hera, asks, ' How is the war to end ? Shall we set
the men fighting, or permit peace ? '—on the basis of the
oaths taken before the duel. 20–30. The duel, if its conditions are adhered to, has ended the war. This must not
be, so the intervention of the Gods is brought in. Hera
replies fiercely. 30–49. Zeus threatens to destroy Hera's
favoured cities ; she insists on the fall of Troy. 30–67. Hera
proposes that they should compromise matters, and Athene
should be sent to make the Trojans break the oaths. The
result, it is implied, will be the wreaking of her grudge on
Ilios. Zeus may retaliate by ruining Argos, Sparta, and
Mycenæ. 73–104. Athene bids Pandarus shoot treacher-

ously at Menelaus (104–147). Menelaus is wounded (147). Agamemnon sees at once that the cause of Troy is lost by this perfidy. 'The day shall come for holy Ilios to be laid low . . . and Zeus shall brandish over them all his ægis, in wrath at this deceit' (157–168). The physician tends Menelaus (213–219). The ranks of Troy approach (221–223). Agamemnon visits the various bodies of men, encouraging and rebuking. Among others, he taunts Odysseus and Diomede, who have hardly become aware that a general engagement is at hand. Odysseus replies angrily, Diomede is silent. Agamemnon apologises to Odysseus (358), the battle begins, Apollo encouraging the Trojans, and Athene the Greeks.

In all this there is reference (512) made by Apollo to the absence of Achilles, Thetis' son, but none to Zeus's promise to Thetis. The general story of the siege is however, much advanced, the ruin of Troy has been finally decided on by Zeus, and the fall of the city is determined, as Agamemnon recognises here, and Diomede in vii. 400, by the breaking of the oaths. But Zeus is not intent on straightway giving honour to Achilles, by letting the Trojans have an advantage. It is therefore open to the seekers for the original Iliad to deny the originality of book iv. This point is seized on by Mr. Leaf (introduction to book iv.).

Zeus regards the conclusion of the siege, when the book begins, 'as an open question.'

Why not? As to the future of the war, Zeus had decided nothing. The Trojans had not yet broken their oath. In book i. he merely promised Thetis to give temporary success to Troy, 'until the Achæans do my son honour.' Nor, in that book, did he acknowledge to Hera that he had promised even so much as this. He merely teased Hera as he does again in book iv., 'with vexing words, and speaking maliciously.' He then, at Hera's request, sends

Athene to make a Trojan break the solemn oaths of truce,
taken in book iii., before the duel. Mr. Leaf thinks that
this device 'is strange'—it is on a par with the sending of
the baneful dream, and with familiar events in the careers
of Ahab and Pharaoh. Mr. Leaf adds that the perjury
' has no effect whatever upon the future development of the
story, and is, indeed, barely alluded to in a few lines which
are themselves gravely suspected.' [1]   What more effect
could it have ? Agamemnon sees at once in this treachery
a pledge of the future fall of Troy—' Of a surety I know
this in heart and soul.' Mr. Leaf says the offence ' is indeed
barely alluded to in a few lines which are themselves gravely
suspected,' and refers to v. 206-208, and to vii. 69, 351, 411.
Here (vii. 69) Hector says, ' Our oaths of truce Kronos' son
accomplished not.' ' The lines are rejected by a large proportion of critics, and seem intolerable in the present place.'
Again, the oaths are mentioned in vii. 351. Here Antenor
says, ' Let us give back Helen, and the property stolen with
her, for now fight we in guilt against the oaths of faith.' Bergk
(i. 585) supposes the story of the council in which Antenor
makes this proposal to be by the promising young poet who
told of the duel of Paris and Menelaus. Here there is a
difference of opinion on a point of grammar, but the perjury is
assuredly influencing the development of the story. Antenor
would give up the cause of the war, so discouraged is he.
Paris will not permit the return of Helen ; he offers a compromise—he will give back the treasure of Agamemnon, but
Helen he will not restore. Idæus is sent from Troy with
this message, but Diomede, strong in his certainty that
perjured Troy must fall, exclaims, ' Let no man now accept
Paris's substance, neither Helen's self ; known is it, even to
him that hath no wisdom at all, how that the issues of destruction hang already over the Trojans' (vii. 400-403).

[1] Namely, v. 206, vii. 69, 351, 411.

Agamemnon adds, ' and, for the oaths, let Zeus bear witness '
(vii. 411). Surely this is enough. The Greeks believe that
the fall of Troy is now only a question of time. All chance
of peace is lost. And Pandarus the oath-breaker is slain
(v. 286–296), though, as Mr. Leaf remarks, his crime is not
mentioned in that place. But what was the diaskeuast
about, that he did not interpolate it ? And, if a reference
were made, what would prevent any critic from calling it an
interpolation ? Pandarus's sin is now on the head of all the
Trojans, and they know it, and the Greeks know it ; but, as
all atonement is declined by the Greeks, there is nothing
left but a gallant death-struggle. From that hour of the
broken oath, the ends of death are made fast on the Trojans,
and Hector may fight, and the women may pray, but ' it is
known even to the fool,' as Diomede says, that the end is
certain. The broken oath has made reconciliation impossible. The Trojans might conceivably have restored Helen
and the treasures, but now even that offer will not avail,
and Ilios is doomed. ' Father Zeus will be no helper of
liars ; as those were the first to transgress against the oath,
so shall their own tender flesh be eaten of the vultures, and
we shall bear away their dear wives and little children in
our ships, when once we take the stronghold ' (iv. 234–239).
For these plain and sufficient reasons, we cannot agree with
Mr. Leaf that the oath ' has no effect whatever on the
future development of the story.'

We have shown that, if the Iliad may be taken as it
stands, the perjury is a crucial point in the story. It decides the fate of Troy, and this is recognised on all hands.
Mr. Leaf argues that it is completely forgotten except in
v. 206, vii. 69, 351, 411, all of them ' gravely suspected of
interpolation,' while the interpolator who introduced these
lines omitted any mention of the broken oath, when telling
of the death of Pandarus, the traitor. Such an omission

by an original author Mr. Leaf thinks 'hardly possible.' In that case it is equally impossible that the interpolator should not have added what was wanting. Mr. Leaf imagines that v. 206, Pandarus's boast of his archery, was probably added after the composition of book iii., to avoid the strangeness of not mentioning Pandarus's deed.[1] Then why did not the interpolator complete his work, by another allusion to the oaths, on the death of Pandarus? There is little force in objections to Hector's brief allusion to the broken oath (vii. 69); he could not dwell with complacency on the subject. Mr. Leaf makes no objection to Diomede's refusal of compromise, based on all men's certainty that Troy must fall, though we regard this as a distinct allusion to the perjury (vii. 400-403). In brief, the argument is that if we have no allusion to the oaths made in book iii., that proves that the original poet did not know book iii. If we have allusions, they are interpolations, and as interpolations are excised the very passages which give weight and tragic effect to the oaths. This is not a valid kind of reasoning.

In truth the perjury has the very greatest and most tragic effect, unless we are to hold the poet tightly to his bond, insisting that he shall sing of the Wrath and nothing but the Wrath. The most extreme instance of this criticism is displayed when Fick rejects, for example, book xvii., because the first lines of the Iliad say that 'the Wrath gave the bodies of heroes to the dogs and birds. Therefore there is to be no fight for the body of a hero!' A critic who can seriously advance such a theory simply proves that he is incapable of understanding what poetry is.[2] On the night of a

---

[1] *Companion to Iliad*, p. 116.

[2] Fick, *Ilias*, p. 2; Leaf, *Iliad*, ii. p. 179, where Mr. Leaf says that Fick's objection 'is not foundation enough for so sweeping a conclusion' as that the Prologue of the Iliad excludes all burying of the dead.

battle there would be 'more birds than women' round
many a dead hero whose mangled remains might yet be
interred in the great burial-howe.

Fick's is an extraordinary specimen of criticism, of keeping a poet to the bare letter of his bond. But many of the
excisions of books and passages from the original Μῆνις are
based on this theory, that the poet must be kept strictly to
business, that business being the story of the Wrath. As well
might we excise most of *Paradise Lost* because no summary
of many events is given in the prologue to the heavenly
muse.

After the oaths, in the fourth book, Mr. Leaf objects
to the Ἐπιπώλησις, or review of the troops by Agamemnon.
The course of events was this : at the bidding of Athene,
Pandarus treacherously shot at and wounded Menelaus.
This was wholly unexpected by both parties—it was, as
Homer says, the act of a fool. What would naturally
follow ? The Trojans would be taken aback, not eager to
make themselves partakers in this iniquity, anxious to see
how the offended Achæans would conduct themselves.

This is what we expect; but a Greek, not a Trojan, is the
poet, and he makes the Trojans attack first (iv. 221). The
Greeks are partly taken by surprise ; Agamemnon hurries
about among them, praising the ready, and taunting even
Odysseus and Diomede, who were scarcely aware that the
fray had begun. The speeches are long, and extremely
interesting as indications of character in the spirited reply of
Odysseus, the respectful silence of Diomede, the chivalrous
withdrawal of his angry words by Agamemnon. His temper,
we must remember, had been stirred by the disloyal attack
on his brother. Mr. Leaf argues that the passage retards
the action, that the speeches are prolix, and that the taunts
of Agamemnon are 'out of keeping with his character,'
though he admires the modesty of Diomede. The occur-

rence is referred to by Diomede in book ix. 34–36, so it cannot be later than that book. As to Mr. Leaf's objections, then, we admit that the action is retarded, but we add that a great deal of rhetoric under arms is characteristic of Homeric manners. We do not think Agamemnon's impatience and fury out of keeping with his disposition, considering how his temper had been irritated. The replies of the heroes are extremely characteristic.

The battle now begins, and is continued in book v.

As we understand Mr. Leaf (introduction to book iv.) this battle came at one stage in the evolution of the poem where the Catalogue of the Ships now stands (ii. 483). This was Mr. Leaf's opinion in his first volume, but we have seen that he has now dovetailed book xi. 61 on to ii. 483. Mr. Leaf must apparently have changed his mind, and after at one time regarding the battle in book iv. as part of the 'original Μῆνις,' must have determined later to give it up, and to go on to the battle in book xi.[1]

A number of other objections are urged against the fourth book. Lachmann finds in it fragments of brief lost lays. About these 'lays' we have really no knowledge, the attempts to discover their traces are futile. Bernhardy says that book iv. has no reference to book iii. Jacob and Genz, admitting the connection between the books, fancy that iv. is by a different poet. Bergk finds in the duel and perjury one of the earliest amplifications, but a diaskeuast has been busy with the whole till fighting begins (iv. 422). The oaths of

---

[1] I quote Mr. Leaf's words, *Iliad*, i. 115, as I am not certain that I understand his meaning. 'The beginning of the battle' (in book iv.) 'is what we should have expected after the account of the arming in book ii. (483). 422, as Lachmann observed, can follow 483 or 780–785, without a break of any sort being discoverable. This was, in my opinion, the actual sequence in one point of the evolution of the Iliad from the original germ.' The difficulty of *un beau page d'algèbre* is trifling to that of picking out the lost junctures in the poem.

book iii. and iv. 158, cause searchings of hearts, because, among other reasons, Homer is supposed to know nothing of punishments in a future life.[1] Petty objections are made to iv. 98. Paris would be glad if he saw Menelaus shot, and brought to the funeral pyre. 'Now Paris is not on the field, so how could he see it?' And why should Pandarus wish to win favour from Paris, who has just been spoken of, after his flight from the duel, as hateful to the Trojans (iii. 454)? It is extraordinary that men, professionally busied with literature, should write treatises on points like these. Agamemnon's speech (iv. 155–183) is canvassed as if it were a clause in an important piece of legislation. Agamemnon, in his anxiety, says that Zeus will certainly ruin perjured Ilios, sooner or later, but that will be small comfort if Menelaus leaves his bones in the Trojan land and the Achæans withdraw in discouragement. Rhapsodes and diaskeuasts and fragments of old lays ill-joined are appealed to, by way of accounting for all this. People who criticise Homer should have some inkling of what poetry is. Then, why did the Trojans move first, after the treacherous arrow-shot (iv. 221). Possibly they thought it well, in Scotch phrase, to take 'the first word of flyting.' Mr. Monro says, 'perhaps the intention is simply to represent both sides beginning the advance, but the poet looks at it from the Greek point of view, from which the Trojan movement is more conspicuous.' The review is explained as an old fragment, stuck in at random. The remarks of the irritable Agamemnon to Odysseus and Diomede have already been commented upon. They are certainly long, and there may have been a local patriotic motive for interpolating a lengthy story about Tydeus (iv. 370–400).

---

[1] See xix. 258, iv. 270 ; Odyssey, xi. 570–600, is disposed of as an interpolation. The Erinyes occur in book xix., not in the oath of book iii.

But it was customary to encourage men by references to their illustrious ancestors.   Moreover, granting a local patriotic motive in a single poet, we can see no reason why, if the tale had been interpolated in one minstrel's recitation, or in one text, it should have been accepted.   Let us try to imagine how such an interpolation could be made, and could keep its ground.   Say that the epic was preserved in memory. A very famous Homerid might add this or that passage, might hand it down to his successor, but then the interpolation, unless it had rare merit, would only be known in the reciter's circuit.   Outside that circuit, when copies came to be made, how would it win recognition and acceptance? Or, if there were several early texts, from the generation following the poet's, how would recognition be secured by this one example which contained the interpolation?   The passage, let us say, redounds to the glory of Athene.   It might have pleased in Athene's own city, Athens; the Athenian recension may have been the dominant one. But this brings us almost to the Pisistratean hypothesis, which is very commonly abandoned.   We simply flounder in morasses of conjecture, as a rule, when we pretend to detect interpolations.

CHAPTER VII

THE COMPOSITION OF THE ILIAD

BOOKS V, VI

THE fifth book of the Iliad, with part of the sixth, was
known, as early as Herodotus's time, by the name of 'The
Aristeia of Diomede.' The great deeds of Tydeus' son, in
the battle which followed the breaking of the Truce, occupy
the book. But it also contains pictures of the *mêlée*, the
general combat, and accounts of the parts played by the
gods in the battle. These must be carefully considered.
They illustrate the natural confusions of mythological
fancy when busy with gods, now looked on as supernatural
powers, now as fettered by human conditions. The inconsistencies in the narrative will seem to be the results, not of
interpolations, interruptions, and additions, but of the
mythopœic imagination, itself essentially confused. Indeed,
all through the Iliad, the problems which give most trouble
to commentators are caused by the very nature of mythology.

The fifth book opens with the inspiration lent to
Diomede by Athene. She sends him forth to conquer, and
then (31–34) leads Ares out of the fight, bids him shun the
anger of Zeus, and seats him on the bank of the Scamander.
In Homer Ares is always treated as a bully and coward.
The *mêlée* is described in the next passage ; then Pandarus
(99) wounds Diomede, who prays to Athene. She hears

him, whether from afar or on Scamander's neighbouring
bank does not appear. She speaks to him, saying that she
has taken the mist from his eyes that he may know gods
from men (124-132). He is to fight no god but Aphrodite
only. As a rule, in Homer, any stranger *may* be a god ;
on departing from human converse, however, the gods
usually give some sign of their true character. From lines
177-178 we learn that Æneas thinks Diomede may be a
god wroth with the Trojans. Pandarus thinks he is Diomede, but is not certain. 'I struck him, yet I vanquished
him not ; surely it is some wrathful god.' In this passage
(207) Pandarus refers to his treachery. He has merely
wounded Diomede and Menelaus, and casts the blame on
his bow. Æneas and Pandarus now attack Diomede, who
says, 'Pallas Athene bids me not to be afraid.' Athene
guides his spear, which slays Pandarus. Diomede makes
no reference to his treachery (286-296). This is not really
strange, as the Greeks do not know what Trojan shot the
fatal arrow (iv. 196, 197). The strange thing would be if
Diomede had known. Agamemnon himself does not know
whether the archer was a Trojan or a Lycian. The poet
might have stopped to moralise on Pandarus's punishment ;
he could not consistently make Diomede do so. Aphrodite
now rescues Æneas, her son, from Diomede (312-314).
Diomede wounds her (330). Iris leads her to Ares, who is
sitting on the left of the field, with his spear resting on a
cloud. Aphrodite mounts his car, and Iris drives the
horses to Olympus. The gods sometimes move by a mere
effort of will, sometimes drive, and occasionally walk. In
Olympus Dione cherishes Aphrodite. Athene is there,
now, and with Hera mocks at Aphrodite. Meanwhile (440)
Apollo protects Æneas from Diomede, who, in spite of
Athene's advice, three times assails the hero. Leto and
Artemis heal the wounded Æneas, whom Apollo has car-

ried to the Trojan citadel, leaving a wraith of him lying on the field (449). Apollo now addresses Ares, apparently in the midst of the *mêlée*, bidding him divert Diomede. Then Apollo sits down on the heights of Pergamos, where was his temple. Ares, in the guise of a Thracian ally, encourages Priam's sons. Sarpedon arouses Hector. All this Ares can do, as Athene has departed (510). Apollo sends forth Æneas again. The mellay continues, Ares leading the Trojans (592), and Diomede shudders at sight of the gods whom (604), by virtue of Athene's gift, he is able to recognise. The mellay continues. Sarpedon kills Tlepolemus, but is wounded by him. Athene arouses Odysseus against the Lycians. This she seems to do from Olympus. Ares is now leading the hosts of Troy (702). Hera and Athene take their chariot (722). Athene arms herself; they drive to consult Zeus, who is on the crest of Olympus, apart from the gods (754). By permission of Zeus, to restrain Ares, they drive down to the junction of Simois and Scamander, where they leave their horses. Athene encourages Diomede, who tells her that, on her own advice, he does not encounter Ares. Athene, by aid of the helm of Hades (the 'cap of darkness'), makes herself invisible to Ares (845), and she drives Diomede's spear into the belly of the god (856). Thus Athene, not Diomede, really wounds the deity. He flies to Olympus, where he is rebuked by Zeus. However, he is healed by Pæeon, while Hera and Athene return to the mansion of Zeus.

It is necessary to follow the story into book vi., for book v. ends with the return of the goddesses. In vi. (1) the mortals are left by the gods to their own devices. The mellay goes on; the Trojans have the worst of it. Helenus, the augur, bids his brother, Hector, rally them, and then, returning to the city, send Hecuba with the elder ladies to supplicate Athene. She may stay the fury of

Diomede. Hector rallies the Trojans with divine success
and skill (108). The Achæans take him for a god. He
then sends his mother to supplicate Athene. But, as he is
on his way, Diomede, meeting Glaucus the Lycian, asks
him if he is a god : 'then will I not fight with immortal
gods' (128). Glaucus replies with the history of his lineage,
and the story of Bellerophon. He and Diomede, recognising each other as ancestral friends, exchange armour and
courtesies. Leaving Hector to urge the unavailing ritual
of Athene, to arouse Paris, converse with Helen, and con-
sole Andromache, we must now examine the objections to
this Aristeia of Diomede (v. vi. 1–235).

In the first place, both Achilles and the Promise of Zeus
are out of sight.[1] Thus the passage is not absolutely necessary
to the main idea of the poem. If, however, we admit that
the original poet may have been anxious to celebrate other
heroes, this objection is not important. On the other hand, if
additions were made to the poem at all, the *aristeiæ* of
heroic ancestors are precisely what a new poet would be
anxious to interweave. Doubtless he might find material
in old lays of family minstrels, but it is no less undoubted
that of such lays, their length and character, we know absolutely nothing. The *aristeia* of Diomede may be based
on them ; that it contains one of them, interpolated *en
masse*, we have every reason to disbelieve.

The chief critical difficulty detected by Mr. Leaf is the
remark of Diomede in book vi. 128, where the hero doubts
whether Glaucus is a god, and where he declines to fight
against gods, giving the story of Lycurgus's resistance to
Dionysus, itself probably late, as a proof of the danger of
such impiety (vi. 130). Mr. Leaf finds this cautiousness
unintelligible in a hero who has just vanquished Aphrodite
and Ares, while the doubt is inconsistent with Diomede's

---

[1] Achilles is *mentioned*, v. 788, vi. 99.

recent gift of recognising gods (v. 127–8). But, as we have seen, Diomede was expressly warned by Athene to fight no god except Aphrodite. His experience of Apollo when he attacked Æneas was discouraging. He knew that Athene's hand, not his, had wounded Ares. But Athene is not now with Diomede ; she is in Olympus, withdrawn from war, and, if her gift to Diomede has departed with her, there is no 'glaring inconsistency' at all. The gift had lasted while the gods were on the scene ; we are not told that it was to be permanent. The gods never act in Homer without producing inconsistencies. Mr. Leaf accounted for the anomaly about Diomede by supposing that his *aristeia* is probably the earliest addition to the original poem, perhaps by the original author, while the episodes of the wounding of the gods are later additions to the *aristeia*. Of course, if the *aristeia* is by the original author, it is vain for us to ask whether it is later than the main part of the Iliad. Internal evidence is of no value in such a matter. Commentators will take one side or the other in obedience to their general theory of the original poem. Then, as regards the 'machinery,' the gods and their interventions, we must ask, What motive could any one have for adding it ? What was gained by recasting a simple story, for the purpose of adding later machinery ? The behaviour of the gods here, notably of Athene and Ares, is consistent with their general characters in Homer. Mr. Leaf now 'feels that the unity of spirit of the whole book is a stronger argument than any on the other side.'

If inconsistencies are to be explained as interpolations and the results of *remaniement*, we may imagine how the critics of a future age will treat *Pendennis*. In that romance Master Clavering grows, in six years, from four to thirteen. Mrs. Bungay's Christian name is changed twice in two consecutive pages. In vol. i. p. 25, we learn that Pendennis's mother is 'alive to this day '—namely, when the history is being written. In the seventeenth number of the tale, Pendennis's mother dies.

Now, if *Pendennis* had been worked over by later authors, their first care would have been to remove these inconsistencies, which a competent proof-reader would have detected. On Scott's proof sheets we see James Ballantyne's hand, pointing out to him errors like Diomede's doubt as to whether Glaucus is a god. Homer had no proofs, nor proof-readers. However, if the Homeridæ, or any other successors, followed by Pisistratean editors and later editors, did not correct such slips, what did they do? We have daily instances of blunders quite as great as Homer's inconsistencies, made by authors rejoicing in many 'revises.' Such errors, therefore, are not greater than a writer may commit with all modern appliances to aid. Why should they be thought wonders only to be explained as interpolations, in the work of a poet who, if he wrote at all, must have used rather rude materials? Mr. Leaf thought, but has changed his mind, that the wounding of Aphrodite is earlier, the wounding of Ares later, an attempt to 'outbid' the former exploit.[1] Bergk (i. 578) thinks that the 'old Iliad' had the fight with Ares, a younger poet added the wounding of Aphrodite, and altered the scene with Ares (432–444).

Such is the Higher Criticism ! Meanwhile, parts of the interesting conversation between Diomede and Glaucus, as the comparison of men to forest leaves, are among the most Homeric lines in Homer. The speech was familiar to Simonides, who quotes it. The new plan is simply to excise vi. 128–142, where Diomede refuses to fight a god and tells the tale of Dionysus and Lycurgus.

So much for ' one of the most glaring inconsistencies

---

[1] *Companion to the Iliad*, p. 113. Compare his *Iliad*, Introduction to Book V.

in the Homeric poems.' If this be among the worst, we
need scarcely fly to a theory of interpolation which itself
involves us in so many unanswerable problems as to the
motive, date, authorship, and method of the interpolators.

Surely it is not difficult to imagine, either that the poet
made a slip, or that the mist which had been withdrawn from Diomede's eyes while the gods were present
was allowed to fall on them again when the gods retired.

Omitting some minor points, we may notice an opinion
of Mr. Leaf's on the sixth book. He has much difficulty in
placing the lines 313–482—the conversation of Hector in
Troy with Paris, Helen, and Andromache. But the passage
has clear reference to iii. 454, to the wrath of the Trojans
with Paris, and is a necessary continuation of book iii., if
Paris is to be brought back into the action. In the
speech of Hector, apparently referring to iii., 'none of the
allusions exactly suit.' Mr. Leaf suggests that the duel
in iii. may have taken the place later of the incidents
referred to in vi. The 'anger' alluded to in vi. 326 seems
to us to be the indignation of the Trojans in iii. 454. Again
in book vi. 1–72 are censured. Helenus bids Hector
exert himself to rally the Trojans, and proposes prayer to
Athene. *Why*, as Diomede has only killed a brace of men
in seventy-two lines? But his example has encouraged the
Greeks; Menelaus and Euryalus have each killed a brace,
and Diomede is still pursuing.

There are, as usual, many minute critical objections to
book v. For example, if Zeus is keeping his promise to
Thetis, he should not let Hera drive Ares out of the field,
where he is engaged in fulfilling that very promise (v. 757–
767). Several mythical legends in the book are peculiar
to it : Dione, Enyo, Pæeon, are examples. Haupt would
excise 711–792 ; the long account of Hera and Athene, their

<hr>

[1] Leaf's *Iliad*, ii. 11.

I

preparation for reaching the battlefield, because they do not do much when they reach it, and their return is described briefly.   Here there is want of 'symmetry.'   One is reminded of the Scotch laird, who had to put one man in the 'jougs' on one side of the gate, and placed an innocent person, 'for symmetry's sake,' in the jougs on the other side.   Croiset, on the other hand, excises several passages for their 'symmetry'!   Hentze also is convinced that the passage is un-Homeric.   No motive is found for the rather abrupt action of Athene when (v. 30) she removes Ares from the field.   And why does Athene tell Diomede to fight Aphrodite only of all gods ; how does she know Aphrodite will appear to rescue her son, Æneas?   All this is only difficult if we forget that the gods are sometimes prescient and omniscient, sometimes almost as limited as mortals.

Mythology is only consistent in inconsistency ; when it ceases to be inconsistent it ceases to be mythological. The gods hardly ever appear without troubling commentators, who expect them to act like rational beings.   Are we to imagine that all the divine machinery was introduced later, like the machinery in the *Rape of the Lock* ?   Why should any poet have introduced any of it ?   If an interpolator worked it all over, why did he not excise what was inconsistent with his interpolations ?   It is just as easy to believe, where slips occur, that the original poet made them, as Scott and Thackeray made them, as to believe that interpolators themselves blundered.   These remarks apply to all the cases where the gods cause difficulties. They cannot appear, being what they are, without causing difficulties to modern readers.   Their very nature is a 'bull' and a swarm of inconsistencies.   When we find a goddess hiding herself from a god by the Cap of Darkness, we are clearly in topsy-turvy land, where anything may happen. As to book vi., especially the beautiful passages on Helen and Andromache, there is only one thing to be said. If these are not by the original poet, we encounter a double miracle. It is miraculous enough that two poets should have been so great in the great manner : it is contrary to the doctrine of chances that each should have been exactly the complement of the other. The first was inspired to sing of men, the second to sing of women ; of Helen's shame and repentance, her shame bidding her send her lover into the fight ; of Andromache's tenderness, impelling her to bid her warlike husband tarry within the walls. Nature does not practise this economic arrangement of genius, nor enable one poet exactly to fill up the defect in another poet's inspiration.

By far the weightiest argument for late work in these books is the legend told by Diomede about the enemies of Dionysus (vi. 130–139). Dionysus only occurs twice or thrice in Homer, and the other passages, as in Odyssey, xi. 325, xxiv. 74, are suspected by some. He was confessedly, and according to all myth, a *parvenu* among the gods, but as to the date when his worship was introduced we have no certainty. He is a peasant god, and so is outside of Homer's ken, but his introduction is assigned to the heroic age, and it would be rash to say that he either emerged from rural mysteries, or came in from abroad, later than the date of Homer.

BOOK VII

The seventh book begins with the welcome reappearance of Hector and Paris on the field (1–17). It may be said that Paris does little ; the truth, perhaps, is that, if we were to see Helen again, Paris could hardly be left at home ; he must be brought back from her bower. The battle might go on till one side conquered, but it is not in the poet's interest to end so abruptly. He, therefore, to retard the

I 2

action, falls back on his machinery.   Apollo and Athene
meet ; she comes (with no chariot) from Olympus, he from
Pergamos, and they decide to stop the fight by making
Hector propose a single combat.   Helenus is inspired by
them to suggest this, and Hector agrees (16-53).   Apollo
and Athene look on in the guise of vultures.   There is no
reason in the world why they should act thus, except that
they are gods, and, as such, 'shape-shifters.'   Hector
issues his challenge ; he does not stake the issue of the war
on the duel.   'Our oaths of truce Zeus accomplished not'
(69) ; the proposal is merely chivalrous.   All the Greeks
are silent, Menelaus reproaches them (95) and will fight
himself.   He dons his armour (103), and commentators
may ask when and why he ever took it off?   Agamemnon
tells him he is no match for Hector, and (122) his armour
is taken off again.   Nestor upbraids the Greeks (123-160)
and proposes that the nine heroes who now answer his
appeal shall cast lots.   The Greeks hope that Agamemnon,
Aias, or Diomede will draw the winning lot.   That of
Aias leaps out.   The absence of Achilles is more than once
lamented, as in 228.   They fight : Aias has the best of it,
the heralds sunder them, night is at hand, they exchange
gifts, Hector is taken to the city, Aias dines with Agamemnon (312).

Here a natural break occurs in the narrative.   What
has preceded is criticised severely.   We have now seen two
duels in one day, and the second duel is fought in spite of
the treachery that followed the first.   Hector's allusion to
the broken oath (69-72) is 'almost cynical,' and for a
reason of textual criticism is regarded as unauthentic.   On
the other hand, Agamemnon, like Hector (iv. 160), laid the
weight of the broken oath on the will of Zeus.

Mr. Leaf supposes that this duel in book vii. is older
than that in book iii., which consequently was unknown

to the author of the present combat of Hector and Aias.
The very opposite opinion is held by several German
critics. The lines alluding to it are a later interpolation.[1]
To all this it may be replied that the poet addressed an
audience which liked plenty of fighting, and would be
pleased by the variety of a duel. Though the two duels
occur in one day, they are separated from each other by
three long books, as far as the audience is concerned.
Moreover, as Mr. Leaf says, they are duels of different kind
and character. The inconsistency of the duel does not
strike Mr. Monro so strongly.[2] ' As to the repetition of the
duel .episode,' he says, ' it may be enough to say that *the
two occasions differ in almost every respect*, and that they are
separated by the long interval, poetically speaking, of the
aristeia of Diomede.'

To this one or two observations may be added. Our
modern taste is really no infallible touchstone of inconsistency in a poet of an age, a religion, manners, and ideas
alien to ours. The gods caused this second duel, and
inspired Helènus to propose it. It is inconsistent with our
ideas that the gods should change into vultures, as they do
here, and watch the duel from a convenient tree (vii. 59, 60).
We have already remarked on the incongruities which invariably occur, when the gods mix themselves in the war.
Such are the beings, then, who suggest the duel. But in
itself the duel would not have seemed so inconsistent, nor
Hector's remark so cynical, to men in the Homeric age.
' Zeus has made our oaths of no avail. We must fight
à outrance.' But I conceive him to mean, ' though *one* duel
was spoiled by the gods, there is no reason why we Trojans
should not show, in another, that, man for man, we are
your match.' Once given, the challenge cannot be declined

[1] It is alluded to again in book vii.
[2] *Iliad*, vol. i. p. 320.

without shame, so the Greeks do not refuse on the ground
of Trojan disloyalty.   They do object to the broken oaths
(vii. 400) when a question of a treaty and compromise is
broached.   They do *not* object when 'a gentle and joyous
passage of arms' is proposed.   It is thus that we would explain the second duel.   A duel is usually an interesting incident, and this one, as Mr. Monro says, is, poetically speaking,
separated by a long interval from the other.   We cannot
imagine a critical listener, of the poet's time, saying, 'They
could not have had *two* single combats in one day, especially after the affair of the oaths.'   As men listened to the
reciter, and waited to hear how such a splendid *holmgang*
as that of Aias and Hector would end, one does not believe
that a single thought of criticism arose.   Does anyone
believe it ?   We must estimate Homer by his age and
his audience.   These refinements of criticism belong to a
later age.   An interpolator, if he had introduced the first
duel on the model of the second, would have probably
joined his passages more carefully.   Mr. Leaf himself says
that 'the two duels are separated, to a hearer, by a sufficiently long interval to make their inconsistency the less
obvious.'   Yet ' to hold that they were composed in their
present form for their present places, in a poem conceived
from the first as a whole *is hardly within the bounds of
reason.*'

To tell the truth, ne objections of Mr. Leaf would
never have occurred to us, who have the advantage of reading, and do not listen to, the poem.   I believe that no
hearer of Homer's time, as I have said, would have dreamed
of a critical objection.   Now, Homer was composing for an
audience of eager warriors, not for a public of professors,
poring over his work with spectacles.   If the inconsistency
were not obvious to the audience, why should it have
struck the poet as incompatible with its place in the poem?

And suppose there were critics in Homer's audience who made objections (a supposition almost incredible), the backs of the gods, who suggested the second duel, were broad enough to bear the burden.

It has been said that no man can criticise a novel fairly who has read it, not for pleasure, but with the set purpose of reviewing it. Much more is this true in Homeric criticism. They who pry into the inconsistencies of this or that passage, they who actually have a professional motive, and a name among the learned to win by discovering a slip or blunder, are as remote as mortals can be from the position of Homer's original hearers. For them, for warriors, he sang ; not for spectacled young German critics on their promotion.

It is not possible here to enumerate all the objections that have been made, and all the hypotheses that have been suggested. Now we have fragments of old lays, interwoven unskilfully ; now we have later interpolations ; now the rhapsodist, now the diaskeuast is invoked. As we know nothing whatever about ancient lays, which may have preceded the epic, as we know nothing about diaskeuasts, rhapsodes, and editors, down to Plato's time at earliest, the inventions of scholars on those matters resemble the industry of the Rabelaisian chimæra—*bombinans in vacuo*. There is nothing solid to found a theory upon. Certain expressions, as οἰόθεν οἶος, αἰνόθεν αἰνῶς (39, 226, 97), are peculiar, but afford no certain indications of date. We can only say, with Mr. Monro, ' such forms are rare in Homer, hence it is singular that there are three instances in this book.'

Lachmann found vii. 1–312 so closely connected with vi., that he recognised them, on his system, as the component parts of one lay—his sixth lay. Christ [1] makes

[1] *Homeri Iliadis Carmina*, i. 68, 69. 1884.

vii. 8–312 (the duel of Hector and Aias) his thirteenth lay,
and supposes it to have been composed later than his
twentieth to twenty-fourth lays. His reasons are characteristic. The poet of book xiii. (one of Christ's lays
twenty to twenty-four) had never heard of the duel between
Aias and Hector : therefore the duel is later than book xiii.
Christ proves his point by quoting the speech of Aias
(xiii. 79, 80), 'I am keen to meet, even in single fight,
the ceaseless rage of Hector.'   Again, in xiii. 810, Aias
challenges Hector. But how does this prove that the two
heroes had not already met, as in book vii., in an un-
decided duel—a kind of tournament? They had not, in
book vii., like Glaucus and Diomede, vowed never to
fight again. Such arguments could hardly be advanced in
any other field of discussion, except, perhaps, mythology.

As to the two duels, Christ (i. 38) is in doubt whether
Hector's reference to the first single fight (vii. 69–72) is
genuine or not.   There is nothing against the lines :
Mr. Leaf takes an objection, Mr. Monro does not ; we
may either excise them, or, admitting that the two duels
are inharmonious, lay the fault of Trojan perfidy on Zeus,
as Hector and Agamemnon do. Though there is nothing
against these lines, in Christ's opinion, in Mr. Leaf's they
are 'intolerable in this place,' and Heyne assigns them to
a rhapsodist. Lachmann defends them, Haupt says they
stand where they should not, and, if they are to be expelled,
then the author of the duel between Aias and Hector is
said to know nothing of the duel between Menelaus and
Paris in book iii. But here the commentators once more
begin to quarrel among themselves. Kayser regards the
duel between Aias and Hector as an interpolation, caused
by the national conceit of the Athenians, ' which insisted
on dragging Aias into the *Volksepos* by the head and ears.'
Aias is not an Athenian, but a chief of Salamis, and the

authenticity of ii. 557, in which he is said to have pitched his camp beside the Athenians, was contested by the Megarians, who claimed Salamis for their own.[1] Some critics are as certain that the author of the second duel had the first for his model, as others that the author of the earlier duel modelled it on the second. 'We have a rational ground for holding that we have here (in book vii.) the oldest form of the duel incident, subsequently developed into that between Menelaus and Paris' (book iii.). This is because we 'must undoubtedly begin by cutting out' 69–72, for which Christ (vol. i. p. 38) sees no occasion.

Such are the edifying diversities of the Higher Criticism.

After the duel in book vii., the Greeks dine, and Aias receives the meed of honour (322). Nestor then proposes, 'as many Achæans are dead,' to burn them, erect one large howe over them, and build high towers with gates, while a fosse is also to be dug as protection against Trojan assaults (335–344). The chiefs assent. The Trojans themselves hold a confused assembly. Antenor proposes to give back Helen, for 'now fight we in guilt against the oaths of faith' (351). (The oaths were made in book iii., and broken in book iv.) Paris refuses to restore Helen, but her wealth he is ready to restore. Priam urges that a herald be sent with the compromise of Paris to the Greeks, and with request for an armistice that the dead may be burned. To the proposal of Paris Diomede makes answer : 'Not even if Helen be sent back will the Achæans abandon the siege ; it is known, even to the fool, that the ends of destruction hang over the Trojans,' because of their perjury (402). Agamemnon gives the same answer, but accepts the armistice. At dawn the dead are gathered and burned by

[1] See collection of authorities in Hentze's *Anhang* to Homer's Iliad, i. p. 142.

both armies. On the following morning, apparently (433),
but without mention of the intervening night, the Achæans
erect a great howe over the dead, and thereto build a wall
(436) with towers, gates, a fosse, and palisades. The
gods meet, and Poseidon expresses jealousy of a work which
will cause the walls of Ilios, built by himself and Apollo,
to be forgotten. Zeus tells him that he can destroy it after
the siege. Then (465) the sun went down, and the toil of
the Achæans was accomplished ; ships come in with wine
of Lemnos from Jason's son, Euneus ; both sides feast and
sleep.

Without 'seeking a knot in a reed,' we may observe and
acknowledge the difficulties in these passages. Thucydides
remarked that this precaution of the wall should have been
taken nine years earlier : at the beginning of the siege.
Mr. Grote held that this present account of building the
wall 'seems to be an afterthought arising out of the
enlargement of the poem beyond its original scheme. The
original Achilleis, passing at once from the first book to the
eighth, and from thence [*sic*] to the eleventh book, might
well assume the fortification and talk of it as a thing
existing, without adducing any special reason why it was
created. . . . But the case was altered when a new poet
parted asunder the first and the eighth books in order to
make room for descriptions of temporary success and glory
on the part of the besieging army. The brilliant scenes
sketched in the books from ii. to vii. mention no
fortification, and even imply its non-existence ; but as no
notice of it occurs amidst the first descriptions of Grecian
disasters in the eighth book, the hearer who had the earlier
books present to his memory might be surprised to find a
fortification mentioned immediately afterwards, unless the
construction of it were specially announced to have intervened. At least so thought the poet, who introduced that

account which we now find in the seventh book. ' [1]   Mr.
Grote sees no adequate reason for building a wall at this
juncture if there had been none before.   Mr. Leaf's theory
of the original Μῆνις is not the same as Grote's, for he does
not include in it book viii.   But he makes the same objection as Mr. Grote to the account of the wall-building in
this place.   He thinks that an older piece of poetry may
have been thrust in here.   One obvious defence of the
whole passage is that the description of the building is a mere
example of early poetic perspective.   In old Italian paintings
we see all parts of the story illustrated going on at the same
time.   Homer makes Helen, in the third book, name to
Priam the Achæan heroes, though he must have been
familiar with them for years.   This is a mere licence of
poetic perspective, and the same might be said in defence
of the wall-building in book vii.   It is, perhaps, a more
serious objection that the work of the fortifications is
described in eight lines (vii. 432–441).   Now the
Homeric manner is to give such descriptions in detail, as
in the building of the Raft of Odysseus, in the mooring of
a ship, the performance of a sacrifice, and so on.   'The
pace of the proceedings passes all belief.' [2]   Are we, therefore, to decide that this wall-building is un-Homeric ?   Or
shall we say that Homer had no conventional 'run,' no
long formula to describe so rare a work as a large fortification, and that he cut down the details so as not to impede
the process of the story ?   We are left to a balance of probabilities.   Mr. Monro says [3] 'the building of the wall
round the camp may be intended as an anticipation of the
battles of which it is the scene, and also as a mark of the
difference made by the absence of Achilles, compare his

---

[1] *History of Greece*, i. 249, 250, ed. 1846.
[2] Bergk, i. 585, 586.
[3] Introduction to book vii., *Iliad*, i. p. 320.

words (ix. 348–355), "without mine aid Agamemnon
hath built a wall and dug a foss about it wide and deep, and
set a palisade thereon : yet even so can he not stay mur-
derous Hector."'

BOOK VIII

The eighth book is, in some ways, one of the most
puzzling in the Iliad. This book, or another equivalent,
is absolutely necessary to the development of the narrative as it now stands ; but there is something in the
tone and manner of the book which to certain readers
does not seem entirely harmonious and consistent. The
canto ends with one of the most famous scenes in Homer
—the description of the moonlit midnight heaven brooding
peacefully above the firelit plain, where the Trojans camp,
awaiting the divine dawn, and expecting the destruction of
the Achæans. But not much of the book is on this poetic
level. That, in itself, is not strange ; but the numerous
repetitions of lines and *formulæ* must astonish every reader.
This question of repeated lines and sequences of lines in
Homer is enigmatic enough. Like almost all early poetry,
like our own old ballads, like the Celtic tales, like the
Song of Roland, Homer has certain 'runs'—*clichés* of verse
—inserted where an event recurs, or where a message
is textually repeated. But in book viii. these echoes are
especially numerous. 'Out of 461 lines, 203 occur elsewhere in the Iliad or Odyssey.' The habit of repetition is either a rest for the reciter's memory, or was carried
on into literature by the poet, as a survival from an age of
composition unaided by writing. The repetitions here are
in undue proportion. We might explain this, more or less,
by saying that many of the events, and sequences of events,
have occurred before in this epic. Having once got a
phrase for a purpose, the poet economically repeats it

whenever he has the same purpose in his mind, and this, as we said, is a mark of archaic composition. If we try the opposite view—namely, that the repetitions are the work of an interpolator—we encounter new problems. This is Mr. Leaf's theory : the main part of the book was added, late, to lead up to book ix., itself, in his opinion, a late addition ; but it is plain that an ambitious interpolator would be too conceited to make mere centos of old phrases, like a school-boy writing Latin verses by aid of tags from Virgil. He would rather aim at originality. Again, who could wish to lead up to book ix. except the author of book ix., one of the most brilliant in the Iliad? That book could not well have existed as a separate lay ; it is only of value in its place. It is hardly conceivable that its author would be satisfied with tagging old verses. In these circumstances we can only state the problem ; there exists no certain test of any proposed solution. Much of the book, to my own taste (no man's taste is a criterion), seems to show an air of fatigue. If one may say so, many parts of it are mere ' business ' ; they are necessary for the poet's purpose ; but the poet here is not inspired. But similar passages are common enough in all imaginative literature, and do not imply diversity of authorship.

The purpose of the eighth book is to show how Zeus began to fulfil his promise to Thetis—namely, that he would glorify Achilles by a defeat of the Achæans. As we saw, this promise was originally made in a manner somewhat hesitating and diplomatic. Yet its fulfilment, reckoning by time, has not been long delayed. On the day after his promise Zeus sent the dream to Agamemnon. The dream led, when the king awoke, to the duel, and the broken oaths, and to more fighting ; then followed a day of truce, and the wall was builded. The eighth book is separated only by one day's war and one day's armistice from the

day of the promise to Thetis.   In the day occupied by
fighting, the gods interfered on both sides.   Now, when
we consider the hesitation of Zeus in his promise, and when
we remember what this deity was – how, like Miss Austen's
Mr. Bennet, he took a humorous pleasure in the absurdities
of his wife and children—it really is not extraordinary that
he should let them disport themselves for a day, before he
began to fulfil a promise which he had given without en-
thusiasm.   If we make these human allowances for a very
faulty human character, the innumerable volumes written
about the delay in the keeping of his promise will seem
rather superfluous.   Day dawns after the burial of the dead
and the building of the wall ; Zeus calls the gods together,
and announces that now he will severely punish any inter-
ference.   Yet he admits to his pet daughter, Athene, that
his words are not to be taken quite in earnest (39-40).   He
then retires to topmost Gargarus and looks on.   The hosts
arm ; there is equal fighting till (75) Zeus terrifies the
Greeks by flashes of lightning.   They all fly ; even Odysseus, for once, retreats ; but Diomede takes Nestor in his
own chariot, and retires fighting.   Zeus, by another bolt
(135), takes the heart out of Nestor.   Hector pursues,
and rails at the Achæans for building the wall (178).
There follows a curious passage (185–197), where he addresses his *four* horses, and reminds them of their messes
of wheat and wine.   Now we never hear of *four* horses in
a war-chariot.   Aristarchus objected to this, and all the old
critics were aghast at the idea of giving wine to horses.
But the old critics had never kept chargers actively engaged
in daily battle.   Old 'Dictator,' some twenty years ago,
always had his bottle of port before a race.   In the
Memorials of Montrose (Maitland Club, 1848), p. 123, we
read ' Item, to my Lord's horse after his hunting, a pint of
ale and a loaf, 2s. 8d.'   We also remember how Gustavus

was Dalgetty's *commensalis*. There is another objection : Hector mentions a golden shield of Nestor's, and a breast-plate of Diomede's, which we do not hear of elsewhere. If all this be interpolated, the interpolator's motive is not conspicuous, and, as the poet here deals largely in repetitions, it is odd that he should also break out into unexampled oddities.[1] Hera now wishes to interfere ; Poseidon restrains her ; Agamemnon prays ; Zeus pities and sends him a favourable omen ; Diomede, encouraged, leads a sortie from the wall ; Teucer, till wounded by Hector, shoots from beneath his brother's shield ; Zeus urges on the Trojans ; Hera and Athene wish to interfere, but yield to Zeus. Night falls on the Achæans, deeply discouraged and besieged within their wall, while the triumphant Trojans camp on the plain, in the famous night scene, anticipating the destruction of the leaguer.

Thus the despondency of the Achæans, and the remorse of Agamemnon, lead to the embassy to Achilles in book ix.

Lachmann divides book viii. into three separate pieces by three separate poets. Hentze thinks the author a very third-rate minstrel, inconsistent, and careless of providing satisfactory motives. The canto does not belong to the old original epic. Düntzer and Friedländer think that it does, but hold interpolations. Bergk recognises ancient fragments *remaniés*. Kayser looks on the book as a palimpsest, written over and almost hiding something more antique. Christ believes it is late, and meant to introduce book ix. Genz regards the prowess of Teucer as an older lay. Her-

---

[1] Mr. Leaf suggests that the line about wine given by Andromache to the horses before her husband dined may have been introduced by an interpolator, because, otherwise, Hector would seem to have been fed on grain. Leaving the line out, the passage would read : 'Andromache set before you honey-hearted wheat sooner than for me.' But the addition of the wine does not remove the wheat. Hector clearly means 'she gave you your food before she gave me my dinner.'

mann places bits of it, with bits of xiii. and xiv., in an antique song of his own invention. Any number of such theories can readily be devised, if we wish to be original.

BOOK IX

The ninth book of the Iliad, taken in connection with the sixteenth, is the strength, or the weakness, of disintegrative criticism. It is maintained that the conduct and language of Achilles in book ix. are utterly irreconcilable with his language in book xvi. Consequently, the two books cannot be by the same poet. Both books are of conspicuous excellence, but we are to understand that the author of the original 'Wrath' composed book xvi., while another later poet, no less excellent, composed book ix., and yet xvi. and ix. are in glaring contradiction, according to the disintegrators. As the contradictions only appear in a very few lines of xvi., we naturally ask why the new poet, who freely added book ix., did not remove the brief texts in the older xvi., which, on the showing of commentators, stultify both works. The answer is, that the new poet's conduct in adding a contradictory episode, and so making the old poet's hero behave inconsistently, while at the same time the new poet neglects to remove the absurdity by a stroke of the pen, or by simple omission in recitation, is 'a striking proof of the conservative forces which guided the construction of the Iliad from its first elements.'[1] To add to a poem inconsistently, to botch it, and patch it, and make it self-contradictory, and needlessly leave it so, is an example of 'conservative forces.' This kind of criticism seems rather arbitrary ; but on this kind of criticism the theory of disintegration relies.

We must now examine the so-called inconsistencies,

[1] Leaf, *Companion to the Iliad*, p. 268.

which are said to prove separate authorships. The ninth
book opens thus :—

Agamemnon, ' weeping like a waterfall' (ix. 14), addresses the host. Zeus has blinded his heart. He advises
instant flight. Diomede says that, whosoever flies, he stays.
Nestor suggests a meeting of the Council of Chiefs, in which
he proposes making atonement to Achilles. Agamemnon,
confessing his folly, declares that he will make amends ; will
send gifts of horses, women, gold ; will return Briseïs as she
came to him, and will give Achilles the hand of his daughter,
with seven cities for her dowry. Nestor takes him at his
word, and advises sending to Achilles his old tutor, Phœnix,
with Aias, Odysseus, and two heralds.[1] ' The twain '
(Odysseus and Aias ?) enter the hero's hut ; he is singing
' the renowns of men,' but welcomes the envoys courteously.
After they have eaten, Aias nods to Phœnix (223) ; but
Odysseus takes the word. It is doubtful, he says, if they can
save the ships, ' if thou put not out thy might.' Agamemnon
offers worthy gifts, which are enumerated. But, even if he
and his gifts be hateful, yet pity the Achæans (301).

Achilles, in reply, urges his old grievances against
Agamemnon. He has many resentments, and not his loss
of Briseïs alone. Besides, he cannot trust Agamemnon.
' Let him not tempt me that know him too well : he shall
not prevail' (345). Let him keep fire from the ships for
himself, if he can ; he has already built a wall which he
never needed while I was in the field. Already (in book i.
409) Achilles had said that he must see the Achæans
' hemmed among their ships' sterns given over to slaughter '
before he relented. Not till then would he fight, when his
own ships were endangered (xvi. 61–63). This glutting of
his vengeance is not given him till book xvi. ; and then he
cries, in bitterness of heart at the irony of the gods, ' My

[1] There are considerable difficulties about Phœnix.

K

prayer hath Zeus accomplished ; but what delight have I therein, since Patroclus, my dear comrade, is dead?' (xviii. 79–83). Now he threatens to sail away on the morrow. Let them carry this message openly to Agamemnon, 'that all the Achæans likewise may be wroth' (ix. 370).

He has been deceived once, and once suffices. Not for all the wealth of Egyptian Thebes will he relent, till Agamemnon has 'paid back all the bitter despite' (387)— that is, 'in humiliation, not presents.'[1] As yet he is not paid. Let the Achæans turn to some other counsel. Phœnix may stay in his hut for the night, and return with him to Phthia, or not, as he pleases (429). Phœnix now, with tears, beseeches him not to return to Greece, telling tales from his own history and that of Meleager, to show the folly of relentlessness. In Meleager's case, he relented so late, that his fellow-citizens did not give him the gifts of atonement. Achilles runs risk of dishonour if he also relents late, and fights, on a sudden, before atonement has been made (432–605).

This reception of atonement is a point of honour in Homeric as in old Icelandic manners. It is not the value of the gifts, but the disgrace of relenting 'unatoned,' that Achilles is asked by Phœnix to consider.

Achilles replies : he need not consider the technical point of honour : he is already 'honoured of Zeus.' He asks Phœnix to stay with him : in the morning they will discuss the question of return homewards (620).

Aias now speaks, a man of few words : 'Let us be going. Other men accept atonement even for a son's death, but the spirit of Achilles is implacable, merely for one girl's sake' (636–7).

Achilles answers : he will not fight till Hector comes

---

[1] Leaf.

to his own ships, and smirches the ships with fire (655).
That, indeed, is his private point of honour throughout the
whole epic, till Patroclus falls. 'But about mine own hut
and ship I ween that Hector, for all his eagerness, will be
refrained.'

Odysseus returns to the council and reports his ill-speed.
Aias and the heralds are his witnesses (688–9). Diomede
says that they must let Achilles be. He will fight when
'his heart biddeth and God arouseth him,' that is, after the
death of Patroclus—one of the half-conscious presentiments
common in the Iliad. The chiefs will fight in the morning.
Then men turn to sleep.

The argument of Mr. Grote, Mr. Leaf, [1] and others, is
that all the splendid scene of the Embassy is inconsistent,
first with the speech of Achilles, next day (in book xi. 609),
when the battle goes against the Greeks. '*Now*, methinks
that the sons of the Achæans will stand in prayer about my
knees, for intolerable need comes upon them.' We need
only lay stress on the '*now !*' and there is no inconsistency
in Achilles' enjoyment of his triumph. As Mr. Monro
says, in his note on the line, 'it is possible that Achilles
intends an insulting reference to the Embassy.' To ourselves it seems not so much probable as unmistakably
obvious.

The passages in book xvi. supposed to be inconsistent
with the account of the Embassy are to the following effect.

Patroclus comes weeping to Achilles (xvi. 3). The best
of the Greeks are wounded ; but Achilles is implacable.

'Surely the grey sea bare thee and the sheer cliffs, so
untoward is thy spirit.'

Patroclus asks leave at least to don the armour of
Achilles, and lead the Myrmidons to the rescue.

Achilles replies, first, by recounting his wrongs. 'But

[1] *Companion*, pp. 170, 171, 212.

K 2

we will let bygones be bygones.   No man may be angry for
ever, only I deemed that I would not cease from my wrath till
battle came to my own ships' (xvi. 60).   This he had said in
book i.   ' But thou, Patroclus, don my armour, and lead
the Myrmidons.   The Trojans would not tarry when they
saw me, 'if mighty Agamemnon were but kindly disposed
to me' (xvi. 72).   Now, if Achilles, in this remark, has
merely in view Agamemnon's offers of atonement, the inconsistency is glaring.   But does not Achilles mean, ' the
Trojans would not be here about the camp at all, if
Agamemnon's heart were right towards me'?   He had for
very long been on ill terms with Agamemnon ; the affair of
Briseïs had only brought an old enmity to a head.   Besides,
the argument of Mr. Leaf and Mr. Grote (on this point)
does not hold water.   They reason thus.   Achilles, in
book xvi., says, ' If Agamemnon were but friendly to me,
our sorrows would never have happened.'   But Agamemnon
is friendly, they say : he has offered priceless atonement.
Therefore the poet who put these words into the mouth of
Achilles in xvi. knew nothing of the offer in ix.   Therefore
the book in which the offer is made is later than book xvi.

    But this is only convincing if by the words

εἴ μοι κρείων 'Αγαμέμνων
ἤπια εἰδείη—

if by the ' kindliness' Achilles meant the feelings implied by
Agamemnon's offer.   But he does *not* regard that offer as a
proof of such feelings in Agamemnon as he desires.   In
book ix. 345 he denies the sincerity of Agamemnon : ' Let
him not tempt me that know him full well : he shall not prevail. . . . He hath taken my meed of honour, and hath
deceived me.'   Thus, if book ix. be genuine, the words of
Achilles in xvi. are not inconsistent.   He is angry with
Agamemnon's whole conduct towards him, culminating, as
it did, in the seizure of Briseïs, and the offer of atonement

seems to him insincere. Nothing but utter defeat and humiliation will appease his anger.

There remains another so-called inconsistency in Achilles' speech (xvi. 82-86). He is giving advice to Patroclus : ' But do thou obey, even as I shall put into thy mind the end of my commandment, that in my sight thou mayst win great honour and fame of all the Danaans, and they may give me back again that fairest maiden, and thereto add glorious gifts.' His counsel is that Patroclus shall do no more than merely drive the Trojans 'from the ships,' and then return, not fight longer, apart from Achilles, for 'thereby wilt thou lessen mine honour.' Moreover, there will be danger from Apollo, a protector of the Trojans—another example of unconscious prediction. Then Achilles wishes that Trojans and Achæans might perish together, while he and Patroclus alone survive to 'undo the sacred coronal of Troy.' Here Mr. Leaf insists that the passage on the restoration of Briseïs is inconsistent : her restoration and the gifts have been offered already. ' Those who would defend the unity of the Iliad have therefore to expel these lines, but without the slightest warrant.'[1] And here occurs a humorous example of criticism. Even Colonel Mure, for once untrue to his glorious colours, would like to regard the lines on Briseïs (85, 86) as an interpolation, so inconsistent with the offer in book ix. does he hold them to be.[2]

Meanwhile Hentze and Fick also would excise the lines as inconsistent with their private theories. Mr. Leaf thinks their reasons 'the result of a *parti pris*.' But he suspects the lines in xviii. and xix. which refer to the Embassy, they being contradictory of his theory (xviii. 448 ; xix. 141) The passages where they occur are 'later accretions.'

There is, obviously, no end to this method, if partisans

[1] *Companion*, p. 272.
[2] *Literature of Ancient Greece*, 2nd edition, vol. i. p. 282, note.

of either side are to cut out just whatever they find inconvenient. In truth, the passage in book xvi. 85, far from being
inconsistent with the Embassy, actually refers to it. In
the first place, though Achilles refused atonement from
Agamemnon, before fire came on the ships, there is no reason
why he should not accept it now from all the *Danaans* at
large, *after* fire had come on the ships, and as a tribute to
the valour of his beloved Patroclus. The total change of
circumstances may naturally produce a change of temper.
The resolution framed in one mood (like the resolve to sail
homewards) may be altered (as after the speech of Phœnix
in book ix.) in altered circumstances and in another mood.
So much for the alleged inconsistency.

Again, there is clear reference in book xvi. to the Embassy
and to the speech of Phœnix therein. Achilles was there
warned by the example of Meleager, who, on account of his
late relenting, never received his promised atonement at all.
This Achilles remembers, and bids Patroclus confine himself to driving the foe from the ships (xvi. 87). Patroclus is
thus restricted in his action for two reasons : first, if he gain
too decisive a victory, Achilles, like Meleager, will risk losing
his atonement ; secondly, Patroclus will be in peril of the
wrath of Apollo, before which, in the event, he fell.

With this interpretation (and the meaning is perfectly
clear, if we understand heroic ideas of the point of honour),
there is no inconsistency in the passages of books ix. and
xvi., but rather the closest agreement.[1]

---

[1] This had been written before the writer observed the same
opinions in Mr. Monro's note to xvi. 84-86, where Mr. Monro also
points out the connection between the words of Phœnix in book ix. and
those of Achilles in book xvi. Mr. Monro, however, thinks that lines
84-86, about Briseïs, may have been interpolated by some rhapsodist,
and may have been suggested by the words, in 90,

ἀτιμότερον δέ με θήσεις

('thou wilt lessen mine honour ')—

So it appears to us : we see no inconsistency when
a passionate hero changes his mind with a change of circumstances. We see absolute consistency of sentiment and
manners, just where glaring incongruity of facts startles a
number of critics. But we must ever beware of the *idola
specus*—the fallacies of personal prepossession. Our prepossession, as lovers of poetry, is in favour of the unity of the
Iliad. The prepossessions of Mr. Leaf, Mr. Grote, Mr. Jebb,
and other critics are in favour of separatism. Thus Mr. Leaf
writes that the speech of Achilles, in xvi. 60–61, 71–73,
84–86, ' is not a mere superficial inconsistency . . . it is a
contradiction at the very root of the story, as flagrant as if
Shakespeare had forgotten in the fifth act of *Macbeth* that
Duncan had been murdered in the second. To suppose
that the same intellect which prepared the Embassy to
Achilles by the eighth book, and wrought it out in such
magnificence of detail in the ninth, could afterwards compose a speech, so different and yet so grand, in entire oblivion of what had gone before, is to demand a credulity
rendering any rational criticism impossible.'

Who is to decide ? Mr. Monro, and we ourselves, find
no incongruity, but, on the other hand, close congruity
of character and manners, and an actual implicit reference
to the scene of the Embassy. Mr. Leaf says that such
credulity renders any rational criticism impossible. Again
it is Mr. Leaf who, to us, seems credulous.

He imagines a great poet adding a magnificent scene to
a whole epic composed by a predecessor. And he supposes
this second great poet to have introduced a blunder as
glaring as it is superfluous—a blunder so great that it must

' which some rhapsodist wished to make more explicit.' No excision,
at all events, is necessary in the cause of consistency, nor could seem
necessary to anyone who understands the heroic temper and the
manners of the heroic age.

be recognised by every rational listener or reader.   Now, if
it were, in any unexplained way, at any date, possible for a
new poet to introduce books viii. and ix., that poet must
have had every freedom of action.   A stroke of his stylus,
or needle, or pen, if he wrote, would have scratched out the
'inconsistencies' of Achilles's speech in book xvi.   If he
did not write, he would omit them in recitation, and it
seems to be the hypothesis that his version was, somehow,
preserved in oral tradition.   Then why did he leave the
lines in book xvi., to ruin the whole structure of an epic
in which he was so much interested that he sank his own
fame and his own work in it, rather than win glory by a
distinct new poem of his own ?   Mr. Leaf seems to satisfy
himself on this head by the excellence of the *purpureus
pannus* (book ix.).   Its introduction, 'at the expense of
subsequent inconsistencies, is intelligible enough, for such
a poem has every right to be regarded as an end in itself.'
Elsewhere, Mr. Leaf attributes the blunder to the 'conservatism' of the Homeric school.   Now, if any dramatic
poet had interpolated into *Macbeth* (to use Mr. Leaf's own
example) the most magnificent scenes, turning on the
denial that Duncan had been murdered, and if he had at
the same time let the scene of the murder stand, no good
nature could tolerate the absurdity.   No sane poet could
contemplate such a meaningless outrage.   But the poet of
book ix., on Mr. Leaf's theory, did this very thing.   He
must have been a mischievous mocker, for he stultified himself along with the author in whose work and fame he
merged his own.   He did not take the obvious precaution
of excising the few lines which, in Mr. Leaf's opinion, make
the obviousness of his interpolation a thing not to be discussed 'by rational criticism.'   Or was this his cryptic
method of affixing his private mark to book ix. ?

    To ourselves it appears that book ix., the Rejection of

the Embassy, is not only not inconsistent, it is inevitable, necessary to the tragic development of the plot, necessary to our intelligence of the hero's character and to the propriety of his punishment.

We are taking Achilles as Homer shows him to us— that is, with the passions of an early age. He has a touch of the Maori or the Iroquois. Mr. Grote says that the passages in book ix. ' carry the pride and egotism of Achilles beyond even the largest exigencies of insulted honour, and are shocking to that sentiment of Nemesis which was so deeply seated in the Grecian mind.' This is all quite true ; but—such a man was Achilles. Moreover, the word Nemesis, in the Herodotean sense, is unknown to Homer. Again, Nemesis (as the later Greeks understand it) does fall on Achilles. He is punished by his own sin. Patroclus falls—Patroclus, more dear to him than Briseïs, dearer than a wilderness of gifts and fair maidens. Mr. Grote complains of the ' implacability' of a hero who is proverbially *inexorabilis*. We venture to say that when commentators call books ix. and xvi. ' inconsistent,' they understand neither Achilles nor Homer, neither the heroic age nor even the conduct of the poem.

Although the Homeric Greeks did not use the *word* Nemesis in the Herodotean sense, meaning the revenge of God and of circumstances on overweening pride, the *idea* was familiar to them. In the conduct of the Iliad, taking the poem as a whole, Nemesis falls on Achilles because of his superhuman and inexorable pride. This is avenged by the death of Patroclus, entailing his own. He alone, of the great Achæan heroes, is slain in Troyland. Now, according to Mr. Leaf's and Mr. Grote's theories, this Nemesis seems far too heavy a punishment for Achilles's offence. What is Achilles's offence in Mr. Leaf's theory? First (book i.), he stands out of the fight. Next, he prays Zeus to bring de-

feat on his countrymen.   Then in book xi., which, on Mr.
Leaf's hypothesis, follows hard on book i., the Achæans
have, on the whole, the worst of the battle.   In spite of the
deeds, the *aristeia*, of Agamemnon, they are driven to the
ships.   They do not lose the wall, for the wall, on this
theory, is not there to lose.   The twelfth book is regarded
by Mr. Leaf as a later composition.   Of the ·thirteenth
book only forty lines (795–837) are left.   The fourteenth is
late.   Of the fifteenth only two hundred and thirty-one
lines, or less (515, or rather 592–746), are left, containing
the wrath of Hector, and his rush on the ship of Protesilaus ;
but that rush is checked by Aias with the enormous spear
for repelling boarders.   Then comes book xvi., in which
Achilles at once yields to the tears of Patroclus, relents,
and sends his friend into battle.   Achilles, then, as Mr. Leaf
reconstructs the poem, has withdrawn from war ; he has
brought the Trojans to the ships by his family influence
with Zeus.   But he no sooner learns from Patroclus that
three Greek heroes are wounded, than he lets bygones be
bygones to a great extent.   We admit that he has sinned ;
but, if we cut out book ix., he has not sinned against the
prayer of the humiliated Agamemnon.   He has been angry,
but not implacable.   The ninth book, making him implacable, *inexorabilis*, deaf to prayer, ensures his Nemesis,
makes his punishment intelligible ; yet that book is excised
as no part of the original epic !

On Mr. Leaf's theory the famous Wrath, as described
by the original poet, only lasted for twelve days, apparently
of peace, in book i. and for part of one day's fighting,
when it was swallowed up in pity on the first serious
defeat of the Greeks.   Does this wrath, brief and broken in
effect, deserve the terrible Nemesis, the loss of Patroclus,
the death of Achilles, consequent on his revenge on Hector ?
Is *this* the implacable, inexorable Achilles ?   Clearly the pun-

ishment would seem, to an Homeric mind, out of all proportion to the offence. The crime of Achilles, on which all
turns, is, we repeat, the refusal of the ' Prayers ' of the
Embassy, which Mr. Leaf, and many modern commentators,
cut out of the original poem, thereby depriving it of its
raison d'être. There can be no stronger argument against
this mutilation of the Iliad.[1]

Given book ix.—the refusal of the prayers—and
Achilles's conduct is 'shocking to that sentiment of Nemesis
which was so deeply seated in the Greek mind,' as Mr. Grote
says. Take away the book, and his conduct, as Mr. Grote
seems to agree with us, is *not* shocking to the sentiment of
Nemesis. So Mr. Grote excises the very passages which he
sees to be necessary, because the sentiment of Nemesis
must be shocked before its punishment is provoked.

Mr. Grote declares that the conduct of Achilles, admitting book ix., is ' breaking the bruised reed.' Exactly :
Achilles was not a Christian. Mr. Grote, again, says that,
in the original prayer of Achilles to Thetis, Achilles only
asks for honour, redress, and 'victory to the Trojans until
Agamemnon and the Greeks shall be bitterly sensible of
the wrong which they have done to their bravest warrior '

---

[1] I had written this before noticing that Nutzhorn, in his *Die
Entstehungsweise der Homerischen Gedichte*, p. 171, has taken the same
very obvious point :

'If the death of Patroclus and the sorrow of Achilles is to be
" motived," Achilles himself must have sinned. This he does by rejecting, in book ix., the gifts promised by Athene in book i. 212—

καί ποτέ τοι τρὶς τόσσα παρέσσεϯαι ἀγλαὰ δῶρα.'

Hence, as Nutzhorn says, arises the tragic motive, as in Herodotus
and Sophocles (p. 178).

All this appears manifest enough to anyone who reads Homer as
literature. Whoever bases his opinions on a mass of German names
will find plenty of support for what our literary instinct should tell
us unaided (Hentze, *Anhang zu Ilias*, iii. 122 ; vi. 10).

(book i. 409-509). ' Hem them among their ships' sterns about the bay, given over to slaughter,' is what Achilles really asks for (i. 409). This is what Zeus promises (viii. 473-4), ' when these shall fight amid the sterns in most grievous stress ;' and this is what Achilles gets, to his sorrow. He 'has no joy of it.' Thus, before the Embassy, Hector 'thought to make havoc of the ships ;' but Hector did not reach the ships, and fire one of them, till just before Achilles sent out Patroclus to war. Achilles gets his prayer fulfilled to the letter, and to his bane.

To support his case, as we have said, Mr. Grote needs excisions in later books. The first is xviii. 448, 456 : ' the elders of the Achæans entreated him, and offered many gifts' —a plain reference to the ' interpolated' Embassy. Mr. Leaf pronounces this ' a later accretion,' and it certainly seems to differ from the narrative in book xvi. In xviii. 448, Thetis is telling the story to Hephaestus, and speaks, Mr. Leaf thinks, as if Achilles had sent out Patroclus in consequence of the Embassy. Her words are, ' Then albeit himself he refused to ward destruction from them, he put his armour on Patroclus, and sent him to the war.' Mr. Grote says that those places, with xix. 192 195, and xix. 243, 'are specially inserted for the purpose of establishing a connection between the ninth book and the nineteenth.' But, if it were easy to doctor the epic thus, why were not the equally needful excisions made, as in xvi. 86? It is really impossible to understand these old interpolators. They make this and that *callida junctura*, and yet they neglect other passages which also they should have handled. In xix. 140-1, Agamemnon says, 'I will send the gifts Odysseus promised yesterday,' really the day before yesterday—that is, in book ix., which Mr. Leaf excises. Mr. Leaf says that this passage, which contradicts his theory, is an interpolation. In xix. 192-5, Agamemnon tells Odysseus to convey to

Achilles 'the gifts promised yesterday'—that is, in
book ix. In xix. 241, the gifts are carried to Achilles, ' the
tripods Agamemnon had promised.' About all this Mr.
Leaf remarks : ' Allusions to the gifts offered in the ninth
book are found scattered through the scene of the oath,
and this therefore is also late.' It is 'late' merely because
it does not suit the theory of Mr. Leaf and Mr. Grote. The
ancient Alexandrine critics objected to none of these lines.
There is no linguistic ground for the charges against them.
They are simply inconvenient. Mr. Monro points out that
Mr. Grote must excise more, if he is to excise at all. ' If
192–195 are to go, we cannot keep 238–249, nor 271–281.
Homer could not make Odysseus go to the tent of Agamemnon and fetch the gifts without being first commanded by
Agamemnon to do so, and this command is given in lines 192–5.
It is significant, too, that Ulysses is not told what gifts he
is to fetch. He simply goes to bring ' the gifts,' and he
finds everything ready to his hand, in a way that would
be unintelligible unless the episode of book ix. had preceded.'

Thus book ix. appears to be a natural and necessary part
of the story, and, indeed, essential to a knowledge of the
character of Achilles, and as an explanation of his heavy
punishment. On the other hand, if we reject it, we are
driven to make excisions at our own will and fantasy. The
system which needs these least is, so far, the least unscientific.

The objection of Bergk (i. 590), that the tone of true
Homeric poetry is not recognisable in the ninth book, is
a question of literary taste. The speeches of Achilles are
famed as the most glorious examples of Homeric rhetoric.
Are they too rhetorical in the case of a hero outraged in
his dearest affections and in his honour? This has not
been the opinion of the world for three thousand years.

We cannot object to a poet because, when rhetoric is
needed, his rhetoric is good.

'The position of the ninth book in the economy of
the Iliad is, as Mr. Leaf says, 'a point of cardinal importance in the Homeric question.' We have, therefore,
examined it with some minuteness, as far as the plot is
concerned. We have agreed with Mr. Monro, that Mr.
Grote's arguments about the temper and demands of
Achilles are based 'on modern, or at least post-Homeric,
sentiment.' Mr. Monro thinks that if the book is an
addition 'it is at least a skilful and effective one.' Now it
cannot be skilful if it is glaringly and needlessly inconsistent.
Mr. Leaf, on the other hand, as we saw, thinks the inconsistencies between books ix. and xvi. so great that to attribute
them to the same author 'demands a credulity rendering
rational criticism impossible.' We have endeavoured to
show that no credulity is required ; that we have only to
read Homer in an Homeric, not in an academic and modern,
spirit, to see how well books ix. and xvi. agree ; in fact, how
indispensable each is to the other and to the whole poem.

It is not on plot alone, however, that the objections to
book ix. depend. The language is also said to be later than
that of the original Μῆνις. Mr. Monro has pointed out
lines in which the language agrees rather with the Odyssey,
and with books xxiii., xxiv., than with the rest of the
epic. To readers who attribute all the Iliad and the
Odyssey also to Homer, or, at least, to his age, this matters
little. The linguistic peculiarities noted by Mr. Monro
occur in five lines of book ix. (42, 143, 337, 417, 684).
In the first (42) is a grammatic form, ὥς τε νέεσθαι, occurring
only once in the Iliad, and once in the Odyssey.[1] Next,
'the use of ἐν with abstract words is commoner in this book
than in the Iliad generally.' Thirdly (337), δεῖ. This is

[1] Od. xvii. 21.

the only instance of the word in Homer,' so, of course, it cannot attach this book to the Odyssey. Fourthly (417), the 'use of the 1 sing. opt. is very rare in the Iliad.' Lastly (684), we have here 'the only instance of ἄν with an infinitive in Homer,' which, again, cannot connect the book with the Odyssey. These and one or two other linguistic peculiarities are also noted in Mr. Monro's ' Homeric Grammar.' The mention of Egypt and of Pytho (Delphi) (382, 405) are supposed to show that ' the geography is later than that of the Iliad.' This consideration may influence persons who believe that Delphi and Egypt were discovered by Greek geographers after the composition of the original Μῆνις, and before the composition of the Odyssey. If the white barbarians from the North on the temple walls at Medinet Habu represent early Greeks, and if the prehistoric remains of Greek pottery in Egypt are correctly dated, of course the geographical objection, as far as Egypt is concerned, falls to the ground.[1] Mr. Leaf, at least, cannot urge it, for he believes in the early dates of Greeks in Egypt as assigned by Mr. Flinders Petrie. ' The legend of the choice of Achilles between two destinies ' (ix. 410, xi. 794) is not, to our mind, inconsistent with his description of himself in book i. as 'short-lived.' He has made his choice of 'one crowded hour of glorious life ' (book i. 352). However, this is open to doubt.

Such are the main arguments against book ix., and they may be weighed by the reader. To our mind the book is necessary as an exposition of the character of Achilles, and also because, if it is to go, we must make many excisions in later books at our private pleasure and fantasy. Do the linguistic and geographic objections, such as they are, out-weigh the completion of the character of Achilles and the necessity for arbitrary excisions?

[1] Cf. Flinders Petrie, *Journal of Hellenic Society*, xi. 2, 271.

There remains, in book ix., a passage of curious interest. This is the introduction of Phœnix, an old Myrmidon, whom Peleus sent as a kind of governor or adviser of Achilles (ix. 438). As a member of the embassy, he tries to move Achilles by a singular story of his own youth. There is decidedly nothing like this tale in Homer, and it would furnish matter for an Homeric 'realistic' novelist, if such a being were imaginable. The father of Phœnix had a mistress, which distressed Phœnix's mother. She bade her son make love to the mistress, which he did successfully. His father then cursed him that he should never have a son. Phœnix fled to Peleus, at whose court he was employed to bring up Achilles. 'Oft hast thou stained my doublet with sputtering of wine,' says Phœnix, in the spirit of the Æschylean nurse of Orestes. Phœnix implores Achilles to accept the gifts, and warns him by the example of Meleager, who, in similar circumstances, came too late to the rescue of his countrymen, and never got the gifts that had been promised. Achilles is bidden not to risk the gifts by too late repentance.

This is a curious passage, and Phœnix is strangely introduced. At the council in Agamemnon's hut, when it is determined to send an embassy, Nestor says (ix. 168), ' Let Phœnix lead,' accompanied by Odysseus, Aias, and the heralds. What was Phœnix—a Myrmidon, and not of the first rank—doing at a meeting of the great chiefs? There is a linguistic difficulty later (182, 192–8). In describing the faring forth of the embassy, Homer says 'the twain went along the seashore.' What twain? Mr. Monro explains, ' Aias and Odysseus, who are the envoys proper.' Again, when they reach the hut of Achilles, he is singing. Then we read, 'the twain went forward, and noble Odysseus led.' Why only two, as Phœnix, Odysseus, and Aias were the representatives of Agamemnon? We might

say that 'the twain' are the two heralds, but of the heralds
we hear no more by name. What became of the heralds?
But, however we take this—and others explain the dual by
saying that Phœnix was not originally in the embassy—the
whole passage is unusual in every way, above all in the
abrupt and unepic fashion of introducing Phœnix. But
what could be the motive here of an interpolator? Phœnix
often appears later in the Iliad, and is always regarded by
commentators as a suspicious person. We can offer no
theory as to the singularly broken manner of his introduction ; it is natural to suspect that something has been lost,
or that much interesting matter has been abruptly introduced.

BOOK X

After a defence, successful or unsuccessful, of book ix.,
it is less necessary to examine very minutely the objections
against the later books. If our opinion be accepted, as far
as book ix. is concerned, we have 'the inexorable' Achilles,
whom all the world knows, restored to us as the creation of
the original poet, and this is our chief concern. We find,
too, if our argument about book iii. and book vi. is
accepted, that he who drew this Achilles is also the painter
of Helen and Andromache—that there are not two poets of
this genius, but one. The remainder of the Iliad, however,
cannot be neglected.

The tenth book is almost universally recognised as an
addition, and, by some apparently, as a late addition. The
story, briefly, is this :—After the news of Achilles's refusal to
listen to the embassy, Agamemnon cannot sleep. He hears
the flutes and pipes of the Trojans round their fires on the
plain. Menelaus, too, is wakeful. The pair waken the
other chiefs, inspect the sentinels, and hold a council
outside the moat. They determine to send spies to the

L

Trojan camp. Odysseus and Diomede set forth ; they
catch Dolon, a Trojan spy, whom Hector has bribed by
the promise of the horses of Achilles. From him they
learn that Rhesus, the Thracian king, has just arrived in
Troy, that he and his goodly horses are unguarded. They
slay Rhesus, and drive his horses into camp, to the en-
couragement of the Greeks. There is a legend that if these
horses once drank the water of Xanthus, Troy would be
safe. Homer says nothing of this.

This episode does not advance the story, except in so
far as it does hearten up the Greeks, and inspirit, for next
day's fight, the despondent Agamemnon. But the adventure is not referred to later, unless we find a reference in
the close companionship of Odysseus and Diomede, in
book xi. The Iliad can do without the story, as both Mr.
Grote and Colonel Mure see : the story cannot do without
the Iliad. It is useless, except as a portion of the Iliad.
This some of the ancients noted. Though the famous
Alexandrines say nothing about it, Eustathius, a Byzantine
of the twelfth century, remarks that, 'according to old
writers, Homer made this lay separately, and Pisistratus
added it to the Iliad.' This evidence is vague. If it has
any value, then it implies that Homer did not compose a
mere series of lays, but an epic, and made this canto
'separately.' Mr. Leaf remarks that the whole story about
Pisistratus is later than the days of Aristarchus, and, as a
piece of serious history, is now generally discredited. Nor
would the canto have any meaning as a separate lay. It
was meant for its place here, whoever its author may have
been, and whatever his date.

As to the character of the book, Mr. Leaf says that the
style stands almost alone as being 'distinctly mannered.'
Effects are produced 'by violent contrasts,' a criticism
passed on book xxiv. ; but what artist does not produce

effects by contrasts? Homer is full of contrasts; so is
Scott. The motives of the story are much confused, and,
indeed, the tale seems to need the later myth about the
horses. 'The author takes quite a peculiar delight in the
detailed descriptions of dress and weapons.' There is
nothing 'peculiar' in this. Homer everywhere rejoices, as
in the very next book, in detailed descriptions of weapons
and dress. 'The linguistic evidence' contains 'pseudo-
archaic forms,' as Mr. Monro says. But these, we may
reply, are merely the result of false analogy, an undying
principle in language.[1] Mr. Leaf points to such a possible
'sham archaism' in x. 346. 'It looks as though the poet
thought that the -σι, which is so often found in the subjunctive,
was an arbitrary affix, which might be appended also to the
optative.'[2] We need not imagine that the poet, who certainly
was an early poet, reasoned about the -σι ; even now half-
educated people unconsciously use such false analogies.
Conscious reasonings and forgeries belong to a much later
and more pedantic age. But, if the book is really crowded
with such instances—for example, 'the post-Homeric use of
the article '[3]—that is a more serious consideration. Mr.
Leaf[4] says that there are ' numerous instances of false
archaism.' In Introduction to book x. he mentions two,
'probably' a third, ' with several other possible cases.' The
words which are ἅπαξ λεγόμενα—used only once—may be
reasonably accounted for by the rather peculiar and hasty
equipment of an unpremeditated night expedition, the singular helmets and other gear, which the poet has to describe.[5]

[1] *Sounds and Inflexions in Greek and Latin.* King and Cookson,
pp. 19, 22.

[2] La Roche reads παραφθήῃσι, which would remove the objection,
but there is no MS. authority.

[3] Monro, introduction to book x.   [4] *Companion*, p 191.

[5] The phrase πτολέμοιο στόμα may be ' curious,' but it recurs in xix.
313.

But we cannot, with Mr. Monro, regard the ruthlessness of Dolon's slaughter, and the midnight havoc, as 'akin to comedy' and 'a farcical interlude out of harmony with the tragic elevation of the Iliad.' The humour is as cruel as that of an Icelandic saga.

On the other side, we might point to a passage of touching sublimity, as where Agamemnon tells Nestor that Zeus has planted him 'above all men for ever among labours' (x. 89). Compare the words of the weary Charlemagne, in the *Chanson de Roland*, 'Deus ! dist li Reis, si peneuse est ma vie !' Again, consider Agamemnon's anxiety about Menelaus. Him he has not the heart to send as a spy (x. 240), just as he was in terror for his sake, in book vi., when Menelaus wished to accept the challenge of Hector. As an archaic touch, notice lines 152, 153, the spears are set upright on their spiked butts, beside the sleeping Greeks.[1] Now we know, from Aristotle, *Poetic.* xxv., that this piece of drill was by his time disused in Greece, though it survived among the Illyrians. Again, it is an Homeric note where we are told that the newly arrived horses of Rhesus 'were not yet used to dead men,' and had to be led carefully, while Odysseus dragged the dead out of the way. Very Homeric, too, is the remark that Dolon, the horse-loving spy, was an only son, among five sisters. The whole episode, as Col. Mure says, 'might naturally suggest itself to the mind of a patriotic bard, to relieve a gloomy interval, and cheer the drooping spirits of his countrymen.' Homer, if we may parody Dr. Johnson, cannot bear to 'let the Trojan dogs have the best of it.' Virgil[2] thought the episode worth imitating, and did not imitate it well. The episode, as Christ says, is certainly a *pannus haud spernendus*, and the reader may choose between the objections which we have stated and the defence which may be urged.

---

[1] Compare iii. 135.   [2] Æneid, ix. 167.

The whole question of book x. is of no great importance, except in one regard. If it were possible, somewhere, somehow, to foist a whole book into the sacred text of Homer, then it would also be possible to foist many others. But how, when, where, and by whom such liberties were taken with the literary inheritance of Greece, especially as the labours of Pisistratus are given up for unhistorical, is precisely what we do not understand. Bergk, admitting that Pisistratus made an edition, thinks the tradition not improbable.[1]

BOOK XI

After the eleventh book there is no longer the same general agreement between the ideas of Mr. Leaf and Mr. Grote. Mr. Leaf retains nearly all book xi., fitting it in, as we have seen, to book ii. The book tells of the battle, the valour of Agamemnon, his wounding, the assault led by Hector, the flesh-wounds of Diomede, Odysseus, and Machaon. Achilles, who, on Mr. Leaf's showing, is in the full tide of wrath, sends Patroclus with kind inquiries for the wounded Machaon, who is lunching with Nestor, and Patroclus, instead of returning, stops to attend to the wounded Eurypylus. The stay was not, in Mr. Leaf's view, really long, for he now boldly cuts out the wall (built in book vii.) and the fighting at the wall altogether. The Greeks had been so reckless as not to fortify their position. Thus all the twelfth book goes at a blow, taking with it Sarpedon's famous address to Glaucus, and Hector's contempt of omens—' one omen is best, to fight for our country.' On any consideration of ' the grand style,' these passages, of course, are the true Homer's, but they must go, and we must congratulate the poet on his late collaborator. Of xiii. only forty-two lines are left ; of xiv. nothing ; of xv. one hundred and forty-two lines (Hector's attack on the

[1] See Appendix, B.

ship of Protesilaus, and the defence of Aias), and so we reach xvi., where Patroclus appeals to Achilles, with tears and is sent into the war, with all the command of Achilles, the Myrmidons. We thus lose from the original poem, among other things, the celebrated scene in which Hera, with the cestus of Aphrodite, beguiles Zeus to love, sleep, and forgetfulness of the war.

The chief reasons for this wholesale excision are the discrepancies as to the confused fighting about the wall. We might say, with Thirlwall, that, if the current of the poem could make even Wolf forget his critical difficulties (as Wolf admits), these inconsistencies 'might as easily have escaped the poet's attention.' Mr. Leaf admits that 'when it suits his purpose the poet forgets all about the river which runs between the Greek camp and the city of Troy.' [1] Why should we expect him to be more mindful of the wall? Of confused fighting the description is apt to be confused, as all history shows, and as most fiction attests. 'Hard were it for me, like a god, to tell all these things,' says the poet in a passage objected to by Zenodotus. It is hard, and rather too hard. But critics have pardoned the poet. Mr. Grote thinks that in the original Μῆνις the existence of the wall was taken for granted; its building was not described, as in book vii. of the actual epic. Mr. Grote, therefore, retains books xii., xiii., xiv., xv. 'I shall not deny,' he says, 'that there are perplexities in the detail of events as described in the battles at the Grecian wall and before the ships, from the eleventh to the sixteenth books, *but they appear only cases of partial confusion,* such as may reasonably be ascribed to imperfections of text; the main sequence remains coherent and intelligible. We find no considerable events which could be left out without breaking the thread, nor any incon-

[1] *Companion,* p. 16.

gruity between one considerable event and another.' He
recognises 'congruity of structure, and conformity to opening promise.' Mr. Leaf, on the other hand, sees far
greater discrepancies. To his mind it is easy to account
for these by ill-contrived additions and ill-made junctures,
and it is also easy for Mr. Leaf to believe that the excellence of the poetry was within reach of a new poet. This
Mr. Matthew Arnold was unable to suppose. 'The matter
affords no data for arguing, but the grand source from
which conviction, as we read the Iliad, keeps pressing in
upon us, that there is one poet of the Iliad—one Homer—
is precisely this nobleness of the poet, this grand manner.'
The Iliad ' bears the magic stamp of a master.' [1]

But this is a question of taste, not of argument. [2]

The language and style of the tenth book, then, certainly
did not shock the orthodoxy of Mr. Arnold. Several
Isaiahs he admitted, not several Homers.

On the earlier part of book xi., and its supposed
connection with the beginning of book ii. as part of the
original poem, we have already spoken in treating of
the second book. The book received in old times the
name of ' The Aristeia of Agamemnon.' In lines 1–283
the hero behaves with courage and wins great success,
driving the Trojans from the plain to the Scæan Gates. He
is wounded by Coon on the arm and retires into camp.
Hector, who has held back in obedience to Zeus, while

[1] *Lectures on Translating Homer,* i. 45.

[2] It is curious to find Mr. Jebb arguing that what Mr. Arnold
meant by the ' grand manner ' is only the conventional epic diction.
Mr. Arnold might seem to have guarded himself partly against this
objection by his remarks on the hexameter as superior, even in the
hands of Quintus Smyrnæus and Coluthus, to the verse of the
balladists. Quintus has the epic diction, the epic instrument, but
Mr. Arnold does not claim for him 'the grand manner,' though he
calls Quintus ' a poet of merit,' as he certainly is.

Agamemnon raged, now comes forward, but is repulsed
by Diomede, whom Paris wounds on the foot with an arrow.
Odysseus alone and staunchly upholds the fray ; indeed,
in this stand Odysseus fights a losing battle more resolutely
than almost any hero of either side. He is wounded, is
succoured by Menelaus and Aias, and retires. Machaon,
on the left, is wounded by Paris, and, in Nestor's company,
he withdraws to Nestor's camp. Hector comes up from
the left to engage Aias. Eurypylus, arriving to aid Aias, is
wounded by Paris. Achilles sees Nestor and Machaon
retiring, and calls out Patroclus from the hut. '*Now*,
I think,' he says, 'the Achæans will stand in prayer about
my knees, for need no longer tolerable comes upon them'
(xi. 608-610). He then sends Patroclus to inquire for
Machaon, 'and this to Patroclus was the beginning of evil.'
When he reaches Nestor's hut he declines to sit down, but
Nestor very characteristically tells a long story of his youth,
and ends by reminding Patroclus how Menœtius, his father,
had bidden him counsel Achilles wisely. Now is the time
for him to urge Achilles to the war. At the least, Achilles
might send Patroclus to lead the Myrmidons, and might
lend him his own armour, 'if perchance the Trojans may
take thee for him' (796, 800). This advice is a turning-
point, leading to the death of Patroclus, to Achilles's reconciliation with the Greeks, and to the death of Hector.
It is obnoxious to Mr. Leaf, as, in his opinion, the wearing
of Achilles's armour by Patroclus (book xvi.) is late, and
was merely composed to lead up to the description of the
new arms, made by Hephæstus in book xviii. Patroclus then runs with the message to Achilles, but, meeting the wounded Eurypylus, he takes pity on him, and tends
his hurt, as one surgeon is wounded and the other is fighting. Patroclus cuts out the arrow and remains with Eurypylus all through the fights in books xiii., xiv., xv. 'The

sending of Patroclus is itself an anticipation of the all-important change in the temper of Achilles. Thus it prepares us for that development of the story which we have in books xvi.–xxii., and upon which the incomparable dramatic interest of the Iliad mainly depends' (Monro).

According to the theory of the original Μῆνις this change of mood occurs rather early in the first day of recorded fighting after Achilles conceived his anger, or, at least, after his long-cherished grudge came to a head. If we believe that the Iliad as it stands is, on the whole, the original poem, the Wrath has endured longer, and is much more implacable. There are passages in book xi. which the believers in the possibility of disengaging the original Μῆνις are obliged to expunge. The long story of Patroclus with the wounded Eurypylus is objected to by Bergk (i. 600). There is here an 'unnatural dislocation' of the story, 'contrary to all rules of the poetic art.' These passages, therefore, must be from a later hand, though why the later poet should be more ignorant of, or indifferent to, the laws of art than an earlier poet we are left to guess. Idomeneus, who takes a share in the fighting in book xi., is regarded as an interpolated hero of the dia-skeuast's. The words of Achilles, ' Now will the Greeks stand in prayer about my knees,' disregard, it is urged, the fact that, according to book ix., the Greeks have already implored his compassion. With this objection we have already dealt. The drinking scene in Nestor's hut is the diaskeuast's—' here he is quite at home.' He has interwoven an old lay on Nestor into his ruthlessly tedious speech. He has introduced the wounded Eurypylus to find a motive for the long stay of Patroclus. Old work and new are loosely combined.

Mr. Leaf also admits, as we have seen, the existence of unoriginal parts in book xi. The *aristeia* of Agamemnon

followed the dream-scene in book ii. The long yarn of
Nestor is 'one of the clearest cases of interpolation in the
Iliad. It is singularly out of place at the moment when
Patroclus has refused even to sit down, owing to the urgency
of his mission.' If Mr. Leaf has never met an intelligent
old bore, whom no one could check by refusing to sit down,
we envy his inexperience of misfortune. The endless
reminiscences of Nestor are, in fact, most peculiarly in
place when they are 'singularly out of place.' The remark
that the story is 'full of words and expressions elsewhere
peculiar to the Odyssey' is a graver objection, at least to
those who ascribe the epics to different authors. But 'full
of words and expressions peculiar to the Odyssey' is rather
a strong statement of the facts. In ninety-seven lines
(665–762) Mr. Leaf notes five such examples ; one of them
also occurs in book xxiv., which is supposed to be closely
related to the Odyssey. They are (677) ἤλιθα, (688)
δαίτρευον, which the Odyssey uses (in another sense), (695)
ὑβρίζοντες, which the Odyssey naturally, on account of the
wooers, has occasion to use seven times ; (735) ἠέλιος
φαέθων ; (774) ἄλεισον, a chalice, used in Odyssey and
Iliad, book xxiv. If this be an interpolation, the motive of
the interpolator is obscure, especially if 'an old lay' of
Nestor[1] was used, for then he had not even the motive
of vanity, which might make him insert his own composition. Mr. Leaf conjectures it is 'designed to glorify
Nestor,' by representing him, we suppose, as bestowing
all his tediousness on a person in a hurry. Perhaps it may
be suggested that the glories of Nestor were inserted by
Pisistratus, as a descendant of Nestor's family. But Mr.
Leaf does not believe in the Pisistratean recension, and the
old opinion is that Nestor, being an aged man, is naturally
garrulous about his early exploits. Fick attributes the piece

[1] Bergk, i. 601.

to a poet of Colophon, a colony of Pylos, Nestor's city.
The truth is that Nestor is one of Homer's bores, answering
to 'Scott's bores,' people like the Baron Bradwardine, of
whom it is complained that Scott gives us too much. And
Homer gives us a great deal of Nestor. Perhaps the
Germans will argue that the Baron's speeches in *Waverley*
are interpolated by a diaskeuast, probably a Forbes of
Pitsligo. Mr. Leaf is uncertain as to Bergk's theory that
Eurypylus is merely brought in to account for Patroclus's
long absence from Achilles—an absence needed for the
introduction of books xii.–xv. His lingering 'is not inconsistent with the character of the "kindly" hero.' It may
be observed that in an admitted part of the original Μῆνις
(book xi. 62) occurs a form not elsewhere read in Homer,
but read in the late Hesiodic *Shield of Heracles*. Had
this only been found in what the theory required to explain
as an 'interpolation,' much play would have been made with
it, as a proof of late insertion. But the author of the original
Μῆνις is a privileged person. The whole book, according
to an army of German commentators, is a mere patchwork
of interpolations. The conduct of Zeus in withdrawing
Hector (163, 164) and in sending Iris with the command to
abstain from war while Agamemnon rages (186) gives rise
to many objections. The different appearances of Paris
and Hector in different parts of the field also cause disquisition, 'but these difficulties are not removed by
Lachmann's separate "lays," nor, indeed, by any theory
of the Iliad ' (Monro).[1] A singular theory of the wounded
Odysseus is advanced by Usener. In line 489 Aias
slays four Trojans—Pandocus, Lysandrus, Pyrasus, and
Pylartes—all which names Usener regards as titles of
Hades, king of the dead. He therefore infers the exis-

---

[1] 'In details such as this it is useless to look for exact accuracy '
(Leaf).

tence of one old lay, in which Aias, who rescues Odysseus, fights Hades. Now Odysseus is here compared to
a stag wounded by an arrow, and pursued by jackals ; after
which the jackals are driven off by a lion. Usener discovers
that works of art in which a lion devouring a stag is
attacked by an archer existed in old Assyrian art ; that the
Phœnicians and Cyprians understood the lion to be the
god of the under-world, who fights for the dead with the
good genius ; the archer (Heracles) is the good genius,
who rescues souls from the God of Death. Thus Hades,
like a lion, is seizing Odysseus, Aias is the god who
rescues him from the lion in some ancient lay, and all this
is connected with figures on early coins of Phocæa, derived
from Phœnician myths. Consequently this part of the Iliad
is based on an old Phocæan lay.[1] This picturesque hypothesis may be left to the taste and fancy of the reader.

It may be remarked that Mr. Leaf [2] regards the account
of Agamemnon's shield from Cyprus as an anachronism and
an interpolation. Cyprus is mentioned in Odyssey viii. 363,
where Aphrodite goes to Paphos in Cyprus. But this is a
' very late passage,' and except in such passages, ' Cyprus is
quite unknown to both Iliad and Odyssey.' Yet Temesê,
in Cyprus, is the place whither Mentes is sailing for copper,
in Odyssey i. 184. Hence, indeed, comes our ' copper '—
Kupfer, *æs Cyprium*. Is Odyssey i. 184 also ' very
late ' ? [3]

This is an example of the method of criticism. Some
point is to be ' unknown to Homer.' This is proved by
alleging that all passages which include the point are later
interpolations. But this process occasionally leads a critic
rather too far, and he must give up his theory, or proclaim

[1] Hentze, Iliad, xi. 490 (*Anhang*).
[2] *Companion*, pp. 119, 203.
[3] See Ameis's note, Od. i. 184.

that Odyssey i. 184 is interpolated, or late. It is, according
to Wilamowitz Moellendorff, but he places Temesê in Italy.[1]

BOOK XII–XV

THE BATTLE AT THE WALL

The battles beside the ships and the wall as described in
books xii.–xv. of the Iliad are confused, indeed, and the
description of them is not very clear. But the story is
brief, the skirmishes are few, the account is lucid, compared
with the battles of the commentators on the subject, where
Lachmann wars upon the left, and Nutzhorn on the right.
Benicken and Baeumlein, Holm and Düntzer, Gerlach and
Cauer, Köchly, Jacob, Kiene, Giseke, Genz, Bernhardy,
Bergk, are but a few of the heroes in this conflict, every
man fighting gallantly for his own hand over the pro-
strate body of Homer. The poet is torn and mangled worse
than Hector's corpse ; excisions, fragments of early lays,
huge cantles by diaskeuasts (corrupters and interpolators)
are all mentioned, and the cantos are carved and re-
arranged by everyone in accordance with his own theory.
Before attempting to examine the objections, it must be repeated that the cantos on confused fighting are naturally
confused. Further, as Mr. Monro insists, we know nothing
of the tactics of Homeric war in such remarkable circumstances as a retreat on a fortified camp protecting ships
drawn up on shore, which themselves are used as cover by
the Greek besiegers, now besieged in their turn. Once
more, unluckily, the gods have many a stroke in the
battle.

It has already been said that the inconsistency of the
mythical conception of the gods makes their action always
puzzling. Their limited omniscience and omnipotence are

[1] *Philol. Untersuch.* pp. 6–27.

constantly bewildering us, merely because the poet was in-
evitably without a clear idea of their nature.   Consistency
cannot be expected from gods, would be suspicious if it
were found, and would be contradictory of the very nature
of mythology.

As to the confusion in the narrative it cannot be cleared
up, as Mr. Monro says, ' by any theory of the Iliad.'
One thing we must remember.   General Marbot, in his
memoirs, declares that he could not understand the accounts
which military writers give, even of the battles in which he
himself was engaged.   It is no wonder, then, if we find it
difficult to understand a peculiarly intricate fight as described by Homer.   The reader must fix his attention
closely on the text of the poet, observing two points :
first, the part played by the wall in the struggle, next
the probable time occupied.   At the end of book xi. we
left Patroclus attending to the wounds of Eurypylus in
Nestor's hut.   Meanwhile the tide of war was surging
round the fortifications.   In xv. 390–410, Patroclus rises
from his surgery and conversation, to find the Trojans
rushing on the wall itself, and a panic among the Greeks,
though the Greeks are not absolutely broken and the
Trojans have not yet penetrated ' among the ships and
huts ' (409). How long may the battle have been going on ?
How are we to understand the details of the attack ?

One difficulty is that we have not a clear account of the
wall.   In vii. 438, we learn that the Greeks made gates in
it, with a causeway for driving chariots across.   Now, Aristarchus held that there was but *one* gate, ' with much show
of reason,' says Mr. Monro.[1]   On the whole, opinion is in
favour of several gates in the wall.

The description of fighting in book xi. at the moment

---

[1] See Leaf, notes in xii. 120, 175, 340, insisting on *several* gates,
but the last passage was condemned by Zenodotus.   On line 340,

when Nestor and Eurypylus left the mellay, shows the
Trojans pressing the Greeks in spite of the stubborn
defence of Aias. Some change in the battle would
occur in the interval occupied by the scenes in Nestor's
hut. The twelfth book opens by alleging that the wall did
not long protect the Greeks, and diverges into an account
(presumed to be late) of the destruction of the wall by
Poseidon, after the fall of Troy. We then hear that Hector
cannot urge his horses through the fosse (xii. 50) and the
palisade. We must conceive, first the sea-bay, then the
shore, with the Greek ships drawn up, probably in a double
row, the huts occupying ground between the vessels of the
inner row. Then there would be some space of ground,
then the wall, the palisade, the fosse, through which, at
the gates, opened causeways. Polydamas advises Hector
to dismount his men and attack on foot, leaving the horses
to the charioteers. This is done, and five companies are
arrayed. It cannot be pretended that a clear military account of these five battalions is given throughout. (1) Hector and Polydamas lead the first company ; (2) Paris, the
second ; (3) Helenus and Deiphobus, his brothers, command the third, with Asius; (4) Æneas leads the fourth
body ; and (5) Sarpedon the allies.[1]

One warrior in the onslaught does not dismount. This
is Asius, of company three, who drives his chariot over the
bridge, against the gate at the left of the Greek camp.
(xii. 120). The doors are open, but two sons of the Lapithæ

Mr. Leaf decides against Aristarchus, and in favour of several gates.
Mr. Monro here agrees with Mr. Leaf.

[1] The allies are more numerous than the Trojans (ii. 130), according
to Mr. Leaf, though the passage which he refers to in book ii. does
not assert this in so many words. 'The sons of the Achæans out-
number the Trojans. But allies from many cities are therein, and
they hinder me perforce.' But the inference may be correct.

rush out, and Asius, in baffled anger, appeals to Zeus (xii. 164–172).[1]

Meanwhile (xii. 199) the company of Hector, in the centre, are still craning at the fosse, and the warriors are terrified by the omen of a snake and an eagle. Polydamas bids Hector withdraw his troops ; the Greeks, even in Periclean times, were the slaves of omen. Hector answers in the noble words, ' one omen is best, to fight for our own country.' We should be sorry to refuse this speech to Homer. Hector therefore leads on and the Greek towers are injured, but their wall of shields is unbroken. Meanwhile the two Aiantes are ' everywhere ' on the wall (265) nor would Hector have broken the gates, had not Sarpedon come on, with his famous address to Glaucus, ' I would not fight, were we to be immortal, this battle once escaped, nor send thee to war, but, since ten thousand fates of death on every side beset us—On !' So (290–492) he drags down a strip of the battlement, leaves the wall bare, and 'makes a path for many,' a path which they did not hold (399). By this time (340) all the gates had been shut. Menestheus, whose tower was threatened by Sarpedon's men, sends a messenger to the Aiantes for aid, and the Telamonian Aias, with Teucer, speeds to Menestheus, thereby relieving Hector in the centre. Teucer wounds Glaucus, a wound that still maims him in book xvi., when Sarpedon, in that book, has fallen before Patroclus. The Aiantes repulse the Lycians under Sarpedon, and Hector leads a new attack on the central gates, bursts them in with a heavy stone, and enters, while the Danaans flee among the ships. Here ends book xii.[2]

---

[1] This 'leads to nothing whatever' (Leaf), 'and the Iliad does not know the name of the Lapithæ' (Hentze), though Nestor, in i. 263, mentions Pirithous, the father of the two Lapithæ of book xii.

[2] In this book Nitzsch, though converted to conservatism, would

In the long book xiii. there are assuredly some difficulties in the conduct of the poem. The question is, are the difficulties to be ascribed to interpolation, and that very unskilled, or must we allow for ' our ignorance of the conditions of Homeric warfare, and the tendency to lay

have excised all the passage about Sarpedon (290-429) as an interpolation. Mr. Leaf points out that Hector first actually entered the fort, whereas in xvi. 558, Sarpedon is spoken of, when dead, as he who first ' leaped within the wall.' Apparently he only ' opened a path.' which he could not hold. He did not force a gate, but made the wall easier to climb. He may have been just within when Aias thrust him out. ' He gave ground a little from the battlement.' A modern military controversy about General Roberts in his youth may remind us how difficult it is to insure absolute accuracy on such a point. The discrepancy can hardly be called a discrepancy. Had Hector and Sarpedon lived, their friends might, as in modern times, have squabbled about their precedence. ' Such is the appearance of war,' as the Maori epic says. In xii. 438, it is said of Hector, as later (by a Greek) of Sarpedon, that he 'first leaped within the wall.' Really the point should give no trouble. Patroclus (xvi. 558) may surely describe the feat of Sarpedon in the same words without vexing the souls of commentators. Possibly an objection might be taken because Menestheus, the Athenian, is mentioned. The Athenians were suspected of having interpolated the praises of their hero in the ' Catalogue,' ii. 552-556. But the Athenian share in the war is so small that it is an argument *against* Athenian interpolation. If large interpolation was possible, here was the occasion for it, and here, in the Athenians of letters, were the men who could have done it. But there is no *aristeia* of Menestheus. In book xiv. 136-672, is a long glorification of two Cretans, Idomeneus and Meriones. This ' strongly suggests '—to Mr. Leaf— ' an interpolation for the special glory of Cretan heroes.' ' The Cretans were always liars,' but if interpolations to please national vanity were going, the Athenians were much more likely people to foist in an *aristeia* of their man, Menestheus, especially if Pisistratus and the noted forger, Onomacritus, had such an opportunity as Wolf declares, and really *made* the Iliad. The absence of any Athenian *aristeia* is a strong proof that interpolations for the glorification of national vanity were not made at all. But see Leaf, note to xiii. 685, where the Athenians are chiefs of the Ionians, here only mentioned.

M

undue stress on isolated expressions'?[1]   The gods, too, intervene now with the usual results.

The story of book xiii. runs thus :—Hector and his following are now within the wall, on the centre.   Are the other Trojans, those of the left brigade, also within the wall?   Certainly many of them are.   They are said to have poured in at the gates (xii. 469-471) and 'climbed over it in their multitude' (xiii. 87), taking advantage of the diversion by Hector.   At the opening of the book, Zeus, for no particular reason, turns his eyes from the war, and amuses himself by watching the Northern races, who drink mare's milk.   He believes that his threat will keep the other gods from interfering.   Poseidon, however, who has not intruded before, leaves his watch-tower in Samothrace, and comes out from the sea to encourage the Greeks, in the form of Calchas.   He also takes other shapes.   He urges on the Aiantes.   Oileus's son recognises him for a god by 'the tokens of his feet and knees,' whatever that may mean (among some savage races supernatural beings have their legs turned the wrong way about), 'and the gods are easy to discern,' which contradicts what we gather from Athene's opening the eyes of Diomede to know gods (v. 127).   Poseidon, in any case, gathers the Greeks round the Aiantes in the centre.   They repulse Hector, who, having entered, was making for the ships, and Meriones, breaking his spear on the shield of Deiphobus, goes to his tent for another.   Now Deiphobus is of the third company, so some, at least, of that company, who were originally on the left, are now within the wall.   The strife goes on, and Poseidon sends Idomeneus who, oddly enough, is not armed, to array himself and fight.   The Homeric heroes, like Menelaus in book vii., and other examples to be noted later, arm and disarm with singular celerity.   Idomeneus

[1] Monro, Introduction to Book xv.

has here been tending a wounded comrade—curiously, anonymous. Meriones, his companion in arms, and he, now, after much parley, join the battle on the left, leaving Hector to deal, in the centre, with the Aiantes. The *aristeia* of Idomeneus lasts from 330 to 672. Mr. Leaf says, 'the wall is here treated as non-existent.' Naturally, for the fight here is (xiii. 333) 'by the sterns of the ships,' within the wall, which the Trojans (xiii. 87) ' have climbed in their multitude.' Asius, somehow, has got his chariot in ; and why not, as the gates had been entered (xii. 469–471) and they had causeways for chariots.[1] Asius is now killed by Idomeneus ;[2] his chariot is taken by Amphilochus ; he is partly avenged by Deiphobus, and, Idomeneus coming against him, Deiphobus calls for aid to Æneas, of the fourth company. Clearly the Trojans, 'in their multitude,' are within the wall, for Paris, and Agenor, of the second company, are all here (xiii. 490). It is also apparent that the attacking parties have become blended, an occurrence frequent even in modern warfare. The battle rolls to and fro, Meriones, Idomeneus, Helenus, and Æneas, being chief antagonists. On the whole, the Greeks have the advantage on the left, whither Idomeneus and Meriones carried their swords. Hector, in the centre, is ignorant of this (xiii. 674). From line 683, we learn that chariots are now engaged here (inside, apparently), 'where the wall was built lowest.' This is an obvious confusion. Mr. Leaf ascribes it to 'the unskilfulness of the interpolator,' who, really, as he had the text before

---

[1] xii. 340. There is a various reading. Aristarchus read πᾶσαι γὰρ ἐπῴχατο, meaning ' the whole gate was shut,' for he believed that there was only one gate. The ordinary reading is πάσας γὰρ ἐπῴχετο, ' the noise had reached all the gates. πᾶσαι, says Mr. Leaf, must mean 'all the gates. There is no point in saying the whole gate.'

[2] See Mr. Leaf's objections, xiii. 384, *note*. He supposes that there was no wall in the original.

him, must have been little better than an idiot. On the
whole, an error on the part of the original poet is at least
as probable as a mistake by an interpolator. But the
mention of Ionians (685) for the only time in Homer, and
of the Phthians, with the immense effect produced by the
fire of the light-armed Locrians (the Locrian Aias only
wears a linen corslet, ii. 529), under cover (721) certainly
donne furieusement à penser. Bowmen may do much in
Homer, when Paris or Teucer is the archer ; but to ascribe
a great effect to the artillery of nameless men is most
unusual. Still, we know little of Homeric tactics. When the
ships were in danger, the whole force would fight as it could,
whatever its defensive armour. Thus, several facts combine
to make all this passage at least suspicious. Mr. Leaf
suspects ' false archaism.' The interpolator, he thinks, calls
the Locrians light-armed archers and slingers, because, in his
own time, they were *not* light-armed. But this is, perhaps,
to consider too curiously. Still, what with the unusual fact,
the unusual name, and the introduction of chariots where
we expect none, the passage needs defence.[1] As to the
chariots, however, we have often remarked that as Hector
had broken down the gate, and as the gate certainly had
a carriage-way, or bridge, leading to it, chariots may have
been driven across. The motive for interpolating the passage is sadly to seek.[2] Polydamas, in the distress of the
Trojans under fire, advises retreat and a council of war. He
fears that Achilles may come out on the confused army.[3]
Hector rushes to the left to collect his chiefs, and finds all

---

[1] See chapter on ' Homer and Archæology.'

[2] Mr. Leaf suspects Athenian patriotic fraud (xiii. 685 *note*, and
Companion, p. 237).

[3] The Trojans, according to Mr. Leaf (737), have only ' come into
the neighbourhood of the wall.' So, where is the difficulty about the
chariots ? According to Mr. Monro, they have ' passed over the wall.'

wounded but Paris, who alone sustains the fight.   Hector
addresses Paris, 'with words of shame,' which are quite inappropriate.   Paris answers with dignity ; the pair rally their
forces, attack the position of the Aiantes, and Mr. Leaf
admits that, to the end of the book, '*it is impossible not
to believe*' that we have part of the original attack on the
ships.   In his *Companion*, however (p. 240), he withdraws
this opinion, so rapidly does the impossible become possible
to the Higher Criticism.

On the whole, considering the confused character of
such an encounter, where a fortified position is assailed in
more than one place by ill-disciplined forces, and where
gods take a hand, book xiii. seems consecutive enough.
The only really suspicious part we have remarked upon,
and, if it be an interpolation, we fail to detect the motive
of the interpolator.   One general objection has been
urged.   The poet describes many ghastly circumstances of
war : a spear rises and falls with the last beats of a wounded
man's heart ; a hero's bloody eyes are dashed out at his
feet, and the fallen are bitterly taunted.   'This is not at all
Greek,' as modern critics, ignorant of Greek, would say.
However, it is not very un-Homeric, though, here, we have
more of it than usual.[1]

The thirteenth book ends with a spirited rally of the
Greeks, under Aias ; they 'abide the onslaught, and the
cry of the two hosts goes up to Zeus.'   The Battle of the
Wall takes a long time in the reading, because events
which occurred simultaneously have to be described in
sequence.   These events are, the dismounting of the

---

[1] There is a difficulty in line 764.   Hector finds that some Trojans
are lying in death among the sterns of the ships, ' but some were
within the wall wounded.'   Mr. Leaf says the wall is that of Troy.
Compare line 538, where a wounded man is carried to the city.   The
use of ' wall ' here is confusing.

Trojans, their formation into five attacking bodies, the
charge on the wall—in which Sarpedon is partly, and
Hector wholly, successful—the bursting of a gate or gates,
the entrance partly by the gateways, partly over the wall,
the rallies under Poseidon, stimulating Idomeneus and
Aias, the wounding of Hector, the flight back across the
ditch, the restoration of Hector by Apollo, the rally and
advance of the Trojans, the retreat of the Achæans, terrified by Apollo, the throwing down of the wall by Apollo,
the onrush of Troy, the fight about the ship-sterns, and the
firing of a ship by Hector. The sequence, the speeches, the
similes, the single combats, the doings of the gods, make
all this long in the telling ; in fact, the occurrences may
have occupied no great space of time. There is a storming
of the fort, the place is not held, it is retaken : that is the
whole story. There are difficulties in language, as xii. 23,
where the heroes are styled ' men half divine.' This is in
the account of the destruction of the wall by Poseidon,
after the siege. The term does not occur elsewhere, and
the passage does look like a late addition made to explain
the absence of traces of the wall. We have parallels in the
Icelandic sagas. Line xii. 176, with what follows, the poet
introducing himself, was suspected in antiquity. But compare ii. 484, 761, and Odyssey, i. 1. In all these places the
minstrel makes a personal appeal to the Muses for aid. If
Odyssey i. 1 is spurious, what is genuine?

BOOKS XIV–XV

The fourteenth book of the Iliad has been regarded as
a collection of patches, unskilfully joined by short passages
of transition. The thirteenth book ends, ' And the clamour
of the two hosts went up through the higher air to the
splendour of Zeus.' The fourteenth book begins, ' Yet the

cry of battle escaped not Nestor, albeit at his wine,' which
he is drinking with the leech, Machaon (xi. 642), himself
engaged in attendance on Eurypylus, to inquire for whom
Achilles had sent Patroclus. The clamour is that of the
hosts as Hector leads the Trojans against the Greeks, who
have rallied under the Aiantes. But when Nestor goes
out he sees 'a deed of shame, *the Achæans fleeing in rout,*
and the Trojans driving them, and the wall overthrown.'
This certainly does not correspond to the situation at the end
of book xiii., if the cry heard by Nestor is that very cry mentioned at the end of book xiii. Or is it the cry mentioned in
xiii. 41 ? [1] However, the main thing for Nestor, at his wine,
is that the wall is down. He sets out for the distant hut
of the wounded Agamemnon, whom he finds in despair.
Agamemnon suggests flight, and is rebuked in a famous
passage (xiv. 82) by Odysseus. 'Thou shouldst lead some
other inglorious army, not be king over us, to whom Zeus
hath given it, from youth even to age, to be winding the
skein of grievous wars till every man of us perish.' Diomede,
after some remarks on his father, suggests that he, Odysseus,
and Agamemnon, all of them wounded, should go down
and encourage the host. This they do, and Poseidon
meets them in the guise of 'an aged man' unnamed. In
the Iliad, though not always in the Odyssey, disguised
gods put on the semblance of some known person.
Zenodotus added a line out of his own head to the effect
that the old man was Phœnix, the friend of Achilles.
Any ancient interpolator might have done as much, but
nobody did it (xiv. 136). Poseidon then utters a divine
shout, not much in accordance with his disguise, but rather
reminding us of the conspirators' song in the *Rovers*. Now
(153) Hera bethinks herself of beguiling Zeus to love and
sleep, that he may not observe Poseidon. It has been

[1] See *Companion*, p. 243, 244.

suggested that this famous passage (154-358) should come *before* the first arrival of Poseidon.   On the other hand, she may have been encouraged by the success of Poseidon. ' The thwarting of the will of Zeus (which is the ground idea) arises in an unexpected quarter.' [1]

Critics have differed much in their theories of interpolation here.   After the craft of Hera is accomplished, and Zeus has slept, Poseidon (370-388) bids the Achæans change their armour, the best men taking the best weapons. This is very odd advice in the midst of war, though the heroes armed and disarmed with amazing celerity, so Lachmann, Kayser, Benicken, and others excise the lines (370-388), Koch removes most of them, Bernhardy cuts out all between 361-401, and there are other attempts at im-

---

[1] Monro, introduction to book xiv.   Mr. Leaf's theory is that all this account of the wiles of Hera is 'meant as an alternative to the *aristeia* of Idomeneus (in book xiii.) after the wall had been introduced by the author of the twelfth book.'   In the original recitations, either the fight of Idomeneus or the wiles of Hera would be given, not both.   A ' diaskeuast ' (corrupter or interpolator) 'amalgamated the two alternative pieces, kept them both, and added *juncturæ*.'   We are, as usual, puzzled to know how all this was done, and when, and how the mixture won general acceptance.   We do not know whether all this manufacture was performed before or after the use of written texts. Let us suppose that the original poet, whether he used a written copy or not, recited till his poems got a strong hold on Greek audiences. After his death, or in his absence, did other rhapsodists recite his poem, with such variations and alternative lays as they pleased ?   Did one version win general acceptance, and, if so, how did the diaskeuast manage to foist his patchwork on the public, so that it became canonical, as it were, and remain unsuspected even by the sceptical critics of Alexandria ?   For all this, some such committee of revision as Wolf fancied, was necessary.   The Pisistratean commission of recension and the text they made are the key-stone of Wolf's theory.   It is now almost universally abandoned, and we are left wholly at a loss as to how poems, widely known in ancient Greece, and much revered, were patched and altered, and how the various States came to accept the patchwork as authentic.   Mr. Leaf's theory of a ' School' we have already criticised.

provement. The passage is a puzzle, but it is as puzzling to conjecture why any interpolator inserted it. If he merely wished to keep Poseidon before the audience, he need not have made the god give such extraordinary advice. 'The whole passage is a clumsy piece of work,' as Mr. Leaf says, whoever composed it, or, at all events, it seems clumsy to modern readers. Aristarchus understood it no better than we do, and set his critical mark against it. The dread sword of Poseidon (385) is perplexing, too, like the mysterious weapon often spoken of in Irish epic tradition. But all this may have been intelligible to an Homeric audience. That a passage is obscure to us, or to the Alexandrine critics, by no means proves that it is spurious. There must have been a time when it was intelligible enough. The book ends with a fight between Aias and Hector, deferred since the close of book xiii. Here, again, is a difficulty. Aias knocks Hector senseless with a large stone; Hector is removed to the banks of Xanthus, and book xv. opens on the Trojans in full flight across the palisade. Hera and Poseidon have, in fact, thwarted for the moment the will of Zeus, who is still asleep on Ida, under the cloud of gold. The poet cannot bear to 'let the Trojan dogs have the best of it.' He constantly rallies his dear Greeks, and so defers the issue. It may be that this frank boyish spirit is the cause of various passages which delay, or defy, the modern critics, whether in Alexandria or Bonn or Berlin. If ever the Trojans do score a success, it must be by the aid of Zeus or Apollo, with all the consequent mythical confusions.

As to the difficulties about the wall, Mr. Leaf partly explains them.[1] 'The river appears and disappears just as suits the poet at the moment. This is only one instance of the freedom with which the details of topography are

[1] *Companion*, p. 252.

treated in the Iliad.' Why should the poet of the Iliad be
more particular about the great wall than about the much
more permanent river?

The fifteenth book has given commentators an enormous
amount of trouble. Perhaps the truth is that they consider
too curiously. If Homer had been describing the fights in
a military examination paper he might have been more
clear in his statements. But he has before his eyes the
flux and reflux of battle, a stream of chariots and men pouring
back and forth from the wall and fosse, between and among
the ships, and even rearwards to the huts. Here a rank keeps
its ground ; there is a knot of men attacked on all sides ;
here some send their spears from the openings between the
ships ; warriors leap into and out of chariots and barques ;
there is all the confusion of a mellay, intermingled with the
coming and going of gods, the crash of thunder—an
ambiguous omen—and the panic that streams from the
shaken ægis. Homer shows us all this : the war shifts and
shines before us, and this ought to suffice. Doubtless it
did suffice his audience, as it satisfies any reader, except
those who pry with microscopes into the exact sense of isolated expressions, and detect discrepancies, which suggest
interpolation. 'We must not expect a degree of accuracy
which would be without poetical value' (Monro). There
may be, there probably are, some interpolated lines, but the
whole battle-piece, read in a proper spirit, is its own justi-
fication. For the Iliad is literature, ancient and warlike ;
it is not a chapter of scientific military history.

In the opening of the fifteenth book Zeus awakes in the
arms of Hera to see Hector wounded (thanks to Poseidon and
Hera), and the Trojans driven in rout from the wall. Zeus
rebukes Hera and announces his decision. Let Iris bid
Apollo help Troy, till the Achæans flee and fall among the
ships (63). From 63 to 77 Mr. Leaf brackets the lines as

spurious. The lines continue the speech of Zeus. He says that the Achæans shall fall among the ships of Achilles, who shall rouse Patroclus (ἀνστήσει). Patroclus shall slay Sarpedon, Hector Patroclus, and Achilles shall slay Hector. 'From that hour will I cause a new pursuit from the ships' till Troy falls. Till that hour Zeus will not cease from anger, nor suffer gods to interfere, 'before I accomplish that desire of the son of Peleus.' The Alexandrines placed the critical sign of falsity against all this passage. Mr. Monro, as well as Mr. Leaf, marks it spurious ; so do almost all the modern Germans.[1] However regretfully, we must acknowledge that the lines do look like an interpolation, though for what purpose, and why the interpolator did not take the trouble to get up his facts, it is not easy to conjecture. Iris bids Poseidon leave the war, where the Achæans 'miss him sorely,' and Apollo, by command of Zeus, encourages the reviving Hector. The description of his return to fight is a verbal and uncalled for repetition (263–268) of the simile about Paris, in book vi., and is probably inserted by some error. The Greeks are alarmed by Hector's return, and Thoas bids them fall back on the ships, the chiefs covering the retreat. Commentators object that the Greeks needed all their forces, but the retreat covered by 'all the best in the host' seems natural enough. It is later said that the Achæans abode the attack ἀολλέες (312), 'in close ranks,' but there is no wild inconsistency in that, nor (319) in πίπτε δὲ λαός, 'the folk fell.' The foes are not at close quarters. The best warriors, covering the retreat, are in close array ; the 'folk' fall when the arrows reach them, but they are so far off that many spears are thrown, and only reach 'half the distance' (316). 'The contradiction, perhaps, would disappear if we knew how an army in Homeric times would effect its retreat behind fortifications.'[2] It is, no doubt,

---

[1] Hentze leaves in 56–63, 72–77.   [2] Monro.

the rapidly retreating multitude, galled by arrows and by the better thrown spears, that are compared to a herd of kine in confusion (323).[1]   The close fight (between the champions covering the retreat and the Trojans) breaks up, the Achæans are driven within the wall, and have no time to man it, for Apollo dashes the banks into the fosse, fills it up, and the Trojans stream in, horse and man.   Nestor prays ; Zeus thunders, the Trojans accept the omen, and there is fighting from ship-board and from chariots.   The great jointed spears are used to repel the attack.

The story now goes (xv. 390) to Patroclus, who has long been tending the wounded Eurypylus in his hut.   He sees the Trojans 'rushing over the wall' (395) and goes off to rouse Achilles (404).   No doubt, it is odd that the first successes at the wall did not attract the attention of Patroclus, but he may have been then absorbed in his surgery ; now he is merely conversing with Eurypylus.   It is also objected that, in 387, the Achæans are *on* the ships ; in 408 the Trojans cannot break their phalanxes and pour in among ships and huts.   Mr. Monro remarks that it does not follow that *all* the defenders had mounted the ships.   We may imagine that there were all sorts of combats going on.[2]   On the whole, the divers descriptions of the fighting seem as consistent as we have any right to expect.   The bowstring of Teucer is broken, there is a rally of men, 'a ring of bronze' about the ships.   Hector assails it ; Aias leaps from deck to deck with his long spear ; Zeus waits for the blaze from a burning ship, the fulfilment of his promise to Thetis ;

---

[1] Hentze and others do not accept this view, and think great doubt lies on the originality of the passage.   They seem to consider too curiously, but there is nothing of essential value in the lines (Hentze, p. 103).

[2] In 393 and 405, occurs the words λόγοις and σοφίης (art).   The latter is only here found in Homer ; the former only here and in Odyssey, i. 56.

Hector seizes the barque of Protesilaus ; Aias drives off
those who come up with burning torches.   So ends the
book.

About this book, it may be said, with almost perfect
assurance, that it does contain apparent interpolations.
Again, these are, in one or two cases, very awkward and
senseless, unless they be rude attempts at *juncturæ*.

Once more, in some cases, the passages suspected for
their matter display unusual forms of diction, and the
coincidence strengthens the suspicion.[1]   The lines which
we must admit to be interpolated are not, in our view, very
many or important.   We have endeavoured to show that the
general view of the fighting is less inconsistent than many
commentators have thought.   But the admission of any
interpolation confesses the possibility that others *may*
occur, and drives us back on the problem : how, when, or
where were the undeniable interpolations made, and how
did they secure acceptance in the many old copies which the
Alexandrian critics handled ?   Perhaps no critic is so conservative as to deny seriously that there are interpolations
in the Iliad.   But it is not enough to admit this vaguely.
We must make up our minds as to what is to be rejected,
and how far the innumerable passages which have been
attacked may be honestly defended.

Our own position is that there are traces of dislocation
in books xiii.-xv., and a trace of something omitted, while,
perhaps from our ignorance of Homeric warfare, there are
passages not clearly intelligible, and it is possible that
attempts to remedy this state of things may have introduced
other blemishes.   By way of making all this clearer, we
may restate briefly the sequence of events, after Hector, at

---

[1] Friedländer says that, by the new critical methods of Geist,
Düntzer, and others, there is hardly a word in Homer that could escape
objection (Nutzhorn, p. 119).

the end of book xii., leaped within the broken gate, while other Trojans climbed the wall, and the Greeks ' fled in fear among the hollow ships' (xii. 471).

Next (xiii. 1–9) Zeus withdrew his eyes from the battle. This was Poseidon's opportunity : in a magnificent passage he speeds from the crest of Samothrace to Ægæ, thence drives to a cavern in the sea deeps, and thence, again, goes to the Achæan host.   In manner this piece is closely akin to the later description of the sleep of Zeus and Hera. Poseidon, in guise of Calchas, rallied the Achæans who were fleeing before Hector, within the wall.   The two Aiantes recognised him as he left them, to hearten the other Greeks, despairing among the ships.   They rallied, therefore, around the Aiantes, and there

> The stubborn spearmen still made good
> Their dark impenetrable wood ;
> Each stepping where his comrade stood,
> The moment that he fell.

On this group Hector sped, like a loosened rock leaping from a hill.   Through the scattered ranks he smote and slew, but was checked by the spearmen round the Aiantes, and called up his men.   They rally to him ; Deiphobus breaks the spear of Meriones, who goes to his hut for another.   Here the *élan* leaves the fight ; the Trojans do not break through the square 'in fashion like a tower,' nor are they wholly repulsed, for the victors on both sides fall to stripping the dead.

Poseidon, in wrath for a scion of his line, again urges on the Greeks, and chiefly Idomeneus, who has been aiding a wounded comrade, and has disarmed.   All this seems absurd to Northern men.   When Gunnar and Grettir warred, they fought the battle through.   But Homer's heroes constantly disarm in mid combat — constantly saunter out of the mellay.   We must take them as we find them.

Poseidon, disguised as Thoas, returns to the fight round the group of the Aiantes, Idomeneus arms, meets Meriones, who has now procured a spear. After a long dialogue, the pair decide not to aid the Aiantes, who can give Hector toil enough, but to go to the left wing. Here they fight by the very sterns of the ships.

Meanwhile, Zeus is perhaps watching the battle, and Poseidon, in the likeness of a man, is heartening the Greeks (xiii. 345-360). To us it is absurd that Poseidon should thus deceive Zeus by a flimsy disguise ; but the gods are of very limited acuteness. The *aristeia* of Idomeneus, on the left, now engages the poet. Idomeneus slays Asius, whose charioteer also falls. Deiphobus urges Æneas against the elderly Idomeneus, who retreats slowly. Menelaus and Antilochus now do most of the work, and on the left, practically, the Trojans have the worst of it. Hector does not know this, he is still in the centre, where he first broke in, and the Bœotians and Ionians and Athenians and Locrians have rallied against him. The heavy fire of these light-armed archers and slingers, under cover of the ships, apparently, is of great service to the Aiantes, who are opposing Hector.[1] Indeed, the Trojans would have given way ; Polydamas, therefore, bids Hector 'withdraw and call hither all the best of the warriors.' Hector springs from his chariot, whereas it is unlikely that his charioteer can have rejoined him ; but the best MS. omits the line (749). Hector rallies whom he can to the central battle ; Paris explains to him that many are dead or wounded. With all he can collect, Hector tries to break down the Aiantes, and the cry of both hosts in the renewed struggle goes up to Zeus.

Nestor hears the cry, or a cry, and sees, not a sturdy

[1] For the cover they shoot from, see xiii. 721.

clash of equal foes, but 'the Achæans fleeing and the
Trojans driving them, and the wall overthrown.'

Here we, for our part, first detect confusion. Is the
story going straight on, or has the tale turned back to the
end of book xii., where Hector first leaped through the
gate? In any case, Nestor goes to the wounded chiefs,
Diomede, Agamemnon, and Odysseus. After a parley, by
Diomede's advice, they go behind the fight, to encourage
the Greeks. Here Poseidon appears again as an aged man
(xiv. 150), shouting terribly, to hearten his friends the Greeks,
and here begins Hera's design to lull Zeus in love and
slumber (xiv. 153–351), while Sleep goes to bid Poseidon
seize his opportunity. Now, if there is anything in internal
evidence and the testimony of style, the poet who told in
xiii. of Poseidon's seafaring tells here of Hera's wooing.
There is an immortal splendour in his descriptions ; he
seems to revel in such a change after a mere record of grey-
goose shafts and handy strokes. But why is the device of
Hera needed? Poseidon, in xiii., worked his will unhindered
of Zeus, who, indeed, at first was watching the Scythians.
But (xiii. 345) Zeus appears to have turned his attention
again to the war, and Poseidon (xiii. 356) had to work 'by
stealth.' One might conjecture that he has returned to the
sea (xiii. 352), and stolen forth 'secretly' *again*; though
Mr. Leaf regards the statement as 'a mere recapitulation.'[1]
If it be not a recapitulation, but an indication that, when
Zeus again took an interest in the war, Poseidon retreated, but
returned 'secretly,' then, indeed, we require the wile of
Hera that Zeus may sleep and Poseidon may regain his
freedom of action. Undeniably the passage is far from the
usual clearness of the epic. Nitzsch has suggested that the
action of this book xiv. is not subsequent to but parallel

[1] Leaf, note, xiii. 351.

with that of book xiii. This certainly could be discovered by no listener, and by no ordinary reader.

Mr. Leaf suggests that the poem originally ran thus (xiii. 1-125):—Zeus is not watching; Poseidon comes and rouses the Greeks (xiv. 1-362). Nestor heard the cry raised when the wall fell, and as Poseidon was encouraging the Achæans; he went to the wounded heroes; Poseidon, as 'the aged man,' shouted; and Hera beguiled Zeus. Then came xiii. 795-837, the rush of the rallied Trojans, under Hector, against the Aiantes; then xiv. 402-522, Hector assails Aias, is knocked down by a stone, and Aias routs the Trojans, xv. 1-366. Zeus wakens, restores Hector to strength, and the Achæans are driven once more through the fosse, while Hector cries 'Leave the spoils, and burn the ships.' All this original structure was broken up by introducing the *aristeia* of Idomeneus, to please the Cretans. They must have been easily pleased, for Idomeneus talks much, does little, and is so elderly that he can hardly run away when his mind urges him to do so.[1] If Mr. Leaf is right, the passage (xiii. 345-354) which looks rather as if Zeus had really restored his attention to the war, must be an interpolation, or a passage which has gone astray. It is impossible for any honest unionist, perhaps, to deny that there has been a confusion made somewhere. But this is so manifest that we are all the more inclined to doubt the theories of diaskeuasts and recensors. If they existed at all (and the diaskeuast is the *deus ex machina* of commentators), why did they not put this passage straight? It was their very business to free these beautiful contrasted descriptions of love and fighting from the difficulties which tend to make them incoherent.[2]

[1] *Companion*, p. 244.
[2] A defence of the delay of Hera is offered by Nutzhorn, *Entsteh-*

N

When Hera's purpose is accomplished and reported to Poseidon by Sleep (xiv. 361), he again encourages the Greeks. The obscurities in his advice have been dwelt on; 'it is a clumsy piece of work,' and we, at least, can see no reason for its existence, original or interpolated. We need not recapitulate the fighting in xv. (1–366), when Hector has been restored to force, and when Apollo has overthrown the wall. It is plain (xv. 385) that there was space for charioteering within the wall, and so vanish the difficulties about the chariots. In the earlier fighting, they came in by the gates; here, over the ruined wall. In xv. 668–673, a 'wondrous mist' is suddenly removed by Athene, though we never hear of its arrival. The ancients noticed this blot; there must be a *lacuna* somewhere, and the diaskeuasts, as usual, were idle just when their assistance was needed. The book closes with Hector carrying fire against the ships.

On the whole, then, in books xiii.–xv., we are obliged to recognise what we may call dislocation. The poem can scarcely have been composed exactly as it stands, and the persons who are supposed to have 'redacted' it failed to do so successfully. But we do not recognise a large late addition to the original poem. The new elements, Poseidon and Hera, supply 'gradation' or thickening of the plot, which is essential to dramatic effect.[1] The absence of Achilles is recognised (xiv. 50 and 366). 'These references make us feel that he is uppermost in the minds of the Greeks.'

BOOK XVI

In the beginning of the sixteenth book it is generally admitted, even by the most sceptical, that we re-enter the

ungsweise, p. 160. She has been frightened by Zeus in book viii., and dare not stir, till she is encouraged by the success of Poseidon.

[1] Monro.

stream of the original Μῆνις.   Patroclus, weeping, asks the
implacable Achilles, as Nestor had suggested in book xi., to
let him lead the Myrmidons into the war, like Harry Blount
charging at Flodden, and to wear Achilles's armour.   Achilles
consents.   We have already shown that this passage, and
the remarks about the maiden and the gifts (promised by
Athene in book i.), are not inconsistent with Achilles's
refusal in book ix.   In the present passage, Patroclus says :
'Pitiless thou art.   The knight Peleus was not, then, thy
father, nor Thetis thy mother, but the grey sea bare thee,
and the sheer cliffs, so ruthless is thy spirit.'   This pitiless-
ness may well refer to the refusal of the Embassy.

Mr. Monro asks, 'Why does Achilles allow Patroclus
to aid the Greeks, but will not aid them himself?'   A man,
he says, cannot always be angry ; 'though I deemed that I
would not cease from my wrath until *to my own ships* came
the war-cry and the battle' (62).   Mr. Leaf hints that this
phrase suggested the similar vow of Achilles in ix. 650.
'I will not take thought of war till Hector come to the
Myrmidon's huts and ships, but about mine hut and black
ship, I ween, Hector, though he be very eager for battle,
will be refrained.'   Anything may be argued in this manner.
A late book refers decidedly to an early book, therefore the
early book is really late, and was suggested by the late book,
which is really early.   Thus, if there are no cross references,
the books are unconnected ; and, if there are cross references, they are only by an interpolator, and prove the case
for disintegration.

Achilles, then, will keep the letter, though not the spirit
of his vow in book ix. ; that is his motive for letting
Patroclus fight.   Moreover, his credit will be increased when
it is seen that even his companion in arms can save the
Greeks.   'That Hector, too, may know whether my squire
hath skill to war even alone' (xvi. 243).   Again, Mr. Monro

asks, ' What is the necessity or ground for the determination of Zeus that Patroclus shall be slain ? ' That, we reply, is the Nemesis of the haughtiness of Achilles in book ix. It was suggested at the moment when Patroclus left the hut, to inquire for Machaon. 'This to him was the beginning of evil' (xi. 604). Mr. Monro says that 'the art of Homer conceals the want of motive,' but really the motive is manifest enough. In xi. 796, Nestor had suggested that, if Achilles will not fight, he might send Patroclus in his place. Again, the death of Patroclus has an additional motive, if one is needed, in his rejection of the warning of Achilles, not to go too near Troy (xvi. 94), lest Apollo step in and slay him.

The connection with the ninth book having already been defended, we may examine the other 'interpolations' in book xvi. The story is that Patroclus wears the armour of Achilles, that he is at first successful, that he kills Sarpedon, but is killed by Apollo aiding Hector, who, to our ideas, plays a most unworthy and unchivalrous part. Mr. Leaf very ingeniously conjectures that the description of the new shield of Achilles in book xviii. is an interpolation, and that the interpolator devised and added the wearing of Achilles's armour by Patroclus, to make room for that famous passage. He also thinks that Sarpedon was not in the original poem, but he, and his death scene in this book, 'may have been added by the original hand.' We have already said that additions by the original hand will suffice us, as original enough, though we doubt the possibility of discerning between the first and second draught.

As to the wearing of the armour of Achilles by Patroclus, it is a point of considerable interest. Here we have a motive, and an approximate date for the so-called additions. The supposed interpolator cannot be late, because, as all recent archæological evidence shows, the shield of Achilles (to introduce which the interpolations about change and loss of armour were, *ex hypothesi*, made) is in accordance with the art of the Homeric age. Mr. Leaf believes that inlaid metals were used, as in the bronze daggers found at Mycenæ.[1] Now, these very ancient daggers are, in the style of their inlaid pictures of the chase, what we may call pre-Phœnician. We have no examples of Phœnician work in this inlaid manner ; there are Egyptian examples of it, about 1600 B.C.[2] Nor are the designs on the bronze daggers of Mycenæ at all Phœnician in style : the landscape of papyrus swamps with cats hunting wild-fowl is Egyptian ; not so the style of the figures introduced. The technique of the shield in book xviii., if it really corresponds to the Mycenæan daggers, is thus pre-Phœnician: such work is as old as the seventeenth century B.C. The scheme of ornament in bands, on the other hand, resembles later and Phœnician work on bowls.[3] Thus a difficult question arises. Is the poet describing work not Phœnician, and earlier than Phœnician influence in art, or is he 'combining his information'? Is the work of the Egypto-Mycenæan inlaid style, with Phœnician arrangement?

In any case, such art as that of which an idealised account is given in the Shield is extremely ancient, if it be as old as the inlaid bronze daggers of Mycenæ. But now we must remember that on the theory of interpolation there already existed a text, or a careful oral version, into which passages of two lines in length could be neatly dovetailed, in several remote books, so as to admit of, and lead up to, the long interpolation of the shield. If the text was merely

[1] They are excellently copied in colours and gold in *Bulletin de Correspondance Hellénique*, 1886, pt. ii.

[2] See below, on 'Homer and Archæology.'

[3] See Leaf, *Iliad*, note on xviii. 478, and *Companion*, p. 310.

'in oral transmission,' as Mr. Monro thinks,[1] we find it quite impossible to conceive how reciters, in many distant places, were induced to accept these little dovetailings. The addition, if addition it be, 'belongs to the same period.' If there were written texts, it is not much more easy to understand how one poet prevailed on Greece to welcome his private additions and judicious corruptions of familiar passages. It is the easiest thing in the world to go cutting out what does not suit our systems, but the hardest to explain how the pieces which we cut out were sewn in, and were accepted. For all this, in the case of the Shield and the dovetailings which give it a *raison d'être*, must, *ex hypothesi*, be very ancient indeed, in the full time of Heroic art and manners. That so many poets of the highest class, and using 'the grand style,' should have existed, and have preferred interpolating an old work to making original lays, is, of course, a literary difficulty, felt by critics like Goethe and Mr. Matthew Arnold. In the case of the French *chansons de geste*, a close analogy, the late continuators are a very feeble folk, and the grand style, even as found in the *Song of Roland*, is far from them. Greece was more fortunate in possessing many great self-denying poets, satisfied with compiling sequels. Content to do good work by stealth and blushing to find it fame, they, like Poseidon, disguised their genius under the shape of the παλαιὸς φώς, 'the Old Man,' and were pleased, by artful dovetailing, to escape renown, and be blended in glory with the author of the original Μῆνις. But all this happened before the age of Hesiod, who distinctly tells us that 'potter is jealous with potter, and poet with poet.' A poet of this temper would not hide his light under a *diaskeuê*. We are not dealing, let it be remembered, with mere ballad-mongers, whose names are indifferent to a popular audience. We are to

[1] Introduction to book xviii.

think of great poets in an age when there was probably poetical rivalry, when Thamyris sang against the Muses.[1]

They are poets of this early age, who, on Bergk's and Mr. Leaf's theory of the arms of Achilles, were content to sink their individuality in that of a predecessor, and to conceal their merits by ingeniously thrusting in lines here and there, up and down, about the Μῆνις. The nature of men, and especially of poets, not to mention the difficulties of the operation and of securing acceptance for the additions, really makes the theory very hazardous.

We are to believe, however, that a later poet composed the brilliant description of the Shield of Achilles. Far from being proud of the achievement, his first care was to conceal his merit, and to palm it off as part of the work of another. He, therefore, had to lead up to it, by foisting verses containing motives for the change of arms into earlier books. First he took the canto which is now book xi., and made Nestor, in that book, advise Patroclus to borrow the armour of Achilles (xi. 798).[2]

The interpolator has next to introduce Patroclus's request for the arms, and the grant of them by Achilles (xvi. 40–64). Lines 130–144 must next go, for they describe Patroclus arming in Achilles's gear. The description of the lance of Peleus, which Patroclus does not take, as it is too heavy, was rejected by Zenodotus, because it recurs in xvii. Aristarchus preferred it in this place, but Mr. Leaf and Bergk agree with Zenodotus. The opinion of Aristarchus is usually admired ; but why should not Homer indulge in textual

---

[1] ii. 595.   This is from the Catalogue, and, whatever may be thought of the age of the Catalogue, it at least illustrates heroic manners. Mr. Leaf believes that ' it was composed in Achæan times,' on the mainland of Greece, and was thus earlier than the Dorian Conquest.

[2] Fick thinks that they are an interpolation here, borrowed from Patroclus's request for the arms in xvi. 36–49.

repetition, a note of all early poetry, from ballad to epic?
Again, when Sarpedon doubts who it is that leads the
Myrmidons (xvi. 423–4), we are not to suppose that Patroclus is taken for Achilles. But, if he were not, what could
there be any doubt about? He had the well-known horses
of Achilles, two immortal and one mortal; but Bergk cuts
them out also, ' because there was no room for them ' ! [1]
Again, xvi. 796–800, where we are told that not before had
Achilles's arms been stained with dust, is a device of the
author of the Shield. [2]

Not including Sarpedon's doubt as to who wears the
armour (xvi. 423–4), there are four or five passages in xvi.
which have to go out, on Bergk's theory. Lines 41–43
disappear, because they repeat (as we should expect from
Homeric usage) the words of Nestor in xi. 799–803. Again,
141–144 vanish, that we may agree with Zenodotus, rather
than Aristarchus, about their recurrence in xvii. 388–391.
It is said that the change of armour produces little effect,
though ' the Trojans wavered, deeming that Peleus's son had
cast away his wrath ' (xvi. 282), and though Sarpedon did
not know whom he was fighting with. The appearance of
the Myrmidons, and of the deathless horses, might cause a
momentary confusion, but there can be no question that
the doubt which Sarpedon felt and solved was chiefly
produced by the armour.

Let us follow the ' interpolator ' (whose object is to describe the arms, and then fit them in) into the later books.
In the seventeenth book Apollo warns Hector not to pursue

---

[1] *Griech. Litteraturgesch.* i. p. 617.

[2] Here, perhaps, is an allusion to the belief that, when Hector wore
Achilles's arms, taken from Patroclus, he was doomed, as they were
only to be worn by a man of divine birth. Yet Aias and Odysseus
contended for Achilles's new mail, and Odysseus got it without any
nemesis. Od. xi. 546.

the horses of Achilles, 'hard to be driven by mortal man.'
Why should Patroclus have taken such dangerous beasts,
which only Bergk grudges him, except to carry out the
illusion caused by the armour of Achilles? Hector approaches Patroclus, Menelaus withdrawing in fear, and
sends the armour into Troy. He changes his mind, however, when urged into battle over Patroclus, by Glaucus,
and, running after his messengers, dresses himself in the
harness of Achilles (xvii. 188–197). According to the
scholiast, his change of mind was caused by his desire for
the arms. He could not part from them. This movement
seems odd—as it is—to Mr. Leaf, who finds here 'disastrous
confusion.' But, strange as it is, it greatly influences the
story. Zeus remarks (xvii. 201) that now Hector is doomed
and never will return to Andromache, but grants him 'great
strength' for the moment. If this avails him little, it is
simply because Homer cannot bear to let the Trojans have
much the best of the fight. Hector now (xvii. 214) seems
to all of these allies like Achilles. Mr. Leaf would have
expected 'a more marked effect'—what kind of effect we
know not. Hector could not have scared them as an apparition of Achilles, for he had told them what he meant
to do (xvii. 183–187).

The fight is keen over dead Patroclus. The divine
horses weep. Zeus pities them, and pities men, and declares that Hector, as he has the arms of Achilles, shall not
have the horses also (xvii. 450). Alcimedon mentions the
fact about the arms to Automedon, the charioteer (xvii. 472),
but does not say they are Achilles's. An allusion in xvii. 711
Mr. Leaf thinks it 'arbitrary to excise.' Nevertheless, 'it
will be necessary to reject it.'[1] As the fight reels this
way and that, Menelaus sends Antilochus to tell Achilles

[1] *Companion*, p. 296. Compare *Iliad*, vol. ii. p. 180, where the
rejection is described as 'arbitrary.'

that Patroclus is slain, and that Hector wears his armour (xvii. 693).   Antilochus strips off his own harness (they did this very rapidly), and runs with the ill news.   Menelaus tells the Aiantes about his message, but adds that Achilles (unlike Fick's Agamemnon in book ii.) cannot fight un-armed (xvii. 711).   This is the line which it is at once 'necessary' and 'arbitrary' to cut out.   The Greeks then retreat with the body of Patroclus, and the book ends.

It is plain that the interpolator has made good use of his opportunity.   The wearing of Achilles's armour (in-vented by the interpolator) is positively the motive for the death of Hector, if the armour is divine and deadly, an idea unknown to the Odyssey.[1]

In the eighteenth book the loss of the armour leads up to perhaps the most wonderful passage in Homer — the panic caused by the shout of the unarmed Achilles.   Go into the war without harness he may not, but clear as a clarion's cry rang the voice of Æacides.   Thrice he shouted, and thrice the Trojans were confounded.   This passage by itself would justify the change of armour ; but the change, and loss of the arms, now lead direct to the making of the shield by Hephæstus.

Thus, to rob the original poet of the motive for Hector's death, and of the cry of Achilles, and of that peculiarly Homeric work, the shield, it is necessary to make arbitrary excisions in earlier books and later, to seek for 'knots in a reed,' discrepancies where there are none, and to imagine a minstrel, as great as the greatest, who yet is so modest as to hide his work in another's, by aid of crafty interpolations

---

[1] In one of the Cyclic poems, Neoptolemus, on arriving at Troy, receives his father's armour from Odysseus.   This is mentioned in Proclus's analysis of *The Little Iliad*, Kinkel, *Epic. Græc. Fragm.*, p. 37.

[2] *Companion*, pp. 288-9.

introduced (how we are never told) at a very early period—
the period of various coloured inlaid gold on bronze. To
many readers, probably, all this will seem wasted ingenuity.
'Terrible learning !' they will exclaim, with Mr. Matthew
Arnold, and will thank the original poet for his management
of his most admirable scenes.

In an attempt to vindicate for the original poet the
greater part of the Iliad, perhaps the two most important
points are the authenticity of book ix. and of the passages
about the armour of Achilles. As to book ix., the question
is really one of literary taste. Are we to believe in the
truly inexorable hero who refuses the prayers, or are we to
believe in two separate heroes—the Achilles of the original
'Wrath' who received and refused no embassy, and the
Achilles of the second poet who did refuse one? Our answer
greatly depends on our sense of what the heroic temper
was, and this sense will guide our estimate of the meaning
of the disputed passages.

In regard to the Arms and the hypothesis that they
are an addition made late in the third stratum of interpolation and change, we deal with something more tangible. We
ask whether a composition so clearly marked, as Mr. Leaf
thinks, by archæological evidence of great antiquity could,
in a remote age, be first composed and then made plausible
as a piece of the original work by a number of minute
interpolations in the body of the poem? It is only fair to
review and restate Mr. Leaf's arguments as given again in
his *Companion to the Iliad* (p. 269). Mr. Leaf maintains
that 'if it was really the intention that Patroclus should be
taken for Achilles, the result is a singular failure.' The
only allusion to a disguise is Sarpedon's doubt (xvi. 423,
424) as to who the hero may be. We may add that, in
xvi. 543, Glaucus recognises Patroclus after the slaying of
Sarpedon. The general effect, however, has been pro-

duced by the charge of the Myrmidons, led by a warrior in
Achilles's arms, driving the deathless horses of Achilles.
There is here no 'singular failure,' and as the new poet
composed xvii. 201, wherein Zeus asserts that Hector must
die, the whole plot is hastened and foreshadowed by the
'singular failure.' There has been 'a brief breathing time
in battle' (xvi. 40–43), which is all that Patroclus asked for.
To obtain it is not to fail. Not to speak of the advice of
Nestor in the eleventh book, the change of armour is referred to in xvi. 40–43, 64, 134, 140–144, 796, 800, and, of
course, later on in the speech of Zeus, xvii. 201, and elsewhere in xvii. But all this passage about Hector donning
the arms of Achilles, lately worn by Patroclus, Mr. Leaf
'must reject.' Why? 'It is very strange that after
Hector's proud words to Glaucus, whom he has bidden to
stand at his side and see him fight, he should without more
ado leave the field to change his armour.' We have frequently noted the speed with which heroes in battle, like
Menelaus, Idomeneus, and Antilochus, arm and disarm.
It seems curious to us ; we remember Dalgetty's difficulty
in unbuckling his armour after dinner. It appears to us a
dilatory manœuvre, but it is not isolated here, it occurs again
and again, and implies only the briefest delay. Mr. Leaf
thinks Hector's change of arms worthy of 'a passing remark'
from the Greeks. So we might all think ; but nobody does
remark on these things in Homer, except that Zeus bodes
ill for Hector. Moreover, if the effect of astonishment produced among the Trojans by Hector's appearance in Achilles's
arms be less than Mr. Leaf expects, we have still to blame
for that a poet as great as the great original, the author of
the episode of the armour. He was as likely as the
original poet to produce a satisfactory effect. It is no great
argument to say that the whole description of the change,
wherever alluded to, can readily be taken out. Could it

not just as easily be excised if it really were the work of the
original poet? If the original poet, had it been his, might
have made more of it, what prevented as great a poet, the
interpolator, from doing the same thing? Why should so
distinguished an author content himself with 'a singular
failure,' if failure it be? His conduct is just as hard to
account for as the original poet's would have been. The
Trojans, seeing Patroclus in Achilles's gear, and with his
horses and men, 'wavered, for they deemed that by the
ships the fleet-footed son of Peleus had cast away his wrath
and chosen reconcilement ; then each man glanced round
to see where he might flee sheer destruction' (xvi. 278–283).
Nobody thought he only saw Patroclus. There was a 'breathing time in war' (xvi. 302)—all that Patroclus asked for.
Where is the failure? The burning ship was quenched ; no
more was needed at the moment (xvi. 280–312). Even
this passage (281–3) Mr. Leaf thinks 'possibly an interpolation belonging to the change of armour, which never has
any effect but what we find here.' We must repeat that the
effect which we find here is precisely the effect predicted in
Nestor's speech (xi. 794–803) and prayed for by Patroclus
(xvi. 40–44) that 'light may arise to the Danaans, and there
may be breathing time in battle.' It is not failure to produce the very result which you aim at producing. If there
had been any need to amplify the effects, the interpolator
could do it as well as another man.

In book xvi. the references to changes of armour 'may
be cut out ;' in book xvii. they 'must be.'[1] ' In any case
we must omit from this part the forty-three lines which
describe the armour taken from Patroclus as the arms of
Achilles. See notes on xvii. 186–228.'[2] Well, why must
we excise those lines? Because, Mr. Leaf says in the

[1] *Companion*, p. 270.
[2] *Ibid*. p. 287.

note which he refers to, 'as mentioned above, we must
reject some lines here.' This is no strong argument. 'The
idea that Patroclus is wearing the armour of Achilles has
not appeared before in this book.' There has been a
fight for the arms between Menelaus and Euphorbus ;
Menelaus is victorious. Apollo prevents Hector from trying to win Achilles's horses. Hector attacks Menelaus, who
dreads shame if he leaves behind ' those noble arms ' and
Patroclus (xvii. 90–92). Menelaus hurries off, however, to
find Aias, to rescue Patroclus naked, for 'the armour,' τά γε
τεύχε', 'Hector holds.' Hector retreats from Aias, and
sends the armour towards the city, ' to be great glory unto
him.' Glaucus encourages Hector, who speeds after the
armour (xvii. 195)—' Pelides's glorious armour '—and puts
it on. The fact that the arms are those of Achilles might
have been made more of ; but, again, to do so was as open
to the interpolator as to the original poet. Mr. Leaf
argues, as we saw, that Hector's behaviour is odd. We
have shown that it has many parallels. In his edition of
the Iliad (xvii. 186) he says there ' can be little doubt that
the passage is an interpolation by the author of the weapon
making.' But we see no reason for the imperative an-
nouncement that the passage ' must ' be excised, because
it introduces hopeless confusion into a perfectly plain
narrative. That Hector, like other heroes, should be very
expeditious in getting into and out of armour does not
introduce ' hopeless confusion,' and his boyish inability to
let the lovely armour go out of his sight was intelligible to the
scholiast. Among Mr. Leaf's excisions was xvi. 796–800,
containing the beautiful lament for the changed fortunes of
Achilles's armour. ' Not of old was it suffered that this
helmet with horse-hair crest should be defiled with dust ;
nay, but it kept the head and beautiful face of a man divine,
even of Achilles.' In this passage Apollo struck off the

helm of Patroclus, and loosened his corslet. Helm and corslet are supposed to be still on in book xvii., and probably the corslet really was on, even if loosened. But, in xvii. 205, Zeus says that *Hector* has 'unmeetly stripped the armour from his head and shoulders,' though Apollo really struck off the helm and loosened the corslet. Whether an original poet, just as well as an interpolator equally great, might not have made this tiny slip, every reader may decide for himself.

To sum up this long discussion of a crucial point, if the change of armour and its consequences, including the making of the new arms by Hephæstus in book xviii., are by the original poet, we meet the difficulty that the change, though it does all that it is expected to do, does not do as much as the separatist critic would wish. This argument is a little like that of the modern middle-aged philosopher, who posed himself beside the Venus of Milo, in what he conceived to be a preferable attitude. His friend confessed that he 'preferred the Venus.' Even so, we prefer Homer's treatment of the subject to that which his critic would choose. Again, if the change of arms be part of the original poet's work, it is less referred to in book xvii. than it might be; it causes a certainly singular, though not unexampled action of Hector's, which, in some legends, insures his doom, and it is inaccurately described by Zeus, though the slip is not unnatural or momentous. But if Mr. Leaf is right, then, in a very early age according to his archæological system, an age when the inlaying art of Egypt of the seventeenth century B.C. was still in vogue, a new poet, late in the development of the Iliad, was able to introduce a long description of the divine armour-making. He was also able to foist in allusions to it in earlier books, as xi. and xvi. He was able to secure the acceptance of his work, both in the main and in isolated

lines and fragments. So great a poet was he, that his
picture of Achilles at the trench (in book xviii. 187–242)
' is one of the supreme pieces of poetical imagination which
the world has brought forth.'[1]   His whole narrative is 'a
model of vigour, rapidity, and clearness.' Yet he introduced ' hopeless confusion ' when he made Hector change
his armour. Great as he was, he sank his fame in the
work of another, and was content to continue a poem by a
predecessor, and help in making a sequel. The difficulty
of believing in so many supreme poets, and so self-denying,
encounters us everywhere. That such men should also
be clumsy botchers amazes us. As to how the minute
additions were made and accepted—for there is no evidence
for the theory of a ' school,'[2]—we receive no enlightenment.
Are we seriously to imagine a professional school of poets
before 1000 B.C. ? One of them composes the story of the
Arms, he makes the needful interpolations in xi., xvi. ; he
submits it to the Homeric Academy. They like it, and, in
future, teach the whole poem to their pupils with the
modern improvements. Is all this more credible than the
hypothesis of one great peerless and original poet ?

BOOKS XVII, XVIII, XIX

The story of book xvii. has already been indicated. It
is the fight for the dead body of Patroclus, in the course of
which Hector puts on the fatal harness of Achilles. There
are shifts of success. Apollo encourages the Trojans, promising the favour of Zeus. Menelaus sends Antilochus to
Achilles with the news of Patroclus's fall. The body of
Patroclus is carried safely out of the war. The objection
of Fick, that the prelude of book i., where it says that many

---

[1] *Companion*, p. 298.
[2] Jebb, Introduction to *Homer*, pp. 170–171.

heroes were given to the birds and dogs, is inconsistent
with the saving of the body of Patroclus, is characteristic
of the Higher Criticism. It need not detain us. Nor need
we linger over the appearance of Glaucus as no hero of the
original Μῆνις. He may, confessedly, be by 'the original
hand.' There may be a needless and motiveless interpolation in 268–273 and 366–383, where an uncalled-for supernatural mist is introduced. The cloud is very well, and
leads up to the prayer of Aias to die in the light, but the
frequent mentions of it are not beyond suspicion. The
weeping of the horses, with what follows (424–542), is suspected as 'elegiac,' to which we may reply that Homer's
lyre 'has all the strings.' The very merits of the poet are
made accusations. If where rhetoric is needed (as in ix.)
his rhetoric is masterly, then it is 'rhetorical,' and late. If
in a dirge we hear the wail, then it is lyrical, and late. And
if an elegiac passage is elegiac, that also proves lateness.
What was once Homer's distinction, his universality, is now
a proof of interpolation ! The author's 'military wisdom'
in the mouth of Nestor is rejected. True, the 'Catalogue'
dilates on Nestor's military wisdom, but this is matter for the
military critic. The 'futile' performances of Automedon
are censured ; but a man's efforts when he had to drive a car
without a companion to use spear and sword were likely to
be futile. Passages where Phœnix occurs are refused to
the original Μῆνις, as Phœnix, owing to his appearance
with the Embassy, is a suspicious character. We regret
this because he, in his speech in the ninth book, gives us
almost our only view of the seamy side of Homeric domestic
life. And 'it is not necessary that we should be told how
it was that Antilochus came to bring the news to Achilles '
The passage about Idomeneus, ending xvii. 625, 'may be
attributed to the hand which gave us the *aristeia* of
Idomeneus in xiii.' In that case the poet who is sup-

*o

posed to laud Idomeneus here makes him run away in a fright !

The eighteenth book contains 616 lines, of which Mr. Leaf's system leaves 170, or, by admitting the scene where Achilles shows himself unarmed, and terrifies the Trojans by his cry, 200.

The story, briefly, is this : Antilochus brings the news to Achilles ; Thetis hears the voice of his lament, and comes from the sea with the Nereids, who, in the musical catalogue of their names, seem to float up like sea waves. All this of the Nereids is excised. The Trojans nearly take Patroclus's body, but Hera sends Iris to Achilles, who, shining in flame from Athene, shouts thrice on the edge of the trench, and the Trojans fly. Hera shortens the day. The Trojans hold a council of war on the plain ; Hector says he will never withdraw into the city ; Achilles laments Patroclus ; Zeus and Hera have a dialogue (excised) ; Thetis goes to ask Hephæstus for new armour (367-477) ; the making of the Arms is described (478-617). According to Mr. Leaf's theory, these 139 lines are the cause of all the incident of the change and loss of Achilles's arms, and of the introduction of Thetis in this place. We might add that the absence of arms is the reason of the admirable passage on the cry of Achilles from the trench. But Mr. Leaf tries to rescue this ' grand passage ' for the Μῆνις in a curious way. If Achilles had possessed armour, his instinct would have been to rush into the war and rescue Patroclus's body. But he had no armour—his armour clothes Hector. So, when Iris bids him rescue the body, he says, ' How may I go into the fray ? ' for *he* is not ready to fight in sandals and a tunic like Fick's Agamemnon. Iris bids him merely show himself. Now Mr. Leaf suspects that, in the original Μῆνις, he possibly *did* rush out in arms, which, *ex hypothesi,* he possessed (had never lost), and brought in the body.[1]   This theory turns on line 151 :—

Οὐδέ κε Πάτροκλόν περ ἐϋκνήμιδες ᾿Αχαιοὶ
᾿Εκ βελέων ἐρύσαντο—

'Nor might the well-greaved Achæans drag the corpse of Patroclus out of the darts,' had not *what* occurred?   In this place the supposed rescue could have followed.   But the apodosis, the explanation of how the Greeks were enabled to bring in the body, comes in late, in line 166— 'if Iris had not gone to Achilles.'   By excising four later lines about Thetis's command not to fight unarmed, and about the cry of Achilles (216-7, 228-9), the apparition of Achilles might be rescued for the original poem.   But the mere appearance and shout, with the terror they caused, are infinitely more admirable than a sudden charge of the armed Achilles.   We cannot rescue the passage by ruining it.   The strength of the whole sublime passage is in the absence of armour and of onslaught.   The ' interpolator ' greatly added to the beauty and interest of the Iliad if we are really to believe that, for the sake of one hundred and forty beautiful lines on the shield, the whole poem was altered and dove-tailed here and there, and Thetis with her Nereids introduced.   The list of Nereids was objected to, for its 'Hesiodic character,' by Zenodotus, a person of very little taste, and 'the Nereids' names seem to be selected from the longer list in Hesiod's *Theogony,* 243 ff.' Perhaps, on the other hand, Hesiod plagiarised from Homer. We would fain not lose the musical names of that company.

The reason for all this theory is not obvious.   The Shield is confessed to be of the Heroic age.   Why should not the one great poet have composed it?   Why invent

[1] Introduction to xviii. (*Iliad*, vol. ii. p. 221).   This hypothesis is not urged in the *Companion.*

another poet equally great? If it is to account for the
supposed discrepancies caused by the change of armour,
we have shown how little they amount to, and how some
great poet, if slips there be, must have made these slips. The
excised interview with Thetis, again, as Mr. Monro says,
exhibits 'the true crisis of an epic of which "the wrath
of Achilles" is the true subject.'[1] 'The complaint of
Thetis strikes again the keynote of the Iliad, the short-
ness and unhappiness of the life to which the hero is
destined. . . . We see that the prayer of Thetis, which
up to this time has been the main force behind the
action of the poem, can be so no longer. The boon that
she obtained from Zeus has turned to bitterness, and
Achilles has to go back to her for counsel and help.'
He, who an hour ago compared Patroclus to a weary little
girl, praying her mother to lift her in her arms (book xvi.
7–11), has now to pray to his own mother for her un-
wearying kindness and aid. It is this wonderful stroke
of irony and of pity that the commentators deny to the
original poet. They destroy 'the true dramatic περιπέτεια,
of which the remaining events are the natural and obvious
consequence.'

All this they ruin, and they know not what they do.
Even Fick 'endeavours to claim' this scene 'for the
Μῆνις,' Mr. Leaf says—that is, the scene from 35 to 129.
But on Mr. Leaf's theory, if Fick is right, as the purpose of
Thetis's journey is to be omitted, as the arms are out of the
story, 'she comes merely to ask a question of five lines, and
to utter a far from consoling prophecy and a weak truism
of two lines each.' The mother, in our old Homer, comes
to help her son, and enables him to utter his bitterness and
the agony of his repentance. But by the scissors of commentators all is hopelessly mangled and destroyed. The

[1] Introduction to book xviii.

peddling criticisms of some German commentators on book xviii. can hardly be read without pity. Lachmann, indeed, regarded books xviii., xix., xx., xxi., xxii., as a noble whole, the sixteenth of his 'lays.' Others take the most pettifogging objections to points of detail—for example, as to the exact position of the body of Patroclus at the moment when Achilles terrifies the Trojans. Then Thetis (xviii. 454) tells Hephæstus that Apollo slew Patroclus and gave glory to Hector, while the poet (xxii. 323-331) says that Hector slew him. 'They all did it.' Then there is discussion about Achilles's thought of suicide. How could Antilochus hold his hands to keep him from suicide when he has just been described as scattering dust with his hands on his head (22-32)? Is σίδηρος 'the iron,' not a later word for a weapon? Is suicide Homeric? The idea of suicide occurs twice or thrice in the Odyssey. The catalogue of Nereids is attacked, and admirably defended by Nutzhorn and Lehrs : ' with the sound of each separate name comes the vision of their number, the impression that they are many as the sea waves.' In the speech of Achilles to Thetis, Düntzer excises 88-113—that is to say, cuts out the gist of the scene, the peripeteia of the poem : Achilles's determination not to live if he slay not Hector, whose death is to be followed by his own. Then, as Hera sent Iris privately to Achilles, how does Athene know it and aid him with the miraculous flame, with the ægis, and with her voice? And is Zeus on Olympus at the moment, or is he on Ida? He is on Ida, not on Olympus (xvii. 594) ; and so forth. An interpolator, says Bergk, introduced the Trojan council of war (243-315), and Mr. Leaf thinks that the speeches in the council have been 'seriously interpolated, though the scene as a whole cannot be rejected,' because Hector refers to it very touchingly in the hour of his death (xxii. 100). In the eighteenth book Polydamas advises retreat

within the town.   When death is coming on him (xxii. 100)
Hector cries, 'Woe is me ; if I go within the gates Polydamas will be the first to reproach me, since he bade me
lead the Trojans within the city during this ruinous night,
when noble Achilles arose. Yet I regarded him not ;' so he
fights and dies on this point of honour.   There is more
trouble over the 'chronology' of Thetis's visit to Hephæstus.
Did Thetis arrive at his house before or after the sunset
which Hera had hastened?   Did Hephæstus work by
candle-light?   It is enough to say, with Mr. Monro, 'It is
true that several events are placed in the interval after
Thetis leaves Achilles (148–368), and that one of them is
sunset (239) ; but we may suppose that the poet, in returning to Thetis, goes back to the beginning of the interval,
and that the journey of the goddess takes no appreciable
length of time.'

We have often said that the gods, by the very nature of
mythology, cause discrepancies, but this is a discrepancy
which could only puzzle critics of a class for whom Homer
did not sing.

The nineteenth book · is vigorously mangled.   It tells
how Achilles publicly renounced his wrath.   Thetis brings
him the new divine armour (1–39).   He calls the Greeks
to an assembly, corresponding to that which he called when
the wrath began in book i., and urges instant battle.

Agamemnon again offers the gifts, to which Achilles
now attaches no importance.   Odysseus says that the host
had better breakfast before fighting (40–276).   The gifts
are brought by Odysseus to Achilles.   Briseïs, restored
to him, laments Patroclus.   Achilles refuses food ; Athene
strengthens him with nectar (277–355).   The Greeks go
forth ; Achilles arms ; the divine horse, Xanthus, foretells
his death.

In all this, of course, they who think book ix. an

interpolation must reject all references to the gifts, with
Düntzer, and so slight Athene's promise to Achilles in
book i. But gifts of reconciliation are far too great an Homeric institution to be slighted.[1] They make the reconciliation
public and legal, by the offer and the acceptance. In
fact, they must stand in any case ; the allusions to book ix.
are alone obnoxious. The debate on feeding the army is
excised (154–237) as decadent. Agamemnon's remarks on
Heracles (88–136) are probably 'inserted from an old
Herakleia,' we know not why, as no interpolator's vanity
could be gratified by the act. Digressions, like Agamemnon's, far from being unsuitable in an Homeric speech, are
rather favourites with the orators. The speech of Achilles
about his son Neoptolemus, born to him of Deidamia in
Scyros, is certainly not in accordance with the rest of the
Iliad, where Neoptolemus is never alluded to (326–337),
and it has peculiarities of diction. Kammer thinks the
speech of the divine horse (404–423) is a 'conceit' added
by 'a rhapsodist.'[2] It is one of Mr. Matthew Arnold's
favourite passages—indeed, almost all his favourite passages
in Lectures on Translating Homer are interpolations, late
or early. Rhapsodists come rather late into history, and
we do not know how one of them got his 'gag,' as we
may call it, into the accepted text. It is true that Achilles
bids the horses bring the charioteer safe home, and Xanthus
warns him of his own fate. But the 'speaking horse' whose
voice the Erinyes stayed—the Erinyes, guardians of natural
order—is better than a 'conceit.' Mr. Leaf talks as if

---

[1] Odyssey, viii. 400–405.

[2] Naber thinks the passage unworthy of the old singer. Bergk
holds it for a part of the original ancient poem, well worthy of the
great master. Nitzsch feels the tragic force of the prophecy. The
prosaic Düntzer cannot see why Hera should make the horse tell
Achilles what Thetis had told him already.

a speaking horse were 'a purely physical phenomenon.'
The rhapsodist, or Homer, looks on it as an infringement of
the law of the universe.   Mr. Monro remarks on the passage, correctly, as one of the omens and prophecies which
gather and darken towards the end, as in the Odyssey.[1]
The 'conceit' 'gives additional emphasis and solemnity.'
We are, in fact, reminded of the plot of the Odyssey in two
ways, at least.   First, the Iliad, like the Odyssey, turns on
the prayer of a supernatural or semi-supernatural being of
minor rank : here of Thetis ; in the Odyssey of the Cyclops.
Next, in both poems prophecies and omens grow frequent,
and grow darker, as the epics draw to their close.

As to the long speeches, and the question of food before fighting, Mr. Monro rightly argues that though they
may seem to us, or at least to Hentze and others, 'tasteless and out of place,' this is a line of argument which we
must be careful in applying to Homer.   Homer is full of
words, where a blow is more in place, 'where a single
word would seem to be more than enough.'   The speech
of Achilles is intended to reflect his new mood of
impulsive desire for vengeance on the Trojans, ' contrasted with the neutral type represented by Agamemnon,
and with the patience and practical wisdom of Odysseus.'
The Heracleian myth in Agamemnon's speech is probably
meant to draw attention from the awkwardness of his
situation and of his apology.   ' Even Zeus was blinded
on a time by Atê ; and a mortal man, like me, may be
pardoned for yielding to her.'[2]   'This is no time to dally
here with subtleties,' says Achilles, very naturally, and, as
naturally, Odysseus, who is in no mood of passion, men-

---

[1] Compare the *Bride of Lammermoor*.

[2] As Mr. Monro remarks, the personification of Atê is shifting.
First she is a passion, then a person.   Hence comes matter for long
German commentaries.   Hentze, *Anhang*, book xix. p. 11.

tions the instant need of breakfast before battle, and sums the conference up with a few words on the gifts. Part of this is out of our manners, and alien to our taste, but we are not living in the Homeric age. The .oratorical race of the Red Man would be gratified by all the stately and prolix discussion. The motive, on the other hand, for an interpolation from an old *Herakleia* is obscure. But if the *Herakleia* was an *old Herakleia* how came it (93) to contain ' a false archaism, dating from the time when the feeling for the primitive rhythm had died out' (Leaf) ? Yet the *Herakleia* must probably have been ' old,' as Mr. Leaf says, because a late interpolator would not, whatever his inscrutable motive, thrust in a cantle from a poem known to be recent in his own time.[1]

The speech of Briseïs, her lament over Patroclus, beautiful and touching as it is, is taken to be an interpolation. If Homer is not its author, he should have been, in spite of some curious expressions. Briseïs says (298) that Patroclus promised that Achilles would make her his κουριδίην ἄλοχον, his ' wedded wife,' a phrase used only of wedded maids. But Briseïs, who lacerates her face in grief, though that is uncommon in Homer, was a foreign captive and knew no better. She believed what Patroclus told her, Patroclus ' the kindly knight,' and we are not to censure him if he promised more than he could perform. The so-

---

[1] Mr. Leaf's opinion about the *old Herakleia* is that of Nitzsch, Bergk, La Roche, and others. It is urged that a mere mortal, not being an inspired poet, cannot know what the gods said and did, as Agamemnon knows, and that the piece is allegorical in an un-Homeric way ; but Mr. Grote's remarks on allegory and myth seem to apply here. Yet it has seemed well to Germans to excise 90–136, as ' without doubt interpolated.' Hentze, *l.c.* p. 11. An amusing piece of pedantry is the question *how* Agamemnon (252–266) can cut the boar's throat as (xi. 253–265) he has a wounded arm. To consider so curiously is to outdo the most peevish Alexandrine critics.

called non-Epic expressions in her lament are only cases
of the neglect of the digamma.

Probably the best argument in favour of this book, and
of xviii., is their masterly effect in completing the composition of the whole epic.   In the beginning of xviii., in
the interview of Achilles with Thetis, we have the complement of his interview with her in book i.   'The boon that
she obtained from Zeus has turned to bitterness, and
Achilles has to go back to her for counsel and help.'   The
poem, like the Homeric Oceanus, turns back upon itself.
And so, in xix., the poem returns on the original quarrel.
These 'architectonic' merits of construction are beyond
the reach of 'fakers' and interpolators.   This is well brought
out by Mr. Monro in introductions to xviii., xix.

BOOK XX

The twentieth book of the Iliad contains passages—or
rather, is mainly made up of passages—which scarcely admit
of an honest defence.   Here, surely, if anywhere, there are
breaks in the continuity, and here, if anywhere, are interpolations.

The Achæans are arming, when Zeus bids Themis call
a general assembly of the gods.   Rivers, nymphs, Poseidon
come, but not Hades.   Zeus informs Poseidon that, for
fear lest Achilles overpasses Fate and takes Troy, he will
permit all gods to choose sides and influence the war.
This they do, and 'themselves burst into fierce war' (55).
But nothing here comes of the Theomachy, or battle of the
gods.   In place of really warring, Apollo sends Æneas,
much against his will, to encounter Achilles.   Æneas
says he has already fled from Achilles who 'ever keeps
some god by his side.'   He only asks 'a fair field of battle.'
He is like King Padella, when Giglio prodded him with the

fairy sword, which elongated at will.   ' If,' said he to Giglio,
' you ride a fairy horse, and wear fairy armour, what on
earth is the use of my hitting you?'   Apollo replies to
Æneas that, if the mother of Achilles is a goddess, Æneas
is the son of Aphrodite.   So Æneas goes to war,
but Hera suggests to Poseidon that the fight should be
stopped.   Poseidon says all the gods had better 'keep a
ring' and look on, which they do.   Æneas and Achilles
meet, and behave much like Tom Sawyer and the strange
boy.   They harangue each other at enormous length.
First they exchange taunts, and next Æneas tells Achilles
all about his pedigree, though he admits that this information is already familiar to the hero.   He then hurls his
spear, and 'le bouillant Achille' behaves more as he does
in *La Belle Hélène* than like a furious warrior who has the
death of Patroclus to avenge.   'He held away the shield
from him with his stout heart in fear,' for he did not know
the merits of ' fairy armour,' 'knew not that not lightly do
the glorious gifts of gods yield to force of earthly men.'
Æneas is equally alarmed, but he is rescued, of all gods, by
Poseidon, the foe of Troy.   Poseidon's excuse is the valid
one—that Æneas is both *pater* and *pius*.   ' He is appointed
to escape that the race of Dardanus perish not' (that is, he
is *pater Æneas*), and again, ' welcome ever are his offerings
to the gods,' for he is *pius Æneas*.   Poseidon therefore
lifts Æneas, like Celtic heroes in old Irish sagas, 'over
many ranks of warriors.'   Achilles is chagrined, but returns
to fight, and Apollo bids Hector not to encounter him.
Achilles slays Polydorus, Priam's youngest son, which
arouses Hector.   The two meet in battle.   Athene throws
back Hector's spear.   Hector is hidden in mist by Apollo,
Achilles destroys the Trojan ranks, ' flecking with gore his
irresistible hands '—and the book ends.

The book is, for the more part, unworthy of Homer,

or below our conception of his work. That, in itself, is no
reason why we should refuse it to him. Occasionally
he nods. Again, as has often been said, wherever the
gods take part in the war, instant and inevitable confusion
follows, by the very nature of myth. Homer's religious sense,
when he seems to speak for himself, is pure and high ; even
in mythology his standard is much above that of Hesiod
and of the old temple legends. Homer represents a break
or 'fault' in Greek mythical tradition ; he avoids the tales of
old divine horrors and of bestial amours. But, when his
deities take part in the war, the nature of his task is too
difficult for him. This explains much, but it does not
explain the prologue of the book (1–74) heralding a divine
battle which is not fought in this, but in the next book.
The strange thing is that, when the prologue and the fight
were divorced, the diaskeuast did not join them more skilfully.

The whole passage about Achilles and Æneas (168–350)
would not have appeared so unheroic to an Homeric
audience as to us. All the heroes, except Odysseus, Diomede, and Aias, are capable of fear, and have days when
their courage is unequal to the demands on it. This is
usually accounted for by the action of the gods, a system
which is part, and a confusing part, of Homeric psychology.
The long boasts and speeches, again, answer to the *gabes* of
the heroes in the *Chansons de geste*. When they were composed they were assuredly not thought out of place. The
excuses which Poseidon, the foe of the Trojans, gives for
rescuing Æneas are also valid. But, when Poseidon announces that the seed of Æneas shall not perish, we have
a distinct sign of reference to some princely house which
claimed descent from the pious Trojan (307). In line 219
in the genealogical speech of Æneas we read that Dardanus
begat Erichthonius, an Attic heroic name, and that Dar-

danus had the wind-begotten steeds, elsewhere assigned to
Tros (v. 265). All this may point, as Mr. Leaf suggests, to
an Attic interpolation, a theory which Fick, its author,
supports by certain Attic forms of words in the passage.

As to all this episode of Æneas, the difficulty is one
which we often meet. Whether the poems were, at first,
orally transmitted, or existed in writing, on material probably rude, it is easy to see how some passages might be
lost, and easy to see that reciters or authors might interpolate others. But it is not easy to see how interpolations,
which must have been made by one man, in one place,
and for a personal or local reason, found their way into a
text which must very early have been generally accepted.
We need some such action as the recension of Pisistratus,
whether he was the first to commit the poems to writing,
as Wolf supposes, or whether he and his friend, as Bergk
holds, anticipated the Alexandrians by collecting MSS.
and producing an edition What is the archetypal MS. of
the vulgate, as it existed in Plato's time, and earlier as
Xenophanes and Theagenes knew it? Some such arche-
type must have been accepted, and how did passages of
suspicious and probably local origin, like the episode of
Æneas, succeed in entering the canon? Tradition which
is general, if vague and late, points to Athens as the least
improbable centre of diffusion. But what guided the
selection of the Athenian critics, who, *ex hypothesi*, must
have had extremely various texts before them? Late or
conservative they must have been, or they would have
given more place to deeds of Athenian heroes. We have
already suggested that the Nelidæ, at least, had a motive
for enforcing the praises and enlarging the part of Nestor.
Beyond this even probabilities appear to fail us, nor can we
guess how the twentieth book came to be so formless, and
how or why it admitted 'the .Eneid.'

Still, in this puzzling case, we do see a motive for interpolation.   A royal house in the Troad, pretending to descent from Æneas, had good reasons for foisting in a passage
to his credit, and to the credit of their own claims.   The
problem as to how the interpolation gained acceptance is,
as usual, obscure.   But it is less obscure than common.
The lines xx. 219-230 are pretty obviously an attempt to
connect Athens with the Trojan royal family.   Strabo
avers that the Athenians, for political purposes, claimed a
mythical kinship with Troy, about 610 B.C.   Here, then,
are motives for interpolation, and tradition generally suspects Athens as a place where such interpolation could be
arranged.   Without accepting the Pisistratean legend as
veracious, we can yet see that Athens was likely to have a
hand in producing the original form of the vulgate.   So
the questions about book xx. are almost answered, and
here we can give up much, without committing ourselves
to a wholesale hypothesis of early and late patches and
changes.

BOOK XXI

The twenty-first book contains some of the noblest and
some of the weakest passages in the Iliad.   It is argued
that 'beauty and pathos' are not in themselves enough
to prove the antiquity of the Death of Lycaon (34-138).
To this it can only be replied that a masterpiece, as
Mr. Matthew Arnold says, is not compatible with collaboration.   If the death of Lycaon is not by the original
poet, we must believe in another of equal eminence in
the same manner, and the belief is difficult.   But, if we
are not to think the death of Lycaon necessarily original
because of its excellence, we ought, by parity of reasoning, not to reject the 'Battle of the Gods' (385-513)
because of its badness.   To us it may seem bad, though

a critic in the *Spectator* selects the passage where Hera boxes the ears of Artemis (481–488) as a typical example of Homer's belief in intellectual superiority.[1] When the gods of the Iliad mix with men, or interest themselves especially in the cause of men, modern criticism is lost. We cannot place ourselves at the point of view. It is not so in the Odyssey, and this is, perhaps, as strong an argument as any other for attributing a separate authorship to the two epics. Mr. Leaf regards the Battle of the Gods as 'an early parody'—this is the best excuse for it—' a precursor of the Battle of the Frogs and Mice. To attribute such work to any of the older poets of the Epos is to deny the possibility of any rational criticism in this field.' We fancy that few readers of the Iliad, few who recall the episode of Athene, Aphrodite, and Diomede, will think the divine battle a parody. We must remember what the gods were, and how Zeus kicked Hephæstus and Atê out of heaven, like Ataentsic in Iroquois mythology ; how Zeus challenges the gods to the 'tug of war,' how he ' dashed them about his house ' ; how Ares was once shut up in a huge pot, and so forth. There is no limit to what the gods may endure in the way of despite at each other's hands. Again, we note in the Theomachy, Homer's consistent antipathy to the bully, Ares, a feature of both Iliad and Odyssey. Once more, if we are to deny the Theomachy to Homer because we think it bad, how much more must we deny to Milton the gunpowder and guns in the battle of angels and devils ! If Homer is bad, how much worse is Milton ! It may be argued that Milton is following Homer. That is true ; but he outdoes him in evil, and if Milton followed Homer here, he, a great poet, cannot have regarded the Theomachy with the contempt of Mr. Leaf. The Battle of the Gods leads to nothing, it

[1] *Spectator*, March 21, 1891.

fills up no pause in the story ; altogether, is is artistically indefensible according to our notions of art. But we all do err, and if badness is to be the test of separate authorship, while our estimate is the test of badness, what author can escape disintegration ? If the piece is an interpolation, it is an interpolation without any obvious motive. It connects nothing with anything else ; it gratifies no local, no family, feeling. The story of book xxi. is this : Achilles drives the Trojans to the ford of Scamander, takes prisoners to slay in honour of Patroclus, and kills many, defiling the sacred River, and arousing his anger. He slays Lycaon, son of Priam, in a passage of the most painful grandeur and beauty, full of ruthlessness, justified by a sense of the ruthlessness of life. He also slays Asteropæus. Some genealogy is introduced here, and the death of Asteropæus is criticised as a mere variant on that of Lycaon, and as inconsistently described. Siegfried asks, on which side of the river is Achilles ?[1] This was a difficulty with Zenodotus. Aristarchus was not puzzled by it. The hero is now on one side, now on another, now in the middle of the water, spearing Trojans like salmon. Achilles leaves Asteropæus on the sands (171). The bank is described as ' high,' yet the river carries away the corpse (201–204). Then did the river overflow its high bank ?[2] What happened is as clear as may be. There was a high bank, with footing below it, on the wave-washed gravel or sand. Achilles threw his spear at Asteropæus ; he missed ; the spear stuck in the bank behind Asteropæus ; he tried thrice to draw it out and use it ; he failed, and Achilles struck him with the sword, and left him lying on the wave-washed sand where he had stood below the bank. The affair is as plain as if one saw it. Asteropæus, standing almost in the water,

[1] Hentze, *Anhang*, book xxi., introd. p. 81.
[2] Siegfried, Hentze, *l.c.* p. 84.

on the sand below the bank, throws two spears at Achilles.
The spear of Achilles sticks behind him in the bank. He
tries to draw it forth, and is killed ere he succeeds. Then
he falls forward, probably with half his body in the water,
and is gradually washed into the current. If Siegfried were
an angler he would understand the situation. Far from
being 'a weaker echo of the death of Lycaon,' the poem
here shows us a brave man's death, while Lycaon dies in the
attitude of a suppliant. Objections like that of Siegfried's
only prove an ardent desire to pick holes. A similar desire
is shown in the discussions as to whether the river is angry
because of the taunts of Achilles (136), or because his
Trojan worshippers are slain (146), or because his stream
is choked by the dead (218). These causes are cumulative : one might suffice ; but why should they not combine ? Other difficulties, it may be suspected, have their
source in the bold and impetuous style of the passage,
which leaves little room for fulness and consistency of
detail.[1] The river god rises against Achilles, and nearly
drowns him inglorious, 'like a swine-herd boy crossing a flooded water.' Athene and Poseidon, disguised as
men, give Achilles strength. As in the case where Poseidon
appeared like an old man, we are not told what men they
represent. This may justify the earlier story, or throw
doubt on the later. Scamander and Simois join forces,
Hera sends Hephæstus against them, a fire parches them,
they make peace. The gods now fall to war. Apollo, who
refuses to fight, goes to Troy ; the deities return to Olympus.
Achilles pursues the Trojans ; they rush pellmell through
the gates ; Apollo urges Agenor to war, and then rescues
him, when he has beguiled Achilles from the gate. The
critics who regard the piece as a patchwork suggest many
different ways of extricating the original passages. Hentze

[1] Monro.

P

concludes that the Theomachy and the death of Asteropæus are foreign to the original poem.[1] We may hope that
the Theomachy is ; but there is no proof of it, unless it
be the absurdly mixed metaphor of line 465, and the death
of Asteropæus is an excellent contrast to that unmanly end
of Lycaon.

BOOK XXII

Since the study of Homer began, all commentators have
wished to ' obelise,' or reject, lines and passages not to their
private taste. Had Homer been read in the Middle Ages,
there is little doubt that most of book xxii. would have
been ' excised' by critical knights and minstrels. Nor can
most men of Northern blood, and, with the traditions of
knightly honour in their minds, of knightly honour and
of Northern courage, read it without shame as well as
sorrow. But we do not reject it for Homeric merely because the evidence of all the Muses singing out of heaven
could never convince us that Hector fled from Achilles.
In a saga or a *chanson de geste*, in an Arthurian romance,
in a Border ballad, in whatever poem or tale answers in our
Northern literature, however feebly, to Homer, this flight
round the walls of Troy would be an absolute impossibility.
Under the eyes of his father, his mother, his countrymen,
Hector flies—the gallant Hector, 'a very perfect gentle
knight'—from the onset of a single foe. Can we fancy
Skarphedin, or Gunnar, or Grettir, or Olaf Howard's son
flying from one enemy ? Can we imagine Lancelot of the
Lake, who naked held Guinevere's bower against an armed
multitude, retreating from before a single knight? No
ballad-monger would have been believed who said that the
Douglas or the Percy turned his back on a foe. Assuredly
the hearers of the sagas, the audience of the Trouvère who
chanted that lost fight in Roncesvaux, or the readers of

[1] *Anhang*, on book xxi. introd. p. 98.

Mallory, or Sidney, who loved to listen to *Chevy Chase* from the lips of a blind crowder, would all have rejected the twenty-second book and the story of Hector's flight. We do not, of course, reject it. Homer's world, Homer's chivalry, Homer's ideas of knightly honour, were all unlike those of the Christian and the Northern world. Roland will not even blow a blast on that dread horn for all the multitude of the paynims. But Hector, the hope of Troy, fled thrice round the walls from a single spear.

We must take Homer as we find him. The critics, as a rule, admit that there is much of the original Μῆνις in the twenty-second book. The story is that Hector remains without the Scæan gates when the other Trojans have fled within. Achilles, leaving the pursuit of Apollo in the guise of Agenor, rushes again to the gates, while Priam, seeing him, laments his hapless destiny. Neither he nor Hecuba can move Hector to come within the gates. He is full of 'courage unquenchable,' we are told; but this must be relative to the standard of courage in his time.[1] Had he not declined to listen to Polydamas, in book xviii., he would now enter Troy. But he dare not face the reproaches of Polydamas. This passage (xxii. 99) is, of course, excised by commentators who have already excised xviii. 249, the scene with Polydamas. This is the usual method. If a part disliked by a commentator is elsewhere of importance to the story, both pieces are interpolations. If the passage does *not* affect the later development of the plot, and is not later referred to, then, for that reason, it is an interpolation also. It is not easy, in our age, to satisfy critics.[2] A part of Hector's soliloquy (111–130) is also obelised, and the idyllic touch about the converse of youth and maiden (128) is thought especially obnoxious. Some

---

[1] *Anhang*, book xxii. p. 8.
[2] Bergk, Niese, and others. Hentze, viii. 8.

commentators make the original poem end with line 394 or 393—'We have slain goodly Hector.' Many think the lament of Andromache (477 ff.) an interpolation in whole or in part. The description of an orphan's miseries is thought inappropriate to the son of a prince. Aristarchus had a similar view of 'the becoming.' Perhaps we do not know enough of Homeric society to feel certain on this point. We know that the father of a prince, like Laertes in the Odyssey, might be much neglected in old age. As to orphans, we have only the evidence of this suspected passage. It may be noticed that Priam's proposal to go forth and beg for the body of Hector from Achilles (416–418) seems to lead up to his actual expedition in book xxiv.—a book which most of the critics regard as a later addition to the poem. Bergk recognises in the canto the excellences of the true poet. It is remarkable that when the true poet had to pit against each other a courteous and patriotic warrior like Hector and a young hero who, like Achilles, is really fighting only for his own hand and his private passion, he should have made Hector check our sympathy by his flight, and Achilles even more unsympathetic by the treacherous aid of Athene than by his own relentless and savage revenge. All this should warn us not to judge of Homer's taste and his conduct of the tale by our own standard.

BOOKS XXIII, XXIV

The last two books seem to concentrate all the difficulties that attend the study of Homeric composition. On the one hand, they are for the most part books of extraordinary poetic excellence. The funeral of Patroclus and the description of the games are passages instinct with life and fire. In the twenty-fourth book the long war of passions closes, as with a dying fall of music, in the meeting of the old, bereaved, and ruined Priam, and Achilles, the youth

conscious of his doom. Thus to end an epic of war is
consonant with the genius of Greek art. On the other
hand, it may be urged that the repentance of Achilles, his
permitting the body of Hector to be ransomed, shows
a higher morality than the general tone of the Iliad, where
the corpses of enemies are despitefully treated ; where it is
threatened, for example, that the head of Patroclus shall be
set on a spike above the walls of Troy, like loyal heads in
1746. The language of the two books, especially of the
last, has many peculiarities more in accordance with the
style of the Odyssey than of the Iliad. The two books,
again, are thought 'to represent two different ways of bringing the poem to an end,' and the second episode, it is
said, 'tends to disturb the effect of the first.' [1] But
this, perhaps, is hypercritical, as it is to complain that the
games are described in a cheerful manner, while the last book
is pathetic.

On the whole question the mind is divided between
two difficulties. We cannot readily believe in an array of
poets, each capable of bringing such great qualities to the
enlargement and elaboration of another's work. Against this
must be set the linguistic argument and the apparent advance
in moral ideas. In regard to both these arguments in favour
of a new hand, or new hands, in the last books of the Iliad
and in the Odyssey, one point has rather escaped observation.
We are told that, between the composition of books xxiii.,
xxiv., and of the Odyssey, on the one side, and of the
original Μῆνις on the other, there must have been time for
the development of considerable changes in syntax, in
morality, and in the use of the article. All this seems,
in an age not particularly progressive, to demand many
years, if not several centuries. But Homeric manners and
customs remain all this time practically unaltered. Wolf

[1] Monro.

himself remarks about the poems, 'In them all things agree
in the same character, the same manners, the same way of
thinking and speaking.' He calls it 'a marvellous agreement,' and explains it, in a manner no longer credible, as
a harmony established by the Alexandrine critics.[1] Modern
critics do not admit that there is the same mode *sentiendi
et loquendi* in the last two books. But the unity, the
harmony, and congruity of Homeric manners throughout
Iliad and Odyssey are scarcely to be denied, when we allow
for the different sorts of circumstances with which the two
epics are concerned. Now, it seems unlikely that there
should be time for great linguistic and moral changes without great changes in manners. All these considerations
make in favour of the originality of the last two books, and
for the contemporaneous origin of the Odyssey. If we care
for a poet's opinion, we find Shelley saying that, towards
the close of the epic, 'Homer truly begins to be himself.
The battle of the Scamander, the funeral of Patroclus, and
the high and solemn close of the whole bloody tale in
tenderness and inexpiable sorrow, are wrought in a manner
incomparable with anything of the same kind.'[2] 'In the
face of such testimony,' says Mr. Monro, 'can we say that
the book in which the climax is reached, in which the last
remaining discords of the Iliad are dissolved in chivalrous
pity and respect, is not the work of the original poet, but of
some Homerid or rhapsodist?' We may add that the
Greeks in all ages were keenly interested in funerals ; the
mere remark of Achilles that Patroclus was to have a great
funeral (xviii. 334, xxii. 385–390) would hardly suffice them,
but rather heighten their expectations. Again, if we are to
believe that the twenty-fourth book is the fruit of a new and
higher morality, it seems odd that, when the poem was

[1] *Prolegomena,* 2nd ed. p. 160.
[2] *Essays, &c.,* vol. ii. p. 234.

being altered at will, the ruthlessness and treachery of Athene's conduct to Hector were not removed. If interpolators and Homerids could do so much, it is a perpetual puzzle why they left so much undone. On the whole, the opinions of readers will probably vary, depending much on their own taste, and their preference for the beliefs of poets or the theories of professors.

The objections which have been made to details in the twenty-third book are sometimes rather petty, and almost illiterate. The story runs thus : Achilles sends the Myrmidons to drive solemnly round the body of Patroclus, and orders the funeral feast. In his sleep he sees the ghost of Patroclus, who complains that, till he is buried, he cannot cross 'the River,' the other ghosts drive him away. A pyre is built, and the body is burned. Next day the bones are gathered, and placed in the howe. Achilles then holds the funeral games, and offers prizes. There is a chariot race, a boxing match, wrestling, a foot race, a fencing match 'with sharps,' putting the weight, archery, and a spear-throwing prize, yielded, without competition, to Agamemnon.

A few of the many objections may be noted. In xix. 211, the body of Patroclus is lying in the hut of Achilles. In xxiii. 13, it is on the sands, and Achilles drives his chariot round it. This is a terrible discrepancy, which we need hardly linger over. The appearance of the shade of Patroclus causes discussions. Where is the ghost? He says he cannot 'cross the river' till he has been buried (71–73), yet he 'wanders along the wide-gated dwelling of Hades.' In the Odyssey, the dead Elpenor and the slain wooers mix with the other ghosts before being buried. Patroclus cannot. Elpenor, to be sure, asks for burial, 'lest haply I bring on thee the vengeance of the gods.' But neither Elpenor nor the wooers complain of being excluded. This, at least, would look as if the poet of the Odyssey was not the author of the speech of Patroclus's ghost. In truth, the mythic theories of Hades and the state of the dead are so fluctuating, in all religions, that we need not wonder to find inconsistencies here. The ghost asks Achilles to 'give him his hand,' but, when Achilles would embrace him, vanishes. Such is the manner of dreams. Again, the Myrmidons have their feast (29-34), but Achilles dines with Agamemnon. This is hardly matter for marvel. No man, in his mood, would have cared to dine with a crowd of Myrmidons in a humour of funereal festivity. This consideration may answer Hentze's objection (*l.c.* p. 44) with an appropriate measure of wisdom.

About the games there are difficulties. Nestor gives Antilochus a great deal of advice about turning the post at the mid distance—advice of a nature obvious to the least sagacious charioteer—and implying that Nestor knows what the course will be, before Achilles has chosen it. He also speaks of 'a withered stump and two white stones' as an old goal, or, perhaps, the monument of a man dead. Heyne says that there is no evidence for wooden pillars as sepulchral monuments in Greek antiquity. The poet, or interpolator, must have known more than we do on that head. The oar of Elpenor, in the Odyssey, is to be fixed above his howe, the memorial of a luckless man. Nestor's speech is obscure, and it is prosy, but the Polonius of the Iliad is nothing if not tedious. If the obscurities be not 'of an epic sort,' are we to suppose that the speech was interpolated after epic tradition was lost? Whom would that profit; or are we to imagine that Nestor's speeches are maladroit compliments to the Nelidæ, the family of Pisistratus, in Athens? The speech in no way affects the race, for Antilochus nearly fouls the chariot of Menelaus, but does nothing particular at the turning-point. Sittl defends the passage as charac-

teristic of Nestor, which it really is.[1] The quarrel about
nothing between Idomeneus and Aias is blamed (449-499).
It is much more in accordance with the sullen arrogance of
Aias, as we read of him in the Odyssey, than with his performances as a gallant man of war in the Iliad. He insults
Idomeneus for merely expressing an opinion as to which
chariot was leading.[2] Pappenheim concludes that this
spirited passage is a later interpolation. Bergk thinks it
a true sketch of Greek sporting life, but not in keeping
with the knightly character of the Iliad.[3] As, however, the
games were imitated by Arctinus, in the *Æthiopis*, they
cannot be very late. The objections to the last three contests are, poetically speaking, scarcely to be disputed. They
seem like the work of a later sporting reporter, and it is
easy to conceive that such a person would try his hand,
though it is hard to imagine how he obtained currency for
his work. The courtesy of Achilles, in the whole book,
and the *amende honorable* of Antilochus to Menelaus are
worthy of the poet. The Germans express contending
opinions. Hentze has no doubt that the games are by a
later poet, and foreign to the original epic. Christ, like
Bergk, thinks them older than Arctinus. Fick makes them
not earlier than 680 B.C., but 'before the Ionising of the
Epic' (550 B.C.).

BOOK XXIV

To the original position in the poem of book xxiv. we have
already recounted the objections. The gods weary of the
prolonged brutality of Achilles—and perhaps they might
well be thought to weary, seeing the same hideous spectacle
every day—we need hardly imagine a change in moral
sentiments ; it is enough that the insults to the corpse are

---

[1] Hentze, *l.c.* p. 51.   [2] Pappenheim. Hentze, *l.c.* p. 52.
[3] Bergk, i. 644.

continued. The objection that Hermes is here the guide
of men, as in the Odyssey, is not powerful. Iris appears,
as usual, in this very book as the messenger ; the guide
has a different function. The mention by Helen of her
twenty years' absence from Greece (765) is a considerable
difficulty, but we do not know (except, indeed, from the
Odyssey) how long Homer supposes the Greeks to have
been occupied in preparing their expedition. About the
allusion to the judgment of Paris it may be confessed
that, if Homer was to introduce it, he was likely to do so
more frequently than in this solitary place (29, 30). In the
beginning of the book there are several lines which seem to
be interpolated—for example, 20, 21, where the Ægis is
conceived of as a goatskin, not as a shield. In 29, 30,
words are used in a manner absolutely un-Homeric.
Lines 181–187 are repeated in the message of Iris,
where they should be omitted, for the courage of Priam in
venturing to approach Achilles is increased by his ignorance
that Hermes is to be his guide, and in these lines Iris gives
him this information. For the rest, the language contains
many Odyssean lines and phrases. If, therefore, we are to
regard the Odyssey as considerably later than the Iliad, we
must refer this book to the same period. The difficulties
of either hypothesis have already been stated. It is curious
that opinions and style should change so considerably,
while manners and customs change so little ; and it is
strange that so great a poet as the author of book xxiv.
should have merged his own in another's work. His
description of the hut of Achilles makes it in structure,
though not in splendour of appointments, resemble an heroic
palace. In this, perhaps, there is nothing very extraordinary,
but this argument has been used in favour of an ' Odyssean '
authorship. The German conjectures as to the date and
authorship of this noble canto, perhaps the most dramatic

—assuredly the most pathetic—portion of the Iliad, are numerous and so various that they carry no conviction.[1] The possession of the poem must suffice us, and to credit the original poet with its authorship is, at least, a pious opinion. The only severe test to faith is found in the character of the language. And we cannot believe that our poet would have ended his lay leaving Hector unburied.

CONCLUSION OF ANALYSIS

We have now run through the whole plot of the Iliad, and examined at least some of the more prominent objections to its unity. Reviewing the task, we find that we have felt constrained to abandon the little 'Æneid' of book xx. as a probable interpolation, the date and motive and possibility of which may be approximately explained. We have also had to abandon the later part of the funeral games as probably un-Homeric. About the tenth book, or Doloneia, we see that it may be a separate composition, but, if so, it is one with little *raison d'être*. The books on fighting, from eleven to sixteen, have not improbably suffered somewhat in the course of the ages. The last two books are so admirable, and admirably adapted to their place, that the presence of Odyssean style and phrase need not make us refuse them to the original author. Their matter, and their peaceful action, under the roofs of Priam's palace and Achilles's hut, are more akin than the matter of the warlike books to the nature of the Odyssey. Hence the resemblances of style may also have arisen.

With these main deductions we accept the Iliad as one epic by one hand. The inconsistencies which are the basis of the opposite theory seem to us reconcileable in many places, in others greatly exaggerated. We doubt if they

[1] Hentze, *l.c.* pp. 110-112.

could ever have been detected by Homer's audience of
ladies and warriors. If they do exist, it is more difficult to
account for their escaping the notice of a 'school' professionally busied in preserving and improving the poem
than for their evading the scrutiny of the original author.
A well-known modern novel, *Robbery under Arms*, by Mr.
Boldrewood, opens with a passage referring to the conclusion, but quite contradictory of that conclusion when it
is reached. This at once strikes a careful, or even a careless, reader, but, like misprints in proof sheets, these things
will escape the wearied and over-familiar eye of an author.
Thus it is more likely that Homer occasionally nodded
than that a whole school of Homeridæ were generally sound
asleep. The extraordinary audacity and incongruity which
are detected in their additions are incompatible with the
conservatism' which they seem only to have displayed
when conservatism according to critical opinion makes nonsense. Again, we attribute many undeniable difficulties to
the self-contradictory nature of mythical fancy, and whenever a god appears we look for a perplexity to follow. If it
did not we might suspect later editing. Finally, to us the
hypothesis of a crowd of great harmonious poets, working
for centuries at the Iliad, and sinking their own fame
and identity in Homer's, appears more difficult of belief
than the opinion that one great poet may make occasional
slips and blunders. We are especially disinclined to believe
in the self-denying collaboration of great poets in the Iliad
after 776 B.C., when such poems as the *Cypria* and
Æthiopis began to be composed by individual authors
whose names survive. They did not add to the Iliad and
hide their fame ; they rather strove to write sequels in their
own interest. As to earlier collaboration, under the
auspices of a school, we have no historical evidence, and
nothing analogous in other national poetry, while the

functions of the school, as guessed at, seem to be self-contradictory. Whoever finds his belief in the separatist opinions shaken will have recourse to the ancient hypothesis of a single great genius, who may conceivably have been able to write, or who, in the strength of a potent memory, may have composed the poems without writing, and may have taught them to successors. Where there is interpolation we incline to attribute its survival to the original editors, not improbably Athenian, of the text which Xenophanes may have known, and Herodotus knew. But this is an extremely difficult part of the subject. If we are right, on the whole, we rescue the divine first poet and master of Greece, and we secure an almost unbroken picture of a single age. If we err, at worst we err with the poets.

CHAPTER VIII

ODYSSEUS AND THE EXTANT ODYSSEY

THE Odyssey has been almost universally recognised as a later poem than the Iliad. Longinus, or whoever wrote the *Treatise of the Sublime*, looked on the Odyssey as the work of Homer's old age—an epic bathed in a mellow light of sunset. Modern criticism has noted in the Odyssey wider geographical knowledge, different mythological ideas, a more reverent attitude towards the gods, a more fully developed morality, and a more advanced condition of language—all affording presumption of comparative recency

The hero of the Odyssey is a rather unobtrusive personage in the Iliad. But in the Odyssey he is, in extremely different and in far more trying circumstances, the same man as the hero with whom the Iliad made us acquainted. In both poems his character for staunchness, eloquence, and shrewdness is consistently maintained. Is Odysseus borrowed, then, from the Iliad by the Odyssey, or is it not the character of the hero that is borrowed from the Odyssey by the Iliad? Or did the poems (or the sagas on which they are based) grow like sisters—side by side, perhaps, through a period of centuries?

Before examining the adventures of Odysseus, in the Odyssey, it may be well to consider these questions and to note what part he bore in the Iliad. Unluckily, no certain ground can be won while the Iliad itself is regarded by critics as a patchwork of different dates. In book i. of the Iliad, Odysseus at once appears as a great chief—one of the small council of kings. He restores Chryseïs to her father ; but this occurs in a passage over which doubt has been thrown (i. 440–480). Here he is styled 'Odysseus of the many counsels.' In book ii. he stands desponding by his ship when the host is fleeing, after the 'trial' by Agamemnon. Here Athene appears as his patroness, which is her position in the Odyssey, and bids him stop the rout. Here, too, he styles himself 'father of Telemachus' (ii. 260, and again in iv. 354). Telemachus, therefore, is known to the Iliad, though, according to the higher critics, he and his adventures had no share in the 'original' Odyssey. But book ii. of the Iliad is regarded as 'not original' by Mr. Leaf, Fick, and many others, and we can only say that, when it was composed, Telemachus was already a familiar figure. He may even have had his part in the legend of Odysseus's wanderings, for, apart from the Odyssey, Telemachus has no *raison d'être*, unless we believe in a separate independent, early Telemachus, which is hardly credible. According to Mr. Leaf, the deed of Odysseus, when he prevented a disgraceful panic, in Iliad ii., is one of the 'earlier expansions.'

In the Catalogue (ii. 631) Odysseus is leader of the Cephallenians and Ithacans, with twelve ships. In the third book Helen points him out to Priam as 'crafty Odysseus, of Ithaca,' and Antenor praises his eloquence. He is described as a short, broad-shouldered man ; he arranges the lists for the duel of Paris and Menelaus. In the fourth book he faces Agamemnon, who has ventured to rebuke him. The king shall see how 'the father of Telemachus' can fight. He keeps his word, and makes Hector give ground (iv. 505). His 'enduring soul'—exhibited in the Odyssey—is mentioned (v. 669), and his patroness, Athene, directs his anger where to rage. In the eighth book he shows less than his usual resolution, and Diomede upbraids him for his retreat. In the ninth book he is chief spokesman in the famous embassy to Achilles, and is addressed as ' Odysseus of many wiles,' his Odyssean appellation. In the tenth book he and Diomede, under the special patronage of Athene, carry off the horses of Rhesus, and slay Dolon and many Trojans. In xi. 395–487 Odysseus alone resists the forces of Troy, like a wounded stag among jackals. He thinks of flight, but asks : ' Wherefore does my heart thus converse with herself, for I know that they are cowards who flee the battle ? ' / ' Endure, my heart,' is his motto here, as always in the Odyssey./ He is wounded, but Pallas Athene diverts the spear from a vital part. In book xiv., with other wounded heroes, he watches the war, leaning on his spear. He sternly rebukes Agamemnon, who proposes retreat (xiv. 82)·: ' I wholly scorn thy thoughts.' In book xix. he comes limping to the meeting of Achilles and Agamemnon. He prevents the Greeks from fighting, as Achilles desired, on empty bellies, and suggests the due form of reconciliation. He it is who brings the gifts of atonement to Achilles. He wrestles with Aias in the funeral games—an even match—and Athene helps him in the foot-race.

These are the chief exploits of Odysseus in the Iliad. The most martial is found in book xi. ; in a portion recognised as ' original ' by the most advanced separatists. The hero's place is clearly marked, he is the wisest of counsellors, the least despondent, the staunchest of men, the special favourite, in book xi.—that original document—as elsewhere, of Athene. If then we say, like Niese, that ' without the Odyssey there is no Odysseus,' we must note that, without the Odyssey, there would be no Odysseus in the Iliad, and must make the Odyssey older than parts of the Iliad where Odysseus appears.[1] According to Niese, the patronage of Odysseus by Athene is a late element in the Odyssey, and is borrowed from the ' Doloneia.'[2] But the goddess watches over and saves him in the eleventh book of the Iliad. Thus his relations with her are as old as the so-called oldest part of the Iliad. How, then, could they be omitted in the original Odyssey? Yet Athene's patronage of Odysseus was no original part - so Niese holds—of the oldest poem on the hero's return ! She takes no part in the story he tells of his adventures.[3] That story, then, must be old. The rest where she appears must be a later addition. So, apparently, the oldest part of the Odyssey, where Athene does not befriend the hero, is older than the oldest part of the Iliad, where Athene does protect her favourite. It is a singular conclusion.

It is plain that the character and status of Odysseus are a puzzle. How did a petty chief, in the remotest part of Greece, manage to inherit (as we shall see that he did inherit) the fame of adventures which are widely rumoured not only through Europe, but among savage races? Why did he whose native realm was distant and obscure, come to be more gloriously renowned than Agamemnon, Menelaus, and all the great heads of royal houses in Achaia, in Thessaly, in Bœotia, in Crete? How did the legend of an island Sennachie, or bard, eclipse the lays of minstrels in golden Mycenæ, in Pylos, in Sparta, in Orchomenos, and Thebes? Odysseus spared the life of his minstrel Phemius, when he slew the wooers. Is his celebrity due to the gratitude of Phemius?

---

[1] Compare Niese, *Die Entwickelung der Homerischen Poesie*, pp. 140, 177, 192, 195.

[2] Iliad, book x.

[3] This is accounted for in *Odyssey*, xiii. 341.

Q

These are vain questions. We cannot discover why popular saga neglects the great, and brings into the sun-light of glory the obscure. Roland (Hruodlandus) is known to history from a single line of Eggihard, as warden of the March of Brittany. Legend has carried all over the world the fame 'of Roland brave and Oliver,' while of Oliver history has not a word to say. Roland eclipses Charlemagne, and Oliver outshines the early Frankish kings. We cannot account for the caprices of romance, which have given to a petty chief an undying fame, crowned him with splendour not his own, attributing to him achievements far older than the date of sacred Ilios. An examination of the Odyssey proves it to be, as Fénelon and Perrault said, *un tas de contes des vieilles*, a mass of old wives' fables, or *Märchen* (popular tales) Many of these are found among Germanic, Celtic, Finnish Basque, Slavonic, Asiatic, and American peoples. The extent of their diffusion indicates extreme antiquity. In the Odyssey all these tales are attached to the person and adventures of Odysseus. How and when incidents which elsewhere are told of nameless heroes crystallised them-selves round a single person, Odysseus, we cannot pretend to say. The phenomenon of such crystallisation is familiar ; we see new wits inheriting old jests, we see Charlemagne, Wallace, Roland becoming centres of attraction for legends much older than their own date. It is probable that Odysseus had become the hero of mythical adventures in popular saga, perhaps of ballad, before the poet composed his song, but how much the poet may have added to the legend is a point which escapes us.

The central *Märchen* round which the others now group themselves in the Odyssey is The Return of the Wandering Husband. This tale exists in modern European ballads of Lorraine and Brittany ; it inspires Scott's poem,

The Noble Morringer.[1]   It is also found in China.[2]   In China, the returned wanderer, anxious to test the fidelity of his wife, pretends to be a friend of her husband, as, indeed, Odysseus also does when in disguise.   As the Chinese warrior is somewhat enterprising, the wife throws a handful of sand in his eyes.   She even tries to hang herself rather than accept the embraces of the stranger, who is recognised for the true husband by her own mother.   This *Märchen*, then, is simple.   A returned husband has a difficulty in overcoming the doubts of a chaste and faithful wife.   Penelope is the Faithful Wife, and, originally, there may have been an old Greek tale or ballad to this effect, not including any adventures of the wanderer nor any revenge on the wooers, and not even attached to the legend of Troy.

In Niese's system, indeed, this legend appears to be the original *Nostos*, or return of Odysseus.   We are not disinclined to believe that in some such lost story or ballad we have, indeed, the germ of the Odyssey, but we do not hold that the germ was gradually developed and added to by a series of poets, redactors, and botchers.   Popular fancy more probably combined other *Märchen* into the tale which one poet finally chose as his theme.   Every *Märchen* is an arrangement of incidents, some or all of which may be found, differently arranged, in other *Märchen*.   Popular fancy probably combined several *Märchen*, in the same way, into an Odysseus saga before the poet took it up, and, perhaps, connected the hero with the Trojan affairs.   There may have been an Odysseus before there was an Ilios.

[1] Puymaigre and Villemarqué, in *Barzaz Breiz* (see also Luzel), and in *Chants Populaires du Pays Messin*.   The subject is treated in the author's *Etudes Traditionistes* (Paris, 1890), pp. 66–79, and in Gerland's *Altgriechische Märchen in der Odyssee*.

[2] Dennys, *China and the Chinese*.

This *Märchen* of the wandering husband has no necessary connection with *Märchen* of ' The Shifty Lad,' whose
astuteness in popular tales proves more than a match for
giants and magicians.   One of the wiles of this person gets
the better of a giant, the hero giving a false name, such as
' Nobody' or 'I myself' in the Esthonian version.   This
fable is familiar in Celtic legend, as in ' The Black Thief'
of the *Hibernian Tales*.   In an excursus (ii.) to Mr.
Merry's ' Odyssey,' are collected mediæval, Arabian, Tartar,
Esthonian examples of the story, taken from W. Grimm,
Die Sage von Polyphem.[1]

As W. Grimm says, in this adventure of the Cyclops
Odysseus displays recklessness foreign to his character, both
in approaching and taunting the monster.   But, as the
Odyssey stands, this adventure is now central and essential.
If he had not blinded the Cyclops, the hero would not have
incurred the wrath of Poseidon, and might have reached
home with all his company.   But the absence of his
company is essential to the interest of the story.   As in
the Iliad all turns on the prayer of a minor goddess, Thetis,
so in the Odyssey all depends on the prayer of a son of a
god, the prayer of the Cyclops to his father, Poseidon.
The utterance of this prayer is, in a sense, inconsistent.
The Cyclopes, indeed, put their faith in the gods (ix. 107),
but yet ' they reck nothing of Zeus nor of the blessed gods '
(ix. 276), according to the Cyclops, who, however, himself
prays to Poseidon.   But his boast that his race recks not of
the gods is clearly an individual piece of arrogance, for his
kinsfolk (ix. 412) mention Zeus with reverence and bid
Polyphemus pray to his father, Poseidon.   The inconsistency, therefore, is of no importance.

When once the encounter with the Cyclops had been
attached to the legend of the Returned Husband, and when

[1] Berlin, 1857.

that hero was once regarded as the favourite of Athene and as persecuted by Poseidon, the way was clear for introducing other adventures which would beset the wanderer. Circe, the enchantress, who turns men into animals, is merely the witch of a *Märchen*, and a very close analogy is found in the Indian collection of Somadeva, which collection, as a whole, is of the thirteenth century, A.D. The witch, after transforming a company into beasts, is vanquished by a magical formula in the mouth of a young traveller, whom she then bids to her bed. An Indian parallel to the Phaeacian isle occurs in the same collection. Scylla, again, is a mythical *pieuvre*, as in Victor Hugo's romance, a mere seaman's marvel ; the rocks wandering were familiar to the Aztecs ; the descent into Hell is accomplished by Wainamoinen in Finland, by Conan in Celtic legend, and generally by the heroes of North American and Maori tales, as it is also in the *Chanson de Roland*, by Siglorel. The Læstrygonians are cannibals or 'weendigoes,' such as in Zululand and North America and Europe haunt the forests of faery ; but in the Odyssey they appear to have a Scandinavian colour, and the description of their home on a fiord may be inspired by travellers' tales of the realm of the midnight sun. Æolus, who gives the winds to Odysseus in a bag, is an heroic ancestor of the witches who, down to the present century, sold winds in the same fashion to Scottish mariners.

Thus the matter of the Odyssey is a heap of separate *Märchen* woven into a matchless tissue of romance. The tales are now dated at the epoch of the Trojan leaguer, are partly localised, and are attached to the lord of Ithaca. In what kind of age would this be done? What would be the period of long epic poems? The Odyssey itself shows us court minstrels delivering long poems, so that, on a given occasion, Demodocus recites part of an epic, beginning at a given point (viii. 500)—the point where the city has

fallen, and the Achæans are about to return.   Such a lay
could not really have arisen within ten years of the fall of
Ilios, but the poet transfers into the past the poetical habits
of his own time.   Long poems, as Nutzhorn observed,[1]
followed by Mr. Monro, and Mr. Jevons in his *History
of Greek Literature*, were suited for a court minstrel with
a regular audience, meeting nightly in hall.   On the other
hand, short cantos were adapted to the popular audiences
of a later democratic age assembled only for a brief
festival, and addressed by reciting rhapsodists.   Thus a
remote period of Achæan royalty would foster epics of
considerable length, from which a later democratic age
selected separate cantos for recitation.   If we consider thus,
we are rather inclined to believe that the heroic age
developed lengthy epics, than that old short lays were
strung together about the date of 700–550 B.C. into long
epics for which there was then apparently no audience.
Thus the Odyssey as it stands, with allowance for interpolation and accident, is more likely to be earlier than later.
The great element which does not partake of the character
of familiar popular tales, the element of the wooers, and
the revenge on the wooers, attests an early, not a late and
law-abiding, condition of Greek manners and society.   Law
has little hold in Homer : the only important law here is
that of revenge and the blood-feud, which is very strictly
observed in Scandinavian fashion.   Though unessential to
the mere isolated *Märchen* of the *Returned Husband*
or the *Faithful Wife*, the affair of the wooers was highly
interesting to heroic society, much less so to an age of law.
Greek historical times present no parallel to Ithaca under
the wooers.   Our contention is, then, that a poet of the
heroic Achæan age, with the Tale of Troy for his poetical
environment, and with a mass of stories, songs, and tradi-

---

[1] *Entstehungsweise*, p. 91.

tions for his material, produced the Odyssey very much as it stands now. He employed traditional epic formulæ, and practised that economy in the use of recurring lines, many of them found also in the Iliad, which marks the early ballad manner, and survives into the epic. But we do not believe that he mechanically incorporated whole masses of earlier lays, nor dove-tailed in whole earlier epics. He worked like Scott in the *Lay*, not like Lönnrot in the *Kalewala* ; he selected themes, and composed them into a whole, he did not stitch together pre-existing ballads, lays, and longer poems.

The story of the Odyssey must now be briefly recapitu-lated. The action occupies a space of exactly six weeks, forty-two days, but embraces the narrative of all that Odysseus did after the fall of Troy.

The ordained time has arrived (i. 16) when the gods have decided that Odysseus shall return to Ithaca, avenge himself on the wooers, and recover his own. Pallas Athene, in an assembly of gods, prays to Zeus for his restoration, taking occasion by Zeus's remarks on the folly of men, and the avenging of Agamemnon by his son, Orestes. Why is Zeus angry with Odysseus? Zeus, setting forth the exposi-tion of the story, explains that it is Poseidon (at this moment in Ethiopia) who persecutes Odysseus for the blinding of Polyphemus, his son. Meanwhile Odysseus is detained by a goddess, daughter of Atlas, in her isle, the centre of the deep.[1] Athene bids Hermes be sent to release Odysseus, meanwhile she will go to Ithaca, and hearten the son of Odysseus, Telemachus, to speak his mind to the men who, for four years, have wooed his mother, Penelope, and wasted his substance. Also she will send him to Pylos and

---

[1] The name of the isle Ogygia is taken by Wilamowitz to be really an adjective, meaning 'oceanic,' mistaken by later poets for a proper name.

Sparta to seek news of his father, win renown, and gather manhood by travel. She appears in Ithaca in guise of Mentes, a Taphian chief, and marvels at the rabble rout of wooers. Telemachus explains the state of affairs : Athene then gives her advice in a passage which has been critically censured (i. 269–298). Athene departs in the shape of a sea eagle. Telemachus, returning, finds his mother remonstrating with the minstrel, who is singing of the *Nostos* or return of the other Achæans. Telemachus, now encouraged by Athene, sends Penelope to her room, and warns the wooers that to-morrow, in an assembly, he will call witnesses to his bidding them begone. If they do not obey they will perish, and no blood-price will be paid for them. The wooers are amazed, night falls, they go home, Telemachus sleeps, attended by old Eurycleia, the nurse, an important character.[1]

In the second book, Telemachus calls the assembly, and gives before the whole people as witnesses the warning which he had already uttered in private. Antinous, a wooer, explains the earlier policy of Penelope, the famous tale of the web unwoven. He declares that Telemachus shall have no peace till his mother marries. Just as in Iliad ii. we were shown the feelings of the Achæan host at large, so here we learn, from Halitherses, what the Ithacans in general think of the wooers. Halitherses repeats the prophecy he had made at the beginning of the war that Odysseus would return in the twentieth year—that is, immediately. He is scouted, and Telemachus is told by a wooer that Mentor will assist him in his proposed expedition to Pylos, if he ever goes. Telemachus approaches the sea,

---

[1] The critical objections to all this exposition of the poem will be discussed later. The separatist theory looks on book i., or most of it, as a prelude added *après coup*, and late, by an incompetent redactor, or compiler.

fashioning of a raft ; the voyage ; the wrecking of the raft, the final piece of spite by Poseidon ; the appearance of the sea maid, Leucothea, to Odysseus, with a present of her veil ; the swimming of Odysseus to shore, his difficult landing in Phæacia, his sleep in a wood.

Book v. covers days 8-12-32. In book vi. (day 33) Odysseus meets and is clothed by Nausicaa, daughter of Alcinous and Arete, king and queen of the country. He is asked his name by Arete, but withholds it for the moment and merely explains how he was wrecked on his voyage from Calypso's isle, and how he was clothed by Nausicaa, that most beautiful creation of the poet. Alcinous promises him safe convoy home in the magic ships of Phæacia.

The doings of the thirty-fourth day occupy books vii., viii., ix., x., xi., xii. In viii., the Phæacians hold sports ; Odysseus is rudely challenged, and, by Athene's aid, wins great renown. The minstrel sings part of the Trojan lay ; Odysseus weeps, as he hears the tale of the Wooden Horse ; he is asked for his story, and, in the following books, the 'Apologia,' recounts all his adventures after the fall of Troy, first announcing his name. This, according to Kirchhoff, he should have done at first, in book vii. Lehrs remarks that Odysseus did not do it then because he was not a blockhead, a curt way of explaining that the poet waited for a more telling moment, a nobler *éclaircissement*, when Odysseus was no mere shipwrecked mariner, but famous for his prowess in the games, and the centre of all men's eyes. Kirchhoff, however, holds that his *Bearbeiter* has been meddling and making opportunities for inserting cooked-up pieces of older poems.

The tale told by Odysseus begins with his leaving Troy, and includes a fight with the Cicones, followed by a wind that drove him wandering past Malea, the southern point of Peloponnesus. Nine days' sail at adventure brought

him into fairyland, and out of all reckoning. He reached
the Lotus-eaters, and next the Cyclopes. Here comes in
the source of all his woe—he blinded the Cyclops, Poseidon's son. The adventure is part of fairy tale. Next he
reached the floating isle of Æolus (book x.), king of the
winds, who gave him all winds but a favourable one, in a
bag, as witches use. When close to Ithaca, his comrades
opened the bag, out flew the gales, and drove him back
to Æolus, who rejected him for his bad luck. Seven days'
sail brought him to the Land of the Midnight Sun—
'there a sleepless man might have earned a double wage.'
There he anchored one ship—his own—off the mouth of a
fiord ; his crews in the ships within the fiord were destroyed
by the huge cannibal Læstrygonians. Then he reached
Circe's isle, and, by aid of Hermes, dominated Circe, and
made her restore the men whom she had changed to swine.
He dwelt with her for a year, his men murmured, he asked
leave to go, but first Circe made him visit Hades. At the
side of Ocean, the limit of the world, in the realm of endless
darkness, the home of the Cimmerians, he landed, and
advanced to the poplar grove of Persephone. The sunless
Cimmerian land is, perhaps, the obverse of the land of
endless daylight. Tales of the Arctic North may have
reached the poet, borne with the amber of the Baltic down
the sacred way. The object of this adventure is to receive
prophecy from the shade of Tiresias, who warns Odysseus
against eating the Cattle of the Sun in Thrinacia, foretells
his success against the wooers, and instructs him as to his
later conduct in propitiation of Poseidon. Kirchhoff
recognises most of this book (xi.) as a cooked-up but
otherwise genuine fragment of an old *Nostos*, or Poem of
the Return.

The ancients regarded parts of the book as spurious.
The importance of the book demands a more minute

summary of its contents. Circe (x. 513) had described the place of entering Hades as one where 'into Acheron flows Pyriphlegethon and Cocytus, a branch of the water of Styx ; thereby is a rock, and the meeting of two roaring waters.' In book xi. (22) they come to the place which Circe had described, but no fresh account is given of it. There they dig a trench, sacrifice to the dead, and pour the blood of a sheep into the hole. Ghosts come up, and the sheep are sacrificed to Hades and Persephone. Odysseus, with drawn sword, keeps the ghosts from drinking the blood till Tiresias shall come. The shadow of his friend, Elpenor, recently dead but unburied, asks for his due rites, a barrow on the sea banks, surmounted by his oar. The shade of Odysseus's mother appears, but is kept from the blood. Finally Tiresias comes, and is allowed to drink of the blood, 'that I may tell sooth.' After drinking, he delivers his oracle, as already stated, and explains that all spirits, after tasting blood, will 'tell sooth.' The dead mother now converses with her son ; of the wooers she knows nothing ; she describes the condition of the forlorn Laertes, father of the hero. They strive in vain to embrace. Then (225–332) famed ladies of old times, mistresses of gods, come up and tell their stories.

Here (333–385) comes an 'intermezzo.' Odysseus pauses, his hosts praise him, offer presents, and ask what he saw of the shades of those who fought at Troy. He speaks of Agamemnon—who gave a version of the story of his murder, in which Clytemnestra herself slays Cassandra— and of Achilles, who receives tidings of his son, and his conduct in the Wooden Horse and in battle with Eury- pylus. Aias next appeared, still indignant at the loss of Achilles's arms, still refusing to address Odysseus. These scenes are full of allusions to the later events of the war, not mentioned in the Iliad. If they were known to the poet of the Iliad he could only mention them by way of allusion or prophecy. To the poet of the Odyssey such things as the Wooden Horse, the valour of Neoptolemus, the contest for the arms of Achilles, seem to belong to the past. But those passages are looked upon as proofs of late date. After the heroes of the great siege have withdrawn, in book xi. comes a passage which has been spoken of as an 'Orphic interpolation' (xi. 568–641). Here Odysseus sees Minos judging the dead, beholds the punishments inflicted on great offenders against the gods, like Tityus and Sisyphus, and holds converse with the shadow of Hèracles, whose real self is feasting among the gods. After this Odysseus and his company return to the Ææan isle (book xii.), they do not go back to Circe's house, but pass the night on the shore, while she gives counsel about his future journey to Odysseus. That counsel contains advice as to how to deal with the Sirens (book xii.), the Rocks Wandering, and Scylla and Charybdis ; while the hero is to avoid the Cattle of the Sun on the isle Thrinacia, a warning already given by Tiresias. Circe, however, describes the cattle and the nymphs who herd them, at full length. The rest of book xii. contains these adventures : the crew eat the sacred cattle, and Zeus, at the desire of the Sun, wrecks the ship. Only Odysseus escapes on the keel to Calypso's isle, where he dwells for seven years, and then, as we saw (book v.), lands in Phæacia. The whole course of the adventures narrated by Odysseus work to the one result of leaving him to return 'alone, in evil case.' Gradually his fleet, his companions, and finally his one ship and crew are taken from him, through the anger of Poseidon, and, in the last case, of the Sun. The long stay with Calypso is neces- sary—first to give time for the wooers to gather head, next to test the constancy of him who prefers a rocky isle and an aging wife to immortality and the embraces of a goddess.

In the thirteenth book the Phæacians land Odysseus, not near the town, but in a remote harbour of Ithaca. Athene first deludes him by a mist on his wakening, then helps him to conceal his treasures, accounts for her non-appearance to him while he was under the curse of Poseidon, advises him how to deal with the wooers, gives him an appearance of age to prevent his being recognised, disguises him as a beggar, sends him to the house of his faithful swineherd, and promises to bring back Telemachus from Lacedæmon.

Here, as we shall see, the withering of the limbs of Odysseus by the spell of Athene (xiii. 431) causes great though needless trouble to German critics, while they regard the mention of Telemachus as a mechanical taking up of the thread of their hypothetical *Telemachia*. But how could the two actions be more skilfully interwoven, if we allow for a slip in the prolonged stay of Telemachus in Sparta?

In book xiv. Odysseus, now disguised, visits Eumæus, is kindly treated, and assures himself of the swineherd's loyalty. He tells a false tale of his adventures, giving himself out for a Cretan bastard of good family, who had been taken captive in a raid on Egypt—a passage of much interest (xiv. 246). In this book Kirchhoff thinks that he recognises a basis in an old separate lay or ballad; he often does recognise an old ballad in a fine piece of the poem.

In book xv. Athene rouses Telemachus in Sparta, saying that Penelope's kin wish her to wed Eurymachus. She also warns him of the ambush which the wooers laid for him (in book iv.). Telemachus asks Menelaus to let him go; the hero and Helen bestow gifts on the young prince, and Helen interprets an omen to announce the return of Odysseus and his revenge. In all this passage critics recognise an ill-made resumption of the thread of the *Telemachia*,

broken in book iv. 620.   From Pylos, without visiting
Nestor, Telemachus sets sail, taking with him a homicide,
Theoclymenus of the house of Melampus—a second-sighted
man and an outlaw.   They sail on as far as ' the pointed
isles,' in dread of the ambush, and giving the shores and
isles a wide berth.   Meanwhile (xv. 307) Odysseus in disguise informs Eumæus that he means to beg at the palace.
Eumæus tells a strange and interesting story of how he
himself was kidnapped, as a child, by Phœnician merchant-
men, and sold into slavery.   They go to bed ; Telemachus
lands ; Theoclymenus interprets an omen of the slaying of
the wooers ; Telemachus entrusts Theoclymenus to one of
his friends, Piræus, and himself goes to the house of
Eumæus.   Thence (xvi.) he sends Eumæus to Penelope,
with news of his arrival.   Athene then, invisible to Telemachus, but beheld by the dogs, restores Odysseus for the
moment to his true aspect.   Father and son are at last
united, plan the massacre of the wooers, and arrange for
the removal of the shields and spears from the walls of
Odysseus's hall.[1]

Meanwhile the ship of Telemachus arrives in the port
of Ithaca, closely followed by the vessel of the wooers
who had lain in ambush.   Penelope rebukes the wooers.
Athene, before Eumæus can return from his errand to
Penelope, again gives Odysseus the appearance of age.
His son now knows him for himself, but it is not yet time
to enlighten Eumæus.

In book xvii. Telemachus goes to the town.   After a
few words with his mother, he brings Theoclymenus to the
house.   Here he recapitulates his adventures to Penelope.
The second-sighted Theoclymenus protests that Odysseus

---

[1] Critics complain of this meeting, and of the remarks about
removing the arms (carried out in book xix. 1–50) as work of a botcher,
patcher, or compiler.

is even now in his own islands sowing the seeds of fate for
the wooers. They begin their revels ; Eumæus and Odysseus start for the city from the hut.[1] In his guise of a
beggar Odysseus, walking townward, is insulted by his
faithless goatherd. Reaching his own house, he is wel-
comed by his old hound, Argus, which dies in that welcom-
ing. Eumæus enters the hall ; Odysseus sits down like a
beggar on the outer threshold. Odysseus begs in the hall, is
smitten by Antinous, and wrangles with him. Penelope
hears of, or overhears, the disturbance, pities the beggar,
and bids Eumæus bring him to her. Odysseus promises to
come after sunset ; he dares not pass through the hall
among the wooers. Eumæus goes back to his herds, and
the book ends as the wooers revel, 'for already it was
close on eventide.'

In book xviii. a common beggar, Irus, comes up ; is
jealous of Odysseus ; they fight ; Irus is half killed ;
Odysseus is rewarded with a haggis and the post of beggar-
in-ordinary, *vice* Irus cashiered.[2] Odysseus next holds talk

[1] Odysseus borrows a staff ; now Athene (xiii. 437) had given him a
staff, which he dropped (xiv. 31) when attacked by the dogs. On his
now borrowing a staff, though Athene had already given him one,
German critics found a charge of discrepancy.

[2] This fight leads Kirchhoff to some curious reflections. When
Odysseus has knocked Irus down, he drags the beggar into the court,
props him against the wall, and 'puts a staff in his hands.' He
then 'casts about his own shoulders his mean, tattered wallet, and the
cord therewith to hang it' (xviii. 100–110). Now (xiii. 437) Athene,
when disguising Odysseus, had given him a staff and 'a mean, tattered
wallet, and a cord therewith to hang it.' In xvii. 197 and 357,
Odysseus put on this wallet as he started for the town, and laid therein
the food given him in hall by Telemachus. Now Kirchhoff (p. 516)
does not believe that the fight with Irus is an original invention of the
poet. The ' poet of the continuation ' availed himself of an older lay
or ballad. Traces of insertion of such ballad material remain : thus, in
the original ballad the staff and scrip or wallet spoken of were the
property of the vanquished, which the victor would annex as *spolia*

with Amphinomus, a wooer ; and Penelope, prompted by
Athene, who beautifies her, appears among her suitors, and
extracts presents from them.   The hour has now come
when Telemachus wears a beard, and, by Odysseus's own
counsel, when he left Ithaca for Ilios, she is to take another
mate (xviii. 269).   Darkness falls ; Odysseus ministers fuel
to the braziers in hall ; one of the false maids of Penelope
reviles him ; he has an altercation with Eurymachus, who
throws a stool at him, but misses ; Telemachus chides
Eurymachus ; the wooers go home, and the book ends.[1]

In book xix. Telemachus and Odysseus, as they had
arranged in book xvi., remove the arms that hung in the
hall.[2]   Penelope enters the hall, to see Odysseus at night,

opima and insignia, so to say, of the privileged gaberlunzie, or licensed
beggar. The poet of the continuation, not seeing this, made Athene give
Odysseus a staff and wallet, as in the passages quoted from books xiii.
and xvii.   Readers of or listeners to the story would necessarily believe
that this is the wallet here spoken of.

[1] Wilamowitz excises the scene with Penelope, which does not
satisfy the 'time-test.'   It was growing late when the beggar Irus
appeared, in the end of xvii. and opening of xviii., and many events
occur before Odysseus is left alone with Telemachus in the halls.   The
whole affair of Penelope's visit to the wooers and extraction of presents
is blamed as not original, or not intended for this place, although it
gives her motive for meaning to marry at last, and so to choose a
husband by the trial of the bow.   This is 'motived' by her report of
Odysseus' parting advice, twenty years before, ' When thou seest thy
son a bearded man, marry whom thou wilt, and leave thine own house '
(xviii. 270).   Penelope's appearance before the wooers is called mere-
tricious, and the passage likened to the work of Ariosto rather than of
Homer.   Separate lays on Penelope are invented and invoked (p. 33).
The scene of the presents may have been introduced by an Ionian in
the age of Archilochus.   The fight with Irus is a half-comic travesty of
the single combats in epic poetry, and probably arose among Ionians in
the age of Simonides.   Evidently the fight cannot be both an old
ballad (Kirchhoff) and a comparatively late parody.   Other objections
of almost equal weight have been advanced.

[2] The objections to this passage are discussed elsewhere.

as he had arranged. Her maid, Melantho, again insults the hero. Penelope tells him the story of the web un-woven, and adds, 'Now I can no longer escape the marriage.' Odysseus amuses her with a feigned tale of a meeting with her lord in Crete, and adds that Odysseus is alive, in Thesprotia, giving here a portion of his real ad-ventures and shipwreck after leaving Thrinacia. 'In this same year shall Odysseus come hither, as the old moon wanes and the new is born.' Penelope replies that Odys-seus will never come again. She bids the maids wash the beggar's feet ; he refuses to let a young and scornful girl touch him, but will accept the service of an old woman. He withdrawing into the shadow, old Eurycleia washes him, and recognises him by a scar on his thigh, but he compels her silence by a threat.[1] When the washing is done, Penelope describes a dream, which Odysseus interprets favourably. Penelope announces that to-morrow she will choose the man who can bend the bow of her lord, and shoot an arrow through a row of axe-heads.[2]

In book xx. Odysseus thinks of slaying the faithless maids. As he lies awake, he is comforted by a vision of Athene, who will aid him. Penelope, in the morning, wakes and weeps ; he hears her, and asks Zeus for a favourable omen. Zeus thunders, and a weary woman, grinding at the mill, prays that the meal she is preparing may be the wooers' last. Telemachus goes to the assembly-place ; the hall is cleaned and arrayed ; Melanthius insults the beggar ; Philœtius, the neat-herd, and Eumæus show their loyalty ; Odysseus promises the neat-herd that to-day he shall see the slaying of the wooers (xx. 232), who conceive, but abandon, a new plot for slaying Telemachus ; the feast

[1] The criticism of this recognition is elsewhere answered.
[2] On the axes see Butcher and Lang, Note, p. 418, edition of 1890.

begins ; Telemachus, who has returned from his curious visit to the assembly-place, makes Odysseus sit down beside him, at the higher end of the hall, 'with crafty purpose;' sacrifice is done in the grove of Apollo—this being the second sacrifice of the day (xx. 251, 276), if, indeed, the hecatomb is not only taken to the grove, but sacrificed. There is here—at least to non-Homeric readers—a decided want of clearness. Lines 276–279 seem to us to have no necessary place in the story.[1] Ctesippus now throws an ox's foot at Odysseus, but misses—Odysseus in this passage is seated, in xx. 291 : Philœtius later says that he was ' begging through the house ' when the ox's foot was thrown—a serious inconsistency ! Telemachus rebukes Ctesippus ; the wooers laugh like fey men ; Theoclymenus sees the shroud of death mounting to their heads, and leaves the hall ; the festival goes on noisily.

In book xxi. Penelope brings out the bow and the axes ; Telemachus arrays them for the feat of archery ; he nearly strings the bow, but desists, at a look from his father.   Some of the wooers fail.   Odysseus goes out of doors, and reveals himself, by the sign of the scar, to the neat-herd and Eumæus.   The latter is told to bid Eurycleia bar the inner doors of the hall, which communicate with the women's rooms, and Philœtius, the neat-herd, does as much for the outer gate of the court.   The wooers determine to try the bow on the following day, not on Apollo's festival.   Odysseus asks leave to try his strength at once. After some controversy he gets the weapon, strings it, and performs the feat.   Telemachus draws near him, spear in hand.

Then (xxii.) the hero leaps on the high threshold, threatens the wooers, shoots Antinous, reveals himself, refuses Eurymachus's offer of atonement, and the fight begins;

[1] The objections are dealt with elsewhere.

the wooers vainly looking for the weapons which have been removed from the walls (xix. 1–46). Telemachus brings shields, spears, and helmets from the store-chamber or armoury. Melanthius, by some passage not well understood, also enters the armoury, and conveys arms to the wooers. Philœtius and Eumæus detect and bind him in the armoury; Athene, in guise of Mentor, encourages Odysseus ; finally, all the wooers are slain, but the bard and the herald are spared. Eurycleia is sent for ; the maids are compelled to clean the hall, and those who lay with the wooers are hanged. Melanthius is put to a cruel death.

In book xxiii. Eurycleia tells the news to Penelope, who has been asleep in her chamber. Penelope is incredulous, enters the hall, refuses to recognise Odysseus. He is bathed and clothed, and beautified by Athene (xxiii. 156). By revealing the secret of his bed, wrought out of a growing tree, he is at last recognised, and Penelope explains her long reluctance. He tells her of his remaining adventures, as prophesied by Tiresias, 'and so they came gladly to the rites of their bed, as of old' (xxiii. 296).

Here, in the opinion of the Alexandrine critics, the Odyssey ended. But no Homeric hearer could have been satisfied till he learned how Odysseus escaped the blood-feud for the slain wooers.

As the poem goes on, the hero recapitulates his adventures to his wife, and, at dawn, sets forth to see his father, so often spoken of as retired to a country farm.

In xxiv. the souls of the dead wooers, led by Hermes, enter Hades, and converse with Agamemnon and Achilles. Odysseus, in a charming passage, makes himself known to Laertes, by recalling memories of his own childhood. Meanwhile the kindred of the wooers gather in arms : Athene and Zeus consult about the ending of the feud, the kin of the wooers attack the party of Odysseus, the battle begins, old Laertes slays his man, and, suddenly, Athene interposes and establishes peace.

So ends the Odyssey ; a *dea ex machina* is needed to settle the blood feud ; nor is it easy to see how otherwise the affair could be made up, under the old law of homicide. For, though in book ii. the wooers received fair legal warning, their kin were not likely to let them fall unatoned, or unavenged.[1]

[1] Cowper was not, perhaps, a very good judge of Homer. He complains that the last battle is ' a paltry battle, and there is a huddle in the management of it,' the very term constantly applied by Lady Louisa Stuart to the conclusions of Scott's novels.

CHAPTER IX

COMPOSITION OF THE ODYSSEY

Modern Theories

ACCORDING to Mr. Leaf, the Odyssey is 'a model of skilful construction ; from the first we have the two independent parallel stories of Telemachus and Odysseus, beginning independently, and joining in the same channel at the beginning of the second half of the tale. The way in which we are told the adventures of Odysseus himself—the narrative opening near the end, and then brought back to the beginning in the hero's own words in the palace of Alcinous—is a true masterpiece. And when we are once landed in Ithaca, the final catastrophe is always in view ; at each step we find it drawing nearer, till the interest reaches its climax at the magnificent opening of the twenty-second book. From beginning to end there is not a single episode which does not bear upon a catastrophe foreseen and aimed at without wavering. With the Iliad all is different.' [1]

These opinions, so contrary to the ideas held by Mr. Leaf about the Iliad, are traditional in England. Mr. Grote [2] supposed that, if we only possessed the Odyssey, and had no Iliad, the question as to multiplicity of authorship would never have been raised. The faults marked by Wolf,

[1] *Companion to the Iliad*, pp. 21, 22.
[2] *History of Greece*, ii. 105, edition of 1869.

Thiersch, and Müller, in the Odyssey are so few and un-
important that they would have been explained as the
natural blemishes which assuredly beset, in greater number,
the romances and poems of modern authors, had it not
been for the suspicions roused by the Iliad. Thus the discrepancy as to the length of Telemachus's stay in Sparta,
where he remained longer than he had intended, no explanation being given, may be compared with the faulty chronology of *The Antiquary*. 'The matter of real wonder,' says
Mr. Grote, 'is that this inaccuracy stands almost alone, and
that there are no others in the poem.' Mr. Grote entirely
rejected the hypothesis of a separate and independent
Telemachia, 'The Adventures of Telemachus,' as a thing
without meaning or interest apart from the Odyssey.

Mr. Grote reckoned without the recent German critics.
They make a great deal of work about the *Telemachia*,
and they collect an enormous heap of discrepancies in the
Odyssey. The gist of such works as Kirchhoff's *Die Homerische
Odyssee* (1879), Niese's *Die Entwickelung der Homerischen
Poesie* (1882), and Wilamowitz Moellendorff's *Homerische
Untersuchungen* (1884) may be stated thus : These critics
believe, as a fundamental principle, that where the same
lines recur, identically or with slight modifications, in
different parts of the poem, there is reason to suspect that
one of the passages is the original, and that the others are
borrowed by a later compiler, continuator, or redactor.
They also imagine that criticism can detect the original
passage, and divine the motive of the borrower. However
beautiful the work of the borrower or 'botcher' may seem
to mere literary students, it is assumed that his incompe-
tence compelled him to steal, and to spoil in the stealing,
lines from the work of an older master. By this criterion —
namely, the detection of borrowed passages—are compilers
redactors, and botchers to be tracked and exposed.

These arguments, in spite of Alexandrian precedent, have little or no value for readers of the epics who recognise the epic manner, the economy which employs textual repetition wherever it can be used. This habit is familiar in popular poetry, *Volkslieder*, and ballads, and recurs in the Finnish *Kalewala* (a congeries of ballads), and in the *Song of Roland*. The habit is also to be observed in the curious epic narrative of the Maoris (in *Old New Zealand*) and in Celtic sagas and poetry. The singer has a formula for all recurrent events, as mooring ships, setting forth banquets, and so on, while he textually repeats all messages and speeches. In Homer it may be said that the poet scarcely ever uses a fresh mode of stating a fact, if he can repeat a formula, and his ingenuity in this economy is remarkable. The German hypothesis, however, is that, in face of great poetic excellencies in a given passage, we must detect it as patchwork, if repetition is present, and must imagine that the botcher could scarcely write a line for himself, that he was driven to make ' centos,' as boys do in composing their Latin verses.

If we reject this hypothesis as generally applicable, most of the recent German criticism of the Odyssey will seem to be founded on the sand.

Another standing critical opinion is that the critic can discern what is old, what is not so old, and what is comparatively recent in the elements of the poem. Here he is often guided by his literary taste. The more splendid and dramatic pieces are borrowed from old poems or ballads ; the passages of transition are new. Thus we can detect, first, the original saga of Odysseus, or several co-existing sagas, whatever they may have been. We have then a separate saga of Telemachus. We have also poems of different dates based on these sagas. We have, moreover separate lays, or ballads, or tales, such as the fighting of

Odysseus with the beggar, the story of the youth of Eumæus, and so forth. We have, moreover, separate poems, not popular but artistic, such as the lay of Calypso. We have various combinations, at various dates, and by different hands, of all these materials. We have, finally, the epic as it stands, a very late patchwork, compilation, *Flick-Poesie*, and we have interpolations even into that. All these things are apparent under the critical microscope, but, of course, all critics do not attain the same conclusions. What is old according to one is late according to another ; Kirchhoff derives xix. from xiii., Niese xiii. from xix. Again, slight geographical hints, of a most disputable sort, are made to yield indications of the date and place of composition. Further, hints in the Odyssey about traditions not set forth in full are not to be supposed to be mere allusions to legends. They are often borrowed from the Cyclic poems, which, about 750–600, were composed, by writers whose names are known, on the basis of legends. Thus we can bring the date of the Odyssey, *as it stands*, down to a very late period. The hand which wove the epic was the hand of a late, and larcenous, and incompetent compiler : the unity which Wolf admired is merely mechanical, and is excessively faulty. These are the general conclusions of criticism.

The results of various critical researches are, of course, by no means harmonious, but they have in common a determination to break the epic up into component parts and elements of various dates. According to Kirchhoff, the Odyssey, as we possess it, is neither the creation of a single poet, nor a collection of ancient independent lays of divers periods and authors, now mechanically arranged in chronological order, but rather the deliberate and systematic expansion, in an age relatively late, of an old and *originally* single 'kernel.' This 'kernel,' which Kirchhoff calls 'the Older Redaction,' is the form in which the Odyssey was known till the thirtieth Olympiad, and even partly to the middle of the sixth century B.C. Yet the kernel was not single, but was composed of an older and a later part. The later part is a combination of work of different ages and different poets, and probably the elements were originally composed in various districts of the coast of Asia Minor. The older part is simple in itself and defies further analysis. It was originally an independent piece of artistic epic. The ancient materials, derived from Greek sagas, are skilfully combined. Even the second part is probably earlier than the reckoning by Olympiads—776 B.C. It was composed with a special eye on the earlier kernel, and was meant to absorb and to be absorbed in that, not to exist as an independent composition. The two, taken together, are a 'redaction.' The poetic value of the continuation as a whole was less than that of the original germ ; the details, however, were respectable. The continuator was not very successful in fusing into a whole many epic ballads with which he was acquainted, and which he used as materials. A collection of these ballads is the basis of his work. He does not keep his motive steadily before him, hence arise discrepancies, contradictions, and various degrees of poetic merit. Still, the separate ballads which the continuator used can hardly now be reconstructed.

About the thirtieth Olympiad an unknown hand took up the old redaction, and amplified it by adding the adventures of Telemachus and other matter to about twice its original amount. In this process the old text was altered and *lacunæ* were developed. The amplifier wished to work in other old poems of the same saga cycle, and to gratify popular taste by a happier conclusion. His method was mechanical.   This epic, 'the later redaction,' thus 'worked over,' amplified and generally bedevilled, was the basis of the edition of Pisistratus's commission.

This is Kirchhoff's own summary of his ideas, which are presented partly in notes on the text, partly in separate dissertations.[1]

In the opinion of Wilamowitz Moellendorff, the present form of the Odyssey is the production of a 'Bearbeiter.'[2]

The person who worked over the whole, and brought it to the shape we know, was 'a slenderly gifted botcher.' He lived in Greece about the second half of the seventh century.   The performance is not older than Archilochus, and is later than Hesiod.   Our problem is to disengage this man's work.   He composed out of his own head all of book i., the assembly of gods, and exposition of the fable, and Athene's visit to Telemachus.   He also composed book iv. 620 to book v. 54.   In these passages the wooers conspire against Telemachus, meaning to kill him on his return from Sparta ; Penelope's grief is displayed ; Athene comforts her by a dream or vision ; there is an assembly of gods ; and Hermes is sent to Calypso's isle.   The botcher is also greatly guilty of xiii. 375–381, where Athene bids Odysseus consider how he may lay hands on the wooers ; 412–428, where Athene tells Odysseus that Telemachus is in Sparta, and that the wooers lie in ambush for him ; 439, 440, where Athene goes after Telemachus to Sparta.   In xiv. the botcher introduced lines 158–164, where Odysseus promises Eumæus that the hero shall arrive in that month, attesting his promise by the 'hospitable table of Odysseus, to which I was come ;' also 171–184, where Eumæus laments Telemachus's expedition to Pylos, and the ambush of the wooers.   Next comes xv. 1–79, where Athene rouses

[1] *Die Homerische Odyssee*, pp. vii–x.   Berlin, 1879.
[2] *Homerische Untersuchungen*, p. 228.

Telemachus in Sparta, warns him of the ambush laid for
him, and directs his conduct when he returns. The passage ends in the middle of a speech by Menelaus to Telemachus. Lines 90, 91 are also from this *Flick-Poet*, and
113-119 a gift of a cup, given to Menelaus in Sidon, is here
offered to Telemachus. Lines 285-495, the introduction
of Theoclymenus, and the interesting tale of his own early
fortune by Eumæus, are also by the patcher, for the tale of
Eumæus has no effect on the Odysseus saga. The critic is
so well aware of its excellence that he doubts whether he
can really assign the tale of Eumæus to that wretched journeyman poet, the patcher (p. 96). He is inclined to suppose that the patcher introduced a piece of a fairy tale
about the stolen prince brought up as a swineherd, leaving
out the usual conclusion—the happy restoration of the
prince. The charming narrative is not the botcher's own,
but stolen property—good in itself, but out of place here.
In xvi. 135-153 Eumæus's remarks about Laertes, and
Telemachus's sending of Eumæus with a message to Penelope, are by the botcher; also 302, 303, where Odysseus
forbids Telemachus to let Laertes, Penelope, the swineherd,
or anyone else know of his arrival. In xvii., 31-166 go out
as patchwork. There Telemachus leaves his mother, converses with Mentor, Antiphus, and Halitherses, old friends
of his father's; he entertains his guest, Theoclymenus, the
seer; tells his mother the tale of his voyage, and hears the
prophecy of Odysseus's return from Theoclymenus. In
xviii., lines 214-243 vanish; here Penelope tells Telemachus
about the ill-treatment of the beggar-man, Odysseus in disguise. In xix. we are to excise 1-50, and 476 on to xx. 387.
In 1-50 Odysseus and Telemachus hide the weapons that
hung in the hall, so that the wooers may not use them in
their need. In 476 to the end, Odysseus prevents Eurycleia
from revealing that she has discovered him by the scar on

his thigh, he holds converse with Penelope, and predicts the massacre of the wooers. Penelope then goes to bed. In xx. he is mocked by the maids, hears the startling prayer of the old woman grinding corn : ' They that have loosened my knees with cruel toil to grind their barley-meal, may they now sup their last.' The botcher is here to be congratulated. Odysseus meets the neat-herd, and finds him loyal ; he is assaulted by a wooer. The wooers, becoming fey, ' laugh with alien lips ' ; Theoclymenus sees the shroud of death about them, and leaves the hall. The wooers banter Telemachus.

Now here, at least, we are on fair literary ground. These passages are among the immortal glories of art, and of the Odyssey. A critic who assures us that they are the work of a slenderly-gifted botcher of the seventh century may fairly be said to put himself out of court. The botcher also composed xxii. 205–240, where Athene, in guise of Mentor, heartens Odysseus in the fight with the wooers, and 249, 250, where the wooers notice Mentor, but do not recognise the goddess.

In xxiii. the botcher claims 115, 116, where Odysseus says Penelope despises him for his filthy beggar's clothes, and 153–170, where he comes clean from the bath, in beauty given by Athene, and Telemachus blames his mother for not acknowledging the hero. Finally, xxiv. 439–450, where Medon says that he saw Athene in guise of Mentor in the hall, is the botcher's. The botcher is thus greatly guilty of more than a sixth of the Odyssey.

The botcher, or ' Bearbeiter,' used three epics in his ' compilation,' and these elder epics were by no means pure of mixture. The latest, made in Greece, is not much older than the general compilation.

It dealt only with the victory of Odysseus over the wooers. Thence proceed books xxi.–xxiv., except such passages in them as are later interpolations (such as the scene in Hades, in xxiv.), or are additions by the compiler himself. In xxii. and xxiii., as they stand, parts of this latest composition used in the manufacture of the Odyssey must have been cut out.

One beautiful scene—the recognition of Odysseus by Penelope—must have been borrowed from yet another more ancient source. The poet who made up this part of the Odyssey, some 1,550 verses, had little mastery of the old epic art.

The two other epic poems, recast, curtailed, and patched into our Odyssey, are older than the one just mentioned, but not more ancient than the eighth century B.C. The later of these two, which were fashioned, not in Greece proper, but in Ionia, is the so-called *Telemachia*. To this belong books ii., iii., iv., xv., xvi., xvii., xviii., and xix., as far as 475, where the compiler takes up the tale.[1] Book xviii. 153-303 is later than the original poem, but had been interwoven with it before the time of the compiler.[2] The beginning and conclusion of this poem were cut out by the compiler, to make room for what he meant to use as xxi.-xxiv., and for his general scheme of composition.

The oldest of the poems thus mishandled by the compiler deserves the name of the Elder Odyssey. It contained books v.-xiii. Hesiod and Archilochus knew it,[3] and Eugammon made use of it in his *Telegonia*, in the first half of the sixth century B.C. But even the poet of the Elder Odyssey 'contaminated' earlier materials. Among these was a poem relating the adventures of Odysseus with Circe ;

[1] The break here is in the scene of recognition of Odysseus by Eurycleia while washing his feet. The critic believes that in the original version Penelope also recognised him.

[2] This is the scene where Penelope shows herself to the wooers, and extracts gifts from them.

[3] Arch. *fr.* 72, Odyssey, xviii. 136. (Wilamowitz, *H. U.* p. 229.)

the Læstrygonians ; Æolus ; the Sirens ; Scylla ; the Cattle
of the Sun ; the arrival in Phæacia, and probably the landing in Ithaca.

The tale of Calypso was a separate short piece of 450
lines. There was also a poem, in which Odysseus himself
told of the Lotus-eaters, the Cyclops, and Tiresias. These
belong to the really blooming age of epos, whence most
of the Iliad is derived. The redactor put the whole of
Odysseus's tale into his own mouth, in Phæacia. He also
contrived the transformation of Odysseus by Athene. He
added scenes in Hades, and allusions to the ship ' Argo,'
and he borrowed from the Cyclic poems.

Our Odyssey is thus a perfect hotch-potch of materials,
very unskilfully combined into its present shape.

Niese's theory of the eldest Odyssey may next be
sketched. The poem originally began with the arrival of
the shipwrecked hero in Phæacia (book vi.). He was kindly
received ; he told his name, and recounted his adventures
with the Cicones, the Lotus-eaters, Æolus, the Læstrygonians in Thrinacia, where his men ate the Cattle of the
Sun, and, probably, with the Cyclops. It may be observed
that Kirchhoff rejects the lines in the prologue to book i.
(6–9), which mention the Cattle of the Sun, as an interpolation, made for the purpose of introducing this adventure.[1] Niese[2] will not accept this suggestion. In fact,
with Niese, the epic, and the landing of Odysseus in
Phæacia, began just after the lines in the prologue, which
Kirchhoff looks on as an interpolation. Certainly the
hero's wreck, and loss of all his company, were the revenge
for the insult to the Sun. But for that he might have
brought his men home, and then there would have been no
failure to recognise him, and, practically, no Odyssey.

[1] *Die Homerische Odyssee*, 1879, pp. 165, 166.
[2] *Die Entwickelung der Homerischen Poesie*, pp. 186, 187.

Niese thinks that the Cyclops adventure was, possibly, part of the original narrative of Odysseus to the Phæacians; if so, he must suppose that the prayer to Poseidon was not included, as the introduction of the influence of Poseidon, according to him, and of Athene, is later. Then Odysseus was taken home to Ithaca by the Phæacians, met his wife, at first in disguise, was recognised ultimately, and that was all. The formula, 'thence we sailed on, sad at heart,' occurring in ix. and x., is not repeated in, or after, the adventure with Circe.

But probably, thinks Niese, the Cyclops story, being different in its character, was really the next addition, not part of the original *Nostos*, or Return. Maron, too (ix. 197), will be later, as necessary, with his present of wine, to the overthrow of the Cyclops. Next came into the expanding poem Circe, the Sirens, and Scylla and Charybdis. An important novelty followed when Calypso was introduced, who kept the hero captive for seven years. To be sure, if he had come home seven years earlier, he would have been more easily recognised, and the wooers would not have reached such a pitch of arrogance, while Telemachus would have been a small boy. The gods, Poseidon and Athene, come in with the introduction of Calypso. While the hero is with her, and in consequence of his long detention, Athene moves Zeus to pity him.

Her influence is not obvious in the adventures before he reaches Calypso. Then we ask, in the early *Nostos*, was Odysseus *not* the favourite of Athene? Did that view of him come into the *earliest* Iliad (book xi.), out of the *secondary* Odyssey? If so, we must reconsider the common theory of the priority of the Iliad.

A new poet next brought in Telemachus, who is closely connected with Athene's performances and promises in the assembly of the gods, in book i., and elsewhere. Then

S

did Telemachus find his way into the Iliad from a tertiary Odyssey, or *vice versa*? Telemachus's adventures enable the returns of Menelaus and Nestor to be narrated. The wooers are essential to the *Telemachia*, and now the scenes in Hades, and the prophecy of Tiresias about the massacre of the wooers—are foisted into the original, the oldest, narrative of Odysseus to the Phæacians. Then there is a conclusion. The condition of old Laertes is already described by the ghost of his wife in xi. 187-191.

The second scene in Hades is very late, as, indeed, was held by the Alexandrines, and, still later, perhaps, the episodic lays of Demodocus were introduced. As it stands, the very stay in Phæacia is of later redaction, though something of the sort must always have existed. But even as we possess it, the Odyssey is earlier than the Cyclic poems (say, 776 B.C.),[1] a position denied by Kirchhoff, who brings it down to about 560 B.C. But 'nobody now believes in the complete unity of the Odyssey' (p. 143). Even Aristophanes and Aristarchus ended it at xxii. 296,[2] where Odysseus and Penelope go to bed together. They argued thus because they were Alexandrine Greeks, and recked not of the blood-feud. The preoccupation of Odysseus is, 'How am I to settle the blood-feud with the kindred of the wooers, after I have slain my enemies?' (xx. 42). This was a matter of indifference to the Alexandrine Greeks, but no Greek of the heroic age could have rested till he knew how that question was answered. The same difficulty would have occurred in any Icelandic saga. It needs Athene, *ex machina*, xxiv. 546, to compose the matter.

Of course, it does not follow that we have the conclusion in its original shape ; but a conclusion, composing so great a feud, there must from the first have been. There

---

[1] Niese, *op. cit.* pp. 140, 141, p. 226.
[2] Scholia on xxii. 296.

are difficulties with the wooers in Hades. Has Hermes any right to be the Guide of Souls, *Psychopompus*? The Muses, for the first time, appear as nine in number, answering to the later differentiation of the arts, unless the arts were differentiated into nine, to correspond with the number of the Muses. The White Rock, the Gates of the Sun, the People of Dreams, appear here (xxiv.), not in the Nekyia of book xi. But, we reply, in book xi., Odysseus does not go to Hades by the Path of Souls, but 'in a black ship,' a living man, to the surprise of the shades.

Niese's general conclusion is that the Iliad and Odyssey are the results of a long period of development. The beginnings or germs of both may be nearly contemporary, the Iliad took the lead in later expansions. To ourselves it seems plain that the character of the hero of the Odyssey was either given to both poems by tradition, or is the work of one mind, or is a quite unexampled success as a sequel by an alien hand.

CHAPTER X

WE have sketched the general ideas of the recent critics :
it is now time to examine some of the processes by which
they reach and seek to establish their conclusions. To
begin with Kirchhoff, who is, in a sense, the father of the
later and more revolutionary Odyssean criticism, we find
him introducing some very grave considerations in his first
excursus. Therein he tries to show that there are interpolations in book i.—*e.g.* lines 6–8—while the whole book, after
line 87, is an ill-conceived *cento* derived from book ii.,
which is really older than book i., and part of the original
Telemachia. As usual, repetitions of lines, regarded as
the borrowings of an imbecile, supply much of the proof.
As the poem at first stood, Athene did *not* go to Ithaca to
send Telemachus in quest of news concerning his father.
As the poem stands, in i. 88 she promises to go to Ithaca
to encourage the son of Odysseus, Telemachus, and bid
him call the wooers of his mother to a public assembly,
' speak out his mind ' to them, and then depart to Sparta and
Pylos in search of news and renown. She does go to Ithaca,
appears in the courtyard of Telemachus in the guise of
Mentes, a Taphian chief, finds the wooers revelling, is
greeted by Telemachus, observes the riotous festivity of the
wooers, and asks why they so behave. The poet's design

is to introduce us to the arrogance of the wooers as beheld by a stranger ; the method of introducing them is highly artistic. Telemachus explains the scene, a result of his father's long absence. Athene declares herself to be a friend of his father's, and prophesies the return of Odysseus. This is the first of a series of predictions and omens, which grow in force and sublimity as the catastrophe approaches. Telemachus sets forth the excuse on which the wooers ravage his house. Athene prays for the return of Odysseus. She then (269-305) gives him advice as to his conduct.

'But I charge thee to take counsel how thou mayest thrust forth the wooers from the hall. Come now, mark and take heed unto my words. On the morrow call the Achæan lords to the assembly, and declare thy saying to all, and take the gods to witness. As for the wooers bid them scatter them each one to his own, and for thy mother, if her heart is moved to marriage, let her return to the hall of that mighty man her father, and her kinsfolk will furnish a wedding feast, and array the gifts of wooing exceeding many, all that should go back with a daughter dearly be- loved. And to thyself I will give a word of wise counsel, if perchance thou wilt hearken. Fit out a ship, the best thou hast, with twenty oarsmen, and go to inquire concerning thy father that is long afar, if perchance any man shall tell thee aught, or if thou mayest hear the voice from Zeus, which chiefly brings tidings to men. Get thee first to Pylos and inquire of goodly Nestor, and from thence to Sparta to Menelaus of the fair hair, for he came home the last of the mail-coated Achæans. If thou shalt hear news of the life and the returning of thy father, then verily thou mayest endure the wasting for yet a year. But if thou shalt hear that he is dead and gone, return then to thine own dear country and pile his mound, and over it pay burial rites, full many as is due, and give thy mother to a husband. But when thou hast done this and made an end, thereafter take counsel in thy mind and heart, how thou mayest slay the wooers in thy halls, whether by guile or openly ; for thou shouldest not carry childish thoughts, being no longer of years thereto. Or hast thou not heard what renown the goodly Orestes gat him among all men in that he slew the slayer of his father, guileful Ægisthus, who killed his famous sire ? And thou, too, my friend, for I see that thou art very comely and tall, be valiant, that even men unborn may praise thee. But I will now go down to the swift ship and to my men, who methinks chafe much at tarrying for me ; and do thou thyself take heed and give ear unto my words.'

It is on this passage, which assuredly presents difficulties, that Kirchhoff bases his theory of a large interpolation within the Telemachy, itself a late addition to the Return of Odysseus. Telemachus is bidden to call the Wooers to an assembly on the following day, the gods being witnesses. He is to bid the wooers scatter to their own lands, and, if his mother is so inclined, she is to return to her father, 'and they' (her father's people) 'will make a wedding feast, and furnish the wedding gifts, all that should go back with a dearly beloved child.' The ἔεδνα are the bride-price paid by the wooer. Where the child was very dear, they, or a portion of them, were expended on her, a custom still prevalent in some countries.[1] Now, Telemachus does not succeed in carrying out this advice, or rather, nothing comes of his acting on it. The advice, and its acceptance, are merely *pro forma*. In i. 372, on the evening of Athene's appearance, he says to the wooers, 'To-morrow let us go to the assembly, that I may clearly

[1] See Mr. Merry's note on the passage, and Appendix, Note B, to *Odyssey*, Butcher and Lang.

speak out my saying to you—namely, to leave my halls,
but, if you think it better to waste one man's wealth unatoned, waste away, only I will call to the gods; if Zeus
grants revenge, then shall you all perish in the house—
unavenged.' On the following day (ii. 40–79) he explains
his position to the whole assembly of the people. Antinous
bids him send his mother home, and let her father give her
in marriage. Till then the wooers will waste his house.
Telemachus (130) says he cannot send his mother away
against her will. He then gives the *formal* notice (ii. 139),
'Go forth from my halls,' with the appeal to Zeus and the
threat that the wooers shall perish unavenged.

All this in itself is perfectly clear. The warning, first
given in private, is not expected to make the wooers withdraw. It is a mere legal observance repeated in public
assembly for the sake of procuring witnesses. After this
warning, if the wooers persist, no *wergeld*, no ποινή, or
atonement, will be paid to their kin after they are slain. It
is not expected that they will accept the warning, but the
warning puts it beyond the power of their kin to make
legal claim for atonement.[1]

So far, and so considered, there is no difficulty in
Athene's advice nor in the action of Telemachus. The
first part of the advice is given *pro forma*, and is carried
out in the same spirit. Kirchhoff, however, finds that only
the frivolous reader, who takes a superficial view, can be
satisfied. Yet no earlier critic had complained; that was left
to Kirchhoff. We may surely answer that if the passage has
hitherto satisfied the world for more than two thousand
years, the poet's purpose has been sufficiently served.[2]

[1] Compare Baron Bradwardine's payment of atonement and his
'Letters of Slains' in *Waverley*, and the general course of legal proceedings in the Icelandic sagas.

[2] Kirchhoff, p. 240. Kammer points out that Kirchhoff had been
anticipated—by Jacob.

Athene next bids Telemachus consider how to expel the
wooers (i. 270). But she never shows him how he is to
do this. There is inconsistency and verbal difficulty in
lines 274–278 : 'Bid the wooers disperse, and let your
mother go home and get married.' And certainly Athene's
speech would be much improved if she said, ' For the sake
of legal form, bid the wooers disperse, and offer your
mother a choice of returning to her father. The wooers
will not budge, your mother will not go, and then you must
act as I shall dictate.' If Athene had spoken thus, all
would be plain sailing. The question is whether her
succinctness can only be explained as a mechanical use,
in her speech, of words adapted from a subsequent, but,
in date of composition, earlier, passage, where Telemachus
speaks (ii. 140) in the assembly, and the wooer Eurymachus replies. In Kirchhoff's opinion, the passage in
book i. is a mechanical repetition of the passages in book ii.
We have already said that Telemachus's double issue of the
warning—first in the hall in book i., second in the assembly
in book ii.—is not necessarily superfluous. The legal
formality, with all the people for witnesses, had to be
accomplished. Textual repetition of statements is a 'note'
of ballad and early epic, as in the *Song of Roland*, but
critics constantly regard such repetitions of formulæ, and
useful half lines or lines, as proofs of interpolation. In any
case, Kirchhoff decides that the confusion of the statement
of Athene in book i. is a result of unintelligent transposi-
tion. The verbal difficulties are the necessary ' Nemesis '
of a mechanical rearrangement, by which the words are
squeezed into a strange environment. Hence all that is
essentially connected with i. 270 is later than what follows
from the speeches of Telemachus and Eurymachus.

There are other troubles. The proposal to marry off
the mother before Odysseus's death is ascertained conflicts

with Athene's later advice to seek news of the father. To this we may reply that the advice to marry Penelope is merely formal — that it certainly would not be accepted. After due season and a year's waiting, Penelope might be compelled to make a choice: in the conclusion she actually begins to make one. Again, there are difficulties about the ἕδνα, which were (in the first instance) provided by the wooer, not by the father. Once more Telemachus, after seeking news of his father, is bidden to wait a year, then marry off his mother, and then when, *ex hypothesi*, the wooers have dispersed, consider how he may kill them, openly or by guile, in his own hall (i. 295). But, *ex hypothesi*, they will by that time have left the hall. We may answer that, whether they had left or not, he had his injuries to revenge, his honour to restore, which he might do by giving a farewell feast, and slaying the wooers. The logical sequence of Athene's speech is certainly faulty in the earlier part. But can this only be accounted for by a late author of book i. manipulating what he found in the much older book ii.?

Anyone who 'could build a hexameter' and could draw the noble picture of the wooers' arrogance (and this the despised redactor must have done) could also surely have arranged his matter in a more adequate way. Later we see that, by Kirchhoff's confession, he could dovetail very skilfully. He needed not to steal and spoil a passage. The economy of phrases in the epics is a curious and difficult subject, but the textual repetition of a message or counsel need cause us little trouble. However, the long analysis of Kirchhoff leads him to regard book ii. as the work of a much earlier poet than book i., with all that depends on it after line 86. As a consequence, we seem to have two poets engaged on the adventures of Telemachus, uninteresting as these are, apart from their connection with

Odysseus. It is rather amusing to find that Kirchhoff
(ii. 262) has to explain the prayer of Telemachus to 'the
god who came last night to our house '—namely, to Athene.
—as an interpolation. On his hypothesis, no god had come
to the house at all, and book i., after line 86, was later than
book ii. Therefore, the interpolator who so clumsily and
mechanically wrought book i. by assistance from book ii.
could none the less in ii. 260 make a masterly piece of
dovetailing ! If he could do it, why did he not do it,
except on an artistic theory that he must repeat a piece
of advice textually? But, if that was a rule of epic composition, such repetitions are not suspicious. As usual, a
theory of separatism necessitates arbitrary excision of whatever does not make for it, though there may be nothing
against the passage excised but collision with the theory.
Meanwhile Niese[1] accepts book i. as ratified by the allusion
in book ii. 262.

Yet Niese regards the speech of Athene and her advice
(i. 269–278) as late. If the goddess did not give the
counsel therein, what did she come for, and what did she
do? The goddess performs what she promised (i. 90–95).
Telemachus takes a course of action. What was the
goddess's counsel, if not that which she proclaimed and
he acted upon ?

This consideration militates against Niese's theory that,
though book i. is genuine, the provocation to the wooers by
Telemachus and the much discussed speech of Athene as
Mentes are probably late. As Athene's speech stands, it is
undeniably very awkward, but if she was to advise Telemachus at all, she must have given, in some shape, the
counsel which he took. Niese does not believe that the
Telemachia was once a separate poem, of which the
original beginning and end are lost, nor that the first book

---

[1] *Die Entwickelung der Homerischen Poesie*, p. 148, note 1.

of the Odyssey is later than and was modelled on the second.[1] The *Telemachia* is based on the Odyssey as we have it, and no other *Motivirung* for it is conceivable : the voyage of Telemachus by itself is motiveless, and it has its origin in 'the counsel of the goddess' in book i. The expedition is only conceivable as part of the epic as it stands. Nor are the adventures of Telemachus connected only with book i., but are interwoven with the whole poem. The warning of Telemachus, the prophecy of Athene in book i., point directly to the conclusion—the slaying of the wooers, which, again, is prepared by other prophecies and omens in other parts of the *Telemachia*, as ii. 141-176, and in books iii. and iv. We may add that, through a meeting with Telemachus, the second-sighted man, Theoclymenus, is brought into the tale, and it is he who delivers the clearest and most appalling prophecy of the slaying. Thus, and in other ways, the *Telemachia* is inextricably interlaced with and essential to the Odyssey.

The unlucky book i. has been tattered, as we saw, by Kirchhoff. Wilamowitz gets rid of it altogether. He does not, like Kirchhoff, spare lines 1-87. The book is indivisible, it is intended for the place which it occupies, it gives the 'exposition' of our Odyssey from beginning to end, introducing the old slave and Laertes, who are brought forward at the conclusion, even in book xxiv. From beginning to end, it is a *Flick-Poesie*, a piece of patchwork, and is about the latest element in the whole Odyssey. Moreover, the book is indispensable : without it book ii. has no beginning. The beginning which it once had must have been cut out to make place for book i. Doubtless the old beginning of ii. was destroyed by the author of book i. The beginning of book v. has also disappeared. At present it opens with an uninteresting assembly of gods. The

[1] *Op. cit.* p. 148.

patcher has got rid of the original opening for the purpose of uniting the *Telemachia* and Return of Odysseus into a single poem. He employed his scissors and tailoring skill on the conclusion of book iv. (p. 21).

Granting all this for a moment, we ask why did this tailor of the Muses, or why did Kirchhoff's redactor, undertake his task? What had he to get by making a long epic out of several shorter poems and shoddy of his own in the seventh century B.C.? Where was he to find an audience? There were no longer any royal and heroic halls wherein he could rant through his rubbish; nay, the rhapsodists were probably beginning to recite selected passages to popular crowds on days of festival.

Is it to be supposed that he looked for his reward to a public of readers? The composition of ' Cyclic' epics by men of known names, who, doubtless, got some credit by their labours, had already begun, unless the ' Cyclic' poems, too, were patchwork, made for no conceivable purpose. Why did the anonymous patcher betake him to this industry, to making a long epic? We hear of lack of ' motive' in parts of the poems; the motive of the botcher is more sadly to seek. How his long work won acceptance in an age of lyrics and short ' selections' from epic song is another problem. Why did all Greece adopt it and regard it as inspired, and assign it to Homer? A literary tradition, once established, may conceivably blind us to the faults of a poem. But the Odyssey is not one of the works, like those of Pindar, or like many of the tragedies, which now depend chiefly on tradition and on the taste of the learned for their success. It is enjoyed by children and the unlettered, as well as by scholars. Its innumerable faults, its detestable and mechanical composition, had almost escaped notice till they were spied out by recent criticism, especially by Wilamowitz Moellendorff.

The first book is, as we saw, by 'the journeyman poet,' and is a fair sample of his manner. For example, in book i. Athene disguises herself as Mentes, a Taphian chief. In book ii. (older than book i.) she appears in the form of Mentor, an Ithacan, and a friend of Odysseus. In answer to a prayer of Telemachus, she joins him in Mentor's guise, and he does not suspect her to be a goddess till she disappears as a sea eagle from the feast at Pylos. The name Mentes occurs as that of a Ciconian leader in the Iliad (xvii. 73).

This resemblance of the names Mentes and Mentor, and the similarity of the parts played by the goddess under each name, are stumbling-blocks to the critic. Again, ii. 328, the wooers mock Telemachus, saying that he will go to Sparta, or Pylos, or fruitful Ephyra to fetch a poisonous drug wherewith to destroy them. Now, in i. 259, Athene, in guise of Mentor, tells how Odysseus once went to Ephyra to Ilus, Mermerus's son, in search of poison for his arrows. Ilus gave it not, from awe of the gods, but Mentes's father gave it. In the speech of the wooers, we must look on Ephyra as a 'hypothetically named land'; in book i. it is a definite place with a king, Ilus. In the second book the fetching of the poison is a 'base insinuation'; in the first book it is a matter of fact. 'Can borrowing of book i. from book ii. be coarser or more palpable?' The *Scholia* mention three towns called Ephyra: 1, the old name for Corinth; 2, a city in Thesprotia; and 3, one in Elis. Mr. Merry finds eleven cities so styled; the choice here is between that in Thesprotia [1] and the city in Elis. If we knew where Taphos was we might determine which town Odysseus would touch at in returning to Ithaca from Ephyra. But we do not know. There are traditions of Agamede, daughter of an Elean king, as a sorceress, who

---

[1] Iliad, vi. 152. Mr. Leaf's note.

knew all drugs that earth bears.[1] This would point to
poison-bearing Ephyra as in Elis. But the scholiast says
that Ilus, king of Ephyra, was great-grandson of Jason and
Medea, and a king of Thesprotia. Thus the evidence in
favour of Thesprotia and Elis is about equally balanced,
and equally worthless, being probably invented by later
upholders of one or the other site. But Wilamowitz
Moellendorff (p. 25) decrees that Ephyra and her poisons
are borrowed in book i. from book ii., and *therefore* the two
books do not allude to the same Ephyra. In ii. the Elean
city is meant as being near Sparta and Pylos, whither
Telemachus is going. But the mention of Ilus shows that
the patcher in book i. meant Ephyra in Thesprotia. The
stupid botcher misunderstood book ii., and introduced in
book i. a person, Ilus, a descendant of Medea, from the
later Argonautic cycle. This makes the botcher late, and
defines his home as that of a man interested in Thesprotia.
He knows the western seas ; of Asia he knows nothing,
but that is the country familiar to the earlier poet of the
Telemachia.

To us it seems plain enough that the genealogy from
Medea and the disputes about Ephyra are the work of
persons later than the Odyssey, genealogists who wished to
attach family pedigrees to Homeric origins. Arguments
like those of Wilamowitz Moellendorff are infinitely more
apt to excite suspicion than anything in the Odyssey.
But by dint of such arguments both the badness of the
botcher's work and his late date, as well as his geographical
position, are to be determined.

There are more charges against book i. In line 154 a
herald hands the lyre to Phemius, the minstrel. This
proves that Phemius was blind, in the botcher's opinion.
But (xxii. 331) Phemius catches hold of the lyre for him-

[1] Iliad, xi. 741.

self at the massacre of the wooers, when he appeals for
mercy, or rather he has the lyre in his hands. His blind-
ness is derived from Demodocus in viii. (the critic says
in vii.) 261 by the stupid botcher. Was ever such an argument? It neither follows that a bard is blind because, after
a feast, he lets a herald bring him his lyre, nor that he can
see, because he has his lyre in his hands, when he needs it,
to save his life, as a symbol of his profession. The chances
are that he could see perfectly well.

Next (i. 425), Telemachus has a bedroom ' builded
high in the fair court, with a wide prospect,' perhaps in
a gate tower. *Das ist der reine Gallimathias,* according
to the critic, and is taken from xiv. 6, the court of
Eumæus. Why should it be? We never saw an Homeric
house, and know nothing of such a detail as this. Telemachus (437) sits down on his bed, and takes off his
chiton. But the chiton reached to his feet. How, then,
could he take it off when sitting down? The critic can try
the experiment with his night-shirt; he will be far from
ingenious, if he does not solve the problem. But he decides that the botcher simply stole the line from Iliad
ii. 42, where Agamemnon sits up in bed, and puts *on* his
chiton.

Penelope (i. 332-335) enters the hall to stop the song
of the Return of the Achæans. Two maids go with her;
she veils her face, and stands by the door-post. Borrowing
again, and stupid borrowing! She does the same thing in
xviii. 208-211, but *then*, out of coquetry, to charm the
wooers. But there is no coquetry in i. 332-335; here, then,
is imbecile theft. This is worthy of the other arguments.
In book xviii. Eurycleia advises Penelope to wash and
anoint herself, and charm the wooers. She does not take
the advice; but Athene gives her beauty. There is

nothing coquettish in her conduct in book i. The passage is as clearly a formula as in ballads—

> Stately stepped he east the ha'
> And stately stepped he west.

By these magnificently convincing arguments, with some from Kirchhoff, Wilamowitz Moellendorff demonstrates that the first book and the prologue, so much admired by Horace, are trash—and late trash, and trash from Western Greece.

When was it ever heard of that the gods sent Hermes, as in the prologue, to warn a man from a deed of sin (i. 38)? Why should the gods care about Ægisthus? This is just a stopgap, and serves as well as another. Well, as Clytæmnestra was a daughter of Zeus, and as Ægisthus may have been generous in sacrifice, the gods might well be interested in their common affairs. But the critic finds it all as absurd as the poisoned arrows of Odysseus. 'O le grand homme, rien ne lui peut plaire!' Zeus gives a genealogy of Polyphemus in i. 71, 72, most necessary for the exposition of the story, because the hearer wants to know why Odysseus was persecuted, and the cause of the wrath of Poseidon. In ix. 412 the Cyclopes reveal to Odysseus, by their conversation with the blinded giant, his name, and his relationship to Poseidon. Why should Homer bring that in, if it was he who, in book i., told us who the Cyclops was? Manifestly because, though we know from book i., Odysseus does *not* know, and has to be told. We are to decide that the passage in the prologue, being genealogical, is late, and out of keeping with the passage in book ix. This is to quarrel with the exposition of the poem, because it is an exposition. It does not serve for the poet to let the reader or hearer discover gradually what the hero gradually discovers. The reader or hearer needs to be put in possession of the essential facts from the first, and this is admirably managed in the prologue, the work of the botcher.

Hesiod mentions Calypso in a catalogue of nymphs,[1] and derives her from Oceanus and Tethys. She is a nymph in i. 14, ' the lady nymph Calypso, that fair goddess.' She is also (i. 52) daughter of Atlas. There-fore Hesiod knew book v., where Calypso is a nymph, not book vii. (245), where she is daughter of Atlas, nor book i. She is both a nymph and a goddess in book v. Does it follow that books i. and vii. are later than Hesiod (what-ever the date of the *Theogony* may be), because Hesiod, for genealogical purposes, adopts a different tradition? Again, if the author of i. and vii. be later than Hesiod, why does he not accept Hesiod's genealogical version? On this system, we may as well argue that the author of book i. is earlier than Hesiod, because he does not know Hesiod, as that Hesiod is earlier than the author of book i., because he ' does not know ' book i.

The same pun is made in the name of Odysseus in i. 60 - 62 and xix. 409 : ' das τ ἐτυμολογεῖ, das α παρετυμολογεῖ.' Atlas, in relation to Calypso, is borrowed from the Heracles saga. The botcher's native land is determined, among other things, by his mention of going to Temesa for copper (i. 184). For Temesa[2] is in Bruttium ; hence, far to the west ; hence the botcher is a Western man. Temesa is usually taken to be Tamasus, or Tamassus, in Cyprus.[3] The botcher knew the West ; Asia he did not know. The author of the *Telemachia*, on the other hand, knew Asia, not the West, for he gives a fantastic geography of Pylos, as no-thing is said of crossing Taygetus, in the drive from Pylos to Sparta (iii. 470–497). If the Asiatic author of the *Tele-*

---

[1] *Theog.* 359.
[2] Strabo, i. 6, 6, 255.
[3] *Cuprum* (copper) = *aes Cyprium.* Ameis.

T

machia knew so little of Pylos, he was to blame, for the chiefs of Miletus and Colophon, in Asia, looked on Pylos as their original home. Pheræ in Messenia (Kalamata) the borrower stole from Iliad v. 543, where there is a genealogy of Diocles. Why the botcher, when he was about stealing localities and genealogies, did not steal from Hesiod, in the matter of Calypso's parentage, as he was later than Hesiod, does not appear.

For these reasons, and such as these, book i. is the work of a late incompetent cento-maker, residing in or near Corinth, or Eubœa, while the *Telemachia*, a separate poem mangled by the botcher, is earlier, and was made in Asia Minor. By means of arguments hardly less ingenious and convincing, we are enabled to track the botcher through the rest of his nefarious industries.[1]

[1] The mere literary student cannot but sympathise with Kammer's spirited defence of the true poetic merit in much of book i. (*Einheit der Odyssee*, p. 286). To say, like Kirchhoff, that the book, from 88 to 444, 'is scarcely more than a mere cento,' is to lay oneself open to refutation by any reader of ordinary feeling.

CHAPTER XI

WITHOUT pursuing here the analysis of the Odyssey, book
by book, we may diverge to arguments by which Kirchhoff
and others establish the late date of the epic in the only
form in which we know it. Certain of the reasons for this
opinion are given in Kirchhoff's second dissertation, at the
close of the first twelve books. The second excursus of
Kirchhoff may be said to take its rise from a curious passage in book vii. The hero has been cast on the shore of
Phæacia, after his shipwreck as he sailed from Calypso's
island. He has met Nausicaa, the daughter of the king ;
she has clothed him, and he has entered the palace of
Alcinous. He is first entertained by his hosts, and then,
in accordance with Homeric manners,[1] the Phæacian queen,
Arete, asks Odysseus who he is, whence he comes, and who
gave him the garments which he wears, and which she
recognises (vii. 237-239). Now, the maiden Nausicaa had
given them out of those which she had been washing, for
Odysseus was cast naked on shore. The hero has some
delicacy about mentioning this encounter, before he has
won the favour of her parents. Now, if he merely answered
the queen's first question, 'Who are you and whence come
you ?' by saying 'I am Odysseus, Laertes's son,' doubtless

---

[1] Compare Helen's inquiries of Telemachus, iv. 140.

the queen would be more than satisfied.   But the poet
would miss a much more striking moment for the avowal,
which is only made after Odysseus has won great renown
by his athletic skill, and great sympathy by his weeping
when the minstrel recites a lay on the siege of Troy.   At
that moment (ix. 19), in the full and festive gathering of
Phæacians, with all eyes bent on the mighty and mysterious
wanderer, he says, 'I am Odysseus, Laertes's son.'   The
poet, we think, was justified in keeping his secret for that
hour.   Consequently, when Arete (vii. 237) asks him his
name, and who gave him the garments, he merely says
that it would be hard to tell all his woes, and simply describes the isle Ogygia, and his lonely residence there with
Calypso, after his shipwreck (vii. 240-250).   But, as the
poem stands, after line 250, he repeats his statement
about Calypso (vii. 251-258) in a sufficiently awkward
manner.   In most texts these lines are bracketed as spurious.   He then recites his misadventure with the raft, and
acknowledges the kindness of Nausicaa.   Alcinous promises
him an escort home next day, and he goes to bed without
answering the queen's question, 'Who are you, and
whence?'

  This delay arouses the suspicions of Kirchhoff, who prints
in smaller type as later, and not original, the lines vii. 243-
251; and again, the poem from vii. 297 to ix. 16, where
Odysseus begins to tell his name.   This passage includes
the account of Nausicaa's kindness, as given by Odysseus
to her father (book viii.), with the sports in Phæacia and
the athletic triumph of Odysseus, the lay about Ares and
Aphrodite sung by Demodocus, the presents given to
Odysseus, the touching farewell of Nausicaa—'Remember
me in thine own land ; to me thou owest thy life's price'—
the later lay of Demodocus about Ilios, the tears of Odysseus
as he listens, and thus the leading up to his avowal of his

name. In small type, too, Kirchhoff prints (x.) the story of
the Læstrygonians, by whose enmity Odysseus lost all but
one of his ships, and the tale of Circe, till we reach book xi.
and the adventure in Hades.

All these passages are later, and not original. Kirchhoff cannot reconcile himself to the delay in telling the
name in book vii.[1] This, he holds, is a fault in composition, incident on a later forcing in of new material. The
concealing of the name cannot be part of the original plan.
There must be a gap in the text, the original poet cannot
have composed the speech as it now stands. Then the
doubling of the statement about Ogygia and Calypso (in
vii. 250–259) is suspicious. There is a gap here, and Aristarchus[2] was for rejecting the passage. On the other hand,
ancient critics praised the conduct of Odysseus, in first
winning sympathy by the story of his wreck before introducing Nausicaa, and in concealing his name, till he had
gained renown among the Phæacians.[3] The repetition
about Calypso has been explained as a confusion of two
texts.[4] Kirchhoff, on the other hand, holds that a passage
wherein Odysseus instantly revealed his name was removed
by some redactor, for purposes of interpolation, and that
confusion was caused by this means. The new poet's purpose required the concealment of the hero's name.

When were all these changes made? The greater part
of x., xi., xii.—namely, the Læstrygonian adventure, Circe,
portions of the scenes in Hades, the Sirens, the Rocks
Wandering, the eating of the cattle of the Sun, Scylla and
Charybdis—can be dated by Kirchhoff. 'The motive of
this part of Odysseus's narrative betrays a close connection with the story of the Argonauts' (p. 287). Thus
Circe is a sister of Æetes, the wizard king of the Argonaut

---

[1] Kirchhoff, p. 278.   [2] Scholia on vii. 251.   [3] Scholia on vii. 244.
[4] Friedländer ; *Philologus*, iv. 588, ap. Kirchhoff.

saga. The Rocks Wandering were only escaped previously by Jason's vessel, 'Argo, that all men wot of,' as the poet specially remarks (xii. 70). In the Læstrygonia of the Odyssey is a spring, Artacia. There was such a spring at Cyzicus, and in Cyzicus the Argonauts met giants like the Læstrygonians. This Artaçia is an historical spring; Alcæus mentioned it.[1] These Argonautic details, then, were by a late and arbitrary process foisted into the Odyssey, a poem of the Trojan cycle. Moreover, the passages must be later than knowledge of the fountain of Artacia, and the 'localising' of Argonautic adventures at Cyzicus, consequently, later than the Greek colonisation of Cyzicus. That is dated by some in the seventh, by others in the twenty-fourth Olympiad. Hence, Kirchhoff would not date our present Odyssey as it stands earlier than the thirtieth Olympiad. Indeed, it was known between Olympiads 30–48, when the chest of Cypselus was made, for that chest was adorned, among other works of art, with a representation of Odysseus asleep with Circe.[2]

Now, no doubt, the Odyssey was known in the time of the making of the chest of Cypselus. But the arguments of Kirchhoff are singularly unconvincing. The incidents of the Argonautic legend are of extreme and universal antiquity as fairy tales and heroic legends. The chief of the plot of the saga is found in Samoa, North America, Russia, Finland, Scotland, Madagascar.[3] The Rocks Wandering are known to the Aztecs. The Sirens are familiar in the folk-lore of most peoples. Jason is mentioned in the Iliad in vii. 469, xxi. 41, xxiii. 747. The Læstrygonian giants are placed on a fiord, in the land of the Midnight Sun ; they are clearly derived (as has been said) from vague

---

[1] Apollonius Rhodius, i. 957, scholion.
[2] Pausanias, v. 19. 7. The chest was probably earlier.
[3] See ' A Far-travelled Tale' in the author's *Custom and Myth*.

travellers' tales, borne along the Amber Route from the Baltic. They have no connection with Asia Minor. In brief, this part, like other parts of the Odyssey, connects with its hero a mass of primæval fairy tales of dateless antiquity. The saga of the Argonauts also dealt with some of these, and with some other fairy tales, as of Phrixus and Hellê, and especially with the widely diffused tale of the wanderer who achieves adventures by aid of the magician's daughter. Poems on these topics were known to the author of the Odyssey, but we do not possess the original lays of Argo which he knew. We have only the Alexandrine and late imitative epic of Apollonius Rhodius, and the legend in Pindar, and the so-called Orphic poem, and hints in Hesiod. Because Homer refers to Jason, and knows primitive legends used in the Argonautic cycle, it does not follow that the author of this piece of the Odyssey was using contemporary epics, and working *after* the localising of part of the Argo saga at Cyzicus. In Solon's time Mimnermus did not localise the home of the wizard king at Colchis, but placed it vaguely on 'the brink of Ocean.' The fountain Artacia (from the isle Artacê) has very little to do with the Argonaut saga. The Læstrygonians have nothing to do with Cyzicus at all. The Asiatic coasts were known long before the Greek colonies were planted there. The adventure of the Argonauts at Cyzicus is quite a late piece of poetry.[1] In brief, so sweeping a theory of lateness in the Odyssey has rarely been based on such insignificant evidence. It is very much easier to believe that the poet for good artistic reasons delayed the *éclaircissement* of Odysseus, than that a later poet worked in a huge cantle for the purpose of plagiarising from an Argonautic poem, itself late.

The peculiar subtlety by which Kirchhoff establishes

---

[1] Niese, pp. 223-224.

that parts of the poem once existed in an earlier shape, and
that, as they now stand, they have been mechanically
altered to fit a new purpose, may be illustrated from his
third excursus.

This is based on xii. 374-390. In these lines Odysseus
tells how, after his comrades had eaten the cattle of
Hyperion, Lampetie carried the news to the Sun, who
threatened to leave heaven and shine among the dead.
Zeus avenged him by striking the ship of Odysseus with
a thunder-bolt, and the hero alone escaped. Of what
passed in heaven he heard from Calypso, who had it from
Hermes (xii. 390). The whole passage in the Venetian MS.
is marked with the sign of doubt or rejection. The scholiast has a note asking why the Sun, who sees all, should
need intelligence brought by a messenger? This is merely
an example of that essential characteristic of mythology,
inconsistency, and need not detain us. Then, how could
Odysseus hear the tale from Calypso, and she from Hermes?
She had never met Hermes before, according to the scholion
on v. 79, and when he visited her island to demand
Odysseus's release, only recognised him 'by a divine
instinct.' This is not very evident ; a god can see a god,
though he be invisible to mortals. Hence Athene's use of
the Cap of Darkness in the Iliad. Calypso greets Hermes
kindly as ' dear,' and asks him why he comes now ; ' before
you did not come often' (v. 87), which certainly does not
imply that he never came at all, that she never saw him
before. Odysseus has now been seven years with Calypso,
since his wreck. Though Hermes rarely called, he may
have come once in five years with some gossip from
Olympus. The poet makes Odysseus give his authority
for the scene in heaven, because mortals, not being inspired
poets, are supposed not to know what passes in the highest
circles.

These considerations seem childish; there is no real difficulty in the matter. But Kirchhoff finds here signs of mechanical foisting of matter originally conceived for another purpose into the organic whole of the original Return. He thinks it very unpoetical in a poet to let Odysseus cite his *Quelle*, his 'sources,' but the religious feeling of the epic makes it necessary. We saw in the Iliad how much trouble was caused to commentators when Agamemnon told a tale of what occurred in heaven about Heracles, without giving his authority (xix. 95). Kirchhoff so much resents the introduction of the story of Helios and Lampetie in this place, where it interrupts the action, that he regards it as part of a poem in which this adventure was originally told by the author, speaking of Odysseus in the third person. It had then to be amalgamated with the books in which Odysseus tells his own tale in the first person. The spirit and character of the older lay could not be kept up in the new transformation. The difficulties are not original nor the result of interpolation merely, but come of a mechanical attempt, by an incompetent hand, to dovetail an old poem, told in the third person, into a later poem where, in the first person, the hero recited his own adventures. Kirchhoff, indeed, goes so far as to reconstruct the original poem in the third person. Odysseus wakes with a smell of cooking about him, and cries to Zeus that his sleep has ruined him. So spoke he, and Lampetie went to Helios, the scene in heaven followed, and Odysseus went to the ship. Niese (p. 183) does not see that the passage is rendered less offensive by being told in the third person, and thinks that Kirchhoff lays too heavy a weight on his evidence. To consider as Kirchhoff does is to consider very curiously; to found a whole theory of late 're-daction' on such ideas of æsthetic propriety in narrative is audacious. The later the date, the more democratic the

society, the more lyrical the trend of poetry, the less
temptation there would be to expand an old epic. It could
no longer be recited to a chief and his retainers on consecutive winter evenings; the fashion was in favour of
cutting rhapsodies for recitation out of long epics, not of
lengthening what was already long.

There is more to the same purpose. How, in book x.
277, did Odysseus know that the young man who gave him
a magic herb in Circe's isle was Hermes? A poet might
know, as being inspired, but how could a hero? Why, we
answer, who but a god could it be? No mortals were on
the island. The herb is 'hard to dig for men; to gods all
things are easy' (x. 306). What man, in an island where
there were none, could have done a feat so hard for
mortals to do, and could have laid down the magic law of
a root that constrains goddesses? No mere mortal could
possibly have done all this, and the hero, not being a
dullard, readily recognised Hermes. The 'redactor,' in
a moment of negligence, forgot to make Odysseus give his
authority. Clearly his common sense was his authority.
The poet is blamed where a character gives his authority,
and also when he does not. Odysseus was a hero, not a
commentator. Moreover, he learned later from Circe (x.
331) that Hermes had foretold to her his coming, and the
shrewdness for which Athene praises him enabled him to
combine his information. Then it is to Kirchhoff a very
suspicious circumstance that Odysseus knows the name
of the Læstrygonian fountain, Artacia, where his men par-
leyed with the Læstrygonian woman. A bard might know
it, but how could a hero? There are other criticisms of
a similar weight and obviousness, which all tend to show
that book x., much of xi., and xii. are late patchwork in
their present form. But, even if we admit that they were
once narrated by the poet, not the hero, the Odyssey never

could have existed without the adventures which they contain. Without the Læstrygonians how can we get rid of
the most of Odysseus's ships and companions? Without
the cattle of the Sun how can we deprive him of the ship
which was left, and of his remaining comrades? Without
Circe how is he to reach Hades and hear the essential
prophecies? It is necessary that he should arrive in Ithaca
alone ; the plot and interest demand it. The end is achieved
by the aid of books which, in their present or an older
form, must always have belonged to the epic.

As we are now concerned with these deathless ladies,
Circe and Calypso, we may examine critical opinions as to
their connection with the Odyssey. Wilamowitz [1] has practically destroyed the authority of book i., where Athene
tells us all about Calypso, how she is the daughter of the
wizard Atlas, and dwells in an isle, the navel of the deep.
What book i. and other books and passages wrought by the
botcher say 'is not evidence,' we can only get evidence
about Calypso from book v. This only is genuine. The
author of book v. practically created the part of Calypso,
'The Concealer.' When he ceases, the Concealer falls back
into concealment. Calypso is a creature of *fiction*, artistic
fiction ; Circe, the daughter of the Sun, is a child of real
saga, ancient popular legend. Though the circumstances
of the two ladies are very dissimilar, it is inconceivable that
the two are not essentially identical, that one of them is not
modelled after the other. Now, Calypso, a thing of *fiction*,
is the later ; Circe the earlier. There was a time when
legend knew of Odysseus's residence with Circe, but did
not know of his stay with Calypso. Yet, astonishing as it
seems, *our* Circe, in the poem as it stands, borrows from
our Calypso, not our Calypso from our Circe. The process
appears to be of this sort : —

[1] *Op. cit.* 115–129.

1. Circe is known to saga.

2. Calypso is based by an independent poet on Circe, in saga.

3. That poet's Calypso is followed by the poet who did the books on Circe in our extant Odyssey.

These brilliant combinations are thus justified. In book xii. 312, Odysseus has landed, against his will, on Thrinacia, where pasture the sacred cattle of the Sun. 'And when it was the third watch of the night, and the stars had crossed the zenith, Zeus, the cloud-gatherer, roused against our company an angry wind, with wondrous tempest, and shrouded in clouds, land and sea alike, *and from heaven spea down the Night.*' As it *was* night already, how could Night speed down from heaven? We may answer that Night dwelling in heaven, draws nearer earth as it grows darker and denser, when the stars are obliterated by cloud. The passage, too, is a frequent formula, descriptive of storm. But Wilamowitz discerns that, when it is night already, night cannot speed down from heaven. Consequently, this passage in book xii. is borrowed, and idiotically borrowed, from some place where it had a proper meaning. Now, xii. 314, 315, is identical with ix. 67, 68, and we may compare v. 293, 294. Therefore, xii. is borrowed from those earlier passages. Book xii. here also contains a false Æolicism, a sign of late date. This, and a comparison of the oaths exacted from Calypso in book v., and Circe, in book x., proves books x. and xii. to be borrowed from book v., where Calypso appears, and therefore 'our' Circe is later than, and modelled on 'our' Calypso. Kirchhoff errs when he adopts the opposite view, that Circe herself is later than Calypso, and not an original figure of the saga, but a copy of Medea in the Argonautic legend. We possess Calypso in the original shape; our Circe reaches us in a later than her original form. As Calypso, however, is a thing of fiction, not of saga, and had in the saga no place at first, it is plain that when Odysseus was wrecked, after the misdeeds in Thrinacia, he could not go to Calypso, but went straight to Phæacia. There was no Calypso's isle for him to go to, she was not yet in existence. In xix. 273–280, Odysseus, disguised as a beggar, is telling a mixture of truth and falsehood to Penelope. There he omits Calypso, and says that Odysseus, after the wreck off Thrinacia, came to Phæacia, ' on the keel of the ship.' In the twenty-third book, however, recapitulating the story of his adventures to his wife, he speaks of Calypso. The whole tale of Calypso was thus originally a distinct poem, by no mean poet, and, later, it was thrust into its present place in the course of compilation and redaction and general botching. The piece is beautiful, but it is not *Volkspoesie*.

None of the epic, to our mind, is *Volkspoesie*. So this distinction of Wilamowitz's does not appeal to us.

He decides that Leucothea, the lady of the sea, who lends Odysseus her veil, is a figure of the Ionian Asiatic coast. She is daughter of Ino, daughter of Cadmus. Now, Cadmus is probably connected with Miletus. Miletus, according to Stephanus, was once called Calypso's isle, a statement possibly derived from Philo of Byblus. All this is very vague, but it is an example of the arguments in favour of the Ionic and Asiatic origin of much of the Odyssey.

We have already examined another instance of this persistent endeavour to make the Odyssey late—the arguments of Kirchhoff founded on the mention of the fountain Artacia. Yet another effort is made by Kirchhoff.

In a long excursus (iv.) based on two texts in the Odyssey, passages in Eustathius and a number of scholia and Hesiodic fragments, he attempts to bring the date of the completion of the poem down to the fiftieth

Olympiad, and below the age of Eugammon of Cyrene, about 570 B.C. It is impossible to give a summary here of many very minute arguments and singular combinations. In Odyssey xvi. 118, to be brief, Eumæus states a genealogy of Odysseus's family, in which it was hereditary to have only one son. Arceisius begat Laertes, who begat Odysseus, who begat Telemachus, and Telemachus, says Eustathius, according to Hesiod, begat Perseptolis, by Polycaste, youngest daughter of Nestor. Now, she is only mentioned in the Odyssey in iii. 464, where she bathes Telemachus in accordance with Homeric custom. On this line some genealogist obviously based a theory of an illicit amour between Telemachus and the daughter of his host, the sister of his friend. It is perfectly plain that Hesiod is later than Homer, for he geographically localised the scenes of adventures which Homer placed in unknown seas.[1] Yet Kirchhoff argues that the so-called Hesiod did not know our Odyssey as it stands (vii. 54), for in that passage the King and Queen of Phæacia are said to be derived from the same ancestors,

$$\text{ἐκ δὲ τοκήων}$$
$$\text{τῶν αὐτῶν.}$$

Nausithoos begat Rhexenor and Alcinous, Arete was the daughter of Rhexenor, and Alcinous married her, his niece. Now, the scholiast on vii. 54 says that Hesiod, in a lost passage, supposed Alcinous and Arete to be brother and sister. Therefore, in Kirchhoff's theory, Hesiod did not know the genealogy by which Homer makes the pair uncle and niece. Of course, if the passage is later than Hesiod, because he did not know it, it is just as easily maintained that the passage is earlier than Hesiod, because to the Odyssey Hesiod is unknown. But Kirchhoff argues that this part of the Odyssey did not exist when the Hesiodic genealogy

[1] Strabo, i. 23. See Kirchhoff, p. 319.

mentioned by the scholiast was constructed. We might also reply that the Hesiodic genealogist was careless and misunderstood the Homeric phrase 'from the same parents,' or that he followed a tradition according to which Phæacian marriages of brother and sister were permitted, as in Egypt, among the Incas, and on the isle of Æolus.[1] But, if the latest form of the Odyssey containing the genealogy of Alcinous be later than the scholiast's Hesiod, it is also, Kirchhoff reckons, later than the Greek colonisation of Cyrene in the thirty-seventh Olympiad, for Hesiod is said to have poetised the facts of that settlement. This will place the Hesiodic *Eoæ* about the fiftieth Olympiad, and later than that must be the Odyssey as it stands. Further, Kirchhoff supplies from Hesiod hints of Io's wanderings in the far North and in Egypt. Now this expansion of the Io saga must, he thinks, be later than the opening of Egypt to the Greeks under Psammetichus. But, we answer, recent investigations go to prove that Greece had a very ancient and familiar acquaintance with Egypt, and thus we are not at all forced to conclude that Egyptian elements in old Greek myth are as late as Psammetichus and the thirtieth, or even fiftieth, Olympiad. Other arguments, based on the contradictory fragments of tradition or invention, about sons of Odysseus by Circe, Calypso, and other mistresses, are founded on the sand. The authorities concerning the amour of Telemachus with Nausicaa, whence sprang Perseptolis, about the sons of Odysseus by Circe and Calypso, and so forth, are inconsistent with each other, and are puerile trash. It is manifest that the author of the Odyssey never dreamed of any such children. His hero says no farewell to them, never thinks of, never mentions them. In all this matter, down to the absurd *Telegonia* of Eugammon of Cyrene, in which

[1] Odyssey, x. 7.

one son of Odysseus marries his father's wife, and another son marries his father's mistress, we are obviously dealing with a familiar literary phenomenon, 'the Cyclic mania.' Given a good and popular epic, later ages wish to continue it, to know what became of all the characters, to trace their descendants, to connect them with heroic genealogies. Hence arose in France the later *chansons de geste*, based on the old original poems. The Greeks had the same *manie cyclique*, and they pursued the fortunes of Odysseus and his house till they landed in the absurdities of the *Telegonia*. In the nature of things, and in the normal evolution of literature, all this work must be much later than the epics themselves. But Kirchhoff argues that the tasteless Eugammon was earlier than the *Bearbeiter's* conclusion of our Odyssey. For in the summary of his poem, the *Telegonia*, given by Proclus, he is said to start from the Burying of the Wooers. Now, some of them are reported in our Odyssey to have been buried (xxiv. 417), therefore Eugammon did not know our Odyssey; had he known it, he would not have described the burial of the wooers, a thing already done. We are arguing in the dark, as we have not Eugammon's work, but it is likely that, instead of merely saying, 'the wooers were buried,' as the Odyssey does, he drew a full picture of their obsequies on the model of the funeral of Patroclus. The *Telegonia*, in fact, as Mr. Monro says, reveals the wish to find a place for the genealogies of various families that claimed descent from Odysseus, whom Eugammon therefore obliged to marry a Thesprotian queen, Callidice. This does not demonstrate it to be later than our form of the Odyssey, but it does prove it to be animated by motives which, to our form of the Odyssey, are utterly unknown.[1] The Kirchhoffian argument—that because Eugammon is reported to have described the burial of the wooers, while in our Odyssey the burial of

[1] *J. H. S.* 1884.

some, not all of them, is incidentally mentioned, not described, therefore Eugammon did not know our Odyssey, which thus is later than his date—proves nothing but Kirchhoff's vehement desire to make the Odyssey a late poem at any hazard. The critical temptation to bring down the date of any work of art is almost as prevalent as the common antiquarian desire to thrust back the date into remote ages.

CHAPTER XII

ATTEMPTS TO DISLOCATE THE ODYSSEY

THE purpose of Wilamowitz Moellendorff and other modern critics is to disengage the various elements of the Odyssey as it stands. But are there really elements of various dates, and by various authors? Wilamowitz causes the whole edifice to fall to pieces, first by withdrawing the exposition (book i.)—which he blames because it *is* an exposition—and then by striking out the *juncturæ*, because they are *juncturæ*. Every long poem has necessarily this cement or mortar and junction of plot. The critic gets rid of it (p. 66), and then asks us to mark how the stones fall in ruin, when 'den Kitt schlagen wir weg'—when we knock away the mortar. But even if the epic be by one early hand, it will still contain mortar, still possess *juncturæ*, and, when these are removed, the structure will perish, just as it perishes if the cement picked out be modern. For example, if we take *Marmion*, we find the mortar to be highly suspicious. We are introduced to Marmion—a noble, brave, and open-handed knight —going on a king's errand into Scotland. He is guided by a palmer from the Holy Land, a man of pallid cheek and wasted form. This palmer the knight does not recognise, though within the last three years they have met as rivals for a lady's hand, and as mortal enemies. We are not told that either age or Athene had transformed the palmer. He had not been out of his enemy's ken for twenty years, as Odysseus had been out of his wife's. Yet he is never suspected by Marmion. As they travel, the knight hears a legend of an elfin warrior who haunts a neighbouring plain. He rides out to encounter him, and is overthrown—by the wan and wasted palmer, who takes the place of the spectre ! Now, not long before, in a trial of battle, Marmion had vanquished this man, when in full health and vigour. The statement of the palmer's success, when wasted to a shadow, over an enemy who had defeated him when in perfect health, is absurd, and clearly unworthy of the original *Dichter*. Finally, Marmion is proved to be a forger, who had placed false letters among the palmer's papers, that he might ruin his rival, and win the hand of the lady. Who enabled him thus to secure his marriage ? Why, his own jealous mistress, a girl of furious passions, who carried and inserted the forged letters, all that she might lose her lover, and win for him his bride ! This is clearly a mere tissue of contradictions, interpolations, and *Flick-Poesie*. A brave and generous man does not stoop to forgery. A jealous mistress does not forward her lover's marriage. A man who is a mere shadow of himself cannot overthrow in battle a knight who had easily conquered him when in full vigour. Yet, if we pick out this cement of the plot, regarding it as work of a late and incompetent botcher, *Marmion* falls to pieces, and no longer exists, except as a mass of lays (one of them spurious) and episodes. In the same way, when the removal of the cement leaves the Odyssey in ruins, it does not follow that the cement is the modern addition of a late builder.

We have seen some of the arguments by dint of which Wilamowitz gets rid of the exposition of the Odyssey of book i. We may now examine his success in picking out its cement from the whole edifice.

The eighteenth book is (disregarding the episode of Penelope) a consistent fragment of old and original poetry. Book xvii. was composed to lead up to book xix., and knit it up with xviii.   Book xx. contains a bad imitation of book xviii.   In book xix. the first fifty verses, in which Odysseus and Telemachus hide the weapons that hung in the hall, is a stopgap, and, in book xx., another stopgap runs from line 122 to line 384.   It serves to unite xix. with xxi. and xxii.   In this passage Odysseus promises the neatherd that he shall see the wooers slain instantly, and Theoclymenus, in a famous piece, beholds the shroud, ominous of death, around their bodies.   These lines are by the botcher.

Among proofs of these discoveries of stopgaps and patches we find that Melantho, the insolent maid (xix. 65), reviles Odysseus *again*.   This shows connection with xviii., where she had already insulted him.   Penelope rebukes Melantho, 'Thy great sin is not hidden from me, and thy blood shall be on thy head for the same. For thou knewest right well that I was minded to ask the stranger in my halls for tidings of my lord.'

This refers to xvii. 528, where Penelope sent for the beggar, who was Odysseus in disguise.   'But this is not original' (p. 50).

The reference of Penelope, Wilamowitz thinks, is, not to Melantho's present rudeness, but to her revealing the secret of the unwoven web (xix. 154), and to her amour with Eurymachus (xviii. 325).   This is clearly a case of 'working over,' and re-touching, the reference to book xvii., and to Penelope's sending for Odysseus there, being dragged in. All this, then, is the work of the author of book xvii.   No doubt, it is, as the author of book xvii. is the author of all, or nearly all, the Odyssey, in our opinion.   Penelope means that Melantho's insolence is of a piece with all her conduct.

Odysseus now tells Penelope a feigned tale. He gives himself out for a Cretan, who had seen the hero in Crete, on his way to Troy. He himself has been in Thesprotia, where he heard that Odysseus had been wrecked in Phæacia. The hero is now paying visits and receiving presents ; he is also consulting the oracle at Dodona as to whether he should return secretly or openly. ' In this same year shall Odysseus come hither, as the old moon wanes and the new is born.' Penelope disbelieves him, but offers hospitality. He says he would like some loyal old wife to wash his feet, not one of the insolent maids.[1] Odysseus now sat aloof from the hearth where Penelope was, and, as the old Eurycleia poured out water, it misgave him that she would remember and recognise a scar on his thigh, made by a boar's tusk in his youth. He therefore turned away his face into the shadow, but she did know the scar, and he only stopped her joyful exclamation by nearly throttling her (xix. 385–502).

In all this fable told by the hero, Kirchhoff and Niese see proofs that Odysseus, in an original saga, went to Scheria after his ship was wrecked and his comrades lost, with no tarrying for seven years in Calypso's isle. It is plain that, if this really was so in the original, the whole character of Telemachus must be omitted. He is a very young man in the poem as it stands—say twenty-one— Odysseus having been absent twenty years. If there is no stay of seven years in Calypso's isle, Telemachus would be but fourteen on the hero's return. Now, the wooers did not begin their misconduct till three years, or four years, before Odysseus's return, as the poem stands. Therefore, if there were no detention in Calypso's isle, we have no Telemachus, who would be only a boy, and, probably, no

---

[1] In the wanderings of Prince Charles in disguise, a Highland maid, who had washed his companion, declined to do so for him : ' Why should she wash a Lowland body ? ' she asked.

wooers. The references to Thesprotia in Odysseus's feigned
tale testify, it is urged, to a form of the poem in which
he actually did tarry in Thesprotia, a form employed by
Eugammon.   Kirchhoff thinks the gathering of gifts a
'pitiful' late invention; it really was part of Homeric
manners.   It is decided that xiv., where Odysseus tells a
feigned tale, is borrowed from xix.   The assumption that
all repeated lines and all similar passages are 'borrowed,'
and that a German can tell which of them is the earlier and
original, which the late copy, grows tedious.

To come to higher things. Odysseus, Wilamowitz argues,
tells Penelope in veiled language that he is already here, as
he is to come 'when the old moon wanes and the new is born,'
that is, on Apollo's festival, which is held next day (xix.
305–6).   She disbelieves, 'she does not understand, and he
thinks of another plan' (*Hom. Untersuch.* 54), and selects
Eurycleia to wash his feet, as she will know the scar and will
reveal him.   To be sure, as the poem stands, he is most
anxious *not* to be revealed, and (xix. 390) he suddenly remembers the danger of her recognising the scar.   All this is the
result, we are to believe, of editing and compilation. In the
original, Odysseus meant to be recognised, it was part of his
plan, and he actually was recognised in the original, according to Wilamowitz.   Therefore book xix., after 476, is part
of the botcher's work, according to the inspired Wilamowitz
Moellendorff, for here Odysseus nearly strangles Eurycleia,
and threatens her with death if she announces her discovery.
He asked her to wash him, in the hypothetical original, expressly that she might recognise him.   As the poem stands,
he spoke in hatred of the insolent maids, who must not touch
his body, and he forgot all about the scar.   But here starts
up a fresh difficulty, with a fresh discovery.   In book xiii.
430, when Odysseus had landed in Ithaca, Athene disguised
him so that he might not be recognised.   'She touched him

with her wand : his fair flesh she withered on his supple limbs, and made waste his yellow hair from off his head, and over all his limbs she cast the skin of an old man, and dimmed his two eyes, erewhile so fair, and changed his raiment to a vile wrap and a doublet ' (xiii. 430–435).

Now, on this passage in book xiii. hangs a library of German criticism. In xiii. Odysseus is transformed by Athene. In xix., where Eurycleia washes him, he is *not* transformed, because he still has his old scar that he won in his youth. Therefore book xix., where he has the scar, is not by the poets of xiii., xvi., where he is transformed. As Kirchhoff puts it, the person who laboured to make a whole out of the action of the first and second halves of the Odyssey, and invented books xiii. and xvi. (the places where the magical transformation occurs) borrowed an old account of the scene of recognition in book xxiii., without noticing the contradiction between that and his own invention. He clung so loosely to his own motive that he quite forgot to retransform the hero into his proper shape at the end of his work. He forgot nothing of the kind : see book xxiii. 156, 157, where Athene restores and embellishes the hero. But then this passage is an interpolation even later than the work of the *Bearbeiter* ! [1]

This is a very convenient way of arguing, but it does not avail.

By aid of this wonderful ' criterion,' the transformation or lack of transformation of Odysseus, Kirchhoff and Wilamowitz and others are enabled to tatter the later books and ascribe them to different authors and redactors.

This kind of criticism is called ' ingenious ' even by writers who disagree with the conclusions drawn. To us the ingenuity seems perverted. We are never told by Homer that Athene turned Odysseus into a different man, with

[1] Kirchhoff, pp. 531, 539.

different tissues. She aged him merely ; she 'withered
the fair flesh on his supple limbs' ; she produced the effects
of many years—temporarily and for a given purpose. It is
not as when, in fairy tales, a witch or wizard transforms
a person into an animal. Even then, the wound inflicted
on the woman changed into a hare or a bird (as in Scotch
tales, and tales of North American races collected by
Lafitau, the old missionary) reappears on the reassumed
body of the human being. Naturally, then, a scar on
a fair limb remains a scar on the same limb when withered
either by age or magic. We all know that the scar of a
wound received in childhood remains marked till old age
withers and death seizes a man. Now, as Athene merely
aged Odysseus in outward seeming, necessarily the scar
stayed where it was, and we have not to do with a difference
of authorship, demonstrated by the persistence of the scar,
after the so-called 'transformation.' Yet, even if the transformation had been radical and complete—say, into the
shape of a beast—according to popular belief, the only
evidence attainable, the scar would still mark the new body.
But a great part of Kirchhoff's and of Wilamowitz's criticism turns on their inability or unwillingness to understand
a plain statement. This is their 'ingenuity.'[1] Kirchhoff
displays his in the first excursus to the second half of the
Odyssey (p. 538). To Kirchhoff it seems that magic and
transformation come *late* into fable, that natural causes are
allowed to work in *earlier* poetry. Thus Odysseus, in the

---

[1] The change from youth, or middle age rather, to eld, is made
again in book xvi. : that Odysseus may reveal himself to Telemachus,
Athene restores his appearance, and Telemachus exclaims that only a
god could make a man young or old at will. Before the swine-herd
returns to the pair, Athene makes Odysseus 'an old man again'
(xvi. 457), 'lest the swine-herd should know him.' Finally, she
restores his beauty (xxiii. 157), after the massacre of the wooers, and
before the recognition by Penelope.

old story, was rendered unrecognisable by age and trouble, in the later poem by art magic. To say this is to reverse the order of the development of fancy, and to prove *Tom Jones* earlier in order of evolution than the oldest *Märchen*.

According to Kirchhoff, the old story persists where Eurycleia recognises the scar, and in book xxiv. (usually regarded as very late), where Laertes doubts whether Odysseus be indeed his son, and Odysseus demonstrates his identity by the proof of the scar, and by mentioning circumstances only known to himself and Laertes. As has been said, the scar would persist, though by magic Odysseus were alternately made young and old, man and beast. Yet Kirchhoff detects two wholly separate currents in the second half of the Odyssey—one early, in which years and wars have naturally changed Odysseus ; one late, in which Athene has magically transformed him. This is the higher criticism. Here is 'the invaluable criterium.'

To return to Wilamowitz. Niese, he finds, agrees that Penelope did recognise Odysseus after the scene of the scar, when Odysseus, as Wilamowitz holds, meant to be recognised. But Niese thinks that this originally ended all ; the wooers went quietly home—they did not try to cut the throat of the lonely Odysseus. He let them go home ; he did not revenge their insults to his house. There was no bloodshed. But Wilamowitz cannot go to these lengths. Niese believes that there was originally no Telemachus. Wilamowitz (p. 56) very learnedly proves from Greek laws of inheritance that there must have been a Telemachus. 'Suppose there is no Telemachus, what becomes of the heritage of Odysseus?' A childless wife is not heir to her lord's possessions. 'An Odyssey without a Telemachus is inconceivable.'

Moreover, 'recognitions,' it is said, are 'a fine moral motive, and relatively late.' Massacres and revenges are relatively early.   The 'moral tragedy is younger than the mythical tragedy.'   The massacre of the wooers, not the recognition, is the real end and aim.

As a matter of fact, the widespread popular tale of the 'Returned Husband' does end with the recognition, but it is only one of the many *Märchen* which make up the stuff of the Odyssey, and we do not know how early the slaying of the wooers became an element of the legend on which the poet worked.   Wilamowitz insists, and rightly, that in the epic the wooers cannot be allowed to slink home in safety ; for them the ends of death, the shafts of sorrow are prepared.   Thus, 'even Shadwell deviates into sense,' and Wilamowitz maintains that Niese's Odyssey is 'a mere parody of Homer.'

He next determines that, after Penelope recognised Odysseus by the scar (as he supposes she did), she and the hero arranged the affair of the trial of the bow, and the massacre.   Proof of this he finds in xxiv. 167, where one of the slain wooers in Hades says that Odysseus, in his cunning, made Penelope offer the trial of the bow.   This is a mere inference on the part of the ghost, who knows nothing of the matter.[1]

The criticism advances on the familiar lines.   As the poem stands, Penelope has not observed the scene of the foot-washing.   All the passage which tells how Odysseus got the wound from the boar's tusk is omitted by the critic. When Penelope awakes from her apathy, she speaks of her sorrows, compares her heart to the heart of the nightingale, daughter of Pandareus, debates whether she shall relieve Telemachus by marrying, tells a dream about her geese, and asks for the interpretation.   Odysseus interprets it of the death of the wooers.   Penelope says some dreams are

---

[1] A late and corrupt tale in Hyginus (126) is supposed by Wilamowitz to confirm his opinion.

true, through the gate of horn, some false, through the
ivory gate. To-morrow she will choose the man who can
draw and shoot with the bow of Odysseus. The beggar
says that Odysseus will return before the wooers can string
the bow. Penelope goes to bed. All this (476–604) is
Flick-Poesie. Then (xx.) Odysseus lies down in the outer
gallery. Seeing the maids come out, he is moved to slay
them, but bids his heart endure, as it endured in the
Cyclops' cave. Athene encourages him by promise of her
aid. He sleeps. Penelope wakens, wishes the winds
could carry her away, like the daughters of Pandareus.
She has dreamed that her lord lay beside her. Odysseus
wakes, hears her weeping, prays for an omen. It is given
by the voice of the old woman grinding at the mill, who
prays that the wooers 'may now sup their last.' Clearly
Odysseus must hence learn that this is their latest supper—
this the day of vengeance. Telemachus arises, the house
is swept, the swine-herd brings hogs, the goat-herd insults
Odysseus, the neat-herd welcomes the beggar. Odysseus
promises that this is the day of revenge. 'While thou art
still in this place Odysseus shall come home, and thou
shalt see the slaying of the wooers' (xx. 232, 233). The
wooers enter. Telemachus purposely calls Odysseus up to
sit beside him by the threshold of stone, in the inmost
part of the hall. Ctesippus throws an ox's foot at Odysseus.
Telemachus chides him. The second-sighted man arises ;
he sees the shroud swathed about the wooers' heads, a sign
of instant death. He flies from the hall (xx. 356). The
wooers are 'fey,' and laugh with alien lips. Their last,
least gracious meal is placed before them.

To all this passage it is objected that Penelope's speech
about the nightingale is perverted and interpolated. Her
dream about the geese (which greatly resembles many
dreams in the Icelandic sagas, the interpretation also being

familiar in the sagas) has a parallel in an ominous fact in
xv. 160, where an eagle steals a goose of Helen's, in Sparta.
The poet here has imitated and spoiled that scene in the
Telemachia. Penelope then says she will set forth the bow
and the trial of the bow, and wed the winner. Therefore
the encouragements of the beggar have had no effect on her.

This, we reply, is natural ; it has often been stated that
she is utterly incredulous of Odysseus's return, and heed-
less of the encouragements offered by wanderers. She
likes the beggar, but does not believe him ; her hope is
broken. The usual charges of repetition in details, and
therefore of borrowing, are made. A great blot is that
Odysseus ' does not know,' in book xx., that the day has
come for him to slay the wooers, nor that the axes are to
be exhibited, and the trial of the bow proclaimed. There is
nothing in this. We have quoted the passages where,
answered by the omen of the woman's prayer, Odysseus
tells the neat-herd that the wooers are instantly to die.
His faith only needed divine confirmation, which it received
in thunder from heaven and the voice of the woman. The
botcher, we are told, destroyed the recognition by Penelope
where it originally stood in xix. 476, that he might bring in
the insult of Ctesippus, the second-sight of Theoclymenus,
and so forth. He also composed xv. 31–165, where Theoclymenus is introduced to the house. We could pardon him a
great deal—even book i.—for the sake of the soothsaying of
Theoclymenus. And thus the cement is picked out, and
the botcher is exposed in his naked hideousness, and bits of
' old poetry ' (the pieces which Wilamowitz happens to
prefer) are rescued from the general ruin of the epic.

This discovery of old lays, or ballads, interwoven by one
or other of the many compilers who had hands in stitching
together the Odyssey, is a fascinating task. Let us examine
a portion of Kirchhoff's work, in which he recognises, but

does not profess to be able to disengage, an old ballad
now blended in the account of the Slaying of the Wooers
(xvi.–xxii.). In the sixteenth book, when Odysseus has
been recognised by his son, and when they are planning
the massacre of the wooers, the following passage occurs.
Odysseus bids his son go home, he himself will follow in
disguise, the wooers will shamefully handle him. Telemachus must endure this spectacle ; they will not listen to
his remonstrances, for the day of their doom is at hand.
Then comes this remark : ' Yet another thing will I tell
thee, and do thou ponder it in thy heart. When Athene,
of deep counsel, shall put it into my heart, I will nod to
thee with my head, and do thou note it, and carry away all
thy weapons of war that lie in the halls, and lay them down
every one in the secret place of the lofty chamber.' [1]

' And when,' the hero goes on, ' the wooers miss them
and ask thee concerning them, thou shalt beguile them with
soft words saying : " Out of the smoke have I laid them by,
since they are no longer like those that Odysseus left behind
him of old when he went to Troy, but they are wholly
marred, so mightily hath passed on them the vapour of fire.
Moreover, Cronion hath put into my heart this other and
greater care, that perchance when ye are heated with wine,
ye may set a quarrel you between, and wound one the other
and thereby shame the feast and the wooing, for iron of itself
draws a man thereto." But for us twain alone leave two
swords and two spears and two shields of oxhide to grasp,
that we may rush upon the arms and seize them ' (xvi. 280–
297).

Nothing can be clearer than the purport of this advice.
In Homeric halls, as in those of heroic Iceland, weapons
were arranged, probably in trophies, along the wall. Odysseus

---

[1] ἐς μυχὸν ὑψηλοῦ θαλάμου—obviously the chief's strong room.
Similar chambers occur in Icelandic sagas.

means to act as Grettir did in the Grettis saga, when a house
in which he was living alone, as a guest, with some women,
was entered by twelve robbers. He persuaded the robbers
'with soft words,' to let him put their damp weapons in a
dry place, he then intoxicated them, led them into the
treasure chamber, locked them in, and slew them when they
forced their way out weaponless, having armed himself
with a spear that hung over the bed of his host Thorfinn.
In the same way Odysseus will remove the arms from the
hall, so that the wooers may have no spears, but only their
swords, when the fight begins. Late on the following day,
when the wooers have departed to their own houses,
Odysseus remains alone in the hall with Telemachus
devising the slaying of the wooers. He says :—

'Telemachus, we must needs lay within the weapons of
war, every one ; and when the wooers miss them and ask
thee concerning them thou shalt beguile them with soft
words,' repeating the exact speech which he had suggested in
book xvi. But here he says nothing about leaving two
shields and spears and two swords for themselves. Nor
does he specify the exact spot, 'the secret place of the lofty
chamber,' where the weapons are to be carried, he only says
'within' (xix. 4–13). Telemachus now bids Eurycleia confine the maids in their rooms, till he has laid by the weapons
in the armoury ($\theta \acute{a} \lambda a \mu \upsilon s$ as in xvi.), for he fears they may
rust in the hall, thus giving to Eurycleia the first part of the
excuse prepared by Odysseus for the wooers in case of need.
Eurycleia praises his thrift, and asks who is to light him on
the way, if not the maids ? He replies that the stranger
will light him. Eurycleia withdraws. Odysseus and his
son carry the weapons 'within,' and Pallas Athene magically lights them on the way. In universal belief, from the
creed of the Eskimo to English and Norse popular superstition, the presence of the supernatural is attended by

an unearthly light.[1]   As Odysseus says in answer to Telemachus, 'This is the wont of the gods that hold Olympus.'
Odysseus remains in the hall, Telemachus goes to his
chamber 'by the light of the flaming torches,' whether he
bore them himself, or whether the maids were now permitted to accompany him, as the work was done.

We now pass to book xxii.   Odysseus has achieved the
adventure of the bow, has leaped on the high threshold,
and has shot Antinous.   'Then the wooers raised a
clamour through the halls when they saw the man fallen,
and they leaped from their high seats, as men stirred by
fear, all through the hall, peering everywhere along the
well-built walls, and nowhere was there a shield or mighty
sword to lay hold on' (xxii. 21–25).   Consequently they
are obliged to set on with tables for shields, and using the
swords they happen to be wearing.   Telemachus has a
spear, however, for (xxii. 92) he slays with it Amphinomus.
But he dares not pluck the spear from the body, so he
proposes to go to the chamber (θάλαμος as in xvi.)
where his weapons were lying (xxii. 109) and fetch shields,
spears, and helmets for himself, his father, the neat-herd,
and the swine-herd.   This he does (xxii. 110–125), accidentally leaving the chamber door open ; his party arm
themselves, and Odysseus, having emptied his quiver, grasps
two lances.

In all this the reader perceives that Odysseus has not
exactly carried out the plan he sketched in book xvi.   He
has not reserved spears (or not more than one apparently),
swords, and shields for himself and Telemachus.   The
wooers have asked no questions about the removal of the
weapons because they never noticed the removal, being

[1] Compare Rink's *Tales and Traditions of the Eskimo*, p. 61, with
note in the *Lay of the Last Minstrel* to the ballad of Rosabelle ; and
Theocritus, Idyll of Heracles and the Serpents (xxiv.).

engaged with the bow, till the need for arms arose. The
armoury (θάλαμος) is mentioned in xvi. ; in xix. Odysseus
only says that the weapons must be carried 'within.' These
are very weighty considerations ! Be it also remarked that,
as Telemachus forgot to lock the door of the chamber, when
he brought out the shields and spears, Melanthius is enabled
to reach it by some passage not well understood, and to
bring arms for the wooers. He goes to the strong chamber,
'for methinks it is in that room and nowhere other that
Odysseus and his renowned son laid by the arms.'

To all this part of the tale Kirchhoff devotes an excursus
of thirty-seven closely printed pages. He decides, on the
ground of discrepancies, borrowed lines, and so forth, that
'the scene in book xvi. is the original work of the composer
of this last part of the poem ; the narrative in book xxii.
(the battle with the wooers) belongs in essentials to the
statement of some older ballad, which cannot, however,
now be restored in its original shape.' That undertaking
would be fruitless. Probably—as we have not a shred of
evidence about the nature of detached heroic Greek lays
or ballads. Finally, the author of xvi. 3-52 (the removal of
the arms by Odysseus and his son) is not the maker of the
present connection of the poem.

These are very wide and very minute conclusions to
draw from the evidence before us. The evidence gives us
a sketch of an excellent and necessary plan, which, except
in one small detail, is carried out as far as it is within the
power of Odysseus and Telemachus. They cannot make
the wooers ask the question, the answer to which, if it is
asked, they have prepared. It was not necessary for
Odysseus, as he had proposed, to signal Telemachus by a
nod ; he had a chance of speaking openly to him. Croiset[1]
avers that in xvi. 287 Odysseus contemplates removing the

[1] *Hist. de la Lit. Grecque*, i. 313, note.

arms before the eyes of the wooers.   His words, 'when the
wooers miss them,' indicate the opposite.   They apparently
did not reserve shields for themselves :

> The best laid plans o' men and mice
> Gang aft ajee.

But if this were so great a blunder, the redactor, or
Bearbeiter, or *Flick-Poet*, might easily have corrected it.

The removal of the weapons (xix. 3–52) is denied to be
original or genuine.   What has Pallas Athene to do there
with her light ?   The father and son might very well have
carried their own candles.   The purpose of the goddess, we
reply, with Kammer, was to encourage the hero by her
presence.   Moreover, xvi. 282–294 (Odysseus's advice
about hiding the arms and excusing their absence) is clearly
connected with and dependent on xix. 4–12.   The repeated
passage, Kirchhoff holds, is by some one who knew the
original ; not necessarily can the converse be stated.   In
this case, the original passage is the earlier in occurrence—
namely, that in book xvi.   The second passage (xix. 10)
has

$$\pi\rho\grave{o}s \; \delta' \; \check{\epsilon}\tau\iota \; \kappa\alpha\grave{\iota} \; \tau\acute{o}\delta\epsilon \; \mu\epsilon\hat{\iota}\zeta o\nu \; \grave{\epsilon}\nu\grave{\iota} \; \phi\rho\epsilon\sigma\grave{\iota}\nu \; \check{\epsilon}\mu\beta\alpha\lambda\epsilon \; \delta\alpha\acute{\iota}\mu\omega\nu,$$

whereas, in xvi. 291, we read

$$\theta\hat{\eta}\kappa\epsilon \; K\rho o\nu\acute{\iota}\omega\nu.$$

The first passage runs, 'Cronion hath put it in my
heart,' the second ·passage has, 'some god hath put
it in my heart.'   Now $\check{\epsilon}\mu\beta\alpha\lambda\epsilon \; \delta\alpha\acute{\iota}\mu\omega\nu$ is unusual,
$\theta\hat{\eta}\kappa\epsilon \; K\rho o\nu\acute{\iota}\omega\nu$ is customary.   The former is vague,
the latter is definite.   Therefore the lines in xix.
are expressly altered from their model in xvi., and
are later and by a different hand.   Why all this should
follow, it is not easy for a puzzled reader to understand.
Nor are we more persuaded by the remarkable fact that,
in xix., Odysseus says, 'put the weapons *within*,' and, in

xvi., 'put the weapons in the secret place of the lofty
chamber.' Where else but in the strong chamber could he
safely or naturally bestow them? As he had mentioned
the special place the day before, it is not necessary for him
to repeat that the strong chamber is the best hiding-hole.
So obviously is it the best hiding-place that Melanthius
(xxii. 140) at once guesses that Odysseus has deposited the
weapons there. But this very guess is a stumbling-block
to Kirchhoff. How could Melanthius possibly know where
the weapons were, and how they had disappeared? If
he knew, why did he not earlier warn his friends? Of
course, he only made a necessary inference from the fact
that the weapons had vanished. A number of grammatical
objections are urged against the unlucky xix. 3–52 ; these
we leave to grammarians. The use of the microscope is
now pushed very far. If the weapons were newly stored
in the chamber where Penelope kept the bow, the sight of
them would startle her very much when she opened the
chamber (xxi. 8). Of course we know nothing of the size
or structure of the chamber or of the opportunities for
concealment within it, while Penelope, intent on something
else, need not have noticed a few shields and spears more
or less. This kind of examination would prove every novel
that ever was written to come from various hands. To
take the first convenient example—but let me spare the
emotions of a friend ! Enough that, in a novel where the
plot turns on the colour of the heroine's hair, the author
forgets what that colour is. The author has made a slip,
that is all ; there are not two hands at work. But Homer
really makes no slip where Penelope does not excite herself
about the presence of weapons more or less in a place
full of all kinds of gear. The 'subtlety' of Kirchhoff is
childishly meticulous. We know little about the arrange-

ments of an Homeric *thalamos*, or store-chamber. In
xvi. 285 Odysseus proposes to put the weapons

ἐς μυχὸν ὑψηλοῦ θαλάμου,

'in the secret place of the lofty chamber.' In xxii. 180
that is the very place where the treacherous goat-herd hunts
for the arms,

θαλάμοιο μυχὸν κάτα,

'in the secret place of the chamber.' This, again, as far as
we can discern, is the very 'chamber in the uttermost part
of the house' (xxi. 8) whence Penelope brings the bow. Penelope opened the door by shooting back the bolts (ὀχῆας, xxi.
47). But, when Telemachus brought the gear for Odysseus
during the fight (xxii. 155), as we saw, he unluckily left the
door open. Thus, as he says (xxii. 154), it was by his fault
alone that Melanthius got at the weapons. As far as we
can understand, there is but one *thalamos*, where the
weapons were placed after being removed from the hall,
and where the bow was also kept. There is thus no confusion in the narrative, unless we are to suppose that
Penelope would have been startled by seeing the newly-
introduced arms in the *thalamos*, and would therefore have
unconsciously betrayed the whole plot. Such a subtlety is
puerile. Audacity as well as subtlety is necessary to
Kirchhoff's ideas. Audacity he displays, by removing the
lines in xxii. (24, 25), where the wooers look round the hall
and miss the weapons, as an interpolation (p. 583). Here
the wooers are startled, though they think the shot acci-
dental, and carry swords. But the Beggar had a Bow!
Even line 141 in xxii. must go. Here Melanthius says
during the fight, 'Let me bring you armour from the inner
chamber, that ye may be clothed in hauberks, for methinks
it is in that room and no other [that Odysseus and his

renowned son laid by the arms]. The line in brackets (xxii.
141) must be an interpolation (*später eingeflickt*, p. 586).
The reference to the whole affair in the twenty-fourth book
(165, 166) does not concern us much if that part be indeed
very late and spurious, as the Alexandrine critics supposed.
In that book the ghost of Amphimedon is telling the story
to the ghosts of the heroes of the Trojan war. He says that
Odysseus had endured much contumely in his own halls, but
finally, 'when the spirit of Zeus urged him, by the help of
Telemachus, he took up all the goodly weapons and laid them
by in the inner chamber, and drew the bolts.' These are the
'bolts' which Penelope undid when she went for the bow, and
which Telemachus forgot to close when he fetched out arms
for Odysseus, himself, and the two thralls, thereby letting in
Melanthius. The ghost is telling his story by dint of inference. He is sometimes right, sometimes wrong ; his condition of mind is matter for the Society of Psychical Research.
What the ghost said is not evidence.

Kirchhoff has thus had the good fortune and skill to discover a separate ballad, a piece of *freie Dichtung*, an addition
by a *Bearbeiter*, and some interpolations, where one sees
nothing but plain sailing. He does not expect to convince
'Unitarians,' friends of the unity of the epic; and, indeed,
we are not convinced. Unitarians, if they acknowledge the
facts (which Kirchhoff greatly misdoubts), will attempt to
get rid of the contradictions in question by averring that
Odysseus can modify his plan if he likes, or forget it, or not
find time for it. And, again, they will say that we must
judge Homer by Homeric æsthetic, not by ours, and so
forth. But, in truth, we do not particularly trust Kirchhoff
as an authority on the rules of fictitious composition, either
in modern or ancient art. The story, as it stands in the
Odyssey, is excellently told, and has as much consistency as
is desirable. Odysseus sketched a plan : that plan he

executed, with a single slip—namely, in neglecting to keep defensive and offensive armour enough for himself, his son, and the two thralls, of whose assistance he was not certain when, in book xvi., the plan was conceived. Meanwhile, his oversight is artistically justified, for it makes room for the final treachery, the catching, and the exemplary punishment of Melanthius, the traitor. These could not have been arranged if Odysseus had, as he intended, kept back armour enough, or if Telemachus had been careful to close the door of the chamber. Were we critics who excise, we could dismiss xvi. 295–298, where Odysseus says that they must keep arms for themselves, as an obvious interpolation. But we do not excise lines merely because they are inconvenient to our theory. On the whole, then, ' Unitarians ' need not abandon the unity of the poem, as far as these passages are concerned, in favour of several different poets, an old ballad, a *Bearbeiter*, a still later interpolator, and the other subtle and ingenious discoveries of Kirchhoff. Again, if it be urged that the strength of his case depends essentially ' on the cumulative force of a great number of subtle observations,' we must say that, if this, that, and the other subtle observation be worthless, the sum of these observations has no cumulative weight or force at all. The subtle observation about the shape-shifting of Odysseus, and the contradiction involved in the presence of his scar, was not valid ; not valid, we think, are the remarks on the removal of the weapons ; and so on in the case of the others. No number of cyphers make up a sum, by themselves. For example, the arguments against book xi., the scenes in Hades, are far from cogent.

The close of xi., from 565 to 627, the accounts of Minos, judge of the souls, and of punishments endured by men violent against the gods, the description, too, of the Shadow of Heracles, were doubted by the ancient critics, and are

now spoken of as a late Orphic interpolation. Passing by
this question for the present, it is to be noted that Wilamowitz detects in the earlier part of the *Nekyia* a patchwork
of different dates, stitched together, and partly composed
by some one who inserted the canto between books x.
and xii.   Traces of the process of patching are detected in
the ' intermezzo '—that is, in xi. 333-384.   Here Odysseus,
after speaking of the dead heroines whom he beheld, breaks
off, saying that it is time for sleep, whether he is to lie
down on board ship or in the palace.   This is a natural
remark in a guest who may fear, or think proper to affect
to fear, that he is telling too long a story.   His hosts re-
assure him, offer him presents, and ask him what he saw
in Hades of those who fell in the Trojan war.   Wilamowitz
looks on the ' intermezzo ' as the work of the compiler who
' put together ' all the adjacent books.   His analysis
endeavours to show that, in an older form of the poem,
Circe gave Odysseus no command to descend into Hell,
but at the close of book x. (where the directions for the
journey to Hades now occur) merely uttered the warnings
about the Sirens, Thrinacia, and Scylla, which at present
occur in the opening of book xii.   In that book the hero
does not return to Circe's house after coming out of Hades,
but his men sleep by the sea shore, and the goddess and he
meet apart (xii. 33).   For some reason this arrangement is
not satisfactory to the critic.

It is an *Unschicklichkeit* ; why so, one is at a loss to conceive.   One may even imagine that ' men over-bold ' who
have been among the dead are no fit guests for a goddess.   As usual, formulæ in xi., for instance 636-638, are
said to be ' borrowed ' from ix. 177-179.   The story of
Elpenor, his death by accident in Circe's house, the appearance of his shade, his desire of a mound, with a pillar
to cover his body, is declared to be an ' ætiological '

addition. Somewhere there actually existed such a mound
(as many mounds there be), some one wished to explain it,
and connect it with the adventures of Odysseus : therefore
the Elpenor episode was introduced. The compiler is the
author of this part. The compiler has also added to the
speech of Tiresias (an older fragment) the warning about
the cattle of the Sun (xi. 104-113) borrowed from book xii.
Tiresias's prophecy about the wooers (xi. 113-120) is intolerable in this place, for the shadow of Odysseus's mother
knows nothing of the wooers. She must have died, we
answer, before they drew to a head ; she does not know what
she did not see, but Tiresias, even in Hades, remains a
soothsayer (x. 493). As the story stands, Odysseus has
only been two or three years on the seas, since Ilios fell.
He has still to dwell seven or eight years with Calypso. The
wooers have not begun their suit, they only began it four
years before Odysseus actually returned to Ithaca. Thus
Anticleia's shade cannot know what has not occurred, but
Tiresias, as a prophet, knows what will happen. It seems
odd that Telemachus, a lad of twelve, dines out so much
(xi. 186), but this may not have been odd in Homeric
society. In Tiresias's prophecy lines xi. 114, 115 are
' borrowed ' from the prayer of the Cyclops (ix. 534-535),
' late may he come, in evil case, with loss of all his company, in the ship of strangers, and find sorrows in his house,'
to which Tiresias adds, ' proud men that devour thy living,'
which is an offence to Wilamowitz.[1] To our minds the
repetition in the prophecy of the very words of the prayer
is only a regular part of Homer's poetical technique. According to the critic, the compiler adds the prophecy to
prepare for and lead up to the massacre of the wooers.
When *Old Mortality* was first published, ' clever people '
(as Lady Louisa Stewart told Scott) detected in it the work

[1] *Die Epexegese* ἄνδρας *zu* πήματα *ist recht ungeschickt*, p. 145.

of several hands, and it is easy to see how Wilamowitz would have disengaged, and assigned to a compiler, the successive omens and prophecies in the *Bride of Lammermoor*, and 'Wandering Willie's Tale' in *Redgauntlet*.

Three portions of the *Nekyia*, the interview with Anticleia and Tiresias, the 'Catalogue of Women,' the meeting with the heroes of the Trojan war, make up most of book xi., when Elpenor and the conclusion are withdrawn. As to the Catalogue of Women (225-333), it appears to us to be one of the most magical passages in Homer. A great charm of the old Cymric tales (the *Mabinogion*) lies in hints that half illumine the dark unknown backward of tradition, references to old adventures now forgotten by men, the lady made of flowers, the dirk whereon no handle would remain fast, and so on. A similar charm is cast on us by Odysseus's glimpses of the famed unhappy brides of the Immortals : Tyro, who loved Enipeus, 'fairest of the floods that run on earth,' Phædra, and Procris, and beautiful Ariadne. These were among the mortal ancestresses who, in the embraces of the gods, became mothers of heroic houses of Achaia. Each declared her lineage, and told her tale of sorrow 'wild with all regret.' He who writes has been haunted from childhood by these shapes and voices of the Grecian ladies, and this may be the experience of many readers. But Wilamowitz denies the originality of the whole passage. This 'Catalogue of Women' is not to be considered apart from catalogues of women in ancient Greek poetry in general. Some such catalogues were attributed by the ancients to Hesiod : except for a few fragments, these are lost. Such a Catalogue was the Hesiodic *Eoiæ*, and, of the two, *Eoiæ* and *Nekyia*, the originality here, according to the critic, is on the side of 'Hesiod,' not of 'Homer.' In our catalogue, Leda comes in as mother of the Dioscuri, not of Helen. Now, in the

Cyclic poem, the *Cypria* (770 B.C. ?), Nemesis, not Leda, is
mother of Helen : therefore our catalogue refers to the
Cypria. That poem made Nestor tell long tales of Antiope,
Epicaste, Alcmene, Megara, all named here.   Therefore we
must not say that the *Cypria* and the *Nekyia* use the same
legends, nor that the *Cypria* borrows from the *Nekyia* ;
we must decide that the *Nekyia* borrows from the *Cypria*.[1]
Now it is almost waste of time to deduce arguments from
poems like the *Cypria* and the *Little Iliad*, which we happen
not to possess.   It really seems arbitrary also to dismiss all
passages where Attic heroes or heroines are named—for
example, xi. 325—as Athenian interpolations.   If the
Athenians ever had an opportunity of interpolating Homer's
text, they would probably have done so to more purpose.
The least unscientific plan, on the whole, is not to argue without materials.   As the *Cypria*, the *Little Iliad*, the *Nostoi*, and
other Cyclic poems are lost, as only a battered and brief
prose summary of their contents remains, it is well to suspend
our opinion as to whether their authors borrowed from
the *Nekyia*, or the *Nekyia* from them, or whether both
the Cyclics and the *Nekyia* draw from common sources in
tradition.[2]

Turning to the interviews with Agamemnon, Achilles,
and Aias in Hades, Wilamowitz decides that they are by another hand, because these ghosts speak *without* tasting the
blood.   In xi. 390 they do taste the blood, but Wilamowitz
rejects the reading which contradicts his private theory,

ἔγνω δ' αἶψ' ἐμὲ κεῖνος, ἐπεὶ πίεν αἷμα κελαινόν,

' he knew me so soon as he had drunk the blood,' in favour
of the variant,

ἐπεὶ ἴδεν ὀφθαλμοῖσι,

' so soon as he saw me.'[3]   This seems arbitrary enough,

[1] *Hom. Untersuch.* p. 149.
[2] See chapter on ' The Lost Epics. [3] See Schol. on Od. xi. 390.

but the best defence of the originality of this passage is its
beauty, its 'grand style.' The words so worthy of Achilles,
who would rather be thrall of a landless man than monarch
of all the dead, are among the immortal passages of
literature. On Wilamowitz's hypothesis, they are by 'the
author of the *Telemachia*.' It is easy for him to believe
that many poets might possess this faultless sublimity of
matter and manner. Again, the legends in these interviews, about Neoptolemus, the Trojan Horse, Eriphyle,
the contest for the arms of Achilles, and so on, occurred
in the Cyclic poems, and are not alluded to in the Iliad.
It is a commonplace of the Higher Criticism that whatever
Homer does not mention is unknown to Homer. Applying
this system to Shakspeare, we find that Shakspeare was
unacquainted with the use of tobacco ! The Cyclic poems
know the legends ; the Iliad does not allude to them : therefore Homer did not know them : therefore the scenes with
Achilles and Agamemnon in the *Nekyia* are manufactured
after the Cyclic poems. The account of his own death
which Agamemnon gives (xi. 415–450) includes mention of
Cassandra and of Cassandra's slaying by Clytæmnestra.
The tale of Agamemnon's death is hinted at by Zeus in
book i., told by Nestor (iii.), and more fully by Menelaus
(iv.). Finally Agamemnon, in this place, gives more details,
including the slaughter of Cassandra and the cruelty of
Clytæmnestra. Herein Wilamowitz recognises the matter of
later legends than those in books iv. and v. The Revenge
of Orestes on his own mother is thus made necessary,
though as at the very least she was always an accessory
before and after the fact, he probably had to avenge his
father on his mother in any case. In iii. 310 (in the so-
called *Telemachia*) we find already that Orestes made a
funeral feast ' over his hateful mother and over the craven
Ægisthus.' Yet, as to this revenge by Orestes, Wilamowitz

(p. 156) says 'the *Telemachia* knows nothing of it.' So,
to meet Wilamowitz's needs, line 310 in book iii. *muss
fort*—must get out. How is it possible to argue with a critic
who rejects every line which he finds inconvenient to his
theory? If a fact be not mentioned in a given place, that
is proof of the accuracy of his hypothesis ; if it be mentioned,
it is an interpolation. This is too manifestly the familiar
game of 'Heads, I win ; tails, you lose !' By such methods
the account of Agamemnon's death in the *Nekyia* is brought
down to the period of the Pindaric and Stesichorean
legends. On the whole, the scene with Anticleia and part
of the scene with Tiresias are old, the rest of the *Nekyia* is
by diverse hands, in diverse ages, all blended and partly
composed by the compiler. The warning of Tiresias, that
Odysseus must propitiate Poseidon by wandering till he
reaches men who know not salt, and by sacrificing there,
perhaps refers to an overland journey in Epirus. The
Arcadians, as their coins show, thought that Arcadia was
the scene of this adventure. Here we move in mere mist of
later conjecture. But the strength of Wilamowitz's arguments against the originality of the *Nekyia* as a whole
may be appreciated by the reader. They turn on the
interpretation of recurrent poetic formulæ as traces of
dovetailing ; on arbitrary decisions, based on lost, and to
us unknown, poems ; on wilful excision of inconvenient
lines as interpolations 'smuggled in' ; and on misconcep-
tion of the plot and story, as in the matter of Anticleia,
Tiresias, and the revenge on the wooers.

CHAPTER XIII

CONCLUSION OF THE ODYSSEY

THE ancient Alexandrian critics, as we have already said,
held that the original Odyssey ended with xxiii. 296. The
later scholia to the Odyssey are extremely meagre, and we
do not know the reasons which Aristophanes and Aristarchus assigned for their huge excision. The passages
rejected in xxiii. contain a brief recapitulation of the whole
story as narrated by Odysseus to his wife. Athene has
delayed the Dawn, xxiii. 242, that they may have time for
happiness and for the tale. When Odysseus has well slept,
she arouses the Dawn, and it is childish in commentators to
apply 'time-tests' where a miracle is concerned. Odysseus
and Telemachus waken. The hero bids his wife wait
quietly in the upper chamber and see no man, while he and
Telemachus, concealed by Athene in a cloud, go forth to the
farm of his father, Laertes. The retirement of Laertes had
already been described by Anticleia's ghost, in book xi. 192.
In book xxiv. Hermes conducts the ghosts of the wooers to
Hades. Two objections are urged. Hermes appears for
the first time in Homer as *Psychopompus*, guide of spirits.
Next, the entrance to Hades is not like that in book xi. ;
they pass the White Rock, the Gates of the Sun, the People
of Dreams. We do not know, of course, whether the function of Hermes is really a novelty ; Homer has had no

previous occasion to describe it. As to the path to Hades, that taken by the wooers, as we said before, may have been the usual way of souls. In book xi. Odysseus went, as a living man, by another route. In Hades the heroes are conversing. Agamemnon congratulates Achilles on the manner of his death and burial. ' The Nereids came forth from the waters, and all the nine Muses, one to the other replying with sweet voices, began the dirge.' The golden urn provided by Thetis for the hero's ashes was the 'gift of Dionysus.' It is urged that the Muses were not known as Nine till the arts had been differentiated and classified. But the ninefold division may be due to the number of the Muses. Dionysus, who gave the urn, is always an object of suspicion as a recent god. The whole passage, in any case, is of the rarest beauty : ' Homère a esquissé en traits sublimes ce que furent ces funerailles, ce qu'elles durent être ; la fin de l'Odysée répond ainsi à la pensée même de l'Iliade, et y con-corde par un effet plein de grandeur,' says Sainte-Beuve.[1]

Literary merit does not, perhaps, prove genuineness, but we may set Sainte-Beuve's approval against that of those who denounce ' the wretched conclusion of the poem.' Once more, the shades of the wooers, though their bodies are unburied, consort with the heroic souls ; whereas, in book xi., the shadow of the unburied Elpenor was held aloof by the ghosts. Here is a discrepancy, but all theories of the state of the dead are full of similar contradictions. The shades of the wooers tell their story to the heroes, and Amphimedon says that Odysseus had arranged the trial of the bow with his wife. This is merely an erroneous infer-ence of the ghost's, though much is made of it by the critics who believe that, when Odysseus's feet were washed, Penelope recognised him in the older versions.[2] On this

---

[1] *Etude sur Quintus Smyrnæus*, p. 385, a sequel to the *Etude sur Virgile*.　　　　[2] Wilamowitz, *Hom. Unters.* p. 59

theory xxiv. holds by an older version than xix., and we
have only to marvel that the *Bearbeiter* or botcher or
redactor did not reconcile his statements.

Odysseus and Telemachus reach the farm of Laertes,
who is tended by an old Sicilian woman (xxiv. 211). The
hero, in a false tale to his father, says that he himself came
from Sicania (xxiv. 307). This proves that the geography
here tallies with that of book i., if Temesa be the Metapon-
tine town, as Wilamowitz argues. Finally, Odysseus shows
his scar, and, in a charming scene full of reminiscences of
his childhood, reveals himself to his father. The old man
naturally dreads the blood feud for the slain wooers—the
chief anxiety, as is inevitable, of the later books. They eat
meat ; the kindred of the slain muster in Ithaca ; the dead
are buried, or sent to their island homes. Eupeithes urges
the duty of revenge. Medon and the minstrel come forth
from the palace ; critics wonder that they had slept so
long ! Medon tells how a god, in semblance of Mentor,
had helped Odysseus. As it is decided that this event was
'silly,' the reference to it is a device of the compiler.
Halitherses, the prophet of book ii., says, 'Ye obeyed me
not,' and advises a policy of peace. Eupeithes leads the
others on ; there is a last brief council of the gods (xxiv.
479, cf. v. 23, 24). Zeus bids Athene reconcile the foes.
After a brief conflict, in which old Laertes slays his man,
Eupeithes, Zeus casts a thunderbolt, and Athene, in guise
of Mentor, 'sets a covenant between them with sacrifice.'

Except by a *Dea ex machina*, this feud, according to
heroic manners, could in no wise be reconciled. Some of
the suspicious points have been noted, separately they are
of little moment, their cumulative weight may be more
important. Kirchhoff thinks (p. 532) that the whole conclusion was added by his *Bearbeiter* to satisfy curiosity.
But the more ancient the date, the more secure the old

law of blood-feud, the more anxious would curiosity be.
Whether the piece, as it stands, is by the original poet or
not, we can hardly conceive that he could have left the
story unfinished, and the feud unstaunched.   Kirchhoff
regards the piece as the wilful invention of the composer,
with no traditional foundation.   Wilamowitz, however, points
out that the affair of Laertes is prepared for throughout by
constant references to the old hero—for example, at the
close of book iv., xiv. 173, xv. 353, xvi. 135-153, xx. 41-43,
xxiii. 117-152. He thinks, therefore, that book xxiv., though
late, is earlier than book i. and the general patching of the
Odyssey into its present form (p. 71).   The author of the
conclusion is a compiler and a late poet, but even his late
work has been tinkered over by the *Bearbeiter*.   He it was
who, finding the Laertes episode ready to his hand, worked
in references to Laertes in the passages already enumerated,
so as to give coherence to his patchwork.   He has
blundered by a combination of poems in some of which
Odysseus is not, while in others he is, magically transformed
(p. 79).   We have said enough already about this mare's-
nest of the transformation.   The conclusion is decided to
be a poem of the seventh century, probably composed in
Eubœa or Corinth (p. 81).   The recognition scene (xxiii.
240) is inserted from an older poem, whereof it formed the
conclusion (p. 85).

We have now examined a few specimens of the arguments by which the Odyssey is dislocated, and have
attempted to show that they possess little cogency.   But it
must be allowed that the matter does not admit of demonstration, and that, in the final result, the whole question resolves itself into one of literary taste.   For if we say,
with Comparetti, that 'the organic unity, the harmony, the
relation of all the parts, their co-ordination, their leading up
to a predetermined conclusion, attest homogeneity and con-

sonance of poetic creation, and that all this can scarcely be
the work of different poets at different dates,' we have still
to deal with critics who do not recognise the unity, the
marshalling of incidents towards a given end.[1]   We have to
do with critics who find, in place of unity, patchwork and
compilation, and evident traces of diverse dates and
diverse places of composition.   Thus argument is inefficient,
demonstration is impossible, and the final judge must be
the opinion of the most trustworthy literary critics and of
literary tradition.   These are unanimous, as against the
'microscope-men,' in favour of the unity of the Odyssey.
There may be—nay, there must be—accidents of time,
which beget lacunæ and interpolations, but these it is difficult to detect with any certainty.   The conclusion of
book xi. is dubious : it exhibits a more moral, perhaps a
later, theory of future rewards and punishments.   If this be
Orphic, a work of the time of Onomacritus, it is curious
that the Orphicism is not more distinct and strenuous.
Again, the opening of book v. is weak, but who ever heard
of a long poem, however certainly from one hand, in which
there were no weak passages ?   The objections to the conclusion (xxiii., xxiv.) have been stated, and they are not
inconsiderable, but it may be doubted whether they are
strong enough to invalidate the genuine character of the
passage.   At the junctions of two threads of the story, in
iv. 620 and xv. 295–301, are signs of dislocation.   But
whatever difficulties beset the belief in a long, continuous,
admirably planned epic, the work of a single hand in a
remote age, they are, at least, less manifold than those
which meet us when a critic professes to detect in the
Odyssey an old short epic, a continuation of that epic made
up out of ballads, a dislocation of that continuation for the
purpose of inserting a headless and tailless *Telemachia*, and

[1] Comparetti, *Der Kalewala*, p. 326.

a working over of the whole mass by an incompetent hand, whose motive for his industry is sadly to seek, as are the reasons which induced Greece to accept the late patchwork for the genuine work of Homer. Before we can begin to think of accepting this theory, we must submit ancient work, not to the laws of modern literary criticism, and of Alexandrine criticism, which is essentially modern also, but to such tests as scarce any work of fiction could endure. Where is the novel, where the poem, without discrepancies, and where is the sense of explaining most discrepancies by a theory of multiplex authorship ?

It was easy for coxcombs to vanquish Berkeley with a sneer, and it is true that parody is no argument. But parody may, at least, supply an illustration. Let us conceive that the historical facts about the origin and authorship of *Ivanhoe* are unknown. The romance falls into the hands of a critic, and this is how he treats it.

The germ, or kernel, of the so-called *Ivanhoe* is manifestly an early English mediæval version of the Odysseus saga. This the critic will illustrate by the curious mediæval Irish version of the Odyssey.[1] In the original, Ivanhoe was not the lover of Rowena, but the husband, returned from long wanderings in the East. Jerusalem has taken the place of Ilios. Rowena was not the mistress of Ivanhoe, but the faithful wife, like Penelope. In Gurth, the loyal swine-herd, we recognise Eumæus ; Gurth's dog, Fang, is an echo of Argus. Rowena is beset by wooers, De Bracy, the Templar, Front de Bœuf. In the original, Ivanhoe, aided by Gurth, destroys them, in a fight in his own hall.

This is the kernel. In a later age the chivalric spirit made Rowena the lady-love, not the wife of Ivanhoe, and moved the slaughter of the wooers from the hall of the

[1] *Merugud Ulix Maicc Leirtis*, edited by Kuno Meyer. Nutt, 1886.

V

hero, to that of Front de Bœuf. Locksley (Robin Hood) was introduced under Edward III. ; historically he was a character of the reign of Edward II. This interpolation is to be attributed to a poet of the school of Piers Plowman, probably a Nottingham man. Later a *doublette* of the original motive, a poem on the *Nostos*, or Return of the Wandering Richard Cœur de Lion, was amalgamated with the *Nostos* of Ivanhoe. Hence the anachronism, by which (in our *Ivanhoe*) Robin Hood is made a contemporary of Richard I. Still later, probably at the end of the nineteenth century, when the sufferings of the Jews in Russia were notorious, the group of Rebecca and Isaac of York was interwoven with the old poem and its continuation. A late *Bearbeiter* worked over the whole, introducing the absurd episode of the resurrection of Athelstane. Traces of old *lieder* are conspicuous ; above all is manifest the Death-song of Ulrica. This is addressed to Teutonic and Slavonic gods, Woden and Zernibock, and is probably a composite thing, the English element being earlier than the English invasion; for the Slavonic element it is no longer possible to account. This theory of *Ivanhoe* has really almost as much basis and plausibility as some points in the modern analysis and dislocation of the Odyssey.

CHAPTER XIV

THE LOST EPICS OF GREECE

THERE is no doubt that ancient Greece possessed, in addition to the Iliad and the Odyssey, many other old epic poems. Concerning these we have to ask, how far do they, or rather how far does the very little which we know about them, illustrate the Homeric question in general? The lost epics dealt with a large number of topics, but here we are mainly concerned with those about the Trojan War, and the heroes who fought under Troy. It is certain that Herodotus, Plato, and Aristotle were acquainted with various old epics which dealt with the earlier part of the war, and with what followed the death of Hector, the last agony of Ilios. Though the dates of these poems, as we shall see, are uncertain, they were, at least, very old. Now, is it likely that such epics as the poem called *Cypria*, or that other called *Iliou Persis* ('The Fall of Ilios') or *The Little Iliad*, were composite things, botched up arrangements of still older epics and ballads, strung together, interpolated, and 'redacted,' as criticism supposes the Iliad and the Odyssey to be? In a word, were all the old epics of Greece such mere patchwork as the Iliad and Odyssey are said to be, and, if so, in what possible circumstances could it be worth the while of men, living in an age when there were scarce any reading public, to labour at stitching, botching, and 'redacting'?

Unfortunately, our knowledge of the lost epics is extremely slender. Several proofs may be adduced to show that they were not of the same literary value, had not the same hold of the public, as the Iliad and the Odyssey. It may also be proved that they contained records of customs which Homer never mentions, though he often had occasion to mention them, and that they abounded in a kind of myths which the taste of Homer severely rejected. For these reasons it may be presumed that the lost epics were later than the Iliad and Odyssey in their present form. For, if the view is correct which regards these two epics as things of slow evolution, it is improbable that their later continuators could have avoided introducing the customs familiar to the lost epics and the kind of myths in which the authors of the lost epics take delight. Perhaps this conclusion—namely, that the lost epics are distinctly later than the Iliad and Odyssey, and belong to a different age and stratum of custom and of myth—is almost the only solid ground which we can reach, and even this is disputed.

Our knowledge of the perished poems is derived from sources of several kinds, and the earlier authorities, unluckily, are much the more scanty. The lost epics are quoted and referred to by such authors as Herodotus, Plato, and Aristotle, but these citations are very scanty compared with their citations of the Iliad and Odyssey. In the central age of classical literature the two great epics were already far more familiar, far more esteemed, than the epics which have disappeared. Again, writers of the first and second centuries after our era speak of and occasionally cite the lost epics : such writers are the literary and antiquarian authors, like Pausanias and Athenæus. Next we have citations by the scholiasts or annotators of the elder classics. Of these annotators the dates, of course, are various. We have also the evidence of gems and vases,

and the plays composed by the great tragedians on subjects in the lost epics, but many of these plays have
perished. Finally, we possess fragments of a treatise on
the lost epics, as far as they were represented in a compilation called (in late times) 'The Epic Cycle.' This
treatise is attributed to one Proclus, possibly the tutor of
the Emperor Marcus Aurelius Antoninus. Only fragments,
as we said, remain of a work which was 'a kind of primer
or *résumé* of Greek literature.'[1] Proclus lived, as we do,
in an age of 'primers' and literary short cuts. Our position, therefore, is like that of the critic of the future, if
concerning Chaucer he knows no more than he finds in
a few shreds of a primer of English literature and in a
dozen brief quotations in notes to Shakespeare. Manifestly
on such information it is not safe to dogmatise, especially
as one primer-writer borrowed freely from another, and he,
again, from a still earlier condenser and abbreviator, so that
we may often be far from the original source.[2]

The fragments of the Greek primer of epic literature,
the *Chrestomatheia* of Proclus, exist in five leaves surviving
from an original text of eight leaves in the celebrated Venetian
manuscript of the Iliad, first edited by Villoison (Marc. 454).
A portion of what is lost in this MS.—namely, the analysis
of the epic called the *Cypria*—survives in certain other
MSS. of the Iliad. In the *Bibliotheca* of the patriarch
Photius (of the ninth century A.D.) exists an account of the
other parts of the *Chrestomatheia*, or primer of Proclus,
whereof Photius had only extracts before him. Photius

[1] Monro, *Journal of Hellenic Studies*, 1883, 1884.

[2] A curious modern instance of such successive borrowings is to be
found in the old books on angling. From the treatise ascribed to
Dame Juliana Berners, printed late in the fifteenth century, down to
the middle of the last century, it is a series of borrowings unacknow-
ledged ; perhaps the original source of some of the stock remarks will
never be discovered.

summarises what Proclus had to say about 'the so-called Epic Cycle.' It began with the embraces of Earth and Heaven, and contained a complete mythical history, both of gods and men. The 'Cycle' was 'filled up' out of the works of various poets, ending with the death of Odysseus at the hands of his son Telegonus. Proclus reports that the 'Cycle' was preserved, and had its popularity, not so much for its literary excellence as for the sequence of events narrated in the poems. Proclus also gave an account of the lives of the authors of the poems. He next discussed the authorship of the *Cypria*, which some attributed to Stasinus of Cyprus, some to Hegesinus, others to Homer, who gave it as a dowry to his daughter when she married Stasinus. The conception of literary property thus disclosed has been discussed elsewhere. From another reference to the *Chrestomatheia* it appears that some of 'the ancients' assigned the 'Cycle' to Homer, thus illustrating the use of Homer's as a collective name, if indeed 'Cycle' here means the epic Cycle.

The word 'cycle' has caused some difficulty, because it is used in different senses. In the *Organon* of Aristotle the word is given as an example of 'the ambiguous middle,' a kind of pun.

> Every cycle is a figure.
> The epic (?) is a cycle.
> Therefore the epic (?) is a figure.[1]

But the word here used in Greek is τὰ ἔπη, or ἡ Ὁμήρου ποίησις, and it appears that we cannot here regard τὰ ἔπη as meaning 'the epic,' still less 'the Epic Cycle,' for Aristotle, in the *Poetics*, distinguishes the *Cypria* and *Little*

---

[1] τὰ ἔπη κύκλος; elsewhere, ἡ Ὁμήρου ποίησις σχῆμα διὰ τοῦ κύκλου, *Post. Anal.* i. 12, 10. (p. 77 b, 32); *Soph. El.* 10, 6. (p. 171 a, 10). Mr. Monro cites Brandis' *Scholia in Aristotelem* (p. 217 a, 44 b. 16) for the explanation by Joannes Philoponus.

Iliad (which were parts of Proclus's ' Cycle') from the poetry
of Homer. Mr. Monro decides that τὰ ἔπη and ἡ Ὁμήρου
ποίησις mean, not the epics, but a short poem attributed to
Homer, and known as 'the κύκλος' or as 'a κύκλος.' This
was 'an epigram so constructed that the same line may
form either beginning or end, as in the verses inscribed on
the tomb of Midas.' The people of Cyme, as we learn
from the *Life of Homer* falsely assigned to Herodotus, attributed the epigram to Homer. This is one of two explana-
tions of the Aristotelian phrase given by Joannes Philoponus
in his commentary on the *Posterior Analytics*. The 'Cycle,'
or κύκλος, thus understood, answered, curiously enough, to
the *Rondeau*. In a *Rondeau* the same words are both the
beginning and end of a short poem, and the *Rondeau*, or
'round,' is itself a figure, a cycle, or circle   Thus we might
illustrate the ambiguous middle by saying :

> Every ' round ' is a figure ;
> The *Rondeau* is a round ;
> Therefore the *Rondeau* is a figure.

It is not an uncommon use of words to apply τὰ ἔπη to
a mere *rondeau*, or brief epigram, and it is impossible that
by κύκλος Aristotle understood what Proclus knew as ' the
Epic Cycle.'

The term ' Cycle,' again, is used [1] of ' a work on the Cycle '
by Dionysius of Samos, and Athenæus quotes thence a
prose story of the Cyclops. [2] Clemens of Alexandria quotes
the same book for a tradition about the Palladium, and a
scholiast on the *Orestes* of Euripides (988) speaks of ' Dionysius, the cycle-writer.' His book was plainly a statement in
prose of the matter contained in old epic poems. We have an
analogy for such a work in the history of the French epic.
The exploits of ' every paladin and peer ' of Charlemagne

---

[1] Athenæus, p. 477 d.   [2] Monro *op. cit.* p. 22.

were originally sung in epics, or *chansons de geste*, such as the *Song of Roland*. In course of time these old French epics were wholly forgotten, till they were disinterred in the beginning of the nineteenth century. But prose summaries of the French epics remained current in the *Bibliothèque Bleue*, as chapbooks. It is by no means impossible that the prose ' Cycle' of Dionysius superseded, to a great extent, the old epics, which would gradually become obsolete, at what date we do not know—as, indeed, we do not know the date of the prose work by Dionysius.

Another difficulty as to the date of the ' Cycle' is caused by the occurrence of the word κυκλικός, ' cyclic,' in the scholia to the Iliad (as vi. 325), which contain excerpts of the work of Aristarchus in Alexandria. But here 'cyclic' means 'conventional' or ' formal,' ' a piece of epic mannerism.' The same meaning, according to Mr. Monro, attaches to κυκλικόν in a well-known epigram of Callimachus, and to Horace's *scriptor cyclicus*.[1] In the Greek Anthology (xi. 130) Pollianus mocks ' the Cyclic poets who say αὐτὰρ ἔπειτα, and who shamelessly rob Homer.' These were probably archaistic epic-writers of the Alexandrian age, persons like Quintus Smyrnæus in a later day ; perhaps Apollonius Rhodius is meant. Whoever these poets called ' Cyclic' were, they obviously took the advice offered to the Ram in the fairy tale : ' Bélier, mon ami, commencez par le commencement,' and began their poems ' from the egg' of Leda, like Antimachus of Colophon.

In all these senses of ' cycle' and ' cyclic,' then, as used by Aristotle, Horace, Callimachus, and the rest, no reference, according to Mr. Monro, is intended to the ' Cyclic Poems' and ' Cycle' analysed by Proclus.

These poems (so far as Trojan affairs are concerned) are :

[1] *Anthol.* xii. 43 ; *Epist. ad Pis.* 135.

The *Cypria.*[1]
The *Æthiopis.*
The *Little Iliad.*
The *Iliou Persis* (*Sack of Ilios*).
The *Nostoi.*
The *Telegonia.*

These composed what Proclus calls the 'Epic Cycle,' or, rather, they composed the Trojan part of the 'Epic Cycle,' with the addition of the *Iliad* and *Odyssey.* The contents of these two epics Proclus does not analyse, taking for granted that everybody knows them. It is thus obvious that they were infinitely more popular than the other ancient pieces on kindred subjects. There is evidence that, in their places in the 'Cycle,' the other epics were not given in their full original form, but were curtailed and dove-tailed into each other, as the framers of the 'Cycle' chanced to prefer the version of one or another minstrel.[2] This is proved by comparing the list of dramas which Aristotle says were made out of the *Little Iliad* with the contents of the *Little Iliad* as given by Proclus, when describing the 'Epic Cycle.' The framers of the 'Cycle' at a certain point de-serted the *Little Iliad* for the *Sack of Ilios*, preferring the version of events therein contained. It is also plain that, in taking the *Cypria* into the 'Cycle,' the makers of that collection altered a certain passage described by Herodotus (ii. 116, 117) so as to bring it into harmony with the account given in the Iliad. All these operations, and the 'Cycle' as such, are probably later than the Alexandrian school of criticism. They belong to an age of short cuts, like Miss Braddon's abbreviations of the *Waverley* novels. The poems, as they stood in the 'Cycle,' and as they are described by

---

[1] The analysis by Proclus is not in the manuscript known as 'Venetus A,' but missing, and restored from other MSS.

[2] Monro, *op. cit.* p. 13.

Proclus, are probably *not* the poems as their authors left them.

We must now examine the scant remains of the poems, and the brief analyses which tell the gist of their stories. Such analyses, as anyone may observe who reads a perfunctory review of a novel, can give little idea of the literary merit of the lost poems. They do prove, however, that Aristotle was right when he declared that the Iliad and Odyssey were composed on a plan more artistic than the plan of the other old epics.

First in order among the epics, which were included in the 'Cycle,' and which dealt with Trojan affairs, comes the *Cypria*, in eleven books. The analysis of Proclus runs thus :

'Zeus takes counsel with Themis about the Trojan war.' Here we have a fragment of the original poem, quoted in the Venetian scholia to the Iliad, i. 5, 6. Zeus was alarmed by the increase of population. He therefore devised the Trojan war, that the broad-breasted Earth might be lightened of her burden, 'and in Troia were those heroes slain, and the counsel of Zeus was fulfilled.' [1]

The same account of the divine origin of the war is given—probably from the *Cypria*—by Helen, in the prologue to the *Helena* of Euripides.

To continue the analysis by Proclus, Discord throws down the golden apple at the marriage of Peleus and Thetis. Paris decides the strife as to which of the three divine claimants of the apple is the fairest ; he was bribed by the promise of Helen. He builds ships to sail in her quest ; Helenus prophesies evil ; Aphrodite bids Æneas sail with him ; Cassandra foretells doom. Paris is entertained in Laconia by the Tyndaridæ (Castor and Polydeuces), and in Sparta by Menelaus ; Paris gives Helen gifts ; Menelaus

[1] Kinkel, *Epicorum Græcorum Fragmenta*, p. 20.

sails to Crete. Aphrodite brings Helen to the bed of Paris ;
then they sail away with the treasures of Menelaus. Hera
sends a storm ; they are carried to Sidon ; Paris takes the
town, sails to Troy, and weds Helen. Meanwhile, Castor
and Polydeuces drive the cattle of Lynceus and Idas. Idas
slays Castor. Polydeuces kills Idas and Lynceus. Zeus
gives the Dioscouroi immortality on alternate days. Iris
tells Menelaus what has befallen in Sparta ; he consults
with Agamemnon, and goes to Nestor. The old Nestor
tells him many stories about Œdipous, the madness of
Heracles, Theseus, and Ariadne. Then comes the muster
of heroes. Odysseus feigns madness, ploughing the sea-
sand ; he is detected by Palamedes, who lays the child
Telemachus in the track of the plough. They meet at
Aulis. We have the omen of the sparrows and the serpent.[1]
They sail, and, mistaking Teuthrania for Troy, they sack
it. Telephus comes to aid the city ; he is wounded by
Achilles. A storm scatters them ; Achilles is driven to
Scyros, and marries Deidamia. He heals Telephus, who
becomes their guide to Troy. They meet again at Aulis.
Artemis substitutes a stag for Iphigenia, and makes her
immortal. They sail to Tenedos. Philoctetes is bitten by
a snake, and is left in Lemnos. Achilles has a quarrel with
Agamemnon. Protesilaus is slain in the landing at Troy.
Achilles slays Cycnus, son of Poseidon. The embassy goes
to demand Helen of the Trojans ; she is not given up ;
there is an attack on the walls. The Greeks ravage the
neighbourhood. Achilles has an interview with Helen, by
aid of Aphrodite and Thetis. He drives the cattle of
Æneas, and sacks adjacent towns. He gets Briseïs as his
prize. Agamemnon gets Chryseïs. Palamedes is slain. Zeus,
to relieve the Trojans, causes the withdrawal of Achilles.
There is then given a catalogue of the Trojan allies ; and

[1] Iliad, ii. 308–320.

so ends the *Cypria*, according to the analysis of Proclus. It is not a dramatic ending ; and probably is no more than the arrangement made, not by the poet, but by the framers of the 'Cycle,' so as to lead up to the opening of the Iliad.

The fragments of the poem which survive add a little to the bare sketch of the grammarian. We learn that [1] the shaft of the spear of Peleus [2] was cut by Chiron, the Centaur. A passage [3] describes the flower-scented raiment of Aphrodite, fragrant with crocus and hyacinth, violet, rose, narcissus, and lily. The quotation is from Athenæus (xv. p. 682 D–F) ; he says that the poet was Stasinus, or Hegesias, or—some one else. Probably Aphrodite's arraying was for the judgment of Paris. The fourth fragment displays the procession of garlanded nymphs and graces, walking and singing with Aphrodite along the hill of many-fountained Ida. This also is from Athenæus. In the fifth fragment Castor is said to have been mortal, but Polydeuces immortal. The sixth fragment, of twelve lines, shows Nemesis fleeing from the embraces of Zeus, and taking many shapes to baffle his pursuit,

$$\text{ἐτείρετο γὰρ φρένας αἰδοῖ}$$
$$\text{καὶ νεμέσει.}$$

To make Nemesis *feel* Nemesis, a sense of moral shame, is extremely unlike the manner of Homer. The incident has its parallels in the *Mabinogion* and in the *Arabian Nights*, and (except in the case of Proteus, Od. iv.) has no analogies in the Homeric epics. A reference of Pausanias to 'him who made the *Cypria*' as authority for a statement about two daughters of Apollo is of no moment. The remark of Herodotus that the *Cypria* brought Paris from Sparta to Troy in three days, while the Iliad makes him storm-tossed

---

[1] Fr. 2.   [2] Iliad, xvi. 140.   [3] Fr. 3.

on his voyage, shows that the poem, as analysed by
Proclus, had been altered so as to make it consistent with
the Iliad.[1]

The ninth fragment, quoted in the scholion to Pindar's
tenth Nemean ode, 114, deals with Lynceus, the brother of
Idas, and enemy of Castor and Pollux. According to the
scholiast, Aristarchus read, in the Pindaric passage, ἥμενον,
not ἡμένους, following the story in the *Cypria*, for the author
of the *Cypria* says that Lynceus spied Castor hidden in the
oak-tree. Lynceus, in the fragment, looked all over Peloponnesus, from Taygetus, and so beheld the Dioscouroi (or
one of them) 'within the hollow oak-tree.' Lynceus, according to the scholiast, could see through stone and earth. In
fact, he is our old friend Keen-eye of the fairy tales. Castor
was slain when thus discovered. The tenth fragment[2] runs:
'Wine, Menelaus, have the gods made the best of things
to scatter the cares of mortal men.' Pausanias (x. 26, 4)
says that, according to the *Cypria*, Lycomedes gave to
the son of Achilles the name of Pyrrhus, but Phœnix
called him Neoptolemus. Now, 'Homer, in all his
poetry, styles him Neoptolemus:' thus Pausanias does not
assign the *Cypria* to Homer. A scholion on Sophocles,
Electra, 157, alleges that the *Cypria* gave Agamemnon four
daughters, adding Iphigenia to the three named by Homer,[3]
'Chrysothemis, and Laodice, and Iphianassa.' Any one of
these three Achilles may marry, in the Iliad; but, if Homer
knew of Iphigenia, he also knew that she was either sacrificed at Aulis or removed by Artemis to Thrace.

Omitting one or two notices of no importance, we
find[4] that the *Cypria* explained how Chryseïs was
captured at Thebæ; she had gone thither, from Chrysa, to

---

[1] Herodot. ii. 117. [2] Athenæus, ii. 35 c.
[3] Iliad, ix. 145.
[4] Fr. 16, cited by Eustathius, Iliad, i. 366, and Venetian scholia.

a sacrifice. The *Cypria* contained another fairy tale of three maidens who could produce corn, wine, and oil at will, and who fed the Greek army—a magical commissariat.[1] Of course, this fable out of the stock of *Märchen* is alien to the taste of Homer.

Still more alien, if possible, is the tale in the *Cypria* that Odysseus and Diomede killed Palamedes when fishing.[2] Homer's heroes are no anglers, nor would Homer thus have maligned Odysseus. The legend is one of the many which traduce the stout-hearted Ithacan. A quotation of Plato's who merely cites 'the poet,' that 'reverence goes with dread,' is attributed by the scholiast[3] to 'the *Cypria*, by Stasinus.' Whether Plato did assign the *Cypria* to Stasinus, or any other named poet, we cannot be absolutely certain.

The names of the composers of the epics are better known to late than to early authorities. It has even been doubted whether such writers as Pausanias really knew the *Cypria* at all, though Pausanias, speaking of the murder of Palamedes, remarks, 'This I have read in the *Cypria*' (x. 31, 2). A reference to the birth of the Gorgons, who dwelt in an isle of Ocean called 'Sarpedon,' is cited by Herodian ; and Clemens Alexandrinus quotes Stasinus for the line, 'Fool, who slays the sire and spares the children.'

These are all the certain references to the *Cypria* which time has spared us. They are few, but enough to furnish strong presumptions in favour of several conclusions. First, as Aristotle remarks, and as the analysis by Proclus indicates, the *Cypria* had not real unity of treatment ; unlike the Iliad and the Odyssey, it yielded topics for many dramas. It was something of a chronicle-poem, not dealing with the adventures of a few days, but wandering over a great space of time and country. Aristotle says it has ' one hero, one

---

[1] *Scholl. vet. ad Lycophr.* 570 ; Kinkel, p. 29.
[2] Pausanias, x. 31, 2.   [3] *Euthyphro*, 12 A.

time, and one action of many parts.' The hero *may* have
been Paris, but Achilles is really as prominent ; the ' one
time ' is time of great length ; the 'parts ' are a string of ill-
connected adventures. For example, when the poet deserts
Helen and Paris on their flight, and returns to the raids and
revenges of Helen's brothers in Peloponnesus, he leaves the
main thread of action with no obvious reason. The cattle
robberies of the Dioscouroi, their death and immortality,
have no connection with the main action except as explaining why Helen's brothers did not pursue Paris. The two
separate meetings at Aulis are clumsy ; 'the purpose of
Zeus ' to reduce population and relieve the burden of Earth,
is un-Homeric in its premature political economy. If the
influence of Aphrodite be the main ethical motive in the
Cypria, we cannot say for certain whether it was a rule of
epic composition to give every poem an interest of this
kind, or whether the action of Aphrodite is an imitation
of the action of Athene, in the Odyssey. But, whatever
he may have imitated, the author or the *Bearbeiter* of the
Cypria did not imitate the unity and concentration of the
Odyssey and the Iliad.

The set of incidents in the *Cypria* raise two questions :
how far did the author expand hints from the Iliad, and
how far have we a right to say that he used legends
'unknown to Homer'? Certain events, such as the
capture of Lyrnessus and Pedasus,[1] the present of a spear
to Peleus,[2] the embassy into Troy,[3] the omen of the serpent
and sparrows,[4] are common to Iliad and *Cypria*. It is
probable that they were suggested by the Iliad, but it is
not impossible that both authors borrowed from a common
stock of legend. We must be cautious in denying that

[1] Fr. 15 ; Iliad, ii. 690 ; xx. 92.
[2] Fr. 2 ; Iliad, xvi. 140.   [3] Proclus ; Iliad, iii. 205.
[4] Proclus ; Iliad, ii. 308–320.

Homer knew the stories in the *Cypria* to which he did not
make reference. Homeric ignorance can seldom be justly
inferred from Homeric silence. He never speaks of the
Apple of Discord, but he may not have been ignorant of
that *Märchen*, where Discord plays the part of the hostile
fairy at the christening. To the judgment of Paris he only
alludes in a suspected passage (Iliad, xxiv. 29). In that text
the gods generally resent the outrages of Achilles on the
dead Hector, except Poseidon, Hera, and Athene. The two
goddesses resent the ἄτη of Paris, who ' flouted them when
they came to his hut, but gave praise to Aphrodite, who
filled his mind with evil lust.' The passage was doubted by
Aristarchus, and, as we have seen, the twenty-fourth book
is under critical suspicion. But, of course, even if the
passage be rejected, we could not argue that Homer does
not know the legend because he does not mention it.

The curious tale of the death of Helen's brothers [1] must,
in part at least, have been known to Homer. From
Iliad, iii. 236, where Helen looks vainly for Castor and
Polydeuces among the Greeks, it is plain that the author
knew that they had died between the flight of Helen from
Sparta and the moment of her appearance on the wall. He
merely says, 'them already the life-giving earth embraced,
there in Lacedæmon, their own dear native land.' Their
alternate immortality is not hinted at here, but need not
have been unknown to the poet. It is mentioned in the
Odyssey, xi. 302–304, where Mr. Leaf regards line 304 as an
interpolation.[2] According to the tale in Pindar, Polydeuces,
as the son of Zeus, was immortal ; Castor, as the son of
Tyndareus, was mortal. But the former hero halved his
immortality with his brother. Of course, the sons of Zeus

---

[1] Described by Pindar in the Tenth Nemean Ode.
[2] *Journal of Philology*, vol. xii. p. 287 ; also Bekker, *Hom. Bl.*
ii. 37.

by mortal women are not immortal in Homer. All the element of fairy tale, in the matter of Lynceus, is ignored by Homer, but he need not have been ignorant of it. He never alludes to Palamedes, and we may be certain that, if the story of his murder by Odysseus had been known to Homer, he would have rejected it. The incident of the changes of shape by Nemesis is as old as fairy tale, but is quite alien, like the story of the girls who produced oil, wine, and corn, to Homeric taste. These girls play the part of the magical Sampo in the *Kalewala*, or of the Gold-spinner in Grimm's *Märchen*. Even Buddhism has its parallel to the corn, wine, and oil producing girls. When Mendaka bathed his head and sat down by his granary, showers of grain fell from the sky ; his wife had only to sit by a dish, and it filled with food. Their son had the purse of Fortunatus.[1] The fable is puerile, yet such fables are very antique, and may well have been within the range of Homer's knowledge, though he never would have used them in the epics.

Thus, in construction and in incident, the *Cypria* is plainly of a lower order of literary merit than the two great epics. It shows traces of having been composed partly on Homeric hints, and to lead up to the Iliad ; but these indications may be partly due to the changes introduced when the *Cypria* was incorporated with the 'Cycle.' We are certain that the poem was inferior in merit to the Iliad and Odyssey ; we are inclined to believe that it was later than these epics. As to its date and authorship we shall speak later. Old it undeniably was, and critics may dispute as to whether it was a botched, patched, and redacted mass of ancient ballads and earlier epics. If it were, the motive of its *Bearbeiter*, his reason for his industry, may possibly be explained by the persons who believe in him.

[1] Coplestone, *Buddhism*, p. 61.

Z

THE ÆTHIOPIS.

According to Proclus, the *Cypria* preceded the Iliad (of which he gives no analysis), the *Æthiopis*, of Arctinus the Milesian, followed it. The *Æthiopis* was a poem in five books. After the death of Hector, Penthesilea, Queen of the Amazons, came to the aid of Troy. She was Thracian by race, and a daughter of Ares. In the midst of her valiant deeds, she was slain by Achilles, and was buried by the Trojans. Achilles slew Thersites, who railed at him and accused him of a lover's regret for the dead girl. The killing of Thersites caused a feud among the Greeks.[1] Achilles sailed to Lesbos, and was purified of the manslaying by Odysseus, after sacrifice to Apollo, Artemis, and Leto. Next came Memnon, son of the Dawn, in a panoply made by Hephæstus. Thetis prophesies to Achilles about the fate of Memnon, who slays Antilochus, son of Nestor, and friend of Achilles. Then Memnon is slain by Achilles, but, on the prayer of the Dawn, is granted immortality by Zeus. Achilles routs the Trojans, follows them into Troy, and is slain by Paris and Apollo. His body is carried off by Aias, while Odysseus repels the Trojans. Antilochus is buried. Thetis and the Muses, with the Nereids, sing the dirge for Achilles ; Thetis takes his body from the pyre, and carries it to the Isle of Leukê. The Achæans build a howe, and hold games ; Aias and Odysseus quarrel about the arms of Achilles. So ends the analysis of Proclus, but probably the *Æthiopis* actually overlapped the *Little Iliad*, and told of the suicide of Aias. The fragments are (1) the Townley scholion on the last line of the Iliad, where some write, 'So they buried Hector, but the Amazon came, daughter of

---

[1] According to Quintus Smyrnæus, who probably followed some old tradition, Thersites was of the kindred of Diomede, who took up the blood-feud.

Ares.' The scholiast on Pindar (*Isthm.* iii. 53) says that in the *Æthiopis* Aias slew himself about the time of dawn. (2) Eight lines about the surgical and medical gifts of Machaon and Podalirius are quoted by the scholiast.[1]

In this poem the incidents known to Homer are [2] the slaying of Achilles, as foretold by Hector. Another version in which Apollo slays Achilles is used by Quintus Smyrnæus. Again,[3] Homer knows that Memnon slew Antilochus. Of the Amazons Homer only speaks in the story of Bellerophon,[4] and iii. 189, where Priam says that he had warred against them in his youth. The Ethiopians, in Homer, dwell at the limits of the world. He does not mention them as the army of Memnon. He knows [5] the lament of the Muses for Achilles, but he contemplates no immortality for his hero in the Isle of Leukê. Nor does he intend that Thetis shall carry away the body of Achilles, who clearly means to be buried, when his hour comes, with Patroclus.[6] The idea of immortality is not unfamiliar to the Odyssey. Calypso offers it to her lover in his lifetime, and Castor and Polydeuces obtain it in a limited form, while Menelaus is to be deathless, as the husband of Helen. But Homer never alludes to hero-worship, such as Achilles received in Leukê, an isle of the Euxine, according to Pindar and later tradition. However late books xi. and xxiv. of the Odyssey may be called, they seem to be earlier than the *Æthiopis*, for, in the Odyssey, Achilles is no hero, but a shadow. A thoroughly un-Homeric point in the *Æthiopis* is purification for manslaying. The rite was archaic or savage: the slayer was smeared with the blood of swine.[7] But Homer, who often mentions homicides, never hints at the ceremony of

---

[1] Venetus B, Iliad, xi. 515. [2] Iliad, xxii. 359, 360.
[3] Odyssey, iv. 187. [4] Iliad, vi. 186.
[5] Odyssey, xxiv. 60. [6] Iliad, xxiii. 245.
[7] *Eumenides*, 273.

purification. It may have existed in his day ; if it did, his taste rejected the ritual. Thus the *Æthiopis* is clearly un-Homeric ; it represents other manners, another treatment of legend, perhaps a wider geographical knowledge. The story, however, follows Homeric lines ; Antilochus is a *replica* of Patroclus ; the contest for the body of Achilles is a *replica* of the contest for the body of Patroclus. Thetis plays her accustomed part ; all ends in a funeral and funeral games.[1] The change in custom (as of purification) and the belief in heroic immortality, point to a period subsequent to the date of the Iliad and the Odyssey. The author, or authors, of Odyssey xi. and xxiv., cannot have believed in the translation of Achilles to Leukê, but of course it may be urged that the author of the *Æthiopis* cannot have known, as he does not follow, the version of Achilles's fate given in the Odyssey. Many diverse legends were obviously in existence, and it is illogical to argue that a poet ' did not know ' the form of the tale which he did not choose to adopt.

From all these indications we may conclude that the *Æthiopis* is later in date than the Iliad and Odyssey. If we grant that the last books of the Odyssey are very late, we shall find it difficult to account for the absence there of so important an idea, to the mind of post-Homeric Greece, as that of purification after homicide. It is familiar in the Cyclic poets, and we can hardly suppose that a continuator of the Odyssey, coeval with the Cyclic writers, would be a conscientious archæologist, and would, therefore, abstain from any reference to the rite as an anachronism.

The *Little Iliad* is ascribed to so many writers—Lesches of Mitylene,[2] Thestorides of Phocæa, Cinæthon of Sparta, Diodorus of Erythræ, and Homer himself—that we may believe the author to have been unknown. The abstract of

[1] Monro, *J. H. S.*, 1884.
[2] Called Lescheos by Pausanias, x. 25, 5.

Proclus omits the closing events, apparently because here
the arrangement of the ' Cycle' deserted the *Little Iliad* for
the *Iliou Persis* or *Sack of Troy*, attributed to Arctinus.
Aristotle, however, mentioning the tragedies taken from the
Little Iliad, enables us to fill up the story. First, according
to Proclus, came the award of the arms of Achilles to Odysseus—a circumstance known to the eleventh book of the
Odyssey. Aias goes mad, and kills himself. Odysseus
catches Helenus, the Trojan prophet, and on his advice
brings Philoctetes from Lemnos. He is healed by Machaon,
and slays Paris, whose body is maltreated by Menelaus
and buried by the Trojans.[1] Deiphobus marries Helen.
Neoptolemus, son of Achilles, is brought from Scyros,
receives the arms of Achilles, and sees the ghost of his
father. Eurypylus is slain by Neoptolemus. Epeius makes
the Wooden Horse. Odysseus enters Troy as a spy, is
recognised by Helen, and, with Diomede, carries the Palladium (not mentioned by Homer) out of the city. The
poem, as described by Proclus, ends with the introduction
of the Wooden Horse. Aristotle[2] adds to our information.
He praises Homer for not telling the whole chronicle of
the war. 'But the others write about one matter, and one
time, and one action of many parts, like the authors of the
Cypria and the *Little Iliad*. Thus, out of the Iliad and
Odyssey, one tragedy can be made, or two only, but many
out of the *Cypria*, and more than eight' (ten, in fact) 'out
of the *Little Iliad*.' These tragedies are the Award of the
Arms, Philoctetes, Neoptolemus, Eurypylus, the Begging of
Odysseus, the Lacænian Women (a chorus of maidens of
Helen), the Sack of Ilios, the Sailing Away, Sinon, and the
Troades.

The fragments of the *Little Iliad* amount to about

---

[1] The legend of Œnone does not occur here.
[2] *Poet.* xxiii.

twenty lines.   Some are parodied by Aristophanes.[1]   Others
speak of the golden vine which Zeus gave to Laomedon, in
atonement for his son Ganymede.[2]   This vine is believed
to be referred to in Odyssey (xi. 521) as 'a woman's gifts.'
Priam bribed with the golden vine the mother of Eurypylus
to send him as an ally of Troy.   Pausanias (x. 25, 5) supposes Polygnotus to have read the *Little Iliad* and illustrated it on the walls of the Delphian Leschê.   According
to Pausanias (x. 27, 1), the poem includes the adventure of
Corœbus, the wooer of Cassandra.   The relenting of
Menelaus at the sight of the breasts of Helen also occurred
here.[3]   The *Little Iliad*[4] adopted the Athenian theory that
Æthra,[5] the attendant of Helen, was the mother of Theseus,
which, as the scholiast says, is chronologically out of the
question.   Neoptolemus carried off Andromache ; he first
threw Astyanax over the wall.   This conduct, no doubt,
was dictated by a desire to avoid the blood-feud.[6]   Neoptolemus killed Priam, not at the altar, as in Virgil, but at the
door of his palace.

Most of the events in the *Little Iliad* are subjects of
allusions in the Iliad and the Odyssey.   The Palladium and
Sinon are un-Homeric.

The *Iliou Persis* of Arctinus, according to Proclus, was
in two books.   The Trojans watch the Wooden Horse,
doubtful about destroying it.   They dedicate it to Athene,
and begin to revel.   The serpents attack Laocoön, as in
Virgil.   Æneas, awestruck, escapes to Mount Ida.   Sinon
lights signal fires, the Greeks return from Tenedos, the men
in the Horse rush out on the Trojans, and the city is taken.
Neoptolemus slays Priam at the altar, Menelaus slays

---

[1] *Equites*, 1056.   [2] Schol. ad Eurip. *Troad.* 821.
[3] Aristoph. *Lysistrata*, 155 and scholion.
[4] Pausanias, x. 25, 8.   [5] Iliad, iii. 144.
[6] 'Oft waxes wolf in youngling.'   Brynhild in *Volsung Saga*.

Deiphobus, and takes Helen to the ships. Aias, in dragging away Cassandra, overthrows the statue of Athene ; the Greeks wish to stone him, but he takes sanctuary at Athene's altar. The city is burned, and Polyxena, daughter of Priam, is slain at the grave of Achilles. Neoptolemus seizes Andromache, Odysseus kills Astyanax. The sons of Theseus take their grandmother Æthra. The Greeks sail away, and Athene contrives for them peril on the sea.

It is plain that Proclus omits the beginning of the *Iliou Persis*, and gives the poem only as it stood in the Cycle. Dionysius of Halicarnassus [1] says that Arctinus here told the legend of the Palladium, the Luck of Troy. A facsimile of the real Palladium was stolen by the Greeks, the genuine one was hidden. The hero of the poem is probably Neoptolemus. Creusa probably appeared here, the wife of Æneas.[2] It was probably said that Æneas kept the genuine Palladium, and the whole poem would coincide in aim with the apparently interpolated account of Æneas in the Iliad.[3] The whole poem, and the *Æthiopis*, bear traces of influence from the traditions of Asia Minor. Arctinus, as Mr. Monro conjectures, probably survived as 'a witness to the Roman national legend,' and he inspired the second book of the Æneid.

The *Nostoi*, in five books, are attributed to Hagias of Troezen. Athene set Menelaus and Agamemnon at odds about the route homewards. Agamemnon stays to propitiate the goddess. This Menelaus neglected.[4] Menelaus, with five shîps, reaches Egypt. Diomede and Nestor return safe home. Calchas, Leontes, and Polypeithes, faring by land to Colophon, bury Calchas there. The ghost of Achilles vainly warns Agamemnon of the dangers that await him. Aias is wrecked in a storm. Neoptolemus, by advice

[1] *Antiq. Rom.* i. 69. [2] Monro, *op. cit.* p. 31.
[3] Iliad, xx. 178–352. [4] Odyssey, iv. 352.

of Thetis, returns overland through Thrace ; he meets
Odysseus in Maroneia. Phœnix dies ; Neoptolemus, in
Molossia, is recognised by Peleus. Agamemnon is slain,
and avenged by Pylades and Orestes. Menelaus reaches
Sparta. The *Nostoi*, according to Pausanias (x. 28, 7) con-
tained an account of Hades. In some way the story of
Medea restoring Æson to youth occurred in the *Nostoi*.[1]

The Anger of Athene is the chief motive in the poem.
The name of the slave-mother of Menelaus's son [2] is given in
the *Nostoi*, which also notes the presence of Odysseus in
Thrace.[3] Un-Homeric are the references to Colophon, an
Ionian colony, and to the Molossians.

The *Telegonia* closed the Homeric part of the ' Cycle.'
It was by Eugammon of Cyrene, in two books.

The wooers slain by Odysseus are buried by their
kindred. Odysseus sails, after sacrifice to the Nymphs, to
Elis, after cattle ; he is received by Polyxenus ; certain stories
are related as episodes.

Odysseus returns to Ithaca, and later performs the sacrifice to Poseidon among men who know not salt. Then he
goes to Thesprotia, and marries Callidice, queen of the
country. In a war with the Brygi, the men of Odysseus are
routed by Ares, whom Athene opposes. Apollo reconciles
them. Callidice dies ; her son by Odysseus, Polypœtes,
succeeds. He goes to Ithaca, where he is slain unwittingly
by his son by Circe, Telegonus, who takes Penelope and
Telemachus to Circe. She makes them immortal. Telegonus marries Penelope, and Telemachus weds Circe.

Here the Thesprotian incidents merely provide the
Thesprotian royal family with a descent from Odysseus.
The rest is a silly sequel, to say 'what became of them

[1] *Argum. ad* Eurip. *Medeam.*

[2] Odyssey, iv. 12.

[3] Odyssey, ix. 39, 197.

all.' And thus the last echoes of the immortal song die away in a mere literary manufactory.

Concerning the authorship of the poems included in the 'Cycle,' it is plain that our information is both scanty and dubious. Arctinus, Stasinus, Lesches, Hagias or Agias, are mere names to us. Athenæus (vii. 277) speaks as doubtfully as we must do about the author of the *Titano-machia*—'Eumelus, or Arctinus, or whoever he may be'— and (viii. 334, xv. 682) admits his ignorance as to who composed the *Cypria*. In Photius, Stasinus of Cyprus, Hegesinus of Salamis, and Homer himself (who presented the book as his daughter's dowry to Stasinus) are mentioned.

Pausanias, the antiquarian, who described Greece in the second century, is copious about the Cyclic poets ; but his evidence has lately been attacked, on the score that the poems had dropped out of sight before his time. He assures us that 'I read' this or that in the epics, but Wilamowitz Moellendorff thinks, to quote Dr. Johnson on Pot, that 'if Pausanias said that, Pausanias lied.'[1] Now, Pausanias, for example, in x. 26, where he describes the pictures of the Trojan war painted by Polygnotus at Delphi, quotes Lesches (whom he calls Lescheos), and the *Cypria*, just as he quotes the Iliad, and, to all appearance, has read what he quotes. When he has not read a poet, like Hegesinus, whose work was lost, he says so frankly (ix. 29): 'it was lost before I was born.' If, then, the Cyclics were lost before Pausanias was born, it is not likely that he would pretend to have read them. He could have deceived nobody, if the poems were not extant. He supposes (x. 28) that, in one passage, Polygnotus followed the *Minyas*. Had he not read the *Minyas*, and, if it was lost, why is he less frank than in the case of Hegesinus? In x. 31, 2, he tells us of the murder of Palamedes, and says, 'I read

[1] *Homer. Untersuch.* p. 338.

it in the *Cypria.*' 'Either Pausanias composed the most learned archæological exegesis of ancient times, or he makes a swindling claim to learning not his own.'[1] In Wilamowitz's opinion, Pausanias cribs his learning from some earlier describer of the work of Polygnotus, to whose mind the *Cypria,* the *Little Iliad,* the *Nostoi,* and the *Minyas* were anonymous.

Pausanias, then, according to Wilamowitz, lives, as it were, on manuals of the past, and has no original first-hand knowledge of the epics. He, and the writers of *scholia,* and so forth, all go back to learned treatises of an earlier day, by Apollodorus, Dionysius Scytobrachion, Aristodemus, and other scholars of 150–50 B.C. The conclusion is that the really learned ancient grammarians distrusted all names assigned as those of authors of epics. The *Chronicle* of Eusebius is dismissed, as no valid authority on Lesches, Arctinus, and the rest. On the whole, 'the ancient grammarians looked on the Cyclic epics as anonymous. The classical period (450–150 B.C.?) 'regarded them as Homeric.'[2] Our oldest allusion to Homer, that of Callinus, quoted by Pausanias, attributes the *Thebais* to Homer. Pindar[3] clearly attributes to Homer the story of the suicide of Aias. It is Pindar[4] who tells how Homer gave the *Cypria* to Stasinus. This rather makes against Wilamowitz's theory, for it is plain that, even in Pindar's time, the name of Stasinus was connected with the authorship of the *Cypria.* Herodotus (ii. 117) doubts the Homeric authorship of the *Cypria,* because of a discrepancy with the Iliad. There criticism begins. It must really have begun earlier, when Pindar could explain the connection of Stasinus with the poem by the tale that it was given to him by Homer as the dowry of his wife. People must have said,

---

[1] *Homer. Untersuch.* p. 340.   [2] *Ibid.* p. 351.
[3] *Isthm.* iii. 53.   [4] *Fragments,* 189, Boeckh.

' Stasinus never could have composed anything so good,' and then the story would circulate that he ploughed with Homer's heifer. We have no reason to suppose that the doubts of Herodotus as to the authorship began with Herodotus. In brief, the classical age has a tendency to attribute *Hymns*, *Margites*, *Thebais*, and everything to Homer ; but there were others who doubted, and the early mention of Stasinus shows that other claimants were not unnamed. As to whether the Cyclic poems vanished about 150 B.C., and were only known in extracts, or (like the French *chansons de geste*) in prose compilations, we must decide according to our view of the good faith of Pausanias, who avers that he read them.

Wilamowitz concludes that 'the Iliad, as it stands, is not the work of one man, nor of one century ; nay, it is not a work at all. The Iliad is nothing but a Cyclic poem. . . . There is no distinction of quality between " Homeric " and "Cyclic"'—between Iliad and *Cypria*.[1] On this showing, all early Greek epic is Homeric and not Homeric. Those who have observed the vast differences in art, method, and manners which sunder Iliad and Odyssey from *Cypria* and *Telegonia* will scarcely accept this sweeping theory. In art, the Iliad and Odyssey are immeasurably superior ; in custom and myth, considerably older than the Cyclics, as even the little we know of these poems reveals. But, on the theory of Wilamowitz, we must, apparently, believe that, in a certain age, floating lays innumerable were *bearbeited*, and cooked, and dovetailed, so as to produce, not only the Iliad and Odyssey, but all the many Cyclic epics. Who took all this trouble, when, where, and, above all, *why* ? How could it possibly pay any mortals to undertake this colossal labour ? For, if Iliad and Odyssey be huge pieces of patchwork, so must *Cypria*, and *Thebais*, and

[1] *Op. cit.* pp. 374, 375.

Æthiopis, and all the rest of them, be. What reward did the forgotten *bearbeiters* and diaskeuasts reap for all their industry? Whatever we may think of Iliad and Odyssey, it is difficult to believe that all the Cyclic poems were, as theorists assert of them, originally tags of lays, reduced into order and sequence by persons without any intelligible motive. The more probable view is the old view, that the Iliad and the Odyssey were the models of ambitious later poets, in the eighth, seventh, and sixth centuries.

CHAPTER XV

HOMER AND ARCHÆOLOGY

THE poems of Homer are rich in descriptions of works of art, of decorative objects in gold, bronze, silver, and ivory. We hear of cups, brooches, adorned shields, baldrics, sword-hilts, and other trappings. Granting that Homer was describing, with a certain poetic licence, things with which he was familiar, the question arises, have any treasures been discovered which answer to his descriptions and give a clue to his date? Before entering minutely into the arguments on this topic it is necessary to ask what kind of works of art does Homer describe ? It is impossible to remark on all of them : typical specimens must suffice. We find xi. 22) the breastplate of Agamemnon, given him by Ciny-ras of Cyprus. Commentators who think that the author of the original poem was not acquainted with Cyprus of course regard this passage as late. It was decorated with ten courses of cyanus, lapis lazuli, or an imitation in glass paste. A frieze of this material is mentioned in the palace of Alcinous,[1] and such a frieze was found at Tiryns.[2] The breastplate had also 'twelve courses of gold, and twenty of tin' ; there were snakes of cyanus on it. The sword had golden studs. The shield had circles of bronze, tin bosses, a cyanus boss bore the Gorgon's head, and the shield was large enough to cover all the body of a man. Can such

[1] Odyssey, vii. 87.
[2] Schuchhardt, *Schliemann's Discoveries*, Engl. transl. p. 117.

a shield, or that of Hector, which hung from neck to ankles, have been circular ?   As to the Gorgon, Mr. Leaf argues that it was unknown to Greek art before the seventh century.   There is, however, excellent reason to believe that it was known to Greek mythology, in the tale of Perseus. Dread and Terror accompany the Gorgon on the shields; and on the chest of Cypselus (circ. 700 B.C.), which Pausanias saw at Olympia, Agamemnon was represented with Terror on his shield, a lion-headed figure.[1]   Allowing the Gorgon's head, for the sake of argument, to be an interpolation later than the whole passage, itself late, this shield is a puzzle. At what age, if any, did Greeks wear shields that covered the whole body, and were decorated with inlaid glass paste ? On a ring found in the Mycenæan graves[2] we see a warrior in a crested helm, and carrying a huge circular shield, which, like Agamemnon's, covers all his body.   The shield of a lion-hunter on a Mycenæan dagger blade[3] hangs, like Hector's, from neck to ankles ; it has a kind of waist in the middle.   Another hunter has as huge a shield, which is oblong.   But on a vase from Mycenæ[4] (apparently later than the shaft-graves) the warriors use small shields of the shape of a three-quarter moon.   In historic Greece the shields were not nearly so large as those in Homeric descriptions and in Mycenæan works of art.   The shields in the Dipylon vases, about the middle of the seventh century, are small round bucklers ; and the ordinary circular shield with heraldic devices, as shown on vases of later dates, are not half the size of Homeric shields.   On the whole the huge shield seems to take us back to an early age of prehistoric Greek armour, beyond that it were unsafe to go. The high-crested helmet is represented on the ring already referred to, but its wearer's opponent has no helmet.   Some

[1] Pausanias, v. 17.   [2] Schuchhardt, p. 196, figure 178.
[3] Schuchhardt, p. 229.   [4] *Ibid.* figure 284.

of the warriors in a representation of a siege, on a silver
bowl from Mycenæ, are naked. Others, unhelmed, have
large pointed shields, unlike those depicted on the dagger
blade.[1] Homer's warriors always wear greaves: there are
no greaves among the treasures of Mycenæ, nor are any
depicted on Mycenæan works of art. On the other hand,
gaiters were worn, clasped with elaborate clasps of gold.[2]

The shield of Achilles, made by Hephæstus,[3] is clearly
an ideal work of art. Homer probably never saw anything
so elaborate, and so rich in various pictures of human
life in peace and war. Some points of detail are notable :
the gods are wrought in gold, and the raiment on the
shoulders of a Fate is '*red* with the blood of men.' A
vineyard is rich in clusters 'wrought fair in gold, black were
the grapes, but the vines hung throughout on silver poles.'
The kine 'were fashioned of gold and tin.' If we are to
understand that these things were inlaid with gold of divers
colours—red and lighter yellow—we find a parallel in the
inlaid dagger blades of Mycenæ and in Egyptian dagger
blades dated about 1600 B.C. But though Homer may
have seen such work, the objects may have been old heirlooms, and he need not have been contemporary with the
art. Meanwhile, as will be shown, others find a parallel to
the decoration of the shield in Phœnician bowls of metal
of the seventh century B.C.

Turning to more peaceful objects, we find Nestor's
golden cup : 'another man could scarce have lifted it when
full,' it had studs of gold, four handles or supports, and
there were doves on the handles.[4] A very much smaller
cup, with rods connecting the handles and the foot, and with
doves on the handles, was found in the royal graves of

---

[1] This bowl is engraved as a frontispiece to Mr. Leaf's *Companion.*
[2] Schuchhardt, p. 228.   [3] Iliad, xviii. 480.
[4] Iliad, xi. 632.

Mycenæ.[1]   Another cup of silver, with a gold rim, is given
by Menelaus to Telemachus.[2]   It was a present to Menelaus
from the King of Sidon, and was the work of Hephæstus.
In places too numerous to mention, works of art are derived
from the Sidonians or Phœnicians, or are attributed to
Hephæstus.   All this looks as if the jewels known to
Homer were of Phœnician importation.   Now, in the
treasures of Mycenæ, Phœnician influence in art is much
less visible than the influence of Egypt.   We may, perhaps, argue that, in the poet's age, the Phœnicians im-
ported work from Egypt, and had not yet struck out their
own eclectic art—half Assyrian, half Egyptian.   But whereas
much of the Mycenæan work is apparently native, though
influenced by Egypt, gold workers, in Homer's day, seem to
have been rare among the Achæans.   The gold brooch of
Odysseus [3] was embossed with a group of a dog catching a
deer, a very common motive in the earliest gems, whatever
their exact date may be.   We are not told whence the
brooch was procured, but 'all men marvelled at it.'

While many of the objects found at Mycenæ, like the
dagger blades and cups, are like things described by Homer,
the costume of the men and women is different ; the
women wear a kind of flounced petticoats ; the men, as a
rule, wear very little but a kind of drawers.   In funereal
matters, we see that the corpses were not burned as in Homer,
but were, to some extent, mummified and buried in deep
graves, not, as in Homer, under tumuli.   There may have
been different arrangements in peace and war.[4]   On the
whole, the art and life in Homer answer to those of no
historically known Greek period, nor exactly to those of the
heroes buried in the deep 'shaft tombs' of Mycenæ.   In

[1] Schuchhardt, p. 241.   [2] Odyssey, iv. 616.
[3] Odyssey, xix. 226.
[4] Leaf, Introduction to Schuchhardt, p. xxvi.

them no trace of iron has been found,[1] whereas, in Homer, iron is used as synonymous with 'weapon,' and the metal is frequently mentioned. It would appear, then, that the age of Homer is between that of the Mycenæan graves and the dawn of actual history. Putting the graves conjecturally at 1500-1300 B.C., this might place Homer about 1200-1000 B.C. ; but all this is very much guess-work.

Throughout this summary sketch it has been purposely taken for granted that the graves of Mycenæ are extremely ancient and 'Achæan'—that is, tombs of men who died before the Dorian invasion, roughly dated 1100-1000 B.C. But this very point has been recently disputed, and must be more narrowly examined.

Before coming to close quarters with the problem, we should remember that antiquarians have been apt to welcome each new piece of evidence as the key to the whole question, forgetting that the pickaxe and spade may at any moment bring fresh and contradictory testimony. For example, a whole theory as to the date of Homeric civilisation has been based on certain Phœnician objects of art, mainly bowls of silver and other metals, which have been thought, as we saw, to illustrate Homer's descriptions of decorative metal work, as in the shield of Achilles.[2] But later discoveries tend to show that the Phœnician metal bowls do not correspond to Homeric descriptions so closely as do certain other relics—namely, the already quoted dagger blades from Mycenæ, for which an earlier date than that of the Phœnician bowls has been claimed. These

---

[1] Schuchhardt, p. 229. The use of iron in Homer was debated by the Hellenic Society, October 1892. In Odyssey, xvi. 294, occurs the proverbial expression, ' iron of itself draws to it a hero.' In Iliad, iv. 123, ' iron ' is used as synonymous with arrow-head. The arrow-heads of the Mycenæan graves are of flint ; at Ialysus they are of bronze.

[2] Iliad, book xviii.

bowls, in which the art exhibits a mixture of Egyptian and
Assyrian influence, are decorated with rows or bands of
figures in *repoussé* work. Many of them were found by
General Cesnola in Cyprus. Cære and Præneste have
yielded similar works of art. The Phœnician bowls were
dated about 720–600 B.C., but it was admitted that they
might go back 'as far as Homer's time,' say 800 B.C. The
advocates of a much earlier period for Homer and Homeric
civilisation reply that the more recent discoveries at Mycenæ,
Vapheio, and elsewhere, show that the art known to Homer
need not have been the art of the Phœnician bowls, but
rather the art of the Mycenæan sword blades of which the
Egyptian models are as early as 1600 B.C.

It is difficult or impossible to fix the period when Sidonian
merchant-men, so familiar to Homer, began trading in metal
work with Greece. Thus Helbig has observed that there
exists an Egyptian wall-painting in which Phœnicians bring
silver vases, in the form of the heads of oxen, to Thothmes III.
(1591–1565). Now, a silver bull's head, with gilded horns
and a gold rosette on the brow, was found in a royal grave
of Mycenæ. Helbig, rightly or wrongly, regards this freely
handled and masterly piece as of Phœnician work, which
would throw back Phœnician dealings with Greece to
the sixteenth century. He also looks on the object as
earlier than the Dorian invasion of Peloponnesus, say
1100 B.C. But the same form—the bull's head and rosette
on the brow—occurs in the pottery of Kalymna, in the
same case as the early pottery of Ialysus at the British
Museum. Now, concerning the date of that very pottery
a battle is raging among antiquaries. The question is then,
Are we to date Homeric civilisation by the Phœnician
bowls, placing them about 800–600 B.C., or are we to admit
that Phœnician trade with Greece may be eight hundred
years older, and date Homeric art by the sword blades of

Mycenæ, perhaps from 1600 B.C. ?   We shall show that such work existed in Egypt about 1600 B.C., but how long the fashion lasted, and whether the Mycenæan daggers in that style were new, when buried, or were old heirlooms, is another question.

The differences of style between the bowls and the inlaid poignards are conspicuous. It may be said that the partisans of the comparatively late date of Homeric art rely on the evidence of the bowls, while the friends of a very early date rest chiefly on the swords, or rather daggers, and of other objects at Mycenæ, which, we think, are clearly not Phœnician in style.   On the Phœnician bowls, as we saw, the figures are arranged in bands, and are represented in relief.   There is no inlaying of various metals.   But Homer, in the shield of Achilles, distinctly describes, as we saw, the effect of parti-coloured inlaid metals in the decoration of the shield.   If, then, the art of the Mycenæan sword-blades is of a very early date—say 1600–1400 B.C.— we naturally get an approximate date for the style of decoration familiar to Homer.   The evidence of the daggers, later found, will modify or upset the theory based on the Phœnician bowls by which the period of Homeric art had previously been determined.   The earlier date is supposed to be confirmed by the researches of Mr. Petrie in Egypt.[1] But, on the other hand, Mr. Petrie's conclusions are censured by Mr. Cecil Torr as illogical and unproved, while Mr. Murray has advanced the hypothesis that the Mycenæan antiquities are not pre-Dorian at all, are not Achæan, but belong to the obscure age of the great Tyrants, such as Pheidon the Temenid—say, from 770 B.C. to 600 B.C. I shall indicate my opinion as to the improbability of this view, even in face of evidence mainly drawn from comparison of style in the remaining objects of Mycenæan art.

[1] *Illahun, Kahun, and Gurob.*

A A 2

But it may not be superfluous first to dwell for a moment
on the extremely precarious nature of archæological evidence as to dates, where unaided by actual written documents, and even occasionally where these exist.   Before
we argue from the style of decoration or pattern, for
example, we must remember that, in certain regions, one
style may persist long after it has disappeared in other
districts.   Again, pottery made for the mass of the population may keep up archaic forms and archaic designs,
while fashions in work meant for more wealthy cus-
tomers may have altered again and again.[1]   Potsherds of
both classes may easily be found mingled in one ancient
rubbish heap, and may cause great searchings of heart as
to dates.   Once more, in the hoards buried with the dead
may be found objects, such as cups and swords and rings,
which were already ancient heirlooms even at the time of
the interment, or which were acquired from abroad, in
commerce or in war.   Hence the same tomb may contain
pieces of most various date and *provenance*.   Again, even
where a date is discovered, as on an Egyptian scarab, for
example, we cannot argue that the grave is as old as the
Egyptian king whose cartouche is figured, because popular
scarabs continued to be produced long after the time of
the monarch whom they chronicled.   A scarab of Queen Ti
(1450 B.C.) was found at Mycenæ, and a scarab of her
husband, Amenophis III., with 'Mycenæan' pottery, at
Ialysus[2] ; but they need not have been contemporary works.
We cannot even argue with absolute certainty that a grave

---

[1] We know that women in the Hebrides still make clay pots without the use of the wheel, and decorate them with incisions made by
the nails or with the point of a stick.   Such a pot, in an age of
modern factories and modern trade, survives, or lately survived, from
a period of unknown antiquity, and exactly resembles the pots found
in our pre-historic graves.

[2] Schuch. p. 294 ; Furtwaengler and Loeschke, *Myk. Vas.* p. 4.

is of the date of the death of its inmates.   Egyptian
example shows that the royal dead might be removed,
for security, to a new eternal home, and Mr. Percy Gardner
has very ingeniously suggested that the corpses and treasures in the ' shaft tombs ' of Mycenæ, within the citadel,
may conceivably have been transported thither for safety
or other reasons from the beehive-shaped tombs outside
the circle of the wall.[1]   Such ' flittings ' of the dead are
neither impossible nor unexampled · and if they ever
occurred, we cannot even maintain that the dead, in a
grave, are never of much earlier date than the latest object
which the grave contains.   For the latest object may have
been accidentally dropped, or piously bestowed, by the
persons who in a later age shifted the corpses from one
to another habitation.   In such cases, however, the grave
usually shows unmistakable traces of having been disturbed.   Thus, during the long ages of time past, many
changes may occur, many new or even older objects may
get mingled with others of a given date.   Ancient styles
of work and art may survive among others much more
modern, and archæological evidence can only be accepted
with all the reserves which these circumstances, and our
own ignorance and consciousness of prepossession, ought
to suggest.   Nor should opinions be obstinately held
which a new discovery, the stroke of a spade, may at
any moment upset.   The questions before us, then, in
the words of Mr. Leaf, are these : ' What is the true relation of the Mycenæan civilisation to the Homeric poems?
and what is its place in the development of classical
Greece ? '

The answers popularly accepted are : First, that the
Homeric poems describe a civilisation descended from and
akin to that of Mycenæ, an Achæan civilisation not yet

[1] *New Chapters in Greek History*, pp. 77–79.

shattered by Dorian conquerors ; and, secondly, that the
Mycenæan culture itself represents an early Achæan style
of art, not free from foreign influences, but prior to the
direct and potent Phœnician influence so strongly marked,
for example, in Cyprus.   Perhaps the only alternative
hypothesis is that to which Mr. Murray inclines.   Going
backward from the better to the less known in Greek
remains, he suggests that the Mycenæan civilisation may
not be pre-Dorian, not Achæan, but that of the age of the
early Tyrants—roughly speaking from 770 to 600 B.C.   In
comparing these two theories, and seeking to find the
more plausible, we may reserve the treasures of the graves
for later consideration, and begin with the obvious architectural relics of Mycenæ and Tiryns.   These are built in
the various styles known as Cyclopean.   The walls are of
huge stones, some as much as ten feet long, by a yard high
and thick.   'Tiryns of the mighty walls,' as Homer calls it,[1]
is clearly in fact as well as tradition the older and ruder of
the two cities.   At Mycenæ there are three styles of
masonry.   There are blocks unhewn, or slightly hewn,
piled on each other ; next there are well-hewn rectangular
blocks laid in regular courses ; finally, there are polygonal
blocks 'fitting together with the most accurate joints.'   The
Lion Gate is of the second kind, but it is unsafe to conclude
that it is later than adjacent walls in the first or rudest
kind, though it shows signs of later adjustment and change.
It may be later, or it may be a piece of more careful work
used in an important position.   Much the same remarks
apply to the polygonal masonry.   This mode of building,
which is also found in the ancient cities of the Incas in
Peru, speaks of an early age, when there was great command
of labour.   As is well known, Greek popular tradition
attributed the walls to the Cyclopes, a race of giants, just as

[1] Iliad, ii. 560.

in Scotland the Devil or Michael Scott, the wizard, is
credited with superhuman constructions. More learned
theory, in classical Greece, assigned the walls and beehive-
shaped tombs or 'treasure houses' of Mycenæ to emigrants
from Phrygia, rich in gold. 'Pelops came from Asia with
much wealth, among needy men,' as Thucydides says.[1]
This was the view of Peloponnesian antiquarians, according
to Thucydides. 'The vaulted shape of the graves is probably to be traced back to the Phrygian style of building,'
says Dr. Schuchhardt, 'and the masses of gold can only
have been procured from Phrygia or Lydia.' It is certain
that the Cyclopean style is mainly found on very ancient
and Homeric sites, as at Athens. It is also certain that
Greek tradition and belief, without any variation, assigned
Mycenæ and Tiryns to the pre-Dorian Achæan age initiated
by adventurers from Phrygia. Now, if Mycenæ and Tiryns,
as in Mr. Murray's hypothesis, were walled as we see them
by despots of 770-600, it would be a most extraordinary
thing if history gave no hint on the subject, and if tradition were of the opposite opinion. But history is silent,
and tradition is positive on the other side. The Greeks,
according to Mr. Murray, could remember the first builder
of triremes, dated 704 B.C., yet they had hopelessly forgotten
the great contemporary builders of Mycenæ. To wall
Tiryns and Mycenæ must have required such forced labour
as the Normans, after the Conquest, extorted from the
English. Could the hardships thus inflicted by the despots,
according to Mr. Murray's hypothesis, have been wholly
forgotten? Could the citadels and tombs have been
ascribed, by the age of Thucydides, to a period infinitely
more remote? Mr. Murray argues thus :—

'It is just possible that a period covering the seventh
century, and extending, perhaps, into the eighth century B.C.

[1] Thucydides, i. 9, 10.

was the time in which the pottery and other antiquities of
the Mycenæ class were produced for the home market of
Greece, and possibly in Greece itself. That period coin-
cides with the rule of the tyrants in Greece—men like
Pheidon of Argos, Kypselos of Corinth, and his son Peri-
ander. Greek history says little of how they ruled ; but
if we judge them by a comparison with Polycrates, the
Tyrant of Samos' (540–520 B.C.), 'then they may be supposed to have maintained their sway by large bodies of
men, who were at their bidding for war, or for the execution of public works, on a magnificent scale, in times of
peace. At such a period we can conceive the great walls
of Mycenæ and Tiryns, together with the vaulted tombs of
Mycenæ, to have been built in rivalry with the tomb of
their contemporary Alyattes, which Herodotus compared to
the wonders of Egypt and Babylonia.' [1]

Homer, as we saw, distinctly speaks of the massive
walls of Tiryns. If Mr. Murray is right, Greek history and
Greek tradition, dating from an age relatively late, entirely forgot circumstances most remarkable. It is precisely as if Robert d'Oily's castle at Oxford were locally
attributed to King Arthur. Again we have the great works
of Mycenæ and Tiryns, where there was no tyrant known to
history except the neighbouring tyrant of Argos ; while
where we do find known tyrants, as in Argos, Sicyon, and
Corinth, we have no remaining works on the scale of
those at Tiryns and Mycenæ. [2] Of Pheidon, the tyrant of
Argos, very little is known, and that on authority very
late. If he really introduced coined money, he certainly
left none of it in the graves of Mycenæ. He was head

[1] *Handbook of Greek Art*, p. 57.

[2] On the date of Pheidon, varying from 895 to 600 B.C., see Grote
(vol. ii. p. 315, note 2, edition of 1869). Grote places him 747 B.C.
See also Gardner's *Types of Greek Coins*, p. 7.

of the Argive confederacy, then the foremost power in Peloponnesus. He may conceivably, perhaps, have fortified
two neighbouring cities, Mycenæ and Tiryns, much more
strongly than he did his own—namely, Argos—but if he
did so, legend and history have been curiously oblivious of
so great and peculiar an achievement. He raised edifices,
on Mr. Murray's showing, which Pausanias compares to the
Pyramids of Egypt, but in three hundred years his countrymen, who remembered minor matters, had forgotten this.
His comparatively recent and extraordinary efforts as a
constructor were lost to memory, and were assigned to a
dim and dubious past and to a fallen dynasty. To believe
in this theory is not easy.

We now turn to the rather enigmatic evidence of
the solitary piece of sculpture in the architecture of
Mycenæ. The famous headless lions of the Lion Gate
(of which there is a cast in the South Kensington Museum)
have always been conspicuous ; not so the very inferior
and barbaric sculptures on the buried stelæ or grave
stones of the tombs unearthed by Dr. Schliemann. The
lions of the gate are carved in relief, on a triangular slab
of hard grey limestone, over the lintel. Their fore-paws
rest on two bases, at a higher level than their hind-paws.
Between them is a column crowned by a 'curious capital,
composed of a fillet, cyma moulding, roll and abacus.'
Over the latter are four round discs, and these again are
covered by a slab shaped like an abacus. ' In Phrygia,
Professor Ramsay has found two lions exactly similar to
those of Mycenæ, on either side of a column above the
door of a rock tomb.' [1] In considering these lions of the

---

[1] Schuchhardt, pp. 141, 142. Mr. Ramsay thinks that the lion
type passed from Phrygia into Greece during the ninth, or more
probably the eighth, century B.C. (See *Journal of Hellenic Society*,
ix. p. 371.) This suits Mr. Murray's age of Pheidon very well.

gate, which Mr. Murray connects with early Greek gems, we reach a rather puzzling point in his argument. As is well known, various gems, both engraved stones and rings with subjects engraved on the gold bezel, were found in the shaft tombs of Mycenæ.[1] The graves must necessarily be later—how much later we cannot tell—than the walls of the citadel. Now, Mr. Murray apparently believes that Homer was ignorant of gems and rings ; hence, we presume, Homer lived before their introduction into Greece. ' Homer,' says Mr. Murray, ' never mentions engraved gems, *though there are passages where he would have been certain to have spoken of them had he known of their existence.* Pliny quotes the silence of Homer as evidence that gem engraving had not been in practice in his day.'[2] If we take Mr. Murray literally, Homer was ignorant of the existence and use of gems and rings. Therefore, he lived before the date of the Mycenæan graves, where rings are plentiful. He also lived before the date of the tyrants who, according to Mr. Murray's hypothesis, built the walls of Mycenæ, the city so familiar in the Homeric poems. This is certain, because ' the beginning of the tyrants would coincide with the date we have arrived at for the earliest class of engraved gems and the vases found with them.' Homer, then, the author who is so familiar with Mycenæ, lived before Mycenæ and Tiryns were walled as we see them now, for he lived before gems, of which he knew nothing, and the earliest engraved gems in Greece coincide with the

[1] Schuchhardt, p. 122. The engraved stones are published in *Eph. Arch.* 1888, Pin. 10, 34, 35. For the rings, see Schuchhardt, pp. 221, 277. Furtwaengler was lucky enough to pick up a similar ring in a Paris curiosity shop. It is engraved in his work on Mycenæan vases.

[2] We have constantly to protest against the reasoning which deduces Homer's ignorance from Homer's silence.

date of the Argive tyrants who built the walls of Mycenæ and Tiryns. This theory of Tiryns, at least, must clearly be given up as untenable, for Homer speaks, as we have said, of its mighty walls.

Mr. Murray probably does not cling to the hypothesis that the Tirynthian walls are of the age of the Argive tyrants, and unknown to the author of the Catalogue, who mentions them. Our difficulty is to believe in walled Tiryns known to Homer, who did not know the Mycenæan walls as they stand, yet did know Mycenæ. That city manifestly dominated Tiryns in Homer's mind. Could the Mycenæans have held it in such force, as against the Tirynthians, without the walls? Not so, we know, could Zethus and Amphion, hardy as they were, hold Thebes.[1]

Mr. Murray's position, then, will be, that at about 1000 B.C. Tiryns was already walled. About 800 B.C. Homer knew Tiryns a walled, and Mycenæ, not yet walled, or not walled as we see it. About 750–650 B.C., and after Homer, come the rise of Argive tyrants, the introduction of gems, the building of the Lion Gate, increased fortification of Mycenæ, and the making of the tombs in the citadel, those tombs which we have regarded as much older than Homer.

A view somewhat akin to Mr. Murray's, but differing on important points, is that of Professor Ramsay, the explorer of Phrygian antiquities.[2] Phrygia, in his opinion, was in close relation with the Asiatic Greeks of Cyme and Phocæa in the eighth century. 'The Phrygian device' (the lions) 'which appears over the principal gateway of Mycenæ was learned during this intercourse, and belongs to the period of Argive ascendency, under Pheidon and his successors.' Mr. Ramsay publishes illustrations of Phrygian lion tombs, where

[1] Odyssey, xi. 264, 265.
[2] *Journal of the Hellenic Society*, ix. 2.

the attitudes of the beasts, though not perhaps the style of art, are closely analogous to the attitudes of the lions on the Mycenæan gate. He believes that the animals are connected with the worship of Cybele, and that they represent guardians who drive evil influences from the tomb or the town. The artists of Mycenæ learned the device from Phrygia, or Phrygia and Mycenæ both took it from a common source. The Lion Gate is thus of the eighth or ninth century. 'Historically there is good reason to assign at least part of the fortifications of Mycenæ to the time when the Argive kings were the greatest power in Greece'— that is, to the period of Mr. Murray's tyrants.[1] But Mr. Ramsay does not hold the same views as to the dates of the royal graves in Mycenæ. These are much older than the Lion Gate, he thinks, and are pre-Dorian. 'The people who built the Lion Gate considered the peribolus with the tombs as sacred, and the heroes buried in the tombs belong to an older time. . . . The Dorian conquerors continued the family cultus of the chiefs whom they dispossessed.' This they did in part owing to the influence of Homer, who had made Mycenæ famous and sacred. In Mr. Ramsay's opinion, then, the Homeric poems, to some extent at least, are older than the Dorian invasion. The Dorians, thanks to Homer's charm, were proud and anxious to be regarded as Achæans, akin to Homer's heroes. Thus, while they built the Lion Gate and decorated it on Phrygian models, in the eighth or ninth century, they still revered the dead in the royal graves, which are much more ancient than the Dorian possession of the city. If Mr. Murray is right in making the lions of the gate coeval with the gems in the graves, then Mr. Ramsay is wrong, and both the gate

[1] Mr. Ramsay cites similar opinions of Wilamowitz Moellendorff, in *Hermes*, xxi. iii., and of Niese, *Entwick. d. Homer. Poesie*, p. 218.

and the graves are of the age of the Argive tyrants of the eighth century.

This point is matter for archæological and artistic criticism of style. Are the contents of the tombs coeval on the whole with the lions of the gates? Are the lions of the gates necessarily so late as the eighth century?

On these points Mr. Flinders Petrie is at variance with both Mr. Murray and Mr. Ramsay. With Mr. Ramsay he believes in the great and pre-Dorian antiquity of the Royal tombs ; but as to the lions he thinks them of the same or older date.[1] 'The lions on the gate are similar in position to a gilt wooden lion broken from some small decoration, which I found dated to 1450 B.C.' This wooden lion is 'in exactly the same attitude.' 'That the design penetrated to Phrygia is nothing surprising, considering the range of Mycenæan culture.'[2]

The diversities of archæological opinion are thus clearly illustrated. We have Schuchhardt, Furtwaengler (in his work on Mycenæan pottery), Mr. Leaf, and current opinion generally in favour of a remote pre-Dorian date for the Mycenæan antiquities, both for walls, gate, and objects in the royal graves. We have Mr. Ramsay, citing Wilamowitz Moellendorff, Niese, and others as believing in a Dorian and Tyrannical date for the Lion Gate, while Mr. Ramsay leaves the graves to the ancient Achæans. We have Mr. Petrie believing that the gate, as well as the graves, is pre-Dorian, founding his theory on Egyptian evidence. Finally, we have Mr. Murray, who assigns walls, gate, lions, and the bulk of the objects in the royal graves to Dorians of the eighth and seventh centuries.

[1] *J. H. S.* xii. 1.

[2] *Op. cit.* p. 203. The reader may also consult Chipiez and Perrot, *L'Art dans la Phénicie* (1890), pp. 110, 220. They hold that Phrygian designs of lions reached Greece, probably on embroidered tissues, not the converse, as in Mr. Petrie's theory.

Mr. Murray's view about the contents of the tombs is based on comparison of styles in pottery, sculpture, gem engraving, and general decoration. In pottery found in the oldest Greek sepulchres the earliest type is the 'primitive.'[1] The handles of primitive vessels are usually 'rudimentary.' The ornament takes the form of 'incised zigzag lines.'[2] The pottery of Mycenæan tombs is of a character later than the primitive. The vases are covered with a 'creamy slip,' and the designs are painted in black. What is the date of the Mycenæan pottery? Is it Achæan, and earlier than the Dorian invasion (1000 B.C.), or is it later, or did it begin early and last through the revolution of society and the change of ruling races? Furtwaengler and Loeschke, in *Mykenische Vasen*, take the Mycenæan vases to be early and pre-Dorian, relying on comparisons with Egypt. The Achæans would imitate pottery which Egypt presented to their view—say in the fourteenth century B.C. This is not the only theory ; Mr. Petrie holds that the vases of the fourteenth century, found in Egypt, were brought there or made there by Achæans. But Mr. Murray, arguing against Furtwaengler, says that Greeks would find in Egypt much the same vases, whether Achæans went thither in the fourteenth, or much later Greeks in the seventh, century. 'Egypt was for centuries an unchanging country' (p. 25) ; yet 'for a long period previous to 600 B.C. Egypt had been sinking into deeper and deeper degradation' (p. 24). Thus the 'unchanging country' had been changing very greatly. This matter little affects the argument. 'One thing the Greeks would not have seen, and that is finely-painted pottery. The ancient

---

[1] 'Pottery is the very key to digging. To know the varieties of it, and the age of each, is the alphabet of work.' (Flinders Petrie, *Ten Years' Digging in Egypt*, p. 158.)

[2] *Handbook*, p. 6.

Egyptians were not skilled in that art.' Thus as far as
pottery goes, if finely-painted pottery is found in Egypt and
dated 1300 B.C., or earlier, either it is wrongly dated, about
which there is a discussion, or the Achæans, as in Mr.
Petrie's view, not the Egyptians, were its makers. Mr.
Murray sets aside the idea, in itself unlikely on all grounds,
that the Phœnicians made and introduced the pottery of the
Mycenæan style.

Mr. Murray's own argument as to Mycenæan pottery
may be stated thus : We ought to begin with the known,
the dated, and argue back. Let us start, then, from vases
of Camiros, with inscriptions in which the character of the
writing gives the date as early in the sixth century B.C.[1]
Here, as may be seen at the British Museum, are human
figures, with written names, on a field which is filled up
with rosettes. Behind this art, earlier than this, comes a
style in which rows of animals are designed, in Assyrian
fashion, and rosettes fill up the field.[2] Greek colonists in
Egypt in the seventh century B.C. might learn this manner
from contact with Phœnicians. The rosette Mr. Murray
claims as specially Assyrian. But it is also frequent in the
Egypt of Rameses III. (1200 B.C.).[3] It is at least open to
argument that pre-Dorian Greece got the rosette from
Egypt—that the rosette did not need to wait for Assyrian
introduction in the seventh century. Mr. Murray's belief,
however, is that the rosettes on these vases were imitated
by Rhodian potters and potters of Naucratis, the seventh-
century Greek settlement in Egypt, from Assyrian embroidery of curtains and dresses. Moving still further
back, we find ornament mainly geometrical in style ; the
vases in which it is most prevalent, accompanied by very
rude designs of men and women and chariots, are called

[1] *Handbook*, p. 28.   [2] *Ibid.* p. 59.
[3] Flinders Petrie, *J. H. S.* xii. 1.

the Dipylon type, as many were found near the Dipylon
gate in Athens.[1]   On these vases are pictures of sea-fights :
soldiers on board are threatening each other with spears, as
in English MSS. of the fourteenth century.   Mr. Murray
argues that ' Homer knew nothing of battles at sea, nor of
ships equipped for that purpose.'[2]   These Dipylon vases,
then, must be later than Homer.   They are thought [3] to be
of the middle of the seventh century.   But to assert in a
popular handbook, and without qualification, that Homer
knows nothing of battles at sea nor of 'ships equipped for
that purpose,' because he did not mention them in an inland
epic, may, not inconceivably, prove misleading.   In the
attack of the Trojans on the ships [4] we read, 'Nor yet did
it please the spirit of high-hearted Aias to stand in the place
whereto the other sons of the Achæans had withdrawn, but
he kept faring with long strides up and down the decks of
the ships, and he wielded in his hands a great pike for ship-
battles (ξυστὸν μέγα ναύμαχον), joined with rings, two-and-
twenty cubits in length.'   These pikes are again spoken of
as 'used in ship-battles' in Iliad xv. 389, where the spears
serve to repel attacks on ships drawn up on land.   Thus
Homer is not ignorant of ship-battles, though he does not
find occasion to describe one.   Mr. Murray obviously
thinks that the long spears were exclusively employed to
repel attacks on ships drawn up on shore, and they are
so handled in the fifteenth book of the Iliad.   But can we
safely confine the meaning of ξυστὸν μέγα ναύμαχον to such
a conflict ?   'The first naval battle that Thucydides was
aware of occurred between the Corinthians and Corcyræans
in 664.'[5]   But wherever and whenever armed enemies met
in hostile ships, there, in the nature of things, would be

---

[1] *Handbook*, p. 32, plate 3.   [2] *Ibid.* p. 39.
[3] *Op. cit.* p. 40.   [4] Iliad, xv. 674.
[5] *Handbook*, p. 40.

fighting, though history did not preserve the records of these engagements. One example, at least, of very early ship-battles we happen to possess. In the reign or Rameses III., about 1200 B.C., certain Northern invaders attacked Egypt. Whoever they were, they were 'Ægean.' 'They came up leaping from the coasts and isles,' says the inscription on the walls of a temple erected by Rameses III. 'A defence was built on the water, like a strong wall, of *ships of war*, of merchantmen, of boats and skiffs. They were manned from stem to stern with the bravest warriors. . . . They who had assembled themselves over against the others on the great sea, a mighty firebrand lightened before them, in the mouths of the river. Their ships and all their possessions lay strewn on the mirror of the water.'[1] This naval battle was not on the open sea, but 'in the lakes of the mouths of the Nile.' The wall-pictures show men boarding ships, and a mast falling, with the man on the mast-head.[2] In these invaders De Rougé, with Mr. Flinders Petrie, sees pre-historic Greeks, contrary to the opinion of Brugsch. Helbig thinks that the invaders were from Asia Minor. In any case dwellers on shores and isles of the Greek sea, as early as the thirteenth century B.C., were contemporary with naval battles. That Homer should have known nothing of such warfare is highly improbable, and we can scarcely believe that the word ναύμαχον was in his time confined merely to a battle for the possession of ships drawn up on shore. This is a digression, intended to illustrate the methods of archæological argument. To return to the Dipylon vases with their pictures of sea fights ; these, we gladly agree, are later than Homer.

Behind the Dipylon vases again, confessedly more

---

[1] Brugsch, *History of Egypt*, English translation, ii. 148.

[2] Chabas, *Etudes sur l'Antiquité*, 2nd edit. pp. 309–313 ; Helbig, *op. cit.* p. 111.

B B

ancient than these, are the pieces of pottery found in the
royal tombs of Mycenæ. Similar vases, with similar decoration, are also found in Ialysus, Crete, Carpathos, Egypt, and
elsewhere. Now, there was an old Argive, therefore Dorian,
colony in Ialysus. But part of the Ialysian territory
was called 'Achaia,' and it may have been Achæan and
possessed old Mycenæan pottery before the Dorian settlement. This pottery has already been described, with its
creamy slip, and paintings in dark brown. But we had not
previously said that the Mycenæan pots are identical with
those of Ialysus in Rhodes.[1] In Ialysus also were many
rosettes of blue glass, such as are found at Mycenæ. The
designs on the vases show rosettes (of Assyrian origin in
Greece, says Mr. Murray), but these rosettes, though
common in glass, are rare on this pottery. The sketches
of marine creatures, dolphins, octopuses, on the vases of
Mycenæ and Ialysus, 'are drawn with extraordinary freedom'—a freedom which also marks some of the Mycenæan
and island gems, and is especially notable in the gold designs
on bronze dagger blades from the Mycenæan tombs, and in
those extraordinary works, the gold cups of Vapheio. But,
in drawing quadrupeds, the Mycenæ-Ialysus potter is unskilled, while the gem engravers are very clever.

We now reach the crucial point. Are we to date the
pottery of Mycenæ by that of Ialysus, and that of Ialysus
by the pottery of Camirus, of the sixth century, as fixed by
the character of the writing on the vases of Camirus? This
appears to be Mr. Murray's view. We shall then have vases
of Camirus, sixth century ; Dipylon vases, seventh century ;
Mycenæ and Ialysus vases, eighth and ninth centuries. So
the royal tombs of Mycenæ, which contain vases of this
kind, will be of the ninth-eighth century, and therefore post-

---

[1] *Handbook*, p. 21. The British Museum is rich in the remains of
Ialysus, the gift of Mr. Ruskin.

Dorian, and even later than Homer.   They will tell us nothing about Achæan civilisation and the dim heroic age. On the other hand, we establish a continuity in Greek art, going backward from the sixth century to the age of the Tyrants.

This, if we rightly understand it, is Mr. Murray's theory, which he also applies to the gems, gold work, and other remains in the royal tombs.

The opposite theory of Furtwaengler and Loeschke, Mr. Percy Gardner, Schuchhardt, Mr. Petrie, and others, takes the royal tombs and their contents to be pre-Dorian, and relics of the Achæan age.   Confronted with the similar relics of Dorian Ialysus, they would probably argue that Argive Dorians retained the style in pottery which they found in Mycenæ, just as the primitive style of pottery was retained even later.   Or they would maintain, with Mr. Leaf, that Rhodes was Achæan before it was Dorian, and that the pottery of Ialysus is pre-Dorian.[1]   Granting a Dorian invasion, it does not follow that a style of decoration in pottery would be destroyed by it : the Dorians might employ and imitate the Achæan potters.   Mr. Murray himself is 'tempted to regard the peculiar shapes of this pottery and the limitation of the designs to aquatic subjects' as notes of 'a local fabric with these special tastes, rather than as indications of a special period.'[2]   As 'primitive' pottery lasted, we are told, till the seventh century, in some places, who can tell how long the style of Ægean pottery lasted, or how far it goes back into antiquity?   It is a curious fact that old Mexican pottery is often, in shape, colour, and decoration, hardly to be distinguished from that of Mycenæ and Ialysus.[3]   There is the same creamy

[1] Petrie, *J. H. S.* xi. p. 271, plate 14.

[2] *Handbook*, p. 28.

[3] There are examples of this Mexican pottery in the British Museum. The author owes many pieces to the kindness of Mr. W. J. Way.

hue, the same form, the same decorative design in a rich
brown bordering on black, and there are even examples in
which rows of deer are drawn on the vases, as in somewhat
later Greek art.   The meander appears in a rudimentary
form.   This does not bear on the question in hand, but is
worth noting as a case of coincidence in culture.   We now
come to a fresh difficulty and a new crucial point.   If Mr.
Flinders Petrie rightly interprets his own discoveries in
Egypt, then pottery akin to that of Mycenæ (Ægean pottery
he calls it) is found in Egyptian places, where it must be,
or is very likely to be, much older than the eighth or ninth
century B.C.   It is not pottery of native Egyptian make.   If
it be as old in Egyptian soil as Mr. Petrie believes, then in
Mycenæ certain examples may be of the thirteenth and
twelfth centuries, others a very great deal earlier.   There is
something that almost baffles the historical imagination in
Mr. Petrie's hypothesis.   At times even people who are
ready to believe in the pre-Dorian culture and its remains
may fear that Mr. Petrie proves rather too much.   He put
forth a sketch of his conclusions in the *Journal of the
Hellenic Society,* for October 1890, and stated his ideas with
more detail in his *Illahun, Kahun, and Gurob.*   The most
emphatic way of illustrating Mr. Petrie's opinions is to bid
the reader go to the British Museum.   Here in the long
gallery on the first floor he will find examples of Greek
pottery so arranged that the visitor who enters by way of
the great staircase from the south passes from the late and
accomplished types of vases, Panathenaic and others, back-
wards to the inscribed vases of Camirus, to the vases with
friezes of animals in Assyrian style, to the geometrically
ornamented pottery, to the pottery of Ialysus, and to similar
fragments from Mycenæ.   Among these he will see potsherds of 'fine, thin, hard, light-brown paste, of Ægean
origin, with iron glaze-bands,' which he will probably assign

to the ninth century, or even to a later age But these
potsherds Mr. Petrie found 'in rubbish heaps which probably have never been disturbed since 2500 B.C.,' rubbish
heaps of the Twelfth Dynasty. If Ægean or Mycenæan
pottery was being made in 2500 B.C., we must attribute that
enormous antiquity to a civilisation which existed on the
shores of Hellas, by whomsoever these shores were then
possessed. Again, at Kahun, Mr. Petrie found a city of the
Twelfth Dynasty, say 2500 B.C. The houses had cellars cut
in the rock. One of these cellars was used, many centuries
later, by people of the Nineteenth Dynasty as a tomb. In
this tomb are eleven coffins, each coffin containing five or
six bodies. In one tomb, the ninth, was an Ægean vase,
decorated with a freely-drawn pattern of ivy-leaf. Mr.
Petrie dates this vase about 1100 B.C.[1] There is in the
coffins an absence of objects earlier than the Nineteenth
and later than the Twentieth Dynasty. This is the general
tendency of the argument, whereby the Twentieth Dynasty
is fixed as the date of the coffin and the Ægean vase. Thus,
if Mr. Petrie be right, we have a clear case of Ægean or
Mycenæan pottery of very ancient date, and, consequently,
this class of pottery with free drawing must be much older
than the date assigned by Mr. Murray. To all this Mr.
Cecil Torr demurs, in the *Classical Review* for March 1892.
Mr. Torr objects that Mr. Petrie argues thus : the coffin at
Kahun is later than the Eighteenth and early Nineteenth
Dynasties, for their work is absent ; earlier than the Twenty-
second Dynasty, for here is none of its work. We might
as well say it is earlier than the Nineteenth, or is later than
the Twenty-second, as Mr. Torr contends. But we understand Mr. Petrie to mean that all the work which can be
dated, except certain obviously older objects, is of the

[1] *Illahun*, p. 24.

Twentieth Dynasty, and so then must be the Ægean vase.[1]
The arguments are too complicated and minute to be stated
afresh in this place. But they leave the impression that
Mr. Torr quarrels less with Mr. Petrie's facts than with his
method of arraying them. Mr. Petrie accepts and makes
much of a 'Græco-Libyan alliance' against Egypt, and of
'Libyo-Achæan' invasions. These were described by De
Rougé, on the evidence of wall-paintings at Medinet Habu.[2]
In the enemies of Egypt from the north, called Lebu,
Aquaiusha, Shardana, Sikelsha, De Rougé recognised
Libyans, Achæans, Sardinians, Sicilians, Etruscans, and so
forth. Brugsch controverted these ideas, and brought the
invaders from Colchis, of all places.[3] All the names of the
invaders of Egypt are really open to dispute ; and, tempting
as it is to connect Aquaiusha with Achæans, and with
Mycenæan or Ægean pottery in Egypt, Mr. Petrie, perhaps,
prejudices his case by the identification.

Here we must leave the evidence of pottery, whether
Mr. Petrie or Mr. Murray be in the right, whether the
vases of the Royal Mycenæan graves are to be dated late,
by reference to Ialysus and Camirus, or early, by reference
to Kahun, Gurob, and other Egyptian graves and rubbish
heaps.[4]

The rival plausibilities of archæological argument are
divertingly displayed in the case of a curious fragment from

    [1] See Mr. Petrie's letter in the *Academy*, June 25, p. 621, and
other correspondence in that journal.
    [2] *Revue Archéologique*, N.S., vol. xvi.
    [3] Brugsch, *History of Egypt*, English translation, ii. 116–124.
    [4] Mr. Petrie has recently brought back from Egypt the remains
which he discovered on the site of Kuenahten's palace at Tel el
Amarna. Here were found many Ægean potsherds ; and, as there is
no reason to suppose that the site was ever inhabited after its destruction on the death of its founder, Mr. Petrie's theory of very early
Ægean pottery seems to be confirmed.

the royal graves.   In the *Ephemeris Archaiologike* for 1891
is published a piece of a silver bowl, dug up by Dr. Schliemann, and cleaned many years later by M. Kumanudes.[1]
Here we see a walled city besieged, women wave their arms
on the battlements, naked men below the towers ply slings
and bows, there are also warriors with shields and spears.
Now, partisans of the late date of the tombs may say,
'Here, in the tombs, is a representation of slingers, a force
unknown to Homer.   Therefore, since Homer wrote, the
sling has come in ; therefore Homer is earlier than the
tombs.'   But, first, is the sling really unknown to Homer ?
In Iliad, xiii. 599, Menelaus wounds Helenus in the hand
with a spear.   'And the great-hearted Agenor drew the
spear from his hand, and himself bound up the hand with
a band of well-twisted sheep's wool, a sling that a squire
carried for him.'   Here the word translated 'sling' is σφενδόνη, the usual Greek word.   The idea again occurs in
xiii. 716, where the Locrian contingent are said not to have
been heavy-armed men, 'but, trusting in bows and well-
twisted sheep's wool, they followed Aias to Ilios.'   Here a
σφενδόνη is made of well-twisted sheep's wool (xiii. 599,
600), and here (xiii. 716) light-armed men are said to trust
'in bows and well-twisted sheep's wool.'   People who want
to make Homer earlier than the tombs where slings are represented, must deny that the σφενδόνη, used in the case
of Helenus as a bandage, was a sling.   Then what was
it ?   Why did the squire of Agenor carry a σφενδόνη for
him ?   Agenor was not a field surgeon, like Machaon.
What was the well-twisted wool in which the Locrian light-
armed men trusted, if it was not slings ?   'We are driven
to the conclusion that slings are alluded to in xiii. 716,'

---

[1] It is engraved in Mr. Gardner's *New Chapters in Greek History*,
p. 66.

says Mr. Leaf.[1] Then Homer does know slings, and the slings of the tombs (which would make capital bandages) are not post-Homeric. So it seems, but then Mr. Leaf takes xiii. 600 as a later gloss, and xiii. 716 as 'a late interpolation,' perhaps a specimen of false archaism, the interpolator endeavouring to give an air of antiquity ' by ascribing to the Locrians a practice with which his own time was unfamiliar.' This was not a very clever interpolator if he thrust in—as old and Homeric—a weapon which Homer never mentions at all, if indeed xiii. 600 be 'a gloss.' He tried to make his interpolation seem Homeric, by being as un-Homeric as possible ! Pausanias (i. 23, 24) took the Locrians in xiii. 716 to be slingers. But how can we argue when our texts are said to be interpolated exactly where they serve our purpose by apparently mentioning slings ? Or how can we argue if σφενδόνη and ξυστὸν μέγα ναύμαχον do not refer to slings and ship-fights, but to other things of the same name?

If, however, Homer does not mention slings, it does not follow that they are later than his date. He scarcely ever speaks at all of the equipment of the light-armed crowd. He obviously despises the bow on the whole, as many passages declare. Now, on the bowl of the tombs the users of the slings are not only light-armed, but actually naked ; the armed men use spears. The sling may well have been in use in Homeric times, whether Homer names it or not. It was the weapon of the unarmed masses, as of David in Israel. Homer might easily leave it unspoken of. Or we might argue that, as Homer (on Schuchhardt's theory) is much later than the royal tombs, the sling had been in use in the age of the tombs, and had gone out of favour in Homer's day. In later Greek it is mentioned by

---

[1] xiii. 600, note.

Archilochus ; it does not exactly follow that the bowl is of the age of Archilochus.

This example shows how difficult it is to argue on the basis of a text which is said to be interpolated, and of antiquities which may be so diversely understood.

Let us now turn to the most curious and beautiful treasures of the royal tombs, the dagger blades. They are of bronze, never of iron, though iron is so commonly mentioned in Homer. The dagger blades are decorated with inlaid work in gold. We see lion hunts : a lion has overthrown a man, and is attacked by warriors with huge shields, as large as that of Aias, slung, not carried by handles.[1] Other daggers show cats (not known in Greece) hunting wild ducks in papyrus swamps ; the subject is Egyptian, the treatment is more free and lively. The gold is of various colours, as in Japanese metal work. Now, Homer is familiar with such work in various-coloured gold,[2] but no such antique art had been known to us before the discovery of the daggers at Mycenæ. A similar dagger is found in the tomb of Aah Hotep, a queen of Egypt about 1650–1600 B.C., and bears the hieroglyph of an earlier king. The partisans of antiquity, then, naturally suppose that Homer was inspired in his description of the shield of Achilles by ancient Egyptian metal work, already in vogue about 1600 B.C. But Mr. Murray attributes the introduction of such work into Greece to Ionian mercenaries in Egypt, about 650 B.C. ;[3] so that Homer, if he lived about 800 B.C., could not have known such inlaid work. But he describes it. Whence, then, did he learn it ? Does any other work, which he may have seen, show anything like it ? As to the tomb of Aah Hotep, where the similar dagger was found, Mr. Murray says that it

---

[1] Shield handles are said by Herodotus to be a Carian invention.

[2] Iliad, xviii. 561, 573, 597.

[3] *Handbook*, p. 51.

also contained gold work, a chain and ear-rings, ' clearly of Greek workmanship of about 600 B.C.'[1]   Late Greek jewelry, we shall see, did not really get into a grave which seems undeniably that of a lady who probably died before 1600 B.C. Egyptology is worth very little if it can make an error of a thousand years about a grave.

The question of the dagger found in the tomb of Aah Hotep is of considerable importance.   Its resemblance to the decorated poniards of the Mycenæan royal graves is very close.   Its blade is of gold, with a centre of bronze, on which are *piqués*, or inlaid in gold, the figures of a bull, a lion, and three locusts or grasshoppers.   The lion is of the same aspect as the lions on the Mycenæan dirks ; the bull is of the same breed, spots and all, we may say, as the bull painted on the wall of the royal house in Tiryns.   A similar bull occurs on a bronze dish found in the cave of Zeus in Crete.   Is there any chance, then, that the dagger in the grave of Aah Hotep is later than the rest of her treasures (dated about 1700–1600 B.C.), and is only of the seventh or eighth century, the date to which the partisans of the Tyrannic period assign the Mycenæan blades?   This question can hardly be answered in the affirmative.   All the treasures of Aah Hotep must assuredly have been buried at the same time, at a date perhaps ten centuries before the age of the Tyrants.   This appears from the circumstances of their discovery.   They were found in 1859 by M. Mariette, whose attention was drawn to their hiding-place by fragments of ancient pottery.   ' The site had never been ransacked before.'   The royal mummy-case was unearthed ' at a depth of from fifteen to eighteen feet.'   The jewels, necklets, dirks, decorative axes, and other beautiful objects were not lying loose in the earth, but were wrapped up within the

---

[1] Mr. Murray quotes Mariette, *Album du Musée de Boulaq*, plates 29–31.

linen folds of the mummy, which, again, was guarded by
the usual wooden and gilt mummy-case. It is impossible
to believe that anyone, in a later age, opened the case, un-
wrapped the swathings, and introduced objects merely for
the confusion of modern archæologists. They must all
belong to one epoch, unless some were old heirlooms, and
that epoch must be the end of the Seventeenth and the
beginning of the Eighteenth Dynasties (1700–1600 B.C.).
In M. Mariette's *Album du Musée de Boulaq* a pair of
Græco-Egyptian ear-rings, say of 600 B.C., are photographed
among the jewels of Aah Hotep. But in M. Mariette's
Monuments du Musée de Boulaq (sixth edition, 1876)
the ear-rings are not included in the Queen's treasure, but
are described among objects 'from various sources.' They
need not, therefore, be considered as bearing on the subject,
The name of Amosis, first king of the Eighteenth Dynasty,
is found on the heads of geese which act as clasps to a
gold chain of Aah Hotep, and the name of Ahmes, his
predecessor, is on the blade of a poniard, near the handle.
Thus, as far as we can see, the dagger which is so exactly analogous to those of Mycenæ must be of the
Seventeenth–Eighteenth dynasties, and those of Mycenæ
must be vastly nearer to that date (1700–1600 B.C.) than
to the period of the Greek tyrants. There really seems
to be no escape, then, from the conclusion that the art of
the Mycenæan graves is not Phœnician, and late, but is
either Egyptian or Achæan modified by Egyptian influence,
and early.[1]

[1] See description and drawings of the Aah Hotep tomb in *Revue
de l'Architecture*, 1860, pp. 98–111 ; also in a volume of coloured
engravings from the treasures, with an introduction by Mr. Birch.
The drawings were made when the treasures were in the Exhibition of
1862. See, too, Brugsch's Photographs of Mummies from Boulaq,
where the pictures are much more distinct than in M. Mariette's *Album
du Musée de Boulaq*.

This discussion might be produced to any length, and would still leave us in wandering mazes lost. Why are only flint arrow-heads found in the Mycenæan tombs, while in the tomb of Ialysus, among vases similar to those of Mycenæ, the arrow-heads are of bronze? Are the beehive-shaped vaulted tombs later than the dug tombs, the royal tombs, as most authors hold, or earlier, as Mr. Flinders Petrie believes? We find ourselves in an almost pathless forest of difficulties and contradictory plausibilities. Has the spade broken into a splendid stratum, a long-lost world of antique Achæan life, or has it unearthed a much later stratum of the eighth century? Tradition and sentiment are strong on the former side, which mainly relies on Egyptian analogies of 1600–1100 B.C. The desire to keep on a cautious path inspires the archæologists who favour the second theory, and who do not, we may think, give sufficient weight either to tradition or to Egyptian evidence. They turn to the Assyria and Phœnicia of 800–600 B.C. for their arguments, while their adversaries favour the older Egypt of the Ramesids. Thus Steindorff, in the *Archäologische Anzeige* (1892, p. 11), has no doubt that Mycenæan art is very ancient ; he even thinks that it influenced contemporary Egyptian art. Winter also [1] lays stress on the cartouches of Amenophis III., twice found in company with Mycenæan objects, and maintains that this cartouche was not reproduced after the monarch's death. But Mr. Cecil Torr [2] disputes the genuine Egyptian character of these very inscriptions. So the learned war sways this way or that.[3] One kind of testimony appeals most to literary

[1] *Op. cit.* 1891, p. 38.

[2] *Athenæum,* July 30, 1892.

[3] See a summary by Mr. Cecil Smith in *Classical Review*, December 1892. The name on the dagger of Aah Hotep 'looks like a mis-spelling of the first name of the founder of the XVIIIth Dynasty (1700 B.C.).'

students ; the professional archæologist, afraid of being
duped, prefers the less adventurous course.   Yet can anything be more adventurous than the opinion that Greece
unanimously forgot the mighty architectural works of
Pheidon or his successors, and unanimously assigned them
to a dateless antiquity ?   This position is so manifestly
weak that it prepossesses an inquirer against the arguments
used in favour of the comparatively late date of the
Mycenæan treasures.

If we reject Mr. Murray's argument, and agree, with
the majority of students, that the graves of Mycenæ are
pre-Dorian, we still do not see any clear light as to the
date of the Homeric poems in pre-Dorian antiquity.   We
may vaguely conceive them to be very much later than
the shaft graves.   But the whole topic rests in suspense.
The very occurrence of a Dorian invasion is denied by
some, and at any moment all 1 ay be illuminated, or more
darkly obscured, by some new discovery.

CHAPTER XVI

HOMER AND OTHER EARLY EPICS

GREECE is not alone in possessing early national and heroic poems. Germany has the *Nibelungenlied*, France the *Chansons de Geste*, England has *Beowulf*, Finland has the *Kalewala*. All these have been examined with the purpose of discovering the secret of their birth, and so finding analogous illustrations of the origin of Iliad and Odyssey. Unluckily history does not absolutely repeat itself. Moreover, the origins of *Beowulf*, the *Nibelungenlied*, and the rest, are nearly, or quite, as obscure as the authorship of the Greek epics.

For a close analogy to the circumstances in which the Homeric epics were composed, we seem to want a warlike and aristocratic society, feeding its imaginative life with the traditions of the past, which exist in lays sung, now by warriors themselves (like Achilles), now by court minstrels, members of an honoured profession. In such a society, at a time when writing may not improbably have become a serviceable instrument, two long epics are produced, which deal with given facts occurring in a brief space of time, and united by their bearing on a great passion, the Wrath of Achilles, and a romantic event, the Return of Odysseus. Now probably the nearest analogy to these circumstances is to be found in the *Nibelungenlied*, and in the earlier French *chansons de geste*, especially *The Song of Roland*.

We shall examine the *Nibelungenlied* first, as the more complex, following Lichtenberger's *Le Poème et la Légende des Nibelungen*,[1] a remarkably lucid and temperate statement. The MSS. of the *Nibelungenlied* are very unlike the condition in which the MSS. of the Homeric poems have reached us. If we agree with Wolf that the text of Homer owes its present shape to Aristarchus and his contemporaries, we must note that the *Nibelungenlied* had, so to speak, no Alexandrian period. The MS. A found in the last century in the castle of Hohenems, and now in the Munich Library, was regarded by Lachmann as the most ancient known text, apparently of the thirteenth century. It contains sixty-three strophes less than MS. B, and is very casually written (*flüchtig*).[2] The MS. A offers the shortest text, the metrical form is the least uniform, the style often more broken, the divergencies between the different parts of the epic more marked than in the other recensions.[3] The most careful, complete, and copious MS. is C. It has a hundred strophes not found in A or B, while thirty not in C are in A and B. Thus Lachmann, using A, has 2,316 strophes in his edition, while Bartsch, using B, has 2,379 strophes. Holtzmann uses C, 'the most perfect MS. as to composition. Contradictions, disparities of tone, style, and metre, disappear or are greatly reduced.' But this text, far from being the most ancient, 'bears all the characters of a comparatively modern rehandling.' As in the *remaniements* of the *Chanson de Roland*, both B and C replace the ancient assonances by rhymes.[4]

---

[1] Paris, 1891.

[2] Fischer, *Die Forschungen über das Nibelungenlied*, p. 7. Leipzig, 1874.

[3] Lichtenberger, p. 57.

[4] Assonance is the recurrence of vowel sounds without regard to consonants. 'Hat' and 'cap' are assonances. Thus—

It is not necessary here to discuss MSS. A, B, C with their dependent groups. It is enough to say that the *Nibelungenlied* has not reached us like the Homeric poems, in texts of a uniformity fixed at least since the age of Aristarchus, and probably since a much earlier period, a point on which further discoveries of MSS. in Egypt may enlighten us. So much for one marked difference between the Greek and the German epic.

Another is not less marked. The Homeric poems, according to Wolf, display unity and harmony of manners and sentiment. This is not found in the *Nibelungenlied*. The characters are Catholics, and go to Mass. There are long descriptions of courts and festivals, of knights and ladies, in early mediæval taste. But their passions break forth in such colossal massacres as marked the great barbarian invasions, the clash of Huns and Burgundians. The blood-feud is the motive throughout, and 'a murder grim and great' is the natural close. A poet well acquainted with chivalrous manners and ideas is dealing with a subject handed down from an age of barbarism, if not of savagery. 'The *Nibelungenlied* is the poem of the great invasions, and under the brilliant embroideries of Austrian jongleurs constantly appears the ancient warp and woof.'[1] There is thus a patent discrepancy between the society and ideas among which the poet lives and the society and

> ' I put my hat upon my head
> And walked into the Strand,
> And there I found another man,
> And in his hand his hat,'

is assonance, while

> ' With his hat in his hand '

is rhyme. In ballads assonance is often found, and it is the rule in the *Chanson de Roland*. Later versions turn the assonances into rhymes.

[1] Lichtenberger, p. ii.

ideas of the age in which the legend first won its way into
romance.   This characteristic divides the German epic
from the harmony of manners and notions in the Homeric
poems.   Homer sings of an age gone by, but he sees it in
the steady light of his own times, and action and thought
are, in his works, harmonious.

As to the condition of poets in Homeric society, our
information, if scanty, is clear.   They were attached to
kings' courts—Alcinous in Phæacia, Agamemnon in Mycenæ, Odysseus in Ithaca, have each their minstrel.   He is
honoured : to him Agamemnon entrusts his wife ; he is
applauded and gratified by presents ; even in the slaying of
the wooers Odysseus spares his minstrel.   We are reminded
of the sennachie of Fergus McIvor, who receives, as reward
of song, his chief's last silver cup.   At the time when the
Nibelungenlied gained its present shapes, the minstrel, or
jongleur, in Germany, was in a much less fortunate position.
He was a wanderer, *sans feu ni lieu*, a parasite, disdained
by the Church.   It was matter of theological knowledge
that no *jongleur* need expect salvation.   Yet it is undeniable
that these vagabonds chanted, in altered forms, lays of old
German heathendom, lays which may, or must, have been
among those which Charlemagne caused to be collected
and written.   The childlike conservatism of the people
preferred the old songs, as children like to hear nursery
tales repeated without variation.   But the love of the new
also made itself felt, and thus many innovations on the old
Germanic legend were certainly introduced in Germany,
while Iceland and the North retained something much
more original, and infinitely more natural and dramatic.

It is the innovations, the inharmonious veneer of
chivalric manners, which mark off the *Nibelungenlied* from
the Homeric poems.   In Austria, towards the close of the
twelfth century, the position of the jongleur improved.   The

C C

Emperor Henry VI. had a jongleur, Rupert ; Leopold V. of
Austria had a minstrel named Eberhard : a convent accepts
a present of a German book from a jongleur named
Wolfker.[1]   Such men as Rupert and Eberhard had probably more leisure, lived a more settled life, and, above all,
were in a position to address a society in which reading
and writing were not very unusual accomplishments.   The
jongleurs were no longer, like the Homeric minstrels, the
only professional poets.   There were Church poets,
amorous and knightly poets, *Minnesänger*.   The stuff of
the epic—the lays—had survived into a lyric age ; so the
manners of the age of chivalrous lyric, the courtly amours,
now colour the ancient legendary songs : we have rich
dresses, feasts, tournaments, embassies.   Finally (according
to M. Lichtenberger's theory) some one redacted the *Lieder*
thus altered and thus coloured, and by omissions, transi-
tions, and so forth, produced a written *Nibelungenlied*.
Obviously the action of this nameless writer answers to that
attributed to the hypothetical *Bearbeiter*, or redactor, who
botched and patched a quantity of diverse materials into the
Odyssey.   But the errors of the redactor of the Odyssey
are only apparent under the microscopes of a few German
savants ; while other German *savants*, like Kammer, frankly
remark that ' Kirchhoff has not the eyes to see the poetry
of a situation.' [2]

    The incongruities of the *Nibelungenlied*, the trailing
construction of that chronicle-poem, are visible, on the other
hand, to every reader.   Neither Wolf nor anyone else can
call it a marvel of composition.   Briefly, the simple,
dawdling plan, trailing across the years has no analogy at
all with the compact Odyssey.   That a court jongleur of
Vienna (to be specific) could redact the *Nibelungenlied*

    [1] Lichtenberger, p. 405.
    [2] Kammer, *Einheit der Odyssee*, p. 580.

does not raise a presumption that any man, out of a mass of lays and brief epics, could construct the Odyssey. We have often asked what the *Bearbeiter's* motive could possibly be : audience for a long epic he could have none in his late day ; the existence of a purchasing public of readers is not assumed. For the motives of the redactor of the *Nibelungenlied*, M. Lichtenberger suggests that some great lord may have wanted the lays in a written copy ; or that jongleurs needed a written copy, 'which would easily find readers, especially lady readers, in the *châteaux*.' Here, then, is a conceivable motive, and here a possible public for the redactor who first wrote out the *Nibelungenlied*. These motives we miss in the Homeric case, or shall we argue that, as writing was coming into use, one of the early tyrants desired to have a written copy? On literary ladies in Greek *châteaux* we need hardly speculate. There remains one very great distinction between the cases of ' the German Iliad ' and the true Iliad. The scheme of the *Nibelungenlied* could be, and demonstrably was, very freely handled, was altered in essential points, and was equipped with large modern additions and brought into conformity with modern manners. We have no reason to believe that any one person, answering to the author or redactor of the *Nibelungenlied*, would ever have been permitted to take such liberties with the Bible and Doomsday Book of Greece—the Iliad.

As regards the *Nibelungenlied*, one fact in particular throws doubt on the idea that it is a ' *recueil factice* of ballads,' redacted into shape. The poem is written in a peculiar strophe, thus :

Uns ist in alten maeren   wunders vil geseit
Von helden lobebaeren,   von grozer kuonheit,
Von fröuden hôchgeziten,   von weinen und von klagen
Von kuener recken striten,   muget ir nu wunder hoeren sagen.

Now this strophe was a novelty in narrative poetry. It appears to have been introduced in lyric poetry, shortly before 1150, by Conrad von Kurenberg, and he is even regarded by some critics as the author of the *Nibelungenlied*, or of an early version thereof. This is extremely dubious, but at least we may consider the strophe as an artistic and not a purely popular form of verse, and thus in the *Nibelungenlied*, even if its materials are popular lays, they have passed through the hands of an artist, working for courtly hearers or readers,[1] and so cannot be merely stitched together. They are fused into a whole, and they wear a new form, with all that these facts imply. If this be true of a whole relatively so loose and inartistic as the *Nibelungenlied*, if to construct even this demanded the hand of the artist who 'chose the lays and groups of lays destined to form part of the collection, who fixed the beginning and close of the poem, united the groups, and probably perfected the whole as to external form, language, and versification,'[2] how much more is a single poetical constructor needed for the Iliad and the Odyssey !

The analogy between the Greek epics and the *Nibelungenlied* would be closer than it is if we happened to possess the story of the Iliad in two, or rather three, different forms, one derived from Thessaly, one from the coast of Asia Minor. For, as regards the *Nibelungenlied*, we have the South German poem in its various texts, and we also have the legend partly in the shape of Northern lays, partly in a prose paraphrase of these, and of other lost lays, known as the *Volsunga Saga*. We shall first examine the Northern, the Icelandic lays, and the saga which gives their contents in prose. This shape of the legend, as any reader must see, is the most ancient ; it bears no trace of Christian influence and few marks of chivalrous mediævalism. The sources

[1] Fischer, *op. cit.* p. 252.   [2] Lichtenberger, p. 410.

are (1) the poetic treatise of Snorri Sturlason, called, for some reason, *The Edda*.[1] This book is commonly styled the 'Prose or Younger Edda,' and contains, *à propos* of a periphrasis for 'gold,' an analysis of the story of the Nibelungen or Niflungs. In 1642 was discovered (2) a manuscript collection of lays, unluckily incomplete, which is now known as Codex Regius (No. 2365 of the Royal Library of Copenhagen). The discoverer, or promulgator, Bishop Brynjolf, styled this MS. 'The Edda of Saemund the Learned'—a mistaken title. This collection of fragmentary lays, usually named 'The Poetic Edda,' or 'Song Edda,' or 'Older Edda,' is not, of course, an epic (as some have imagined), and makes no such pretensions. Its contents are poems and fragments of various ages and characters: even the pieces on the Nibelungen legend are not all of one sort or of one date.[2] Among the passages bearing on the Niflungs, or Niblungs, in the *Corpus Boreale*, derived from the Codex Regius, we find *The Old Play of the Volsungs*, 'the earliest known version of the story of the Volsungs in a dramatic form.' The characters impart to each other didactic advice and mythical lore. Then we have *The Old Lay of Atli*, 'one of the most ancient Teutonic epics'; only 175 lines remain, and these deal with a part of the story near its close. *Hamdis-Mal*, or the *Old Lay of Hamtheow* (137 lines), tells a part still later. Then we have 'the flower of Northern epic poetry,' containing *Helgi and Sigrun*, a poem of the ancestry of the hero of the Nibelung tale. Their feats are also sung in *The Western Volsung Lay*, and now Sigurd (as he is called in the North), the hero, himself makes his appearance, slays

---

[1] See Vigfusson and Powell's *Corpus Boreale*, i. xxvi, ii. 514.

[2] Messrs. Powell and Vigfusson suppose the authors to have been South Scandinavians, residing in the Western Isles. *Op. cit.* i. lxii–lxiv.

a serpent, wins a hoard of treasure, with a curse on it, and wakens a maid, Sigrdrifa, from an enchanted sleep. Next we reach a lay in which the young hero Sigurd has his fortune told him by Gripi, a prophet. It is a summary of the tale by anticipation. Next *The Long Lay of Brunhild* shows how she had Sigurd, whom she loved, slain by her husband's brother, and how she went down to the place of death. *The Lamentation of Gudrun*, for her brother's slaying by Atli, gives an unusual version of that event. In *The Old Lay of Gudrun* (Sigurd's wife) she tells her story to an exile at the court of Atli, her second husband, and her account of Sigurd's murder differs from that in *The Long Lay of Brunhild*. There Sigurd is stabbed in bed, here he is slain in the wood on the way from an assembly. This poem calls Sigurd 'the slayer of Gothorm,' and he himself is slain by Hogni. In *Brunhild* Gothorm kills Sigurd, and is slain by the dying hero. *The Tale of Gudrun* is elegiac, she watches by her dead lord, and cannot weep till one draws the face-cloth from the face. *Gudrun's Chain of Woe* is her lament before she leaps into her funeral fire. She tells of her latest sorrows with her third husband. *The Greenland Lay of Atli* makes Gudrun a Medea. Atli has slain her brothers, she slays her own children by him, and murders him in his sleep.

These are the chief lays, and it is manifest that they are poetical expositions, often discrepant, of the events in a legend. They are not fragments of an epic, but different poets, in different early times (say 850–1100 B.C.), are telling parts of the same tale, but telling it differently.[1]

There came no poet to construct an epic out of these lays, chanted probably by warriors and warrior poets of the North, rather than by mercenary jongleurs, as in the South. But there did come, (3) early in the thirteenth century, a prose

[1] For possible dates see *Corpus Boreale*, i. lxiv, lxvi.

writer, who worked on the known lays, and on lost lays and legends. The result of his labour is the *Volsung Saga*.[1] The prose sagaman did not produce an example of concentrated epic unity. He rather began *ab ovo* with long genealogical accounts of his hero's ancestry. In the earlier part of the saga two points are notable. First, the adventures of the hero's ancestry are, in some parts, like the central story itself, only more briefly told. They turn on destructive blood-feuds between a married woman and her husband's kin. They are like earlier, ruder, and briefer sketches for the central legend. Secondly, the saga, especially in its earlier portions, is barbarous, almost savage. Shape-shifting and lycanthropy (the superstition of were-wolves) play a great part. The supernatural machinery is frankly heathen. The saga, like the lays which inspire it, is thus far earlier in character than the South German *Nibelungenlied*, and gives, no doubt, an older form of the fable. Yet there are German influences at work : we hear of the Rhine, of Goths and Huns.

We now examine the story as it is in the saga, and show how the lays are handled by the sagaman. He begins with a son of Odin, Sigi, and passes through several generations before he comes to his real hero, Sigurd. Sigi, Odin's son, fled from his home for a manslaughter. He becomes King of Hunland, marries, and is slain by the brothers of his wife, thus anticipating the central legend. His son Reris avenges Sigi on his mother's brothers. Reris is childless, and a May, daughter of a giant, brings him a magic apple. His wife eats of it, and bears a child, Volsung, who is for six years in his mother's womb. Volsung marries the Apple-May; his children (besides nine others) are Sigmund, and a daughter, Signy. Sigmund, like Arthur, lightly draws out a sword

---

[1] Translated by Mr. William Morris and Mr. Magnússon. There is a cheap edition (Walter Scott, London, *s. a.*).

which Odin has driven to the hilt in a tree. Signy
reluctantly marries Siggeir, King of Gothland. He covets
Sigmund's sword. He invites Volsung and his children to
Gothland, with treacherous intent. Signy in vain warns her
kindred. Here, again, the story of the Niblungs at Attila's
court is anticipated. All the Volsungs but Sigmund are
slain: he escapes to the woods. Signy sends him her children by Siggeir, whom he kills. By art magic she lies with
him in the shape of another woman. Her son by her
brother is Sinfjötli. After some adventures as were-wolves
Sigmund and Sinfjötli slay Siggeir and his children ; Signy
perishes with them. Sigmund marries Borghild ; his two
sons by her are Helgi and Hamund. Norns prophesy of
Helgi's fame. Helgi defeats King Hunding, loves Sigrun,
fights her affianced lord, Hodbrod ; in this battle Sinfjötli
and one Granmar exchange filthy heathen taunts, in respon-
sive strains, like Lacon and Comatas in the fifth Idyll of
Theocritus. Helgi slays Hodbrod, and marries Sigrun.
Sinfjötli slays the brother of Sigmund's wife ; she poisons
him. Sigmund divorces her, and marries Hjordis. Hunding's son, Lyngi, defeats and slays Sigmund, whose sword is
broken. Sigmund's wife, Hjordis, escapes to King Alf,
carrying the fragments of the sword. She bears Sigmund's
son Sigurd, and now at last we come to the hero of the
Nibelungenlied under his Northern name.

So far, out of old lays, still preserved in the Codex
Regius, the sagaman has used *Helga-kvida*, ' Helgi and
Sigrun,' [1] telling how Borghild bore Helgi, and how Norns
came to that birth, the slaying of Hunding, the wooing of
Sigrun by Helgi, the war of words between Sinfjötli and
Granmar (called Godmund). But the lay gives an account
of Helgi's slaying not in the saga ; he was slain by Sigrun's
brothers. Here, again, the fate of Sigurd is anticipated ; in

[1] *Corpus Boreale*, i. 131.

fact, Helgi and Sigrun, in the lay, are doubles of Sigurd and Gudrun in the central part of the saga. The living Sigrun joins her dead lord, Helgi, in his barrow. All this would have clashed with the central interest, so the sagaman rightly omitted it. We can only conjecture as to whether these forecasts of the central plot are refractions from it, or whether they represent an earlier legend, later localised in Gothland, Rhineland, and Burgundy, and fitted with historical names, such as Atli (Attila).

With the rearing of Sigurd, under Regin, the smith, we begin to reach the real gist of the saga. To understand the sagaman's treatment of his materials, it is well to examine the story as it exists in the lays. *The Old Play of the Volsungs* gives the legend in a dramatic form. One Rodmar had three sons, Fafnir, the serpent, Regin, the smith (Sigurd's tutor), and Otter. This is savage enough, and may have its origin in Totemism. The gods went wandering ; one of them threw a stone which killed Otter. As atonement ($\pi o \iota \nu \acute{\eta}$) was demanded gold enough to cover the Otter's skin. Loki, the mischievous god, caught a rich dwarf in a net, and extorted all his hoard, including his last magic ring. This hoard the dwarf cursed, and it is the fatal Rhine-gold of the *Nibelungenlied*. Rodmar received the gold ; Fafnir, his son, killed him, ousted Regin, and wallowed on the wealth. Urged by Regin, Sigurd slew Fafnir. As he roasted Fafnir's heart, by Regin's instructions, he tasted it (this is a *Märchen* told in Scotland of Ramsay of Bamff), and so understood the talk of birds. Their song warned him to kill Regin, which he did, to keep the gold, and to waken Sigrdrifa, a maiden who lay in an enchanted sleep.[1] In the drama, she gives him moral advice, and there that piece ends.

In the western *Volsung's Lay*, the birds not only advise

[1] *Märchen* of *La Belle au Bois Dormant.*

Sigurd to slay Regin, but to go to Giuki's daughter, a 'battle-fay,' cast into a sleep by Woden, for slaying in fight others than he wished to fall. Here, as before, her name is Sigrdrifa. Her human parentage, as Giuki's daughter, is given. Then the lay ends. In Gripi's or Grifir's lay, that prophet tells Sigurd his fate. After slaying the dragon, and waking 'a king's daughter' unnamed, he is to love Brunhild, Heimi's foster-daughter, really daughter of Budli. To her he shall vow his faith, but, after one night at Giuki's, he shall clean forget her.[1] By art of Giuki's wife shall this oblivion be wrought, Sigurd shall marry her daughter, Gudrun, and win Brunhild for Gudrun's brother, Gunnar, king of the Goths, wearing Gunnar's shape, and lying with Brunhild 'as if she were thy mother.' Gudrun's brothers Hogni and Gunnar shall be bound by oaths to Sigurd, but not the youngest brother, Guttorm. Brunhild shall discover the secret of her wooing, and urge on Guttorm, as unsworn, to kill Sigurd.

Here ends the prophecy. It is not clear, in this lay, that Brunhild is the enchanted maiden whom Sigurd is to awake, for the passage is obscure. In *The Long Lay of Brunhild* she calls the dwarf's hoard 'the hoard of the Rhine,' a river which first makes its appearance here. In a short Brunhild lay we learn that 'Sigurd died south of the Rhine,' slain, not in bed, but in a wood, as also in *The Old Lay of Gudrun*.

Here we leave the lays, at the moment of Sigurd's death by his wife's brothers' hands, and ask, How does the saga-man tell the story up to this point?

Regin fosters Sigurd, forges for him the sword Gram out of the shards of Sigmund's sword, urges him to kill Fafnir. Odin gives him the horse Grani, Grifir (Gripi) tells

---

[1] *Märchen* of *Black Bull o' Norroway*, with many parallels.

his fortune, he avenges his father on the Hundings, slays
Fafnir, tastes the heart, hears the birds, slays Regin, wakes
Brunhild in her castle within the wall of flame. He meets
her again at Heimir's, her foster-father's, where she em-
broiders his great deeds in gold on cloth, like Helen in
Troy.[1]

We are now in a more civilised region. They swear
troth, though Brunhild foresees the end. And thus the
sagaman has knitted his tragedy, for, in the saga, Sigurd
and Brunhild are true lovers severed by fate, while in
the *Nibelungenlied*, Siegfried and Brunhild are nothing to
each other. The saga follows the lines of the *Märchen* in
which a lover quite forgets his lady after infringing some
magical prohibition or taboo. In popular tales she always
wins back his heart : in the saga they are fatally sundered.
Hence arises the nobly dramatic display of character, the
man enduring life as he may, the woman dashing herself
and him on their death in her passion. After Sigurd and
Brunhild have sworn troth, he rides away to Giuki's realm,
' south of the Rhine.' Here we reach the spot where the
Nibelungenlied begins. Giuki's daughter Gudrun answers to
Kriemhild, in Burgundy, with her brothers, King Gunther
and others. In the saga Grimhild is the mother of Gudrun.
As in the *Nibelungenlied*, Gudrun dreams a dream, that
she has a goodly hawk, and again that she has a golden
deer, which Brunhild slays, giving her a wolf-cub, which
besprinkles her with her brother's blood. Brunhild interprets the dream : Gudrun's brother shall bewitch Sigurd,
Gudrun shall wed and lose him, and marry Atli and lose
her brethren and slay Atli. Grimhild gives Sigurd the oblivious potion, Brunhild he quite forgets, and marries
Gudrun. Then he is sent to win Brunhild for Gudrun's
brother, Gunnar, for Gunnar cannot ride through the fire

[1] It seems they had a daughter.

that encircles her castle, and Sigurd, taking his semblance, rides the flames. He lays a sword between them in bed, and Budli brings his daughter Brunhild and his son Atli to Giuki's, where Gunnar and Brunhild are wedded. Then comes the quarrel between Gudrun and Brunhild, and Gudrun proves that Sigurd, not Gunnar, won Brunhild, displaying in proof Andvari's fatal ring, taken from Brunhild's hand by Sigurd. From the outbreak of this quarrel to the slaying of Sigurd in bed by Guttorm, Gudrun's youngest brother, the saga holds its own with the highest and most passionate examples of literature. Homer has no such scene, no such ideas. The mastery of love in Brunhild's heart, her scene with Sigurd, where he ranges through every choice before them, to live as friends, to live as lovers, her disdainful rejection of friendship, her Northern pride of purity, his anguish, her determination to slay him and follow him, her one laugh as she hears Gudrun's first moan over the dead, her death, the mourning of the horse Grani, as of Achilles's horse Xanthus, the lament of Gudrun—all this is mere perfection, all is on the loftiest level of Shakespeare, and has no parallel in Greek or Roman poetry. It is as modern and comes as near our hearts as if it had been written yesterday, and, while men and women love in despite of fate, it is true and moving for all time. Of this magnificent passage the central glory, the scene between Sigurd and Brunhild, is not represented in extant lays ; the wrath of Brunhild, the murder, her death and descent to the Dead, are in the lays, also the lament of Gudrun, and a prophecy by Brunhild.

This prophecy, and another lay, *The Lamentation of Ordrun*, indicate a version of the story which the sagaman did not follow. Ere she dies, Brunhild declares that Gunnar, her husband, shall win the love of Ordrun, Atli's sister, and shall be put by Atli in a dungeon full of snakes.

In the *Lament* Ordrun herself tells the tale. Gunnar was her paramour ; therefore Atli treacherously got Gunnar and Hogni and the other Niblungs into his power, cut out Hogni's heart, and put Gunnar in the adder-close. The sagaman, on the other hand, follows *The Greenland Lay of Atli*. In a passage not based on extant lays, he tells how Grimhild made Gudrun take Atli for her second husband. Atli covets the accursed hoard of Fafnir's gold, now in the hands of Gunnar and Hogni. He invites them to his house, but Gudrun sends a message of warning, cut in runes on a staff.[1] Atli's envoy cuts other runes on it ; the underlying runes of warning are detected by Hogni's wife, but too late. The sons of Giuki, despising many omens, go to Atli's hall ; they are set on, they fight manfully, Gudrun fights on their side. All are slain but Hogni and Gunnar, who are taken. Gunnar refuses to reveal the hiding-place of the hoard under the Rhine till he sees Hogni's heart in a plate. Hogni's heart is cut out, and Gunnar says that now no man save himself knows the secret place of the hoard, and he will never reveal it.[2]

The *Nibelungenlied*, after a scene answering to this, makes Kriemhild (Gudrun), who wishes to know the secret of the treasure, slay Hagen (Hogni) and be herself slain, when the epic ends, leaving Etzel (Atli) in perfect health. The saga, on the other hand, heaps on Gudrun the deeds of Medea and Thyestes ; she slays her own children by Atli, cooks and serves them up to him, and by aid of Hogni's son, Niblung, slays Atli himself. The rest of the saga, following old lays, recounts a third marriage of Gudrun, the awful slaying of her daughter by Sigurd, the vengeance taken for the death of this daughter, Swanhild,

---

[1] The Australian 'message stick ' or ' talking stick.'

[2] *Märchen* of the Last Pict, and the Secret of the Heather Ale, in Chambers's *Popular Tales of Scotland*.

and the destruction of the avengers by the counsel of Odin, and so ends all the house of Giuki and of Volsung.

In the lays and saga the motives are the blood-feud between wife and husband, and the curse laid on the hoard of Andvari. The religion is heathendom ; the manners vary from the savagery of the were-wolves to the gold embroidery of Brunhild and Gudrun. In battle the forces are few. In the fight within the hall Atli has some thirty men, while in the *Nibelungenlied* the religion is Christian, manners are chivalrous, and many thousands of heroes fall in the palace of Etzel (Atli). To turn from the saga and the old lays to the *Nibelungenlied* is to leave art for the artificial, plain prose or noble poetry for a detestably jigging measure, and the succinct telling of a tale for a wilderness of padding and verbosity. The *Nibelungenlied* has not the qualities of true popular poetry ; it is a professional's work, a professional who apparently was paid for his much speaking. The poet introduces us to Kriemhild of Worms in Burgundy, daughter of Dancrat (Giuki) and Uote (Grimhild). Her brothers are Gunther, Gernot, and Giselher (Gunnar, Guttorm and Hogni, though Hagen of Tronje, who plays Hogni's part, is not one of the brothers in the *Nibelungenlied*). Kriemhild, like Gudrun, has a dream of a fair hawk strangled by two eagles ; her mother interprets it of a husband. We are now introduced to Siegfried (Sigurd), son of the King of the Netherlands, Siegmund (Sigmund), who is still in perfect health. From a story told later by Hagen, we learn that Siegfried once met the Nibelungs sharing a huge treasure. They made him umpire and gave him the sword Balmung (Gram) as his fee. The affair could not be settled : he routed them all and seized the treasure, killing hundreds of men, a form of silliness in which mediæval often rivals Hindoo romance. The saga introduces no such nonsense. Next Siegfried overcame a dwarf, Alberich (a dim recollection of Andvari?), and robbed him of the cloak of darkness, and made him warden of the Niflung treasure. This Siegfried, having heard of Kriemhild, rides with twelve men to her father's court, where he swaggers in a boastful manner, is cajoled, aids the Burgundians in war against the Saxons (here is very much conventional fighting), shines in a tournament, presses Kriemhild's hand, lingers sighing in the court, and, finally, goes with Gunther to woo for him Brunhild. She is an athletic maid, who challenges her wooers to put the stone, jump and throw the spear, killing those whom she defeats. Siegfried's prize is to be the hand of Kriemhild. They travel with Hagen and Dankwart. Reams are here written about their new clothes—silks from Morocco and Libya, fish skins, and what not. They reach the glorious castle of Isenstein; Brunhild takes Siegfried for Gunther's inferior. By aid of the cloak of darkness Siegfried vanquishes Brunhild, while Gunther seems to be the agent. Siegfried next brings an unnecessary escort of a thousand Nibelungers to Brunhild's court. After large banquetings and tournays at Worms, Siegfried is married to Kriemhild, and Gunther wedded to Brunhild, who laments that Kriemhild should be mated with an inferior, Siegfried. She spies a mystery, and will not be a bride indeed to Gunther till the secret is confessed. The misfortunes of Gunther on his wedding night, his succouring by Siegfried, aided by the cloak of darkness, Siegfried's theft of Brunhild's ring and girdle, his gift of these to Kriemhild, are well-known incidents. In all this passage, so unlike the tale in the saga, there is plenty of vigour and rough humour. Brunhild, once wedded, is no stronger than any other lady, though in the bridal chamber she nearly murdered Siegfried.

Kriemhild and Siegfried return to their home, and after ten years are invited to visit Brunhild and Gunther. Each

lady praises her lord, but Brunhild insists that Siegfried is
her husband's vassal. On entering church, Brunhild bids
Kriemhild wait and let her pass. Kriemhild announces
that Siegfried has been Brunhild's lover, and shows the fatal
belt and ring. The Burgundian nobles determine to slay
Siegfried. Hagen is the most resolute. He discovers from
Kriemhild that her husband is invulnerable : after slaying
a dragon, he bathed in its blood, a leaf fell on one spot
between his shoulders, there he may be wounded. That
Hagen may know where to guard him in battle, she sews
a little cross on his coat. This, of course, is absurd, as in
battle his armour would hide his coat. Consequently it is
at a hunting party that Hagen slays Siegfried as he stoops
to drink of a stream. Kriemhild remains in Burgundy with
her brother Giselher, who has had no part in the murder.
The hoard, her Morning Gift, is brought to Worms ; Hagen
seizes it, and hides it in the Rhine.

The second half of the poem recounts the slaying of
Gudrun's brothers, in vengeance for her husband. King
Etzel, the Hun, has lost his wife Helca ; he sends
Ruedeger to woo Kriemhild. She at first declines, but
ends by asking Ruedeger if he will swear to avenge any
injury done to her. He takes the oath, she marries Etzel,
seven years pass, when she invites the Burgundians (hence-
forth called Nibelungen after the hoard) to her court, with
purpose of revenge. Hagen foresees doom, omens are rife,
river nymphs prophesy bane, but they set forth, and after
many adventures and friendly entertainment by Ruedeger,
reach the court. Kriemhild shows her hostility ; her
attempts are baffled by Volker, knight and minstrel, a new
character, and by Hagen. One day she takes young
Ortlieb, her son by Atli, into hall, as the beginning of strife.
The squires of the Nibelungen are slaughtered, news of it
is brought into hall, Hagen slays young Ortlieb, the fight

begins. Dietrich of Berne, however, calls a parley, and is permitted to take Kriemhild and Etzel (a weak, well-meaning man) out of the battle. The fight then rages to the end. Legion after legion of Huns is destroyed ; Ruedeger must fight against his Burgundian guests for his oath's sake ; Dietrich and his men, too, must join the fray. All are slain but Gunther and Hagen, who are delivered over to Kriemhild. Hagen says that Gunther must be killed before he tells the secret hiding-place of the hoard. When Gunther is dead, he, like Gunnar, refuses to reveal the secret. Kriemhild slays him, and is slain by old Hildebrand :

ditze ist der Nibelunge-nôt.

The last scenes of the *Nibelungenlied* have the merit of vigour and of a certain ominous fatality which broods over them to the close. When compared with the Northern lays and with the saga, the Southern poem leaves an impression of fatal fluency. Perhaps half of it is occupied by otiose descriptions of dresses, tournays, feasts, ceremonies, and pageants, all mediæval. The topography is copious and minute in places, elsewhere all is vague enough. The geographical horizon is wider and clearer than that of the saga, though even in the saga Brunhild speaks of having warred in Greece. In the south a wife avenges her husband on her brothers ; in the north she avenges her brothers on her husband, as the law of the blood-feud demands. The northern version is, therefore, the earlier. As the *Nibelungenlied* seems too long for recitation (it contains some 12,000 lines), except in very favourable circumstances, we are inclined to suppose that it was meant to be read. The chivalric manners are all of a piece in contradistinction to the sanguinary and long-deferred revenges. The Nibelungen themselves are a vague people of fancy : the Dragon

D D

is much in the background, there is no curse on the hoard, the relations between Brunhild and Siegfried are relations of spite and pride, not of thwarted and hopeless love. Kriemhild's revenge is inconsistent with her usual character as an ideal lady of chivalrous romance. Atli has been changed from a ferocious conqueror into a mild-mannered man enough. The original legend, in brief, has been greatly diluted and half forgotten, while the whole has passed through a comparatively modern medium. The poem is not 'primitive,' nor is it 'popular'; it is meant for an audience of knights and ladies. What older lays were in the author's hands, and how he handled them, for want of specimens of the lays, it is impossible to say.

The whole legend has grains of historical fact in its mass. There was a Gundicar, king of the Burgundians, who, with his people, was exterminated by the Huns about 440 A.D.[1] There existed Burgundian kings—Gibica, Gondomar, Gislahar, and Gundahar. The legend offers three royal brothers, sons of Gibich, named Gunther, Giselher, and Gernot; these, in the traditions, were betrayed to death by King Etzel, Attila the Hun. In the Northern story Atli is slain by his wife, and so Attila, who died on his wedding night, was in some traditions slain by his bride, Ildico (453 A.D.).[2] Both Northern and Southern epic and lays speak of Dietrich, or Thjodrek, at Attila's court; this is Theodoric, king of the Ostrogoths. He was fifty years or so later than Attila, but his father, Theodosius, had been in exile among the Huns.

The story of Sigurd Fafnisbana, or Siegfried, may well be older than those events with which it is combined by romance. He is explained as a sun-myth and as a lightning-myth, but may be merely a hero of *Märchen*, elevated

[1] Prosper Aquitanus, *Chron.* ad an. 435.
[2] See authorities in Lichtenberger, p. 424

by poetry into more cultivated mythology. The legend of the treasure is mysterious. In the Northern versions it supplies a motive; it is under a curse. In the Southern epic it is not even said to be accursed. It may be a mere treasure of fairy tale such as Dwarfs possess, or it may conceivably be part of a moral myth on the evils of great wealth, or it may be the hidden sunlight, as in the theories of solar mythology. But why is it hidden in the Rhine? Can this be a legendary echo of the burying of the hoard of Alaric in the Italian river-bed? We have seen that the lays of Sigurd's ancestry show the central plot, the domestic blood-feud, several times recurring. Probably enough, the original *Märchen* of Sigurd, the dragon-slayer, the wakener of the Sleeping Beauty, ended happily. But the *donnée* of the blood-feud was combined with the *Märchen*; historical events and characters, 'half remembered and half forgot,' were brought into the tale, which began to assume epic proportions, but only won its way into an epic late, and in unskilled professional hands, when the manners of the original narrators were things of a lost world.

The Greek heroic traditions, containing, perhaps, about as much of historical truth as the *Nibelungenlied*, fell into the hands of the divine poet, and were handled with uniformity as regards manners and ideas, with unparalleled nobility of style, and with all the Greek sentiment for harmony and unity.

CHAPTER XVII

THE SONG OF ROLAND

OF all national heroic poems the famous French *Song of Roland* comes nearest to the Homeric example, not by imitation, though the author knows Homer's name, but as a similar result of similar forces and historical conditions. The poem is intended for recitation to an audience of ladies and warriors. It has a central theme—the wrath of Ganelon the traitor, with the ruin it brought on many souls of heroes, the Franks of France. The theme rests on a remote historical fact, altered and magnified by legend. There is even a divine machinery in the interposition of the Archangel Michael. The action is concentrated within narrow limits of time and space. The diction is archaic, and there occurs, as has frequently been said, the note of epic repetition—passages recurring with textual exactness. Above all, as in Homer, the poet chants of a national endeavour, the war of Charlemagne in Spain (778), and of a national disaster, a national hero, a strife with Oriental enemies—the Saracens.

No parallel to Homer is likely to be more perfect than this, and while we can see more or less clearly the social, historical, legendary, and poetical conditions in which the French epic arose, we can also trace the *remaniements*, the re-handlings, of the original poem. Written in the eleventh century, in *laisses*, or tirades of unequal length, in which assonance, not rhyme, is employed, the poem was later re-handled, rhyme was substituted for assonance, and the lines of ten feet were finally exchanged for Alexandrines. In these processes the epic was diluted, weakened, and so altered that it would be impossible to hesitate as to which are new and which older portions. The whole tone and character alter ; between the version of the eleventh and that of the thirteenth century there is a manifest break and gulf of change. So far as analogy is worth anything, this is an argument against the presence of much late work in the Greek epics. Their tone is harmonious ; manners and metre are consonant throughout. The lapse of two centuries, on the other hand, brought a changed measure and new ideas into the *Song of Roland.* Finally, the French literature shows us the ' cyclic mania ' in perfection ; whole epics and cycles of epics are made to complete the old stories, and to connect them with genealogies of illustrious families, exactly as in the case of the *Telegonia* of Eugammon.

The historical conditions in which the French epic arose are these : there was an age of national splendour, and royal, not feudal magnificence, in the reign of Charlemagne. Then occurred the attack on Charles's rearguard by the Basque Highlanders, at Roncesvaux (778). In that fight fell, as Egihard relates, ' Hruodlandus, warden of the march of Brittany.' This is Roland ; history has no other word to say of him whose legendary fame fills the mouth of poetry. It is known that popular lays were sung on the military events of those ages ; thus the popular view of them was handed down through three centuries. But legend fused all the royal Charleses together, in the heroic shape of the aged king with white-flowered beard, though Charles was but thirty-seven at the date of Roncesvaux. Times and events were confused ; for the Basques the Saracens

were substituted ; comparatively modern occurrences, such
as the sack of Jerusalem, were thrown back into the past ;
Roland was said to have conquered England ; the whole
affair was magnified ; and, to account for the defeat, a
traitor, Ganelon, was introduced, in a manner characteristically French.　For three centuries there was *une fermenta-
tion épique*, as M. Gaston Paris says,[1] and thence arose the
epic.

The poems were promulgated by the jougleurs, or
jongleurs, who in some respects answer to, and in others
differ from, the rhapsodes of historic Greece.　M. Léon
Gautier, indeed, avers that the rhapsodes, or *aèdes* (singers)
of Greece, marched at the head of armies and led them
to victory.[2]　But Homer shows us that the *aoidoi*, or Court
poets, were left at home, and Greek history offers no
example of a rhapsode at the head of an army.　The
jongleurs, as a rule, were under the ban of the Church, like
actors, mimes, and acrobats ; but an exception was occasionally made in favour of those 'who are specially called
jongleurs [*joculatores*] and sing the deeds of kings and the
lives of saints '—that is, the chanters of epics.[3]　These
viellatores narrated the exploits of Charles and Roland.[4]
These epics stimulated men to great deeds, and escaped
the general condemnation.　Taillefer sang a song of Roland
in front of the Norman army before the battle of Hastings,
as we read in the *Roman de Rou*.　The dread of a *mauvaise
chanson*, a satirical lay, was a great impulse to valour.
Like the Greeks and Trojans, the French were determined
to be

ἀοίδιμοι ἐσσομένοισιν,

---

[1] *Lit. Franç. au Moyen Age*, p. 36, 1890.

[2] *Epopées Françaises*, ii. 4.　Edition of 1892.

[3] Cf. the *Penitentiel* of Thomas of Cobham, at the end of the
thirteenth century.　Thomas was Archbishop of Canterbury in 1313.
Gautier, *op. cit.* ii. 21, note.

[4] MS. Sermons, Gautier, *op. cit.* ii. 210, note.

to be famed in song in future generations, and to shun the στυγερὴ ἀοιδή, the *mauvaise chanson*, or 'ill song,' that requited Clytæmnestra.[1]

Thus the epic reciters had a certain social standing, and concerning one of them, the author of *Ogier*, we learn that he was of gentle birth.[2] As a rule, these jongleurs recited the poems of others, of *trouvères*, but a few were poets themselves. When a jongleur was a poet, he usually preserved his copyright by keeping his manuscript carefully to himself. Occasionally he taught the verses to jongleurs for pay, or sold copies.[3] Thus we have, as has already been remarked, examples of the value of a written poem in an age when epic verse, as in Greece, was much more frequently recited to an audience than read by individuals for their private pleasure. The jongleurs, as a rule, were wanderers, and would recite in hostelries or at street corners, but some took service with lords.[4] The extravagant rewards bestowed on them, both in money and plate or rich garments, were condemned by the clergy. Some jongleurs, in a very modern way, offered to sell their praises, to introduce the *aristeia* of a living warrior, for a pair of scarlet hose. Arnoud, Count of Ardres, refused this inexpensive immortality, the insertion of his name in the *Chanson d'Antioche*, when offered by a jongleur.[5] The jongleur did not always find it easy to please his audience. They rejected what was familiar, yet wanted what was old. It was not unusual to pretend that a new song had been

[1] Iliad vi. 358. Odyssey xxiv. 200. *Chanson de Roland*, 1466 : ' Male çanson n'en deit estre canté.'

[2]   ' Jouglere fu, si vesqui son eage,
       Gentishons fu, et trestout son lignage.'
Gautier, *op. cit.* ii. 46.

[3] Gautier, *op. cit.* i. 214–218, ii. 48.   [4] *Ibid.* ii. 51.

[5] *Chronique de Guines et d'Ardres*, p. 311, Gautier, *op. cit.* ii. 119, 120.

freshly discovered in an ancient MS.   There was a kind of
school of jongleurs at Beauvais in the Lent of each year,
where they gathered and learned new lays.[1]   The lateness
of these notices of the school at Beauvais, in the end of
the fourteenth century, when the true hour of epic had long
passed, prevents us from detecting here a close analogy
to the hypothetical school of Homeridæ in Chios.   In
knightly halls, as in Homeric Greece, *chansons de geste*
were recited by the jongleurs after dinner.   How long
might a recitation last?   *Huon de Bordeaux* is a poem of
10,495 verses.   At line 4,962 the jongleur says that he is
tired, and requests his hearers to listen to him again on the
following day.   Then, and in another piece, follows a summary of the first day's portion, to revive the memory of the
hearers or instruct those who had been absent.   These
remarks only occur in one MS. of each poem.   M. Léon
Gautier has tried reciting the poems, and finds that not
more than 1,000 verses could be got through in an hour,
even without the interruption of an audience.   By chanting
for six hours a day, the Odyssey could be finished in two
days, but we may believe that it entertained the winter
evenings for a longer period.   As to France, M. Gautier
thinks that the reciter abridged, selected choice passages,
and in other ways, especially by drinking a good deal of
wine, lightened his task.[2]   When we add that there were
jealousies among jongleurs, and that they accused each
other of ignorance and of corrupting the authentic songs,
there is little of essential omitted in the account of these
mediæval rhapsodes.   They by no means answer to the
sacred singer, the *aoidos* of Agamemnon or Alcinous, but
between them and the later Greek rhapsodes there are
obvious resemblances.

---

[1] *Pro cantilenis novis affluentes.*   Gautier, *op. cit.* ii. 176.   But
this was as late as 1402.   [2] *Ibid.* ii. 232-236.

Was the singer of the *Song of Roland,* as we possess it
in the oldest MS.—that of the Bodleian—a poet, or an
'arranger'? M. Gaston Paris inclines to the latter opinion.
'He was more than a mere *renouveleur,* he has *transformed*
an old poem, which we may divine in the *Carmen*' (a Latin
poem later than our MS. of *Roland*), 'and the Latin romance
of the pseudo Turpin' (which is also later in MS. than the
epic).[1] On the evidence of these shapes of the legend,
M. Gaston Paris supposes the poet to have added the introduction and the episode of the death of Alde (Roland's
lady), and to have placed the execution of the traitor at Aix.
There are certain contradictions or discrepancies, as where
Marsile, the Pagan king, says he has no army, and afterwards raises a large force ; certain hostages are claimed,
and we hear no more of them ; Ganelon's character is not
consistent (a point which may be disputed), and so on.
But while these discrepancies may be the result of altering
an older work, we may just as probably conclude that the
poet, 'in aiming at a momentary effect, loses sight of the
ensemble of his composition.'[2] For an author may fail to
make his inventions tally absolutely whether he is working
over an old canvas or constructing a new whole. Not to
understand this, to regard discrepancies as proofs of
Ueberarbeitung, and to criticise fiction as if it were contemporary history, is precisely the fault of many Homeric
commentators. On the whole, it seems unnecessary to
regard the author of *Roland* as anything else than a poet, a
maker, who has materials in legend, possibly in ballad, and
who handles them in a free artistic spirit. As to the ballad
materials, we know that contemporary *cantilenæ* on battles
and heroes had existed, but they are not extant, and it is
impossible for us to discern their presence in the epic. To
disengage *kleine Lieder* is out of the question.

[1] Gaston Paris, *op. cit.* p. 57. [2] *Ibid.* p. 59

As to the date of the existing poem, that is inferred from the absence of allusions to the first Crusade, from the archæology—the arms and equipments are those of the Bayeux Tapestry (1066–1080)—from the system of assonance, from the style of language, all of which fix it at the end of the eleventh century. The authorship is unknown ; the poem closes

Ci falt la geste que Turoldus declinet.

' Here ends the poem which Turoldus ' finished or narrated, but we cannot tell whether Turoldus was a poet who composed, a jongleur who recited, or a scribe who wrote the MS.[1] The action of the poem must be briefly stated.

Charles has conquered all Spain save Saragossa. There Marsile, the Saracen king, is in doubt what to do. An adviser proposes to send large gifts, and promises to come and be baptized, if Charles will leave France. Hostages must be given, and will be slain when the promise is broken, but this must be endured. The embassy goes to Cordova, and finds Charles beneath a pine. Next day he consults his barons ; a quarrel arises, as in the first book of the Iliad. Roland, Charles's nephew, wishes to attack Saragossa. Ganelon, Roland's stepfather, wishes to accept terms. It is decided to send an envoy. Roland, Oliver, Turpin volunteer, and are rejected. Roland proposes that Ganelon shall go on this perilous mission : hence the wrath of Ganelon. He rises in anger, threatens Roland, and departs. On his way the Saracen envoys win him over. Nevertheless, he delivers a haughty message to Marsile ; his life is in peril, he half draws his sword. Ten mules' loads of gold make him change his tone. He returns to camp with a feigned message. Roland leads the rearguard, with the twelve peers, as the French move north, and the main body emerges from the Pyrenees.

[1] Léon Gautier, Epopées Françaises, ii. 391, note. Edition of 1867.

The rearguard hears the earth tremble beneath the feet of a marching army. Oliver bids Roland sound 'a blast of that dread horn' to summon back Charles. He refuses. The battle begins—a series of single combats on horseback. Oliver's spear is broken ; he strikes with the truncheon. Roland bids him draw his sword Hauteclère. Roland at last sounds the horn ; the blood bursts from his mouth. Reinforcements of negroes come up, the French fall, Turpin and Roland alone survive. Turpin is down. Roland blows a last blast on the horn. He is answered by the clarions of Charles. The Saracens hear them and flee. Turpin blesses the dead and dies. Roland strives to break his sword Durendal, lest it fall into Pagan hands. The good sword will not break. Roland crawls on to Spanish soil, lies down above his sword and horn, and dies with his face to the foe. He holds up his glove to God, and the angel Gabriel, descending, bears away the token.

The rest of the poem, nearly half of it, deals with the revenge on the Paynim and on Ganelon. Alde, Oliver's sister, Roland's love, dies at the news of Roncesvaux. Charles is in peace at Aix, but a divine voice tells him that his labours are not ended. ' God !' said the king, ' toilsome is my life.'

The *Song of Roland* is no Iliad, nor its poet a Homer. He has not the wisdom, the humour, the knowledge, the delight in every aspect of life, the strong flow of various verse. He never deals in comparisons ; he does not take all human fortune for his province. His battle-piece is exaggerated in detail, though most spirit-stirring. The patriotic conclusion, the revenge, is long-drawn and dis-proportionate. But the poem is truly national, truly martial, truly religious. The characters are admirably defined. Ganelon, with a grain of honour leavening his corruption, is more subtle than anything in the Iliad, ' a noble baron ' with a felon heart. Roland, impetuous, daring, hot of temper, selling his own life and the enemy's for the point of honour ; courteous when Oliver, blind with blood, smites him by mischance in the last charge of the Franks, is on a level with Achilles in all but rhetorical splendour in debate. Of all his successors in the North, the poet of the Sigurd lays and the poet of Roland are the only true descendants of Homer ; they alone have been taught by the same muse. They have much, but his charm, his variety, his mellowness, his universality, were given to Homer alone. Still, in the poet of the lays and in the poet of Roland we recognise the artist, not the arranger or redactor. What the redactor is, what he can do, we see in the case of the Finnish collection, called an epic, the *Kalewala*.[1]

[1] For general use the best edition of *Roland* is that of M. Léon Gautier, with a translation into modern French. For a fuller exposition than space here affords, the writer may refer to his article on ' The *Song of Roland* and the Iliad,' in the *National Review*, October 1892.

CHAPTER XVIII

THE KALEWALA

THE so-called epic, the *Kalewala*, of the Finns, differs from the Greek, German, and French national poems, because it arose in different social conditions. It is not concerned with kings and knightly warriors ; its heroes are ' magnified non-natural men,' idealised magicians, or medicine-men. We hear nothing of courts, no echo of historic wars loses itself here in legend. There are traces of rivalry with the Lapps ; of history there is none. The songs of the *Kalewala* are chanted by a people without distinctions of rank ; they have passed through the hands of no epic poet singing for a knightly audience. In Finnish poetry there are no varieties of *form*, as in the lyrics and epics of other races. All verse, magic chant, narrative song, love song, songs of all seasons and labours, dirge, and epithalamium are alike couched in the metre of *Hiawatha*, strongly marked by alliteration. The metre is so simple and natural that, as far as form goes, anyone can be a poet. Now the *Kalewala* is a mere string of older and newer lays of every kind, arranged chronologically as far as possible, and eked out and contrived so as to form a sort of whole by the learned Dr. Lönnrot (born 1801). Lönnrot, an erudite and an enthusiast, set himself, between 1830 and 1850, to do for Finnish songs what, on Wolf's theory, Pisistratus did for the scattered Homeric lays. It has, therefore, been thought by some that here we have a practical proof of Wolf's hypothesis. But the conditions and results bear no real analogy whatever. Lönnrot, in a learned age, was consciously acting on a learned theory. About the nature of his materials we have every information ; about the nature of the materials which, *ex hypothesi*, Pisistratus employed, we can know nothing. Finally, Lönnrot's results in the *Kalewala* are altogether unlike the Iliad and Odyssey in structure and character. After a long prologue, the bard speaking in his own person and asking for beer, the *Kalewala* tells the myth of Creation, and only ends with the introduction of Christianity. The intermediate events are strings of disjointed mythical adventures of idealised medicine-men and smiths, while the only unity is given by the presence of Wainamoinen, a being half demiurge and half man, while even he is frequently absent. Obviously we have here no selecting and constructing artist's hand. There was no Finnish epic before Lönnrot ; he found no scattered parts of an original epic, but only scattered lays, all in the same measure ; and while vast portions of the *Kalewala* could be omitted, as many could be added at will, without altering the character of the collection. Hence this interesting assortment of lays— often beautiful, and always inspired by love of nature—casts no light whatever on the Homeric poems. The *Kalewala* contains the story of no united national effort. The heroes fight, like Hal of the Wynd, for their own hands. The gods even do not form a community as in Homer. They are all independent in their own provinces. 'Thus the myth is unripe, and thus the epic is unripe.'[1] The existence of great families, with their traditions and household bards, seems essential to the growth of epic. In Finland there were no such houses.

To make a summary of the *Kalewala* is rather a tedious

[1] Comparetti, *Der Kalewala*, p. 299.

business. In the first rune, an unearthly maiden, Ilmatar, daughter of Air, descends to ocean, is impregnated by the sea, floats for centuries, lends her body as resting place to a duck, whose golden eggs become earth and sky. The child of Ilmatar, Wainamoinen, bursts his bonds, and lands on earth. The myth is much akin to one current among the Iroquois. Wainamoinen, as Culture Hero, takes to felling trees and sowing barley. He has an altercation with a young Lapp minstrel, Joukahainen, from whom he extorts his sister, Aino. She drowns herself; the hare (as in Zululand) brings the tale to her mother. Wainamoinen laments, and, by his mother's advice, goes to seek a daughter of Suomi. Joukahainen shoots him, and leaves him in the water. He lands on the coast of Pohjola, in the domains of a woman named Louhi. She offers to send him home if he will forge for her a *sampo* ; she will also give him her daughter. A sampo is a magical object, the exact nature and meaning of which cannot be determined. Wainamoinen says that Ilmarinen (an ideal smith) can forge it, and Louhi promises *him* her daughter. Waina- moinen on his homeward way learns that three magic words are needful in sampo-making. Now comes the lay of the Origin of Iron, with a magical song of blood- staunching. Ilmarinen forges the sampo, Louhi takes it, but does not give the promised bride.

Now comes in a long lay of Lemminkainen, or Ahti, and his many and unlucky loves. He is slain, chopped up (like Osiris), and thrown into the Finnish Styx,

> The river of Tuoni,
> In the death realm of Manala.

His mother fishes out the pieces, and reunites them by magic songs. Wainamoinen builds a boat, finds the lost magic word, and sails to Pohjola to woo Louhi's daughter.

Ilmarinen, however, wins her by achieving difficult tasks, as in the story of Jason at the court of Æetes. He is aided by the girl. This is the Finnish form of a *Märchen* known in Samoa, Madagascar, North America, and all the world over. There follows a poem on beer, a description of a wedding, and a collection of nuptial songs.

The most superficial reader of poetry must now observe that between the *Kalewala* and the Odyssey there is simply no artistic analogy at all.

After a lay of the Origin of the Serpent, Lemminkainen is reintroduced, doing mischief in Pohjola. Frost is sent against him by a magic spell. But here comes in the legend of Kullervoinen, an evil person slain by Kullervo. Ilmarinen now forges a golden bride, who is unsatisfactory, and again woos fruitlessly in Pohjola. The heroes make an expedition and capture the sampo, but lose it in the sea. Bear-songs, disease-songs, songs of the stealing of sun and moon, follow, and finally Mariatta, a virgin, becomes a mother, and Wainamoinen sails into the sunset.

Obviously the *Kalewala* has no unity, and is no real epic. Lönnrot collected a number of ancient or later songs, but 'he is much more than a singer or gluer together of songs. He is familiar, as none of the Finnish singers were, with the idea of an epic. He was obliged to break up and distribute the different fragments of songs through the poem, as he had conceived it. He had all the variants before him' (they still exist), 'and fixed the text of each not with reference to its goodness, genuineness, and antiquity, but as each would be useful in the texture of his poem.'[1] He used magic songs as well as epic and epico-lyric lays. 'If we observe the course that Lönnrot was obliged to follow in order to construct a poem out of short lays, one feels how absurd is the idea that a Greek of the time of Pisistratus

---

[1] Comparetti, p. 309.

or earlier, that a jongleur, or a monk of the Middle Ages
. . . would ever have thought of undertaking and carrying
out such a work.   Such a proceeding is not even conceivable
for an Indian of one of the many centuries during which
the monstrous *Mahâbhârata* was heaped up.   Yet these
were times of science, of speculation, of grammar.' [1]

Comparetti (p. 106) shows us how Lönnrot worked.   And
here it is to be said that Lönnrot was no Macpherson.   He
left his collections behind him, and worked avowedly as
redactor, composing out of MS. sources.

In Rune I., as printed in Lönnrot's first edition and in
all known variants, Wainamoinen is maker of the world.   In
the second edition, the *Fille de l'Air* is maker ;   Lönnrot
combines a song of creation with a song of Wainamoinen's
birth.   The second rune contains three songs—of Ploughing and Sowing, of the Oak Tree, of Planting Barley—
which are properly distinct.   They are magical songs, for
the good of trees, earth, and grain.   The story of Aino
(whom Wainamoinen wooed) is a romantic mosaic, fashioned
by Lönnrot out of several songs.   Aino is not the sister of
Joukahainen in tradition, and Wainamoinen the Old is not
her wooer.   Lönnrot had to make Aino the sister of
Joukahainen, to hitch her story into the connection.   The
tale of fishing up a salmon which proved to be the drowned
Aino in a new shape—

> Was never salmon yet that shone so fair
> Above the nets at sea --

has nothing to do with Aino.   *This* maiden is a divine
being, like Leucothea in the Odyssey.

A casual flirtation of Wainamoinen with the Maiden of the
Rainbow is brought into connection with the sampo songs
by Lönnrot.   It is not known in Archangel, where sampo

---

[1] *Op. cit.* p. 312.

songs abound. The wounding of Wainamoinen's knee,[1] and
the *Song of Healing* goes usually with *The Making of the
Kantele*, or harp, less commonly with the sampo songs, and
is older than either. In the expedition to recover the sampo,
Wainamoinen is accompanied by Ilmarinen and Lemminkainen, who answers to Paupukeewis in *Hiawatha*.   Now
Lemminkainen in the popular lays does not join the expedition.   The hero who goes has several names ; Lönnrot
called him Lemminkainen, by way of getting a slender
thread of connection with what had gone before.[2]   Many
magical songs of the Bear, of Fire, and so on, were
dragged in by Lönnrot.[3]   The myth of the Maiden Mother
is found all the world over, and may be older than Christianity here, though now wearing a Christian colouring.

In spite of all this redacting there is no organic or original
unity in the *Kalewala*, all its merit, which is great and
peculiar, is found in its deep sympathy with nature, its
natural magic.   This is the gift of native, untaught culture.
This gives happiness and beauty and charm to a hard and
poor life ; this does for the people what civilisation does not
even begin to try to do : this culture civilisation invariably
destroys.

To forge out of the songs of the Finns, with all their
merit, the sampo of Homeric poetry demanded a Homer.
Lönnrot was no Homer.   Had Homer possessed the material, he could have made an epic out of the story of the
sampo, a compact and dramatic poem.   But this was
exactly what Lönnrot did not do.   If we continued the

---

[1] Compare Tsui Goab among the Kaffirs, in Theal's *Tsui Goab*.

[2] Comparetti, *op. cit.* p. 119.

[3] Magic songs (*Karakias* in New Zealand) give the reciter power
over the various objects whose origin they describe.   Magic love-songs
are common among the Ojibbeways.   Much early poetry and early
art had a practical, not an æsthetic, purpose.   See 'The Art of
Savages,' in *Custom and Myth*.

Theogony of Hesiod into the Argonautic legend, threw in an episode or two from the Theban cycle, including a number of magical chants [1] and dithyrambs, and ending with a version of the Gospel as understood and narrated by the Pythoness who uttered the Last Oracle, we should have a Greek composition analogous to the *Kalewala*. An epic needs materials and a poet—materials and an editor will not suffice ; and only in times like ours, inspired by Wolf's hypothesis, could an editor be found for the materials. [2]

CONCLUSION

THIS brief summary of the Homeric question cannot end better than in the words of the distinguished Italian scholar who, in his *Myth of Œdipous*, practically dealt the death-blow to solar mythology—Signor Comparetti. To the Homeric problem he brings not only vast learning and a fine literary appreciation, but, what is even rarer than these, a sense of historical proportion, and common-sense. In his Preface to his work on the *Kalewala* (p. ix) he says : ' The anatomical and conjectural analysis which has been applied so often and so long by classical and unclassical philologues and grammarians to the Homeric poems and other national epics proceeds from an universal abstract

---

[1] ἐπαοιδῇ δ' αἷμα κελαινὸν ἔσχεθον.   Od. xix. 457.

[2] The English reader can study the *Kalewala* in Mr. John Martin Crawford's translation.   (Putnam's Sons, London, 1889.)   The *Kalewala*, as is well known, inspired Mr. Longfellow's *Hiawatha* ; his materials he found in the Red Indian traditions collected by Schoolcraft.   There is a translation of the *Kalewala* in French prose by M. Léouzon Leduc, and one in German verse by Schiefner (1892). Lönnrot's first collection of songs is *Kantele*.   (Helsingfors, 1829–31.) The first edition of *Kalewala* is of 1835, and is described as ' Old Finnish Lays from Carelia.'   The second edition, with many additions, and with Lönnrot's work in altering and composing, is of 1849.

principle, which is correct, and from a concrete application
of that principle, which is imaginary and groundless.

'The true principle, recognised since the end of last
century, separates the "personal" and learned Art-epics,
like the Æneid and the *Gerusalemme Liberata*, from those
which belong to the period of spontaneous epic production,
when Folk-singers fashioned many epic lays, of small or
moderate compass.[1] These epic lays were called "national"
or "popular," not only by virtue of their contents, sentiment,
and audience, but mainly because the poetry which takes
this form is natural, naïf, collective, popular, and hence
"national" in its origin and development.

'The baseless application of this principle is to regard
the national poems not as creations of a single poet, but as
put together out of shorter pre-existing lays, either by a
single person at one time, or by several in succession, until
the final fashioning of the poem.   And this process is conceived of as a mere stringing together, without any sort of
fusion, so that a critical philologist, thanks to his special
sharpness and by aid of certain criteria, would be in a position to recognise the joinings, and to recover the lays out of
which the poem has been made up.

'With this preconceived idea people have gone on anato-
mising the epics; from Lachmann to the present day they have
not desisted, although, so far, no positive satisfactory and
harmonious results have been won.   This restless business
of analysis, which has lasted so long, impatient of its own
fruitlessness, yet unconvinced of it, builds up, and pulls
down, and builds again ; while its shifting foundations, its

---

[1] We may doubt whether Folk-singers often produced more than
the ballads of victory or defeat which French and Scottish girls sang
in their dances, or, at most, a ballad like *Chevy Chace* or *Kinmont
Willie*.   The epic lay is rather the work of the minstrel at a Greek
court, or in the hall of a Frankish or Highland chief.

insufficient and falsely applied criteria, condemn it to remain
fruitless, tedious, and repulsive. The observer marks, with
amazement, the degree of intellectual short-sightedness produced by excessive and exclusive analysis. The investiga-
tor becomes a kind of microscope man, who can see atoms
but not bodies ; motes, and those magnified, but not
beams.

'Thus the Homeric question has not been settled, but
has spread among other national epics. No doubt, before
the epic there existed shorter lays ; but what is the relation
of the lays to the epic ? Is the epic a mere material syn-
thesis of lays, or does it stand to them as a thing higher in
the scale of poetic organisms—does it move on a loftier
plane, attaining higher, broader conceptions, *and a new
style appropriate to these ?*'

The study of MSS. tells us nothing. We have the
Sigurd and Helgi lays of the North, but you could not
make an epic by joining them together. 'Not a single lay
has been found that also forms part of a great poem,'
though some have been found which form materials of a
great prose romance, the *Volsung's Saga.*

So much for the 'little lay theory' (*Kleinliedertheorie*).
But there remains the nucleus theory, for example, of an
original *Achilleis,* expanded by self-denying poets into an
Iliad. Comparetti, though regarding the Greek ἀοιδός as
one who chants not only his own poems but the poems of
other people, does not believe that he would fashion lays
'to be inserted in a greater mass already constructed by
others, nor that he would have done this with so much
respect for other men's work, and with such strict limitation
of his own, that the modern erudite can recognise the joinings, and distinguish the original kernel and each of the later
additions. . . . The difficulty is increased when we have to do
with epics which seem in all their parts to be composed on a

definite plan, which exists in the final poem, not in the supposed kernel. The organic unity, the harmony, the relation of all the portions, which are arranged so as to lead up to the final catastrophe, are such as to imply the agreement and homogeneity of the poetic creation in a common idea, and, moreover, resting on that agreement—a limitation of the creative processes. Now all this, according to our conceptions, can hardly have existed in different poets and at different periods. It appears natural that additions should be made, but natural, also, that these would be numerous, disparate, and manifold, determined by the fancy and feeling of this poet and that, in widely severed places and times, to whom (*ex hypothesi*) it was open to continue or develop a comparatively short traditional piece.' An old *Mahâbhârata* of 8,000 *slokas* might thus be increased to the monstrous agglomerate of 107,000 *slokas*. 'But that in this fashion such rounded wholes as the Iliad and Odyssey, poems so duly restricted in compass, in matter so circumscribed, in structure so well proportioned, could have been achieved is as hard to imagine as it would be in the case of a tragedy or tragic trilogy. Certainly the mass of poetic material which in different ages and places must have gathered round any such hypothetical kernel must have been considerable and disparate. But he who could extract from this mass the epics which we possess, and not a kind of Greek *Mahâbhârata*, would have produced, at all events, such a work of genius that in fairness he must be called not merely the redactor, but the author and poet.' Thus Comparetti's analysis of the *Kalewala* brings him, as far as the Greek Epics are concerned, to our own conclusion : namely, that the Iliad and Odyssey are neither collections of short lays, nor expansions of an original brief epic, but that, on the whole, they are the composition of a poet—'the golden poet,' HOMER.

APPENDIX

——◦◦——

A

The Australian Message Stick

IN the argument on early writing it is urged that the Australian
Message Stick, or Talking Stick, proves that the most backward races are not unacquainted with some species of inscribed
signs. As to the nature of the signs but little is published.
The only Message Stick which the writer has seen is a polished
piece of hard wood, about ten inches long, covered with deli-
cate etching. But the message is chiefly conveyed by means
of pictures. A house, church, and fences convey the news of a
fresh settlement by Europeans ; boomerangs and waddies
(clubs) show that the natives are resisting ; fish indicate that
the fishing season has opened. There are also conventional
lines, which are said to tell a love story of considerable length.
Dr. Harley informs the writer that a European recently
carried a Message Stick from a tribe to their kindred at a
distance. The interpretation was communicated to him by
the sender. On reaching the recipients, he begged one of them
to read the message to him. The man retired into the bush
for a short time, and then explained the message in the same
words as the sender. It is said that the conventional signs
(not pictures) bear a general resemblance to Ogham writing ;
though, of course, we can hardly regard them as characters,
nor are we certain how far they vary among different tribes.

The stick is an open letter—there is no folding up, as in the tablet of Proetus carried by Bellerophon. The conventional marks indicate some advance beyond the picture-writing of the North American Indians.

B

The Tenth Book of the Iliad

IT is argued in the text that to admit this book to be an interpolation opens the door to the general theory of complex interpolation. Mr. Monro points out to the writer that simple interpolation, as of this whole book, is one thing ; complex interpolation, as of the armour in Book xviii., involving many minute changes throughout the preceding books, is quite another thing. ‘A happy addition came to be current, and so got into the *textus receptus*, which was probably formed, not by Alexandrian critics, but by the needs of the Athenian book-market, in the fifth and fourth centuries B.C.’ As an exposition of the modifications introduced into early epic MSS. in France, the fourth chapter of the first volume of M. Léon Gautier's *Epopées Françaises* well deserves study. If similar practices prevailed in early Greece, the present condition of the Homeric text can only be accounted for either by the Commission of Pisistratus or by recourse to some original and recognised version of the poems. But it is probable that these national possessions were never treated with the arbitrariness of the old French copyists.